Care & Repair

of Antiques
& Collectables

Judith Miller

Care & Repair

of Antiques
& Collectables

A Step-by-Step Guide

Mitchell Beazley

Care & Repair of Antiques & Collectables

First published in Great Britain in 1997
by Mitchell Beazley
an imprint of Reed International Books Limited
Michelin House, 81 Fulham Road
London SW3 6RB
and Auckland and Melbourne

Contributors
Chief contributor **John Wainwright**
Upholstery and furniture repairs **Stephen Luker**
Canework repairs **I. & P. Pritchard**
French polishing **Richard Chys**
Leatherwork repairs **Anthony Cullen**
Textile repairs **Frances Page**

Art Director **Gaye Allen**
Executive Art Editor **Janis Utton**
Executive Editor **Judith More**
Project Editors **Nina Sharman, Anthea Snow**
Production Controllers **Rachel Lynch, Christina Quigley**
Designer **Simon Bell**
Editor **Richard Dawes**
Photographer **Hugh Johnson**
Illustrator **Anny Evason**
Indexer **Ann Barrett**

A CIP catalogue record for this book is available from
the British Library

ISBN 1 85732 427 7

Set in Adobe Garamond and Frutiger
Produced by Mandarin Offset
Printed in Singapore

Contents

Foreword	6
Furniture	8
Introduction	10
Tools	12
Materials	14
Cleaning and reviving furniture	16
Removing marks and stains	18
Repairing surface damage	20
Repairing veneer	22
Applying traditional finishes	28
Structural repairs to chairs	40
Structural repairs to tables	52
Structural repairs to case furniture	58
Canework	66
Introduction	68
Tools and materials	70
Restoring a caned chair seat	72
Upholstery	82
Introduction	84
Tools and materials	86
General care and cleaning	88
Making minor repairs	90
Preparing for reupholstering	92
Upholstering a drop-in seat pad	94
Reupholstering a button-back chair	99
Leatherwork	120
Introduction	122
Tools and materials	124
General care and cleaning	126
Restitching	128
Repairing tears	129
Patching repairs	130
Recolouring and regilding	131
Reviving and polishing a leather case	132
Replacing a leather desktop	134

Textiles   136

Introduction   138
Tools and materials   140
General cleaning and storage   142
Removing stains   144
Repairing textiles   146
Displaying and storing textiles   150

Rugs & Carpets   152

Introduction   154
Tools and materials   156
General cleaning and displaying   158
Mending fringes and Kelim ends   160
Repairing splits and tears   163
Repairing side cords   164
Repairing the pile   166
Reweaving   168

Ceramics   172

Introduction   174
Tools and materials   176
General care and cleaning   178
Bonding simple breaks   180
Remaking old repairs   182
Remodelling a broken spout   184
Repairing shell chips   186
Modelling new handles   188
Casting missing components   190
Regilding   191
Painting and glazing   192

Glassware   194

Introduction   196
Tools and materials   198
Cleaning glassware   200
Repairing glassware   202

Metalware   204

Introduction   206
Tools and materials   208
General care and cleaning   210
Washing and cleaning silver   212
Repairing and restoring metalware   214

Jewellery   218

Introduction   220
Tools and materials   222
Cleaning and repairing jewellery   224
Repairing clasps   226
Repairing brooch pins   228
Repairing necklaces, chains and bracelets   230
Repairing earrings   232

Stoneware   234

Introduction   236
Tools and materials   238
General care and cleaning   240

Techniques   244

Furniture   244
Metalware   247
Textiles, Upholstery and Rugs & Carpets   248

Directory of Suppliers   250
Index   252
Acknowledgements   256

Foreword

Antiques and collectables are subject to wear and tear in everyday use. Also, they are vulnerable to surface deterioration and structural damage caused by misuse, accidental knocks and scrapes, and exposure to environmental hazards such as insect infestation, changes in humidity, air pollution and intense heat and light. The purpose of *Care & Repair of Antiques & Collectables* is twofold. It explains how you can care for such pieces so as to prevent or minimize deterioration and damage. In addition, it shows you how to restore pieces that have fallen into disrepair.

The benefits to be gained from caring for and repairing antiques and collectables are functional, aesthetic and financial. For example, a drawer that slides smoothly in and out of a chest is easier and more convenient to use than a drawer that sticks. Equally, all antiques and collectables are more aesthetically pleasing if they are clean, polished and structurally sound than if they are dirty, dull and falling apart. Good condition also makes a major contribution to their financial value, for you will pay or receive much more for a well-preserved or properly repaired piece than for a damaged or poorly maintained one.

Care & Repair of Antiques & Collectables has eleven sections, each covering a major category: Furniture, Canework, Upholstery, Leatherwork, Textiles, Rugs & Carpets, Ceramics, Glassware, Metalware, Jewellery and Stoneware. A few pieces do not fall neatly into one of these categories. For example, to maintain or repair an antique bisque doll, you must refer to the section on Ceramics (for the bisque head or body) and to the section on Textiles (for the doll's clothing).

In addition to an introduction to the different types of antiques and collectables contained in each category, each section includes a descriptive list of the tools and materials required to carry out the maintenance and repair techniques that follow. Where appropriate, these techniques are illustrated by a step-by-step sequence in which each task is explained in detail. In a few cases you are directed to further information at the back of the book dealing with carpentry and metalwork skills, and with repairing textiles and upholstery. Another important piece of advice that appears throughout the book concerns safety. The majority of the tools, materials and techniques that you will use are perfectly safe, but a few are potentially hazardous. To prevent accidents, and to safeguard your health, always read and follow the advice on safe working practices.

All the projects explained in this book are suitable for the amateur with little or no experience of repair or restoration of antiques. However, whenever a task is beyond the amateur's competence, or when an object is rare or valuable, repair or restoration by a professional is always strongly advised. Indeed, when the amateur undertakes such work it is likely to prove a false economy.

Furniture

Introduction

Until the early 17th century, most households contained examples of just four basic pieces of furniture: 'forms' (stools and benches), beds, tables and 'coffers' (chests). Since that time, numerous variations on these simple forms have evolved, but the general categories of classification have remained virtually unchanged. Contemporary collectors, restorers and dealers categorize most antique pieces as seat furniture (of which beds are a subcategory), tables or case furniture (for examples, chests, bureaux and desks).

Seat furniture

Aside from the thrones that were used by the aristocracy, the earliest seat furniture was stools, benches and low chests. The first chairs were produced by increasing the height of one side of a chest to form a chair back. It was then a simple development to remove all the side panels – leaving a frame – and to replace the exposed frame with legs. Later upholstered seats, backs and arms were added to afford greater comfort than that provided by solid wood. Although chairs have been made in a wide range of styles since the second half of the 17th century, they can all be divided into one of three basic types: frame, stick and bentwood. For an illustrated description of these types of chair, see pp.40–1. For an illustrated description of the development of upholstered seating, see pp.84–5.

Tables

The earliest tables – refectory, or 'frame', tables – consisted of plank tops supported on corner and, in some cases, intermediate legs. The legs were joined at their tops by wooden rails, and sometimes by stretcher

Left: Walnut Davenport

The first small writing desk known as a Davenport was made for Captain Davenport by Gillow of Lancaster, England, in the late 18th century. The example shown here is early 19th century, veneered with burr walnut, and of a type commonly referred to as a 'piano top' because of the curved shape of the top of its writing surface. Davenports made in this style were known as 'harlequins' if they incorporated a pop-up stationery compartment, as this one does.

Right: Pine armchair

This is a typical late 19th-century example of a rustic, high-backed, pine armchair. It features a shaped, flat-slatted back and turned legs and stretchers.

Below: Mahogany pedestal table

This English, Chippendale-period, mahogany pedestal table was made c.1755. It has a tilt top, which allows it to be stored upright in a corner or on one side of a room when it is not in use.

rails at their feet. Two variations developed in the 17th century have become standard: the drop-leaf table and the pedestal. Drop-leaf tables have side or end flaps secured to the frame. These can be raised to increase the size of the top when necessary. Pedestal tables often employed a tilt mechanism that lowered the top when the table was in use and raised it when it was not. An illustrated description of these tables appears on pp.52–3.

Case furniture

The term 'case furniture' embraces a variety of pieces that includes chests, wardrobes, sideboards, bureaux, linen presses, tallboys, lowboys and dressers. All these pieces evolved from the coffer and consist of a storage cabinet incorporating doors or drawers, or both. An illustrated description of case furniture appears on pp.58–9.

Care and repair

The amateur wishing to maintain or repair furniture must be aware of the following factors concerning its construction and decorative finish. First, some pieces are made from solid wood; others are veneered – in other words, their surface consists of a thin sheet of high-quality decorative (or 'show') wood applied to a solid wood of lesser quality. Some of the repair techniques described in the chapter are suitable only for solid furniture, and some only for veneered furniture. Explanations and repair techniques appear on pp.22–7.

Second, the methods of joining the component parts of furniture vary: butt-, peg-, dowel-, mortise-and-tenon and dovetail joints have all been used at various times. Most structural wear and tear occurs in these joints, and you must become familiar with their construction before attempting repairs. Illustrated explanations and repair techniques appear on pp.44–7 and 244–7.

Third, wooden antique furniture is traditionally given one of three types of finish: oil, wax or French polish. (In this last case, wax is usually applied as a final finish.) Proper maintenance and restoration of these finishes, and the subtle, lustrous patina that gradually accumulates on them over time, are essential if both the appearance and value of the piece are to be preserved. Care, repair and restoration techniques for surface finishes appear on pp.28–37.

Tools

The wood-working tools listed below are divided into two groups. The first group contains illustrated and non-illustrated tools that you need to complete the projects specified in this chapter. The second group comprises illustrated tools that you may find useful for tackling some of the techniques described on pp.244–6 or if you progress to more advanced repairs (with the help of specialist publications or professional instruction). You will also need a solid work surface – ideally, a carpenter's bench – to which you can clamp a bench vice for securing pieces of work. A well-ventilated work space, with good lighting, is also essential.

Tools

1 Soft-bristled dusting brush Or a make-up brush.
2 Plastic goggles To protect your eyes.
3 Face mask To protect your face and lungs.
4 Hog's bristle brush For removing flymarks.
5 Penknife Or a utility or craft knife or table knife.
6 G-clamps At least two, to secure repairs.
7 Sash clamps Three, to secure repairs.
8 Bevel-edged chisels A selection of sizes for cutting mortise-and-tenon joints and other tasks.
9 Steel ruler For measuring and for a straight edge.
10 Heavy-duty utility or craft knife To cut veneers.
11 Cabinetmaker's scrapers To remove old wax and French polish finishes.
12 Paint brushes At least two, 2.5–5cm.
13 Varnishing brush For applying varnishes.
14 Needle files Beveled, round and flat.
15 Electric drill (plus drill bits) For drilling holes.
16 Screwdrivers Various, straight- and cross-head.
17 Hacksaw For cutting wood and metal.
18 Tenon saw A rigid, general-purpose saw.
19 Carpenter's mallet For striking chisels and for knocking components together and apart.
20 Panel saw To cut thin sheets and across the grain.
21 Pliers For removing nails and wedges.
22 Mortise gauge For marking mortise-and-tenons.
23 Bench plane A general-purpose wood plane.
24 Block plane For trimming end grain.
25 Chisel plane For making chisel-like shavings.
26 Bench vice Clamp this to the edge of a work surface to secure pieces during repair.
27 Wood files Flat, half-round and round.
28 Dovetail saw Similar to a tenon saw, but with fine teeth for making fine cuts.

29 Fretsaw For cutting curves in thin sheets of wood.
30 Measuring tape To make precise measurements.
31 Hammers Use a ball-pein or a cross-pein hammer for driving smaller nails and panel pins; a cabinet or a claw hammer for larger nails.
32 T-square For marking right-angled cuts.
33 Marking gauge For marking cuts with the grain.

YOU WILL ALSO NEED:
Glass jars Two or three, each with a 4-litre capacity.
Chemical-resistant rubber gloves To protect your hands when applying chemical paint strippers.
Plastic basin For mixing cleaning solution.
Wooden spatula To scrape paint off furniture.
Metal container lid For mixing melted wax crayons.
Cigarette lighter For melting wax crayons.
Lolly stick For mixing melted wax crayons.
Electric iron With variable temperature control, for heating glue film and reveneering.
Magnifying glass For inspecting damage.
Teaspoon For applying melted wax crayons.
Saucer Or similar container, for mixing stains.
Artist's brush (fine-tipped) For touching in minor surface repairs.
Scalpel, or utility or craft knife For making fine cuts.
Cast-iron weights For securing veneer while glue dries. Heavy hardcover books are a suitable alternative.
Pencil For marking cuts.
Set square For marking angled cuts.
Cutting board Use with a utility or craft knife or scalpel.
Sanding block Wrap sheets of sandpaper around this to sand large, flat surfaces.
Plastic bucket For mixing cleaning solutions.

Nylon-bristle brush For applying bleach.
Blunt wooden stick For stirring animal glue.
Metal saucepan For heating water when mixing glue.
Metal container For mixing animal glue. It must fit inside the metal saucepan (above).
Shoe brushes For applying and buffing shoe polishes.
Airtight glass jar For storing rubbing pads.
Sable-bristle artist's brush For applying stains.
Small artist's hog's-hair brush For cleaning crevices.
Wood battens Two, straight, for squaring frames.
Sticks Two, small, to tighten a cord tourniquet.
Wrenches Various sizes for dismantling and assembling bentwood chairs.
Electric dehumidifier Use to reduce atmospheric humidity in order to shrink swollen wood.
Small pointing trowel For applying tinted waxes.
Spirit level For checking that furniture is level.
Scissors For cutting cord, rag and masking tape.
Whistling kettle Use with a cork, plus brass and acrylic tubing, to make a steam generator for softening glue.

YOU MAY FIND THE FOLLOWING ITEMS USEFUL FOR SOME OF THE BASIC TECHNIQUES ON pp.244–6 AND FOR ADVANCED FURNITURE REPAIRS:
34 Cutting gauge Similar to a marking gauge, but for marking across the grain.
35 Pincers Useful for removing large nails and tacks.
36 Needle template Use to copy moulding profiles.
37 Punch Use to drive nails below the surface.
38 Cross-cut saw For cutting planks with and across the grain.
39 Coping saws For cutting sharp curves.
40 Keyhole saw For cutting holes away from accessible edges. The blade is inserted into a drilled hole.
41 Bench hook A cutting board with a raised edge against which a piece of work can be rested.
42 Mitre box Guides a saw blade when cutting mitred and angled joints.
43 Spokeshave For smoothing curved profiles.
44 Lathe chisels and gouges You will need a selection of these, plus access to a lathe, if you intend to make turned wooden components.
45 Hand drill An alternative to an electric drill.
46 Bradawl For making starter holes for small screws.
47 Electric jigsaw For cutting curves.
48 Electric sander For sanding large areas.
49 Steel spatula For scraping off old glue.

Materials

You need the materials listed below to complete all the tasks and projects relating to furniture that are described on the following pages. You should bear in mind that a few of these materials are flammable and that others are caustic or toxic, or both. Therefore you must work in a well-ventilated work space; never introduce a naked flame into the area except when its use is specified; use plastic goggles, a face mask and chemical-resistant gloves to protect your eyes, face, lungs and hands; and store all fluids, pastes and powders out of the reach of children and pets.

YOU WILL NEED:

1 Boiled and raw linseed oil Use as specified with other fluids to make cleaners and revivers. Also, both types can be used for traditional oil finishes.

2 White spirit Use to dilute wax crayons, and as a constituent of cleaners and revivers

3 Methylated spirits Use to dissolve French polish, and as a constituent of cleaners and revivers.

4 Coarse and soft lint-free rag Use as specified to apply cleaners, revivers, polishes and grain fillers.

5 Wire wool (grades 0–0000) Use as specified to remove grime, cut back polished surfaces and clean metal hardware.

6 Commercial metal polishes For cleaning brass, copper, steel and iron hardware.

7 Cotton wool Use to apply cleaners and revivers.

8 Masking tape Use to protect surrounding areas when applying cleaning fluids.

9 Beeswax furniture polish You will need both the clear and tinted types.

10 French polish Sometimes referred to as shellac, and commercially available in the following formulations: brown, garnet, button, white and clear.

11 Paint stripper Use the spirit-based, liquid gel type to remove paint from furniture.

12 Coloured wax crayons Buy a selection of the type specifically formulated for touching up scratches and other minor surface damage on furniture.

13 Commercial wood glue Can be used instead of animal glue for making quick minor repairs.

14 Sandpaper Coarse-, medium- and fine-grade for shaping and smoothing wood.

15 Garnet paper Use fine-grade to cut back finishes.

16 Sheets of glue film For securing new veneers.

17 Thick brown craft paper Use to protect veneers when heating underlying glue film with an electric iron.

18 Wood filler To fill holes and splits.

19 Cleaner and reviver To revive wood finishes. Buy pre-mixed, or mix your own (see p.17)

20 Wood stains Available in spirit-, chemical-, water- and oil-based formulations, in a wide choice of colours.

21 Oil-based grain filler Available in various shades for filling open wood grain before applying a finish.

22 Epoxy-resin glue Use to take castings when making repairs to intricate gesso mouldings.

23 Artist's oil paint Burnt sienna.

24 Gold metallic powder For regilding.

25 Liquid gold size An adhesive for metallic powder.

26 Candle wax A useful lubricant for seized-up moving wooden components.

27 Panel pins To secure thin sheets of wood.

28 Sheet of plain paper Tear into strips to pack out enlarged screw holes.

29 Animal glue Traditional adhesive used by furniture makers. Also called rabbit-skin glue.

30 Woodworm fluid A commercial formulation designed for treating woodworm infestation.

31 Buffing mop An attachment for an electric drill, used for polishing large surface areas.

32 Pre-cut wooden dowels Available in various diameters for repairing dowel joints and reinforcing other specified joints.

YOU WILL ALSO NEED:

White vinegar Use to remove specified stains.

Ammonia As above.

Hessian Can be used to apply grain fillers.

Cotton buds Use to clean recessed areas.

Hydrogen peroxide (20 per cent volume) Use to bleach specified stains.

Bleach For evening the colour of wood before restaining.

Tissue paper Use for cleaning where specified.

Borax Use where specified as a cleaning agent.

Washing soda As above.

Water For rinsing off various cleaning fluids.

Sponge Use where specified for cleaning and rinsing.

Terry towelling Use to dry surfaces after cleaning.

Teak oil To re-oil and re-nourish wood.

Microcrystalline wax To polish furniture.

Oil of spike Use this lavender-scented oil, available from herbalists, to remove bloom.

Olive oil Use where specified for removing stains.

Crocus powder For lessening scorch and burn marks.

Crushed ice For removing deposits of candle wax.

Lemon juice For removing specified stains.

Table salt For removing specified stains.

Acetone For removing paint deposits.

'White ring' remover A proprietary fluid formulated to remove water marks.

Potato flour Mix with vinegar to remove water stains.

Shoe polish Use various shades of brown, plus red and black, to touch up damaged wax finishes.

Scratch remover A fluid for disguising scratches.

Block of pure beeswax Can be melted and mixed with stains to fill small holes, cracks and splits.

Wood Blocks of softwood for protecting surfaces when clamping repairs. Pieces of hardwood or softwood to match the original when making replacement parts. Where specified, plywood can also be used.

Sheets of veneer For patching and replacing damaged original veneer.

Plastic sheeting For protecting floors and surrounding areas when making repairs.

Artist's powder pigments A type of earth-coloured pigment to tint waxes when making repairs.

Mild liquid soap For removing dirt and grime.

Gesso paste To repair gesso mouldings.

Latex, epoxy putty Use to make castings when repairing intricately shaped mouldings.

Cork With a diameter that will fit tightly into the spout of a whistling kettle to form a steam generator.

Brass and silicone tubing To make a steam generator.

Strong cord For binding specified repairs, and for making a steam generator.

Screws To replace lost or damaged originals.

Sheet of cardboard For making a template.

Hinges To replace lost or damaged originals.

Casters To replace lost or damaged originals.

Cleaning and reviving furniture

The cleaning techniques described below are designed to remove dust, dirt and sticky grime from furniture. If these are left to gradually accumulate on a piece, they will dull the surface patina and, in extreme cases, may even mask the figuring and grain of the wood. Provided that the underlying surface finish of a piece is basically sound, the recommended techniques will also revive its surface patina. (However, if the surface finish is damaged, you should refer to pp.18–37.)

The cleaning and reviving mixture you need to use depends on how dirty the surface is. Solution A, the stronger of the cleaners recommended here, will be required only if the piece has been neglected for a long time – as was the case with this 18th-century walnut chest-on-stand, which had been stored in a dirty attic for several years. If you prefer not to mix either of the recommended cleaning and reviving mixtures, premixed commercial equivalents are now available.

YOU WILL NEED:

Soft-bristled dusting brush

Two glass jars Each capable of holding at least 500ml of cleaning-reviving solutions A and B.

White vinegar

Boiled linseed oil

White spirit

Methylated spirits

Household ammonia

Coarse, lint-free cotton rag

Wire wool Grade 000.

Metal cleaners and polishes You will need one or more of these if the furniture has any metal hardware (see pp.210–13 for instructions on cleaning and polishing different types of metal, including brass, copper, iron and steel).

Cotton wool

Cotton buds

Masking tape

Scissors

Soft, lint-free rags

Boiled linseed oil, beeswax polish (tinted or clear) or one of the various types of French polish One or more of these traditional finishes, depending on the type of finish to be revived (see pp.32–7).

1 Mixing the cleaning solution

● Remove all dust from the surface of the piece, using a soft-bristled dusting brush. Make sure that you work the bristles into any recessed sections and mouldings to tease out any hidden accumulations of dust.

● Assess the extent of the underlying dirt. If the piece is simply dull and dirty, go to step 3. If it is badly neglected and coated with thick, sticky grime, use a 500ml glass jar to mix about 250ml of cleaning solution A: 4 parts white vinegar, 4 parts boiled linseed oil, 4 parts white spirit, 1 part methylated spirits, and 3–4 drops of household ammonia.

2 Removing sticky dirt and grime

● Dampen a pad of coarse, lint-free cotton rag with cleaning solution A.

● Rub the pad vigorously, in a circular motion, over the piece. The dirt will begin to dissolve and collect on the pad. Keep turning the pad as it becomes dirty, recharging it with solution A, and replace it with a new one when necessary.

● If the dirt proves difficult to remove, exchange the pad for a ball of grade-000 wire wool. Dip it into the solution, squeeze out any excess and rub it very lightly over the surface in the direction of the grain. Keep wiping off the dissolved dirt with a rag, and replace the wire wool when necessary.

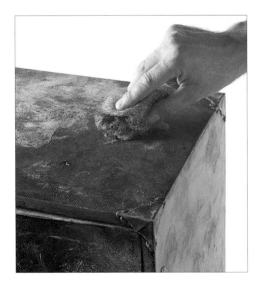

3 Cleaning and reviving

● If you have carried out step 2, the surface will still be slightly cloudy. If you have left out step 2, the surface must still be cleaned. In both cases, use a 500ml container to mix 250ml of cleaning and reviving solution B: 4 parts white spirit to 1 part boiled linseed oil. This will remove any dirt and cloudiness and revive colour and patina.

● Make a pad of coarse, lint-free cotton rag, dampen it with solution B, and work the rag over the surface as in the second stage of step 2. Turn and recharge the rag when it gets dirty, and replace it when necessary.

● Finish by wiping the surface with a new cotton pad dampened with white spirit.

4 Cleaning metal fittings

● Many pieces of furniture have metal fittings, such as hinges, locks, finger plates, pulls and corner brackets. These are made from a range of metals and alloys, but brass, copper (as on this chest-on-stand) and iron are the most common. This is the time to clean this hardware, using the solutions specified under 'Cleaning metalware' (see pp.210–13).

Take care not to get any of the cleaning solutions on the surrounding wood. Apply them very cautiously with a piece of cotton wool. For extra protection, cover the surrounding areas with masking tape cut to the required shape with scissors.

5 Oiling, waxing or polishing

● To further revive and protect the surface, apply a new coat of the original finish with a soft, lint-free rag, then buff it to a shine with another soft, lint-free rag. On antique furniture the finish will be either oil, wax or French polish, the latter often overlaid with wax. To identify the finish, and for advice on how to apply it, turn to pp.32–9. (If you remain uncertain about the finish, consult an antique dealer.) **Note:** The chest-on-stand had a traditional beeswax finish applied over a coat of shellac. After step 4 was completed, it was renewed with a slightly tinted beeswax cream (which is better than a hard beeswax paste for use on veneered furniture such as this).

6 After-care

● If you used cleaning solution A in step 2 to remove thick, sticky grime from the surface, you will know that it is a laborious and messy task. You can avoid the need to repeat this by adopting the following measures.

● Dust the furniture regularly.

● Every month or two, re-oil or re-wax furniture, depending on the finish. Apply the oil or wax very sparingly with a clean, soft cloth. With another clean, soft cloth, buff the oil or wax to a shine.

● Depending on how dusty or dirty the location is where the furniture is kept, repeat steps 3–5 annually or every two years.

Removing marks and stains

In addition to accumulating dust and dirt from daily use and constant exposure to the air, furniture may also become marked or stained, usually accidentally, by various household substances. If it is left untreated, such damage will adversely affect the appearance of a piece and undermine its value. A variety of traditional materials and techniques are available to remedy problems of this kind. The most common and effective ones are described below, under the problems they treat.

Acids

Treat as soon as possible any piece, whether it has an oil, wax or French-polished surface finish, on which any kind of acid has accidentally been spilled.
● Put on protective gloves, goggles and face mask.
● Mix in a large plastic bowl a solution consisting of a level teaspoon of either borax or washing soda and 500ml of warm water.
● Apply the solution liberally with a sponge to the affected area, to neutralize the acid.
● Rinse the area with clean, cold water and pat dry with terry towelling or a soft, lint-free rag.
● If the piece is French-polished and the polish has been damaged, you may be able to reconstitute the finish in the affected area by using the technique described on pp.34–7.
● On waxed or undamaged French-polished surfaces, rub the affected area with a soft, lint-free rag and tinted furniture wax or shoe polish. Buff with a soft cloth.
Note: To treat old, dried acid stains, neutralize them as above, then employ the technique recommended opposite for dealing with water stains.

Bleaching

When a piece of furniture has been exposed to direct sunlight for a number of years, the colour of the wood will usually fade. To treat this problem, known as 'bleaching', proceed as follows.
● Firmly rub a little teak oil into the affected area with cotton wool.
● Leave it to dry naturally for about 48 hours, then repeat the application.

● After a further 48 hours, rub in a little wax furniture polish with a soft rag and buff to a shine.
Note: Use an appropriately tinted wax if the area is still too light. Use clear wax if the teak oil has completely revived the colour.

Bloom

To remove the soft, grey-white bloom (or 'blush') that can appear on waxed, lacquered or varnished surfaces, try one of the two following techniques.
● Rub a little clear microcrystalline wax well into the affected area with a soft rag. Leave to dry for about 20 minutes. Buff vigorously with a clean, soft rag.
● Alternatively, moisten a soft rag with some oil of spike (a lavender-scented liquid available from most herbalists and some chemists). Rub it well into the affected area, leave for 3–4 hours, then wax and polish as described above.

Burns and scorches

If a burned or scorched piece is rare or valuable, ask a professional restorer to treat it. With lesser pieces, try the remedy for discoloration below, but note that unless the mark is fairly superficial and the underlying wood is not charred, you may have little success. Wood that is charred – for example by a cigarette – is best treated by a professional restorer.

It is easier to treat surface discoloration of the finish, which is in most cases caused by heat from a hot bowl or pan that has been left standing on the surface for at least five minutes. Proceed as follows.

● Gently heat 100ml of olive oil in a pan. Slowly stir 30g of paraffin wax into the oil, and blend them until the wax has melted.
● With a soft rag, rub the mixture sparingly into the affected area, then leave for about 1 hour.
● Rub off the excess with a rag and repeat the above procedure as many times as necessary.
● Repolish the area with furniture wax and a soft cloth, then buff it to a shine.
  To treat burns, scorch marks and discolorations that don't respond to the above, proceed as follows.
● With the tip of your forefinger wrapped in a soft rag, gently rub crocus powder into the mark. This cleaning agent is slightly abrasive, so work cautiously to avoid cutting more deeply than necessary.
● When you have lightened the mark, rub in several coats of teak oil with a rag. Leave each coat to dry for 3–4 hours.
● Repolish the area with a tinted furniture wax and buff to a shine with a soft cloth.

Candle wax

If possible, remove candle wax with a clean rag as soon as it falls onto the surface, when it is still soft. However, if it has been there for some time and has hardened, proceed as follows.
● Wrap crushed ice in a plastic bag and place the ice-pack on the wax. Leave for about five minutes, after which time the wax will be very brittle.
● Remove the ice-pack and very carefully scrape off the wax with either your fingernail or the blunt end of a lolly stick.
● Pat dry the affected area with terry towelling.
● Rub on a little furniture wax or oil (depending on the surface finish) with a soft rag. Buff to a shine.

Fly marks

To remove the black specks of dirt, or 'fly marks', that insects leave on the surface of furniture, try the following remedies in the given sequence.

● Brush off the marks with a hog's-bristle brush or a stiff toothbrush.

● Very carefully lift them off with a scalpel blade or by gently scratching with a fingernail.

● If neither of the above remedies works, place cotton wool soaked with linseed oil on the mark, leave for about 20 minutes, then remove. You should now be able to rub off the mark with the tip of your finger wrapped in a piece of soft rag.

Ink

Whatever the type of ink, try to remove it while it is still wet. Do this with a clean, soft cloth dampened with water. If the ink has dried, and perhaps has seeped into the underlying wood, the problem is more serious. The older the stain, the harder it is to remove (see 'Old ink stains', right). One of the remedies below should work, but always try them in the sequence suggested below, wiping off each substance with a damp rag before trying the next.

● Rub on a little white vinegar with cotton wool.

● Rub on a little lemon juice, as above.

● Rub on a mixture of equal quantities of lemon juice and table salt, as above.

● Rub on a weak solution of 1 part 20 per cent volume hydrogen peroxide to 4 parts water, as above.

● After a successful application, immediately rinse off the solution with cold water and pat the area dry with terry towelling, before restoring the finish. In each case, having rinsed and dried the affected area, re-darken it if necessary with a little wood stain of the appropriate colour (see pp.30–1).

● Once the wood stain has dried, reseal the affected area with a thin coat of shellac (see p.34) and polish with furniture wax and a soft cloth.

Acetone

Of all the substances listed on these pages, this is the one that can cause the most damage. Try to remove it as soon as possible, using the following method.

● Dab off as much of the deposit as possible with tissues. (If you are able to remove it all in this way, all that you will have to do afterwards is repolish the piece with furniture wax.)

● If the acetone has penetrated the finish, moisten a piece of cotton wool with white spirit and gently rub over the affected area in concentric circles. The white spirit will dissolve the old layers of polish. When you stop rubbing, the polish will re-form and stabilize over the damaged area.

● Once the polish has re-formed, gently rub in one or two drops of teak oil with a soft rag. Leave to dry.

● Wipe on a tinted furniture wax and buff to a shine.

Oil and grease

Remove cooking oils, animal fats and dairy products such as butter and cream as soon as possible by rubbing on a very small quantity of beeswax furniture polish and buffing with a soft rag. Remove older stains of this type by very gently rubbing with a soft cloth barely moistened with white spirit. Repolish with furniture wax and buff to a shine.

Paint

The amount of damage paint does to the surface of furniture depends both on its type and whether you can remove it while it is still wet.

● Remove wet acrylic paint by wiping it off with a water-dampened rag.

● Remove dry acrylic paint by moistening a rag with methylated spirits and laying it over the affected area for about 30 minutes. Remove the rag and gently scrape off the paint with your fingernail. Then treat as for acetone.

● Remove wet emulsion paint by wiping it off with water- dampened rags.

● Remove dry emulsion paint using the method specified for acrylic paint.

● Remove wet oil paint with a rag moistened with white spirit. Then treat as for acetone.

● Remove dry oil paint by brushing on a spirit-based paint stripper. Leave for no more than 30 seconds, then scrape off the paint and stripper with a wooden spatula. Finish by using the remedy for acetone.

Water

To remove the white rings and spots left on a polished surface by a vessel with a wet base, use one of the following methods.

● Rub in a commercial white-ring remover with a soft cloth (following the manufacturer's instructions). Wipe off the excess and repolish with furniture wax.

● If the above doesn't work, use the olive oil and wax recipe specified for burns and scorches (see opposite).

● If the above doesn't work, mix some potato flour with white vinegar to form a cream-like paste. Wipe it over the stain with a soft rag and leave for about 12 hours. Wipe off the excess with a soft rag and repolish with furniture wax.

Old ink stains

On antique desks it is often better to leave old ink stains rather than try to remove them. Provided that they are not unsightly, they add character to the piece, and are a sign of age (although such signs can be faked).

Fountain-pen ink
An old fountain-pen ink stain on a 19th-century red mahogany desk.

Repairing surface damage

Small dents and holes as well as fine and deep scratches are often found on antique furniture. This minor surface damage is usually the result of accidents or general wear and tear. Various techniques are available for disguising it. However, bear in mind that a rare and valuable piece displaying such damage is usually considered 'honest' by most collectors and so tends to be more sought-after than its repaired equivalent. You are strongly advised to consult an antique expert about what you should and should not do with a fine piece of furniture, particularly if you wish to sell it. With a lesser piece you can make the repair if you find the damage unsightly and are not concerned about its value, because the difference in price between the repaired and unrepaired piece is likely to be marginal.

Filling small holes

Groups of small holes in wooden furniture are the result of infestation by insects, mainly woodworm. This must be treated (see p.244) before you fill the holes. Fine cracks most often appear when wood swells and shrinks in response to changes in humidity. Treat small holes and cracks in the same way, but note that large cracks require a different remedy (see p.64).
• Purchase a set of wax crayons specifically designed for retouching furniture.
• One of the crayons may be a good match for the colour of the finish. If not, combine two or more colours to achieve a match. In either case, place a small piece of a crayon (or of more than one crayon) in the upturned metal lid of a small glass jar. Play a naked flame – such as from a candle or cigarette lighter – over the crayon until it starts to melt. To blend colours, mix the molten pieces with a lolly stick.
• When the wax cools, but before it sets, pick up a little on the blunt edge of a knife and press it firmly into the hole or crack.
• When the wax has set hard, carefully rub it smooth with the back of a sheet of sandpaper. Do not use the abrasive side.
• Repolish both the treated area and the surrounding area with a suitably tinted wax furniture polish (see pp.32–3).

Hiding fine scratches

You can hide very fine scratches in oiled or waxed surfaces by rubbing on a little shoe polish of the appropriate colour with a lint-free rag and buffing it to a shine with a soft cloth. An alternative for waxed pieces is a commercial scratch remover. These work by slightly dissolving the layers of wax, which then re-form to produce a smooth surface. Apply them in accordance with the maker's instructions. To disguise a network of very fine ('moss') scratches in a French-polished finish, proceed as follows.
• Mix in a jar a small quantity of 3 parts raw linseed oil, 2 parts white spirit, 4 parts methylated spirits, and 1 part melted pure beeswax. Blend them together by shaking the jar vigorously.
Note: Don't heat the mixture – it is flammable.
• Dampen a soft, lint-free rag with the solution and gently rub it over the surface of the piece in a series of circular motions.
• Leave to dry, then buff to a shine with a clean, soft, lint-free rag.

Raising small dents

Moisture and heat can be used to raise a minor dent or bruise in a piece of furniture. However, note that the following technique is unsuitable for veneered pieces and should be attempted only on solid wood. Proceed as follows.
• Dampen a lint-free rag with white spirit and wipe it over the damaged area to remove any wax from the surface.
• Cut three pieces of lint-free rag, each slightly larger than the base-plate of your electric iron.
• Dampen the rags with water and centre them – one on top of another – on the dent or bruise.
• Turn on the iron to its lowest temperature setting. When the iron is ready, press it firmly on top of the cloths for no more than 30 seconds.
• Remove the iron and the cloths, and inspect the dent or bruise. It should have started to swell up to the level of the surrounding wood.
• Repeat the above process several times, waiting at least two minutes between each application so that you don't overheat the wood and so damage it. Re-dampen the cloths before they dry out.
• Once the dent or bruise has disappeared, leave it to cool for at least 30 minutes. Finally, apply oil or wax, as appropriate, to the affected area (see pp.32–3).

Hiding deep scratches

Commercial scratch removers and tinted shoe polishes are rarely able to disguise scratches that have cut through the finish to the underlying wood. To treat these deep scratches on waxed pieces, use the method specified opposite for filling small holes. To treat deep scratches on French-polished furniture, such as this early 20th-century walnut side table, proceed as follows.

YOU WILL NEED:
Magnifying glass
French polish See pp.34–7.
Cotton buds
White spirit
Methylated spirits
Teaspoon
Small container An old saucer will do.
Small, fine-tipped artist's brush
Scalpel
Liquid metal polish
Soft, lint-free cotton rag
Tinted beeswax furniture polish

Assessing the damage

● Closely examine the piece, using a magnifying glass if necessary, to assess the colour of the wood around the damaged area. French polish comes in various shades of brown. Buy the shade closest to the colour you wish to match.

Cleaning the surface

● Moisten a cotton bud with white spirit, and carefully rub it back and forth over the scratch. This will dissolve and remove any old layers of surface wax so that the new polish will adhere properly to the surface.

Applying the polish

● Leave a teaspoonful of French polish in an open container exposed to the air. Within 10–30 minutes it will stiffen slightly. Dip a fine-tipped artist's brush into it and apply a thin layer to the scratch.
● The polish will sink into the scratch as it hardens. Let the first layer set for about 4 hours, then build up additional layers, until the last sets slightly raised from, and just overlaps, the surrounding area. Between applications, cover the polish in the container.

Cutting flush

● Let the polish dry for about 12 hours, after which time it will have fully hardened.
● Very carefully position the side of a scalpel blade at slightly less than a right angle to one end of the scratch. Gently push the blade across the surface to cut the polish flush with the surrounding area. Make sure that you don't let the blade slip and cut into the surrounding finish or wood.

Repolishing

● Burnish the new polish by lightly rubbing back and forth along the length of it with a cotton bud moistened with liquid metal polish.
● Using a soft cotton lint-free rag, spread a thin layer of tinted beeswax polish over the entire side of the piece on which the scratch lies. This will help to blend the repair into the surrounding area. (For advice on different types of beeswax polish, see p.32.)
● Buff the wax to a shine with a clean, soft cloth.

Repairing veneer

Nowadays most houses have some form of central heating. Unless a humidifier has been installed, this type of heating will make the air excessively dry. Conversely, when the system is not in use, humidity will increase. Fluctuating humidity has a damaging effect on furniture: as the moisture content of the wood varies, the wood contracts and expands. The effects of this are more marked on veneered pieces than on furniture made of solid wood. In such pieces the veneer and the underlying solid wood generally contract at different rates and so can blister, split or come apart. The damage is exacerbated by the desiccation of the glue that bonds the components together. The remedy that you will require will depend on the nature and extent of the damage.

Repairing blisters

The technique that you should employ to treat a blister that has been caused by contraction and expansion of the veneer depends on the condition of the blister.

If it has split or cracked, and some slivers of wood are missing, you have no alternative but to cut out the damaged area and insert a new piece of veneer (see 'Patching veneer', pp.24–5). Equally, if the blistering is very extensive, you are advised not to make a series of patch repairs across the surface, but to remove the original veneer from the affected side or panel completely and install a new sheet (see 'Replacing veneer', pp.26–7).

If the blister has not split or cracked, you may be able to glue it down by employing the technique specified for 'Raising dents and bruises' (see opposite). Note, however, that this is often unsuccessful because the bonding power of the original glue is lost through age and reheating. If the heat-and-pressure technique fails and the blister reappears, repair it as follows.

1 Splitting and gluing

- Split the blister open using a scalpel. Make the cut parallel to the grain of the wood.
- Place a little wood glue in a saucer. Dip the scalpel blade in the glue and feed it through the slit in the blister. Repeat two or three times to put enough glue between the veneer and the solid wood underneath.

YOU WILL NEED:

Lint-free cotton rag

Electric iron Required only if you are making the repair with the original glue.

Scalpel

Commercial wood glue

Old saucer Or a similar shallow container for mixing.

White spirit

Small block of softwood About 2.5cm thick and about 5cm bigger all around than the area to be repaired.

Masking tape

G-clamp or sash clamp Alternatively, use a heavy weight.

Wax crayons Refer to step 4 to check if you need these. If you do, use the type designed for retouching furniture.

Beeswax furniture polish Select a tint that matches the colour of the finish.

2 Smoothing the repair

- Wipe off the excess glue that emerges from the top of the blister with a lint-free cotton rag moistened with white spirit.
- Press on the blister with a small block of wood and gently rub the block back and forth along the line of the slit to squeeze out more excess glue. Keep the block's face parallel with the blister, otherwise the edges may scuff the surrounding surface.
- As before, remove the glue from the surface of the veneer and the wooden block with a rag moistened with white spirit.

3 Weighting the repair

- Place a small strip of masking tape along the length of the slit to stop any more glue from squeezing out.
- Position the wooden block over the repair and either clamp it in position with a G-clamp or a sash clamp, or weight it down with a heavy object (such as the solid metal block shown here).
- Leave the block in position for about 12 hours. Then remove it, together with the masking tape, and clean the repair with a rag moistened with white spirit.

4 Finishing off

- Examine the repair. It is possible that the slit you made in the blister will be barely visible. However, if a very fine gap is apparent in the middle of the repair, fill it with a very small quantity of tinted wax crayon, using the technique recommended for disguising small holes and fine scratches on p.20.
- Blend the repair into the surrounding area with a fresh application of an appropriately tinted beeswax furniture polish. Apply it with a soft, lint-free rag, then buff to a shine with a clean cloth.

Dents and bruises

To raise minor dents and bruises in veneered surfaces you should employ the technique specified for raising them from solid wooden surfaces (see p.20). However, you must make one important modification to the technique. The application of heat and moisture will soften the glue that binds the veneer to the solid wood underneath. If pressure isn't applied from above as the surface cools and the glue resets, the bond between the veneer and the solid wood may be destroyed and the veneer will lift or blister. To prevent this from happening, proceed as follows.

- As soon as you have removed the dent with the hot iron and damp rag, place on the repair a 2.5cm-thick softwood block cut 7.5–10cm larger all round than the repaired area.
- Secure the block in place with a G-clamp or a sash clamp and leave it in position for up to 12 hours.

Note: If the repair lies in or near the middle of a large surface (such as the top of a sizeable table or desk), you won't be able to secure the block with a G-clamp or bar clamp. Instead, place as heavy an object (or objects) as you can on top of the block. The large cast-iron weights that come with old-fashioned kitchen scales are ideal for this purpose, but a tall, stable column of heavy hardback books is a good alternative.

Provided that you have access to the underside of the surface, an alternative to using kitchen weights or books is to take two planks of wood, position one directly beneath the surface and one directly on top, and clamp them together at the ends with G-clamps or sash clamps.

Patching veneer

Sometimes it isn't possible to glue damaged pieces of veneer down again. Typical examples of this include sections of veneer that have been burned or charred and split or cracked blistered veneer from which small pieces have been accidentally knocked or brushed off. Provided that the affected area is smaller than about 30 centimetres square, you can make a patch repair rather than replacing the veneer for the whole section or side on which the damage lies. However, if the furniture is rare or valuable, you are advised to find a professional restorer to carry out the work.

YOU WILL NEED:

Paring chisel

Sandpaper Medium and fine grades.

New veneer To match the original wood (in this case, mahogany). Wherever possible, try to choose a piece that matches as closely as possible the grain and figuring of the original.

Masking tape

Pencil

Steel ruler To measure and to serve as a straight edge.

Heavy-duty utility or craft knife

Sheet of glue film Available from suppliers of veneers.

Cutting board

Brown craft paper

Electric iron This must incorporate a variable temperature control.

Softwood block About 2.5cm thick.

Lint-free cotton rag To apply stains, waxes and polishes.

Wood stain In a colour to match the original (see pp.30–1).

Beeswax furniture polish Tinted in an appropriate colour (see pp.32–3).

French polish Required only when restoring a French-polished finish (see pp.34–7).

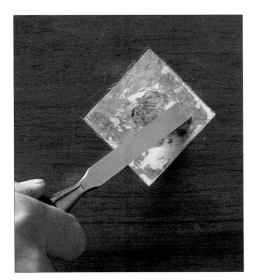

1 Preparing the surface

● Inspect the damaged area. If any part of the damaged veneer has lifted or blistered so that it sticks up higher than the surrounding veneer, carefully scrape away the worst of the damage with the tip of a paring chisel. The aim here, and in the task below, is to produce the smooth level surface required for step 2. When using the chisel, work cautiously and make sure that the blade doesn't slip and cut into the surrounding undamaged veneer.

● Whether or not you have had to level the damaged area with the chisel, sand it with medium-grade sand-paper to smooth the surface. Take care not to rub the finish from the surrounding area.

2 Measuring, marking and cutting

● Buy a piece of new veneer that is about 12mm larger all round than the damage. It must be the same wood as the old veneer, and have close-matching grain and figuring. It can't be thinner than the original veneer, but can be slightly thicker.

● Lay the veneer on the damaged area, with its grain running in the same direction as the old veneer. Secure it along its four sides with masking tape.

● With a pencil and ruler, draw on the veneer a diamond just large enough to cover the damage.

● Using a heavy-duty utility knife and a steel ruler, cut around the four sides of the diamond. Cut through both the new veneer and the old veneer underneath.

3 Scraping off the old veneer

● Peel off the masking tape and carefully lift off the new veneer – both the diamond cutout and the surrounding sheet.

● Using the chisel with the beveled edge facing down, carefully scrape the damaged veneer from within the diamond-shaped cutout. Also use the chisel to scrape away any remnants of old glue to expose the solid wood. Make sure that you don't cut into the good veneer outside the diamond nor gouge the base wood.

● If necessary, sand the solid wood surface with medium-grade sandpaper to create a completely smooth surface. Make sure that you sand into the corners.

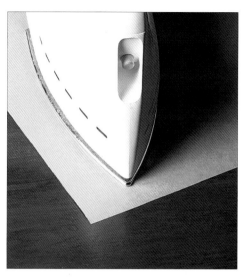

4 Cutting the glue film

● Lay a small sheet of heat-sensitive glue film on a cutting board. Don't remove the thin backing paper from either side of the glue film.

● Place the diamond-shaped piece of new veneer on the glue film and, holding it firmly in place, run a sharp pencil around its perimeter to transfer the diamond outline to the film.

● Lift off the piece of veneer. Place a steel ruler on one side of the diamond outline, and cut along the pencil line and against the ruler with the utility knife. Make sure that the knife doesn't slip. Repeat this cut on the other three sides of the diamond.

Note: Heat-sensitive glue film provides the quickest and most convenient means of bonding the new patch of veneer to the underlying case. However, you could use animal (rabbit-skin) glue instead. (See p.246 for instructions on how to mix and apply animal glue.) If you use this glue, you must make sure that no air remains trapped between the glue and the veneer when the latter is applied in steps 5–6. Thorough rubbing of the veneer with a softwood block, during stage 2 of step 6, will expel trapped air, along with excess glue, from the perimeter of the veneer. Immediately glue appears, wipe it from the surface with a damp rag.

5 Heating and sticking the veneer

● Carefully remove the backing paper from both sides of the glue film.

● Position the film so that it lies flat and fits exactly within the diamond cut-out of the original veneer.

● Place the new veneer on top of the film in the cutout. Make sure that the grain is running in the same direction as the surrounding veneer.

● Lay a sheet of brown paper over the veneer. The sheet must be larger all round than the base-plate of your electric iron.

● Set the iron to its lowest temperature. Press it flat on the paper over the new veneer and glue film to activate the glue.

6 Smoothing the veneer

● Remove the iron from the paper after one minute (no more), then quickly lift off the brown paper.

● Immediately rub a small, 2.5cm-thick block of softwood back and forth over the new piece of veneer. Apply an even, firm pressure for 2–3 minutes, during which time the double-sided glue film will cool and bond the new veneer to the solid wood underneath.

● If the veneer patch stands slightly above the surrounding area, sand it with medium-, then fine-grade sandpaper until it lies flush.

Note: Always use the sandpaper in the direction of the grain to achieve a smooth surface.

7 Restoring the finish

● Stain the new veneer to match the colour of the surrounding original veneer. For advice on staining, see pp.30–1.

● Having stained the veneer, and allowed it to dry thoroughly, apply a wax or French-polished finish to match and blend in with the original finish. For advice on waxing and polishing, see pp.32–7.

Replacing veneer

A section of veneer may be so extensively damaged that it can't be restored with a patch repair. The only thing to do in this situation is to remove the original sheet of veneer completely and replace it with a new sheet. If you have already tried (or read) 'Patching veneer', on pp.24–5, you will be familiar with some of the techniques and materials involved in applying new veneer – although in this case, the size of the task is much greater. The re-veneering technique is demonstrated here on the top of a late 19th-century, mahogany-veneered chest of drawers.

YOU WILL NEED:

Brown craft paper One sheet, larger all round than the top of the piece.

Electric iron With a low temperature setting.

Paring chisel

Sandpaper Coarse, medium and fine grades.

Commercial wood putty

Steel wallpaper spatula

Glue film One sheet, larger all round than the top of the piece.

Pencil

Long metal ruler To measure and to serve as a straight edge.

Scissors

Heavy-duty utility or craft knife

Heavy books Enough hardcover books to completely cover the new sheet of veneer when piled in close columns each about 30cm high.

Sanding block

Soft-bristled dusting brush

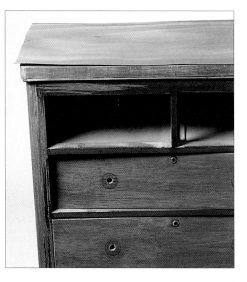

1 Removing the old veneer

● Place a large sheet of brown paper on top of the chest.

● Set an iron to a low to medium temperature. When it is at the right heat, pass it back and forth over the brown paper, pressing firmly. Continue until the paper becomes hot to the touch. This helps to soften the glue that bonds the original veneer to the solid wood underneath.

● Using the chisel with its bevelled edge facing up, scrape off the old veneer. Avoid gouging the solid wood underneath. Reapply the paper and iron as needed to resoften the glue.

2 Preparing the surface

● When you have removed the old veneer, quite a lot of old glue will remain on the surface of the solid top. Cut away as much of this as possible with the chisel. Remove the remainder with coarse-, then medium-, then fine-grade sandpaper.

● Fill any cracks, gouges, or splits with wood putty, applied with a steel wallpaper spatula.

● Leave the putty to dry in accordance with the manufacturer's instructions. Smooth it with coarse-, then medium-, then fine-grade sandpaper.

Note: You must produce a very smooth, flat and even surface for the new veneer. Don't hurry this step, and refill any areas that need filling before moving on.

3 Cutting the veneer and glue film

● Place on a flat surface a sheet of glue film larger than the top of the chest. Measure the top of the chest, and mark this outline on the glue film with a pencil and a ruler. Cut the glue film to size with a pair of scissors.

● Place a large sheet of veneer on a cutting surface. The veneer should be larger all round than the top of the chest. Mark the measurements of the chest top on the veneer with a pencil and a ruler.

● Using a steel ruler and a heavy-duty utility knife, cut the new veneer, either exactly to size or up to 12mm larger all round than the chest top. When cutting against the grain, apply extra pressure on the knife.

4 Installing the veneer

● Remove the backing paper from both sides of the glue film. Carefully align the film on top of the chest.

● Position the new veneer on top of the film. If you have cut the veneer exactly to size, line it up with the four sides of the chest top. If you have cut it slightly large, centre it on the top of the chest.

● Cover the veneer with brown paper.

● Set an iron to a low temperature and press it firmly over the paper. Work from the middle out, then start again, keeping the iron moving until the paper becomes hot to the touch. The heat will activate the glue film.

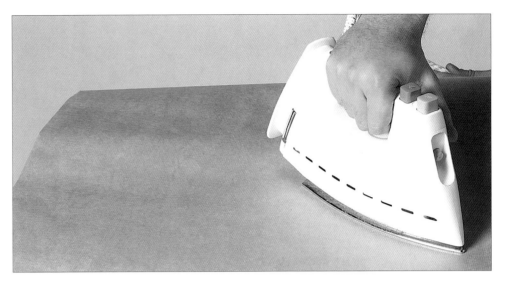

5 Weighting the repair

● Quickly remove the paper and build stable columns of heavy books on top of the veneer. Make sure that each column butts up tightly to those adjoining it, so that there is an even pressure over the entire surface.

● Leave the books in place for about an hour, then remove them.

● Inspect the new veneer, particularly around the edges, to make sure that it has stuck down. If you need to restick an area, repeat the last two stages of step 4 and the first two stages of this step.

6 Trimming the edges

● If in step 3 you cut the new veneer slightly larger all round than the top, place a steel ruler along one edge of the top. Run a heavy-duty utility knife along the outer edge of the ruler to trim the veneer flush with the edge of the top. To make sure that the blade doesn't slip, apply firm pressure with your fingers to the ruler, and continue to do so as you move your fingers along the ruler to keep abreast of the moving blade.

● Repeat the trimming action along the other three sides of the chest top.

7 Sanding

● Wrap a piece of medium-grade sandpaper around a sanding block and smooth the edge of the veneer all round the perimeter of the top of the chest.

● Smooth the edges again, this time using fine-grade sandpaper. Use this also to smooth the top of the veneer very lightly, working in the direction of the grain. Remove the fine dust created by sanding with a soft-bristled brush.

● Turn to pp.30–1 for instructions on filling the grain of the wood and for advice on staining.

● Turn to pp.32–3 for instructions on applying a traditional waxed finish.

Applying traditional finishes

Sometimes it is possible to restore the surface of a piece of furniture by simply reviving, or making minor repairs to, the original finish (see pp.16–23). In most cases, however, more extensive work is required. For example, sometimes a finish is so scraped, scuffed or heat- or moisture-damaged that it must be completely removed and replaced. Similarly, if you have had to introduce a new section of veneer (see pp.24–7), you will need to apply a finish that matches the original finish on the rest of the piece. In these cases, you will use some of the techniques that are described in the following pages: stripping, bleaching, sanding, staining, grain-filling, oiling, waxing, French-polishing and gilding.

However, before replacing an original finish on an antique of good quality, you should do your utmost to salvage it, even if this means employing a professional restorer. Removing the original finish destroys the patina that has built up over time as a result of polishing, exposure to the atmosphere and everyday wear and tear. The patina on a fine piece of furniture makes a major contribution to its value. Many well-meaning amateurs have stripped a piece of furniture and refinished it, only to discover when it comes to selling it they have drastically reduced its value and would have been wiser to have offered it for sale in its original, unrestored condition. Even professional restorers find it very difficult to reproduce an attractive patina in a new finish. So, if the piece to be restored is of financial or other value to you, or if you are in any doubt about the appropriate method to use, do not hesitate to seek professional advice before starting any radical restoration work.

Stripping the old finish

If you wish to strip the original finish from a piece of furniture, the method that you choose should be determined by the size of the piece and how it is constructed, and by the type of finish – oil, wax or French polish. Usually, a combination of two or more of the following methods will prove effective.

Industrial stripping

There are companies which specialize in stripping furniture and wooden items such as doors to the bare wood by immersing them in tanks of caustic soda. This method is quick and relatively inexpensive, but it does have serious drawbacks. In addition to giving the newly exposed wood a dull, slightly grey look, caustic soda tends to both raise and obscure the definition of the grain. In addition, it breaks down traditional animal adhesives that are used in furniture making, such as rabbit-skin glue, loosening joints and veneers. Finally, it strips the natural oils from the wood, which can later cause it to shrink and crack. Unless you are stripping a wooden door or a piece of rustic furniture of relatively crude construction, such as a painted pine chest of drawers, don't use this method.

Scraping

Professional furniture restorers use a cabinetmaker's scraper to remove the finish, particularly on pieces of case furniture, which have large, flat surfaces. This tool is a thin, rectangular piece of steel, about 5cm wide by 7.5cm high, with sharpened edges. Use a scraper as follows.

● Grip the scraper so that one of its two longer edges is parallel with the flat surface of the object. Position your thumbs horizontally across the side facing towards you, and your forefinger and middle finger diagonally across the side facing away from you.

● Apply enough pressure with your thumbs, and enough resistance with your fingers, to gently flex the scraper.

● Starting at one end of the piece, press the sharp edge of the scraper against the surface and push away from you in the direction of the grain. Keep the scraper's edge parallel with the surface; if you allow it to lean slightly, its corners may gouge the wood.

● Two or three strokes of the scraper will remove all the old layers of polish and produce a very smooth surface without disturbing any grain filler (see p.31). Finish off by smoothing the surface lightly with fine-grade sandpaper, working with the grain.

A cabinetmaker's scraper is ideal for removing the finish from flat surfaces, but don't use it on curved surfaces (for example, on a chair) or mouldings as it is very easy to gouge, or produce small depressions in, the underlying wood. For these areas, use a liquid chemical stripper.

Chemical stripping

Solutions for stripping the finish from furniture are available in various forms. Of the paste and liquid-gel types, use the latter, which doesn't have to be kept moist in use. Of the spirit- or water-based types, use the former as it won't raise the grain of the underlying wood or remove the original grain filler. To apply a spirit-based, liquid-gel stripper proceed as follows.

Note: This type of stripper is highly caustic, so keep the work area well ventilated, protect the floor and surrounding areas with plastic sheeting, and wear chemical-resistant rubber gloves, plastic goggles and a face mask throughout the work.

1 With a standard paint brush (2.5–5cm wide, depending on the size of the area to be treated), apply a generous coat of the stripper. Make sure that you work it into any crevices or recessed areas.

2 Leave the stripper until the finish begins to bubble, then carefully remove the stripper and dissolved finish. On flat or gently curving areas, you can do this with a paint scraper, but in recessed areas and on mouldings you should use grade-0 wire wool.

3 When you have removed as much of the old finish as possible, wipe the surface clean with a lint-free rag moistened with methylated spirits.

4 If necessary, apply more stripper, then leave and remove as before.

5 Rub the whole surface with a rag moistened with methylated spirits. When, after a few minutes, the alcohol has evaporated, use fine-grade sandpaper to lightly smooth the surface, working with the grain. If the stripper has removed any of the grain filler, replace this where necessary (see p.31).

Stripping with methylated spirits

Pieces of furniture finished with French polish can be prepared for refinishing with methylated spirits rather than a liquid-gel stripper. The method is described in step 1 of 'Applying French polish', on p.36.

Bleaching

In most cases, once you have removed the original finish, sanded the surface and, if necessary, filled the grain, you can carry out any necessary restaining (see pp.30–1). However, you may find that the stripping process has made the original staining uneven in places. This will make it more difficult to produce an even coloration across the surface of the piece if you have to restain it.

Minor variations in colour contribute to the charm of antique furniture and will appear less obvious once a piece has been refinished. However, on some pieces the original staining is unacceptably patchy and doesn't enhance their appearance. In such cases you can create an even-coloured surface for restaining by bleaching the piece.

Note: Bleach is caustic and gives off toxic fumes. When using it, make sure that the work area is well ventilated, lay down a plastic sheet to protect the floor and nearby objects, and wear plastic goggles, a face mask and chemical-resistant rubber gloves.

1 Dilute household bleach in a plastic bucket, in a ratio of 1 part bleach to 6 parts water.

2 Using a nylon-bristled brush, apply a coat of the diluted bleach over the surface and leave for about 20 minutes. (The surface darkens during this period, but this is to be expected.)

3 Apply a second coat of bleach as before, and leave for 3–4 hours. After about 2 hours, the original colour should be bleached away, but if any remains at the end of this time, apply a third coat of diluted bleach, and leave for another 3–4 hours.

4 Moisten a lint-free rag with water and wipe off any residue of the bleach solution that remains on the surface.

5 Mix a solution of 5ml (1tsp) of white vinegar to 500ml of water. Wipe this over the surface with a lint-free rag and leave to dry for about 4 hours. The vinegar will neutralize any remaining bleach.

6 Use medium-, then fine-grade sandpaper to smooth the wood, working with the grain. Restain the wood, then refill the grain if necessary (see pp.30–1).

Preserving the finish

The antique chair shown right had suffered extensive scratching on its backrest, seat and front legs. However, even this damage didn't warrant stripping off the original finish using one of the methods described above. Instead, the damage was cleverly concealed with wax crayons and tinted beeswax polish (see pp.20–1), preserving the patina that had built up on the chair over the years.

19th-century hall chair
This solid mahogany hall chair was made c.1815, in England. It is stamped on the underside of the seat by its maker, P. Hill. The wax-finished, red-brown mahogany has developed a lustrous patina. This and the maker's stamp contribute substantially to the collectability and market value of the piece.

Staining wood

Some pieces of wooden furniture, such as pine chests and dressers, are not stained before they are oiled, waxed or French-polished because the natural colour of the wood is sufficiently uniform and aesthetically pleasing in its own right. However, most are stained before the finish is applied, and there are two reasons for this. First, the furniture-maker nearly always uses pieces of wood, whether veneered or solid, taken from different cuts or batches, and because such pieces are rarely exactly the same colour, they must be stained to match one another. Second, most cut and planed timber, but particularly mahogany and walnut, look rather dull and lifeless in their natural state. Staining greatly enriches their colouring and, more important, emphasizes or highlights their figuring and grain.

There are four basic types of wood stain: spirit-based, chemical, water-based and oil-based. They all have advantages and disadvantages in terms of colour and ease of application. After you have used a stain, you may need to fill the grain before applying the finish (see 'Filling the grain', opposite).

Spirit-based stains

Professional furniture-makers, polishers and restorers tend to use spirit-based stains on both oily and hard fine-grained woods or before French polishing. These stains are made by dissolving artist's powder pigments in methylated spirits, then adding French polish as a binder, in a ratio of 4 parts methylated spirits to 1 part French polish. They are also available premixed in a wide range of colours from specialist suppliers (see Directory, pp.250–1).

Spirit-based stains penetrate the wood fairly deeply. They produce a duller finish than water-based stains, and it is not easy to achieve evenness of colour during application (which is best done with a brush or a rag) because of their fairly rapid drying times. Consequently, the amateur restorer should restrict the use of solvent-based stains to minor patch repairs, such as when it is necessary to restain a small damaged area before French polishing it again. If you intend to stain the whole of a piece of furniture with a solvent-based stain, you are advised to either employ a professional restorer or refer to a specialist publication on staining and finishing wood.

Chemical stains

Produced by mixing water with chemicals such as ammonia, copper sulphate, bichromate of potash and vinegar and iron, chemical stains react with the tannic acid present in wood and change its natural colour. For example, bichromate of potash turns walnut a pale yellow and beech a light tan, while ammonia gives mahogany a deep-brown tone with a greyish tint and a mix of vinegar and iron turns oak black. A major disadvantage of chemical stains is that it is difficult to assess the level of tannic acid in the wood and thus to predict what colour the wood will be when the stain has dried. Therefore you are advised to entrust the use of these stains to a professional restorer. However, if you wish to carry out the work yourself, you should refer to a specialist publication for advice.

Oil-based stains

The customary description 'oil-based' is misleading, as oil-based stains actually consist of pigments mixed with white spirit and naphtha. Oil-based stains are widely available, premixed, in a choice of wood colours. They provide even coloration, do not raise the grain of the wood or lift old veneers and can be used to tint French polish if you wish to adjust its colour. Different-coloured stains can also be mixed to produce a good colour match with any original staining on another part of the piece, although they are more difficult to shade than water-based equivalents. They are suitable for amateur use, but note that they take 12–24 hours per coat to dry.

Water-based stains

Of the four basic types of stain, the water-based types are the easiest for the amateur to use. Also referred to as 'direct dyes', they are made by dissolving artist's powder pigments in water. They produce quick-drying, clear, vivid colours that can be mixed to create a wide range of shades, and dilution with extra water further extends this variability. Water-based stains can be used with great success on all types of wood, although they work particularly well on light-coloured, close-grained woods such as beech and pine.

These stains have disadvantages compared with oil-based types, but these are not so critical that you should discount their use. First, they raise the grain of the wood unless you prepare it well (see 'Applying water-based stains', opposite). Second, occasionally they lift old veneers from an underlying case. Third, they are absorbed at different rates and to different depths by different parts of the wood. For example, end grain and open grain become much darker than any knots present in the surface. If this happens, you must adjust the colour during application.

Colour-matching

It is unlikely that you will find a premixed oil- or water-based wood stain that perfectly matches the original stain on a piece of furniture. In most cases, to produce the desired colour you must mix two or three different-coloured stains of the same type – that is, either oil-based or water-based, but not a combination of the two. A wide choice of colours is available, but in practice you will find that by combining medium oak (mid-brown), red mahogany (reddish-brown) and walnut (yellowish-brown) in varying proportions you will probably achieve a satisfactory match for most situations. To test the colours proceed as follows.

1 Mix the different-coloured stains in an old saucer to produce a rough approximation of the original colour.

2 With a brush or pad of lint-free rag, apply a thin band of the mixed colour to a test strip of solid wood or veneer (of the same type as the piece of furniture you wish to stain).

3 As the band of stain dries, apply with either brush or rag another coat of stain, but leave about 12mm of the first band uncovered. Then apply a third band of stain, leaving a 12mm strip of the second band uncovered, and so on across the piece of wood.

4 Once the stains have dried, assess the colour match with the original stain on the piece of furniture. If the original stain is still covered with its original finish, apply a coat of that finish (oil, wax or French polish) on top of the test strip before assessing.

5 If you have achieved a good colour match, proceed by applying the required number of coats (of band one, two or three, etc.) to the relevant section of the piece. If the colour is not right, adjust the proportions of the different stains and repeat until you are satisfied.

Applying oil-based stains

Make sure that the surface is clean and dust-free. Using either a fine-bristled varnishing brush or a pad of lint-free cotton rag, proceed as follows.

1 Put a generous quantity of the oil-based stain on the pad or brush.

2 Start at one edge and brush or wipe the stain across the surface in the direction of the grain. Keep an edge constantly wet as you work towards the other edge of the surface, so that you don't leave any dividing or overlap marks between applications of stain. Apply an even pressure throughout the procedure.

3 Leave the surface to dry for a minimum of 6–8 hours between coats. Oil-based stains are absorbed fairly evenly across the surface of the wood, and any patchiness becomes less obvious as you apply additional coats.

4 Leave the surface to dry for at least 24 hours before applying the finish (see pp.32–7).

Applying water-based stains

It is much easier to apply water-based stains with a pad of lint-free cotton rag than a brush. Before you begin, rub a cotton rag dampened with water over the surface and leave the surface to dry. This will raise the grain of the wood, which you should then smooth with medium- and fine-grade sandpaper, working with the grain. By doing this, you will stop the applications of stain from raising the grain. Remove any surface dust with a dusting brush then proceed as follows.

1 Dampen a pad of lint-free cotton rag with water.

2 Pick up a generous quantity of stain on the pad and apply it across the surface, in the direction of the grain, as with an oil-based stain. If you apply too much stain to a particular area, immediately wipe some off with another clean, damp rag. If you apply too little stain, or it is absorbed quickly, apply more stain to the appropriate area.

3 As soon as you have completed the first coat, rub the entire surface with a fresh, dry pad to make the application even and to remove excess stain. Leave to dry for a couple of hours.

4 Using your test strip as a guide to colour, apply as many more coats as necessary. Leave the final coat to dry for 8 hours.

5 Apply a sealer coat of your chosen finish – oil, wax or clear or white French polish.

Note: If you have patched in a small section of new veneer and the grain or figuring doesn't quite match the original, simulate it freehand using a fine-tipped artist's brush and slightly darker versions of the stain used to produce the colour match.

Filling the grain

After stripping the original finish from a piece of furniture, you may find that the grain is filled with flecks of plaster of Paris. This was used to prevent the open grain from making the finish look pitted. You are more likely to find filler on open-grained woods, such as mahogany, that have been French polished or waxed. You will rarely find it on oil-finished oak and teak, where the open grain is a valued part of the finish.

Before you re-finish the surface, seal the filler by wiping over it with a lint-free rag dampened with boiled linseed oil, then leave it to dry for 24 hours. If you need to fill the grain of a new piece of wood, proceed as follows before staining and waxing.

1 Select an oil-based grain filler that closely matches the colour of the wood. Thin it with white spirit until it has a thick, creamy consistency. Adjust the colour with oil-based wood stain, but note that the filler will lighten as it dries.

2 Rub the filler into the grain in a series of overlapping circles with a pad of coarse, lint-free rag (or hessian).

3 Use a clean rag or a piece of hessian to wipe off the excess filler, working in the direction of the grain, before it hardens. Scrape excess filler from recesses or mouldings using a blunt wooden stick.

4 Leave for 24 hours. Smooth, with the grain, using medium- and fine-grade sandpaper, and wipe off the dust.

Wax and oil finishes

Apart from French polish (see pp.34–7), beeswax polish and linseed oil are the two mediums traditionally used to finish antique furniture. Because it is rather time-consuming to apply, oil has fallen out of favour during the past century. However, it is extremely durable, produces a lustrous satin finish and provides very good resistance to heat, liquids, and knocks and scratches. It is also very easy to apply and renew, and is particularly suited to furniture made of pine, and open-grained woods such as oak, teak and all of the Central American or African hardwoods. In fact, it can be applied successfully to any type of wood. If you wish to finish a piece of furniture with oil, or refinish a repaired area to blend with the original oil finish on surrounding areas, refer to 'Applying an oil finish', opposite.

Like oil, wax has been used to finish furniture for centuries. Indeed, pieces made before the beginning of the 19th century were finished with wax or oil; French polish was not invented until later. Although not as durable as oil – it is easily marked by heat, alcohol and water – wax produces a sheen more subtle than the mirror-like finish of French polish. It is also much easier to apply than French polish, although successful results require strenuous effort.

YOU WILL NEED:

Wood stain(s)

Grain filler

Sandpaper Medium- and fine-grade.

Soft-bristled dusting brush

Fine-bristled varnishing brush

Clear or white French polish

Wire wool Grade 000.

Wax furniture polish Either tinted or clear.

White spirit

Metal container To hold a mixture of wax and white spirit. The container must fit in the saucepan listed below.

Metal saucepan

Shoe brush

Soft, lint-free cotton rag

Types of wax polish

A wide choice of high-quality wax polishes is available in clear or coloured formulas. Coloured wax is recommended if you wish to darken slightly the colour of the stained wood. (Coloured waxes will also help you to develop rapidly an antique finish on new wood.) Wax polishes are also available in various consistencies, ranging from stiff pastes to thin creams. The former are most suited to solid wood, the latter to delicate veneers and inlays.

Whichever type of wax polish you choose, it must contain beeswax. If you want a particularly durable finish, it should also contain a quantity of carnauba wax. However, avoid wax polish that contains silicone, which will eventually penetrate the wood and make it practically impossible to apply a new finish if the piece ever needs to be restored. To apply a wax finish, proceed as follows.

1 Staining and filling

● Stain the wood with a wood stain to achieve the required colour (see pp.30–1). In this case, the chest of drawers that had its top re-veneered (see pp.26–7) was treated with a water-based stain. The original sides and front were stained with one coat of a mixture of 3 parts brown mahogany stain to 2 parts red mahogany. The new mahogany-veneered top was then colour-matched to the sides and front with three coats of 3 parts brown mahogany to 1 part red mahogany to 1 part walnut.
● Fill the grain of any new wood, using the technique on p.31. Working with the grain, smooth the surface with fine-grade sandpaper. Remove all dust with a soft-bristled dusting brush.

2 Sealing the surface

● Using a fine-bristled varnishing brush, apply two thin coats of either white or clear French polish. (See p.34 for information on types of French polish. Note that clear polish will not change the colour of the wood, while white polish may darken it slightly.) Allow 12 hours for each coat to dry. Rub each coat with grade-000 wire wool, working with the grain, then use a soft-bristled dusting brush to remove the fine dust. The polish will seal the wood and prevent it from absorbing the wax. If the wood did absorb the wax, the dust and dirt that accumulate in the wax over time would eventually penetrate the wood and make cleaning more difficult.

3 Applying the first wax

● Place equal quantities of wax and white spirit in a small container. Put the container into a saucepan of hot water – the water must be below the height of the container. As the wax melts, mix it into the spirit to form a thick, creamy liquid.
● Keep the wax warm and fluid by renewing the hot water. Brush a thin coat of the wax onto the surface of the furniture with a clean shoe brush.
● Wipe excess wax from the surface with a lint-free cotton rag. Allow the remaining wax to set.
● Lightly rub the surface in the direction of the grain with grade-000 wire wool. Buff it vigorously with a soft, lint-free cotton rag and leave for 48 hours.

4 Applying additional wax

● Build up further thin coats of wax with a pad of lint-free rag. For these coats, take the wax unheated straight from its can, without diluting it with white spirit.
● Leave each coat for approximately 5 minutes before buffing it with a clean rag, and allow 3–4 hours between coats. Apply as many coats as are required to produce a deep, lustrous shine.

Note: It is wrong to think that the more wax you use, the deeper the resulting shine. The secret of wax polishing is to apply very thin coats of wax and buff each one as vigorously as you can – here there is no substitute for hard work if you want good results.

Applying an oil finish

In centuries past, many professional polishers used raw linseed oil to give an oil finish to furniture. However, this substance has a drying time of at least three days between coats, and numerous coats have to be applied if an attractive result is to be achieved. It is not surprising, therefore, that for much of the 20th century, polishers have chosen to use boiled linseed oil in preference to the raw form. It dries in 24 hours and produces very impressive results. To apply a boiled linseed-oil finish, proceed as follows.

1 Stain the wood (see pp.30–1) to a few shades lighter than the colour you want to produce, because each application of boiled linseed oil will slightly darken the wood. Then leave the surface to dry thoroughly.

2 Use a soft, lint-free rag to rub a generous quantity of oil into the wood. Keep rubbing in oil as hard as you can until the wood will soak up no more.

3 Wipe off the excess oil, using a piece of clean, lint-free rag, and leave the item to dry for 24 hours.

4 Repeat steps 2 and 3 once every 24 hours for up to a week. (If you prefer, you can apply boiled linseed oil repeatedly for as long as a month, but most people will not wish to have a piece of furniture out of use for such a long period.)

5 After the final coat of oil has dried, buff it vigorously and with as much pressure as you can, using a lint-free rag. The more effort you put into this stage, the more lustrous the resulting subtle sheen will be.

6 To maintain a boiled linseed oil finish in good condition, apply a further coat of oil every three to six months (depending on how dry the atmosphere is).

French polish

'French polish' is a collective term for a number of different liquid polishes that were developed during the early years of the 19th century. These are all made by dissolving shellac (a secretion from the lac insect) in methylated spirits and adding various other ingredients, including drying and hardening agents. Applied in stages, French polish produces an extremely smooth, mirror-like finish on furniture (notably pieces made from mahogany and walnut, but not wide-pored oak) and enriches the colour and highlights the figuring of the wood. Unfortunately, it is easily damaged, especially when exposed to alcohol, heat or moisture – the latter produces white blotches or bloom on the surface. For this reason, French polish is applied primarily to pieces that are not subject to heavy use, such as occasional tables and pianos, but rarely to dining tables or chairs.

Of the three traditional finishes for furniture – oil, wax and French polish – the last is the most difficult to apply. However, although French polishing may seem intimidating at first, for most people it becomes much easier once they have developed a feel for the method and the materials.

Walnut-veneered side table
An early 20th-century, French-polished, walnut table.

Types of French polish

There are five basic types of French polish, each with a different application. French (or 'brown') polish is the standard type. It is made from flake shellac and can be used on all but the palest of woods. Garnet polish, made from garnet shellac, is suited to mahogany and fine-grained oaks, where a deep, warm, red-brown tone is required. Button polish is made from 7.5cm-wide buttons of highly refined shellac. It makes a more durable finish than the standard type of French polish and gives wood a brown cast with a slight orange-yellow tinge. It is therefore useful for enhancing the colour of golden-toned hardwoods, such as walnut. However, it is not suitable for dark-stained woods, as it can obscure the grain. White polish is made from acid-bleached shellac. Milk-like in appearance, it darkens paler woods slightly. Clear (transparent) polish is made from shellac that has been bleached twice and de-waxed. It is mainly used on marquetry and inlay, where any darkening of the wood would spoil its appearance.

Making a rubbing pad

French polish should be applied to recessed areas and mouldings with a brush (see step 4, p.37), but on flat surfaces it must be built up in thin layers with a pad of soft, lint-free cloth wrapped round a swab of cotton wool to make a rubbing pad. A rubbing pad is essential for French polishing. To make one, proceed as follows.

1 Shaping the swab

● Place the square of clean, lint-free cotton rag flat on a work surface.

● Using your fingers and palms of your hands, tease a handful of cotton wool into an egg-shaped swab with one end more pointed than the other.

● Place the cotton wool in the middle of the cotton rag. Fold back one side of the rag so that it covers the swab's pointed end.

YOU WILL NEED:

Soft, lint-free cotton rag A piece about 25cm square – a clean, white cotton handkerchief is ideal.

Cotton wool An average-sized handful.

French polish For the appropriate type of French polish, see left.

Scrap of wood A small, flat, clean piece.

Linseed oil To lubricate the rubbing pad.

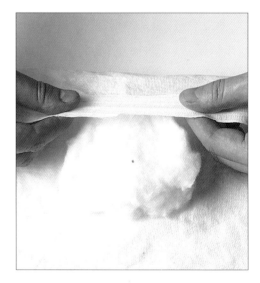

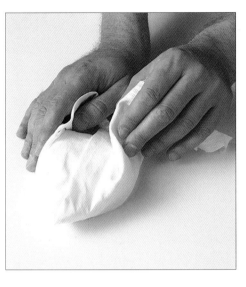

2 Folding in one end of the rag
● At the pointed end of the swab, fold in the sides of the rag to form a pear-shaped point at the end of the rubbing pad.
Note: At this stage you should have covered just over half of the swab; the more rounded end should remain uncovered by the rag.

3 Turning over the sides of the rag
● Using your fingers, start to turn over the sides and end of the rag so that the swab is completely enclosed. Check the underside of the rag to make sure that no creases have formed. If any have, adjust and re-tighten the rag so that you have a flat, crease-free pad underneath.

4 Twisting the top of the rag
● Gently supporting the sides and base of the rubbing pad in the palm of one hand, gather up and twist all the loose material on the top of the pad. This will tighten the rag around the swab and so compress the swab and slightly reduce the size of the rubbing pad.

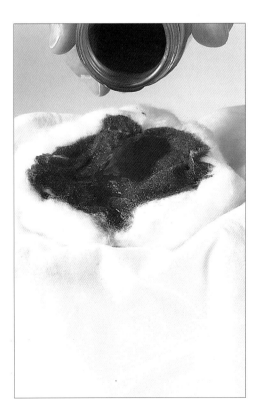

5 Putting on polish
● Secure the pad firmly in the palm of one hand. With your other hand, untwist and unfold the rag to expose the top of the swab.
● Drip a small quantity of polish from its container onto the top of the swab. Keep adding more polish until the swab is saturated, but not overflowing, then refold and twist the rag to again enclose the swab.

6 Lubricating the pad
● Dab the pad of the rubbing pad on a clean, flat scrap of wood to bring the polish from the swab to the surface of the pad. Keep dabbing the rubbing pad to spread the polish evenly.
● To lubricate the rubbing pad and produce a fluent polishing action during application, moisten the tip of an forefinger with linseed oil and rub a very thin coating evenly over the surface of the pad. You are now ready to apply polish to the prepared surface of the piece (see pp.36–7).

Applying French polish

Successful French polishing depends on several factors. First, you must apply the polish with a crease-free rubbing pad (see pp.34–5). Creases in the pad will create drag marks in the finish which you will only be able to remove by stripping off the finish and starting again.

Second, you must always work in an environment that is dust-free, dry and warm. If specks of dust become trapped in the polish while it dries, they will ruin what is supposed to be a blemish-free finish. If you work in a damp atmosphere, the polish will develop a cloudy 'bloom' across the surface of the piece that will detract from the transparency of the finish and obscure the grain and figuring of the underlying wood. Although this bloom may not become apparent immediately, it will inevitably appear after a few days, weeks or months. If you apply the polish at a temperature lower than 16°C, it will not completely harden. This will cause streaks and smears to develop across the surface as you build up subsequent applications of polish.

Third, you must be patient: always work at a steady, even rate, and be prepared to build up the finish with 12 to 20 separate applications of polish.

YOU WILL NEED:

Wire wool Grades 000 and 0000.
Methylated spirits
Soft, lint-free cotton rag
Two rubbing pads To polish. See pp.34–5.
French polish For the appropriate type, see p.34.
Airtight glass jar
Sandpaper Fine-grade.
Soft-bristled dusting brush
Linseed oil
Sable-bristled artist's brush 12mm wide.
Clear beeswax furniture polish

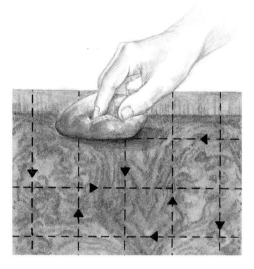

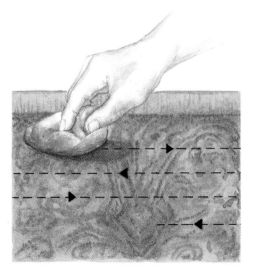

1 Removing the old finish

● Dip a golf-ball-sized piece of grade-000 wire wool in methylated spirits. Gently wipe it back and forth across the surface of the old finish, working with the grain, to dissolve the old French polish. Make sure that you work the wire wool into any recessed areas and mouldings.
● Keep changing the wire wool (and using additional clean methylated spirits) as it becomes clogged with the sticky residue of old polish.
● Moisten a pad of soft, lint-free rag with methylated spirits and wipe it over the surface until no more polish can be removed.

2 Skinning in

● Put French polish on the rubbing pad (see pp.34–5).
● Maintaining firm, even pressure, wipe the rubbing pad across the grain in straight, overlapping strokes. Sweep the rubbing pad onto and off the sides of the surface, and never stop halfway through a stroke, as this leaves marks. Slightly increase the pressure on the rubbing pad if the flow of polish slows up. After using the rubbing pad, put it in an airtight glass jar and leave the piece to dry for an hour.
● Repeat the above, this time working with the grain. Put more polish on the rubbing pad if needed. Put the pad in the jar and leave the piece to dry overnight.

3 First bodying-up

● Lightly rub the surface with grade-000 wire wool or fine-grade sandpaper. Work in the direction of the grain. Remove any dust with a soft-bristled dusting brush.
● Remove the rubbing pad from the glass jar, put on French polish, and lubricate the pad with a small quantity of linseed oil (see p.35, step 6).
● Apply the first 'bodying-up' coat by working the rubbing pad in a series of overlapping circles (as in the diagram) from one side of the surface to the other. Overlap rows of circles slightly until the entire surface is covered. Apply even pressure throughout, increasing it slightly only if the flow of polish begins to dry up.

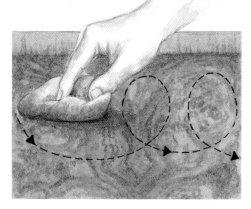

4 Second bodying-up

● Wait for about two minutes after you have finished the first bodying-up. Meanwhile, refill and re-lubricate the rubbing pad.

● Apply the second bodying-up coat by working the rubbing pad in a figure-of-eight movement from one side of the surface to the other.

● Alternate steps 3 and 4 until you have applied another six thin coats of polish. Allow two minutes between each coat, refilling and re-lubricating the rubbing pad between coats when necessary.

● Put the rubbing pad in an airtight glass jar and leave the polish to harden for at least 12 hours.

● Lightly rub the surface with fine-grade sandpaper to remove any minor imperfections. Repeat steps 3 and 4 at least another six times (although you can do more if you want to produce an even more mirror-like finish). For the penultimate coat, dilute the polish as 3 parts polish to 1 part methylated spirits; for the final coat, use equal parts of each. Leave the polish to harden as before.

Note: At this stage, having 'bodied-up' all the flat or slightly curved surfaces, apply one or two coats of the French polish to any recessed areas and mouldings, using a 12mm sable-bristled artist's brush. To make sure that the application is smooth, first moisten the bristles of the brush with methylated spirits. Do not overbrush any areas, as this will leave bristle marks in the finish.

5 Spiriting off

● You will now have a smooth, cloudy finish. The cloudiness is caused by the linseed oil. To remove it, make a new rubbing pad, but this time wrap at least four squares of lint-free rag around the cotton swab. Put methylated spirits on the pad.

● Wipe the rubbing pad over the surface, with the grain, in long, slightly overlapping strokes. If the rubbing pad drags, give it more methylated spirits.

● If you haven't used much linseed oil, after one treatment the surface will clear and not cloud over again soon after. However, in most cases you will have to repeat the treatment up to four times, removing the outer layer of rag from the rubbing pad for each.

6 Waxing

● Leave the smooth, glassy surface for a week to fully harden. Then, either leave it as it is, or apply a thin coat of clear beeswax polish. Use a soft, lint-free rag to apply and buff the polish.

7 Reducing the shine

● To produce a satin, rather than high-gloss, finish, dip a ball of grade-0000 wire wool in clear beeswax polish and wipe it very lightly over the surface in the direction of the grain.

● Wipe off any dust with a clean, soft rag. Apply a thin coat of polish as in step 6 and buff it to a shine.

Regilding a mirror frame

Gilded mirror and picture frames are prone to minor damage, usually as a result of knocks and scrapes. Sometimes just the gilding will be rubbed away, but more often the gesso mouldings of the frame will also be slightly chipped or cracked, as with this late 19th-century mirror frame. If the mouldings have an uncomplicated profile, you will be able to shape the necessary repairs by hand before regilding; if the mouldings are more intricate, you will have to use a casting technique.

Regardless of the degree of damage, if your frame is particularly old, rare or valuable, you should have it repaired by a professional restorer, who will probably use gold leaf for the regilding. However, if your frame is not particularly valuable, you can regild it yourself with gold metallic powders. This frame was completely regilded, but if the damage is confined to a small area, you can restrict the regilding to that, then blend the new into the old, as described in steps 5–6.

1 Repairing the frame

● Remove any dust from the frame using a soft-bristled dusting brush. Wash off any dirt with a soft, lint-free cotton rag dampened with a weak solution of mild liquid soap and lukewarm water. Rinse thoroughly with a clean rag dampened with lukewarm water, then pat dry immediately with terry towelling. Don't allow water to remain on the frame longer than necessary as it can soak into the gesso and soften it.

● Cover the mirror glass with a large sheet of brown craft paper. Secure the paper around the perimeter of the glass with masking tape. Make sure that the glass is covered with the tape right to the edges of the frame, to prevent paint, gold size and gold metallic powder adhering to it during the following steps.

● If there are any small holes or cracks in the frame, press premixed gesso paste into them with the blade of an old table knife. Build up the paste until it stands slightly higher than the old level of each hole or crack and leave it to dry for 48 hours.

● Using a combination of a utility knife, needle files and fine sandpaper, shape and smooth the dry repair so that it is level with, and follows the contours of, the surrounding area.

Note: If an intricately shaped piece of moulding has broken off, you can make a copy from an adjacent section of moulding, using a small artist's brush, latex, epoxy putty, epoxy-resin glue and the press-moulding technique described on p.190.

YOU WILL NEED:
Soft-bristled dusting brush
Soft, lint-free cotton rag
Mild liquid soap
Lukewarm water
Terry towelling rags
Large sheet of brown craft paper
Masking tape
Premixed gesso paste
Table knife
Utility or craft knife
Needle files
Sandpaper Fine-grade.
Small artist's brush, latex, epoxy putty,
and epoxy-resin glue Required only if repairs
to intricately shaped moulding are necessary.
Wire wool Grades 0 and 000.
Two paint brushes 2.5–5cm wide.
Artist's oil paint One tube of burnt sienna.
White spirit
Gold metallic powder
Liquid gold size
Plastic goggles and face mask
Small saucer
Small artist's hog's-hair brush
Soft-bristled make-up brush
**Tinted furniture wax or mid- or dark-
brown shoe polish**

2 Painting the frame

● Lightly rub the surface of the frame with grade-0 wire wool, to make sure that it accepts the oil paint well.

● With a 2.5–5cm paint brush, apply two coats of burnt sienna oil paint over the frame. To make this easier, thin the paint slightly by adding one or two drops of white spirit. Let each coat of paint dry for at least 24 hours.

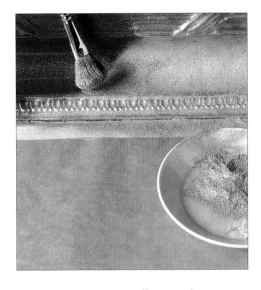

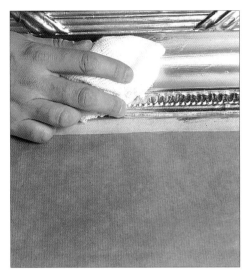

3 Applying metallic powder

- From an artist's supplier, buy gold metallic powder that matches the original gilding.
- Using the other paint brush, apply liquid gold size to the frame. Make sure that you cover it all.
- The size will be sticky in half an hour. Put on goggles and a mask to protect your eyes, nose and mouth, and decant some powder into a saucer.
- Dip the bristle tips of a small artist's hog's-hair brush into the powder. Stipple the powder onto the liquid gold size as soon as it is sticky. Work quickly and make sure that you cover the whole frame.

4 Removing excess powder

- Leave the powder (and the liquid gold size which is drying underneath it) for a minimum of 8 hours, by which time the bond between the powder and the gold size will have fully formed. Then, using a soft-bristled make-up brush, lightly dust off any powder that hasn't adhered to the size.

Note: If you discover bare patches where the powder hasn't adhered to the size, repeat steps 2–4 on the affected areas.

5 Burnishing the new gilding

- Make a flat pad from a fist-sized piece of soft, lint-free cotton rag. Gently rub the pad back and forth over the gilding. A certain amount of powder will come off onto the pad, so re-form it from time to time or, if necessary, replace it with a new pad.
- If you wish, you can rub fairly hard in places, so that the burnt sienna ground colour begins to 'ghost' through the gilding. This process will give the frame an attractively worn appearance. If you like the look of bright, new gilding, stop here.

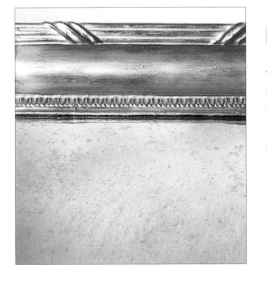

6 Antiquing the gilding

- Give the new gilding an antique appearance by rubbing in a tinted furniture wax with a clean, soft, lint-free cotton rag. (A good substitute for furniture wax is a mid-brown or dark-brown shoe polish.) To give the gilding a more 'distressed' antique look, apply the polish with grade-000 wire wool, which will rub away some of the gilding in a random manner. However, if you do this, proceed cautiously, because rubbing too hard can remove so much gilding that the frame may end up looking unrestored.
- Regardless of whether you apply the tinted wax or polish with a rag or wire wool, leave the wax or polish for about half an hour. Then gently buff it, using a clean, soft, lint-free cotton pad. This will produce a deep, lustrous shine across the surface of the frame.
- When you having finished buffing the gilding, peel off the masking tape and remove the brown paper from the glass.

Structural repairs to chairs

Chairs are more prone to general wear and tear and damage than any other type of furniture. The most vulnerable parts of a chair are the joints that secure the various components together, particularly those that connect the legs and the seat rails. Wear and damage usually occur as a result of excessive loading, especially when a sitter rocks the chair onto its back legs. Initially a loosening of the joints occurs, a process often exacerbated by shrinkage of the wood and drying out of the glue caused by the very dry atmosphere found in most well-insulated, centrally-heated houses. As the joints loosen, additional loading is transferred to the legs and rails. Eventually the joints, and in some cases the legs and the rails, fracture.

In order to carry out some of the repairs to joints and other chair components that are described on the following pages, you may have to dismantle part or all of the chair. The manner and sequence in which you dismantle a chair depends on the nature of its construction. Although chairs are made in numerous styles, the majority of them can be divided into one of three basic categories: frame chairs (which include balloon-backs), stick chairs (which include Windsors) and bentwood chairs. The methods of dismantling chairs are described below and opposite; methods of reassembly are described on p.43.

A typical frame chair
This mid-18th-century Chippendale armchair is made of mahogany and has cabriole legs, ball-and-claw feet and an elaborately carved back splat.

Frame chairs

The Chippendale chair illustrated above right is a typical frame chair, as is the balloon-back illustrated opposite. This style is made of two units: a seat frame and a back frame.

The seat frame consists of a front rail, a back rail and two side rails. The cabriole-style front legs (considered a separate component) are joined to the seat frame with mortise-and-tenon joints. The back frame consists of a cresting (or top) rail, a mid rail or a back splat, the same back rail as the seat frame, and the two back legs. The top rail is dowelled or blind-tenoned to the legs. If used, a mid rail is tenoned between the legs (see balloon-back chair, opposite) whereas a splat is tenoned to the top and seat rails as in the Chippendale chair (above). The two frames join where the side rails meet the back legs.

Angled brackets or blocks are often screwed into the corners of the seat frame to provide stability. On some chairs, further stability is provided by the insertion of stretcher rails between the legs. The configuration of the stretchers varies, but an H-shape is very common. In chairs of this pattern the side stretchers join the front and back legs and are themselves joined by a transverse middle stretcher.

On most frame chairs, the seat is either a drop-in pad or a sprung seat (see p.92). Drop-in seat pads sit on rebates or corner blocks that are glued and screwed to the inside of the seat rails. If the chair has arms, they are usually attached with tenons or dowels. The backs of the armrests join the sides of the back legs, while the fronts join a vertical arm support. In most cases a housing is cut into the bottom of the arm supports and fits over the outside of the side rails.

Before you dismantle a frame chair, you must first remove the drop-in seat pad or stuffed seat (see pp.92–3). Then proceed as follows.

1 Remove any joint reinforcements, as explained on p.42.
2 Work through the chair, softening the glue with steam (see p.42) and separating the joints in the sequence specified below.
3 Work back and forth between pairs of opposing joints, opening each a little at a time so that you don't fracture or jam any of them. If any joint is stubborn, you may have to knock it apart by placing a softwood block against one side and tapping it with a carpenter's mallet.
4 If there are arms, pull the arm supports slightly away from the side rails. Pull the armrests from the back legs.
5 Pull the back legs from the side rails.
6 Pull the front legs from the side rails.
7 Pull the front legs from the front rail.
8 Pull the the top rail from the back legs (and splat, if there is one).
9 Pull the back legs from the back rail (and mid rail, if there is one).
10 Pull the splat (if there is one) from the back rail.

Stick chairs

The legs, back spindles and arm supports of a stick chair (see right) are turned – rounded on a lathe – and tapered at the ends to fit into sockets in the seat, armrests and back rail. The stretcher rails are also tapered to fit into sockets in the legs. All the sockets are blind, with the exception of the through-sockets (see pp.244–5) in the seat that house the larger, outer back spindles. The latter have small tightening wedges driven into them from under the seat. To dismantle a stick chair, soften the glue with steam (see p.42), then proceed as follows.

• Pull the back rail off the spindles, or knock it off by tapping with a carpenter's mallet against a softwood block.

• Twist and pull the spindles out of the seat (and the outer ones off the armrests).

Note: To remove the outer spindles, first cut out the wedges with a mallet and small chisel (see p.42, step 4).

• Pull or knock the arms off their spindles, then twist and pull the latter from the seat.

• Twist and pull the legs from the seat, then the stretchers from the legs and each other.

Bentwood chairs

Most of the parts of a bentwood chair (see right) are screwed or bolted together. The exceptions are the seat, which is glued into the seat frame, and the front legs, which are glued into sockets in the seat frame. These joints are often reinforced by a screw. As a result, apart from softening the glued joints with steam (see p.42) and pulling them apart, you can dismantle a bentwood chair with a wrench and screwdriver. However, in many cases the screws are countersunk and their heads are covered with wooden plugs. Remove the plugs with a chisel (see step 2) to gain access to the screw heads.

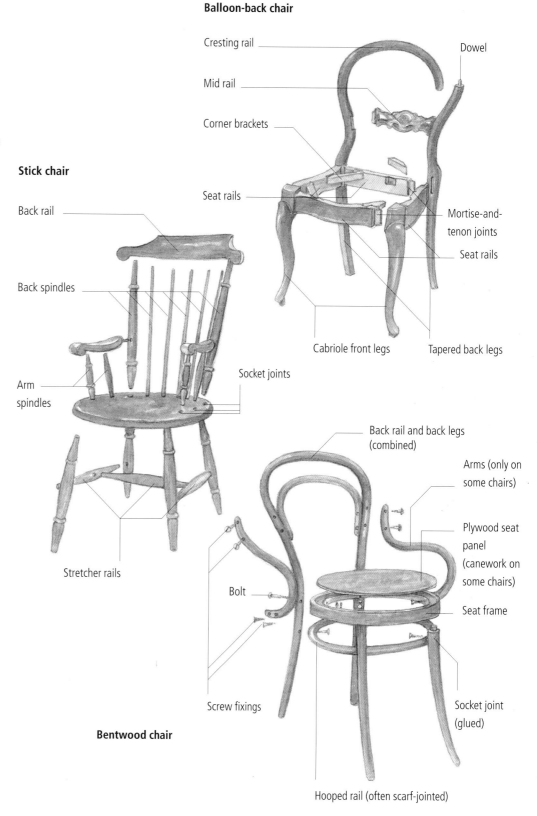

Balloon-back chair

Cresting rail

Dowel

Mid rail

Corner brackets

Seat rails

Mortise-and-tenon joints

Seat rails

Cabriole front legs

Tapered back legs

Stick chair

Back rail

Back spindles

Arm spindles

Socket joints

Stretcher rails

Bentwood chair

Back rail and back legs (combined)

Arms (only on some chairs)

Bolt

Plywood seat panel (canework on some chairs)

Seat frame

Screw fixings

Socket joint (glued)

Hooped rail (often scarf-jointed)

Removing joint reinforcements

Many of the joints that you encounter on antique chairs – particularly mortise-and-tenon joints – will have been reinforced either during manufacture or later. Before you can dismantle joints, you must remove these reinforcements. The most common types, and the methods used to remove them, are described below.

1 Removing corner brackets
• Use a screwdriver to remove the retaining screws from any corner brackets found on the rails under the seat.
Note: The illustration shows a steel corner bracket, as seen on many 20th-century chairs; on earlier chairs, you are more likely to find screwed wooden blocks.

1 Removing plugs and screws
• Check whether wood screws have been used to reinforce the joints. A small wooden plug inserted on top of the countersunk screw, and lying level with the surface, is a telltale sign. Before removing the screw, first carefully cut out the plug with a small, bevelled-edged chisel.

1 Removing dowels
• Carefully drill out any wooden dowels that have been inserted through legs, joints and rails, in order to lock the seat-rail tenons into their mortises. To do this, use a drill bit with the same diameter as the dowel.

1 Removing open wedges
• Check all 'through' tenons (see pp.244–5) to see if they have thin wedges driven into them. The wedges spread the tenons and make them fit tighter within their mortises. To loosen the tenon, gouge out the wedges with a narrow chisel.

1 Removing hidden wedges
• You won't be able to see if 'blind' tenons (see pp.244–5) have been spread with wedges, but their presence will become apparent if you try to remove the tenon and it jams halfway. To release the tenon, cut off its top and bottom by inserting a hacksaw blade between the rail and the leg.

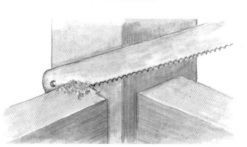

Softening animal glue

If the animal glue that bonds a joint in wood hasn't lost its adhesive qualities, you must soften it so that you can dismantle the joint. The easiest way to do this is to use an improvised steam generator.
1 Use a metal hacksaw to cut two 10cm lengths of small-bore brass tubing.
2 Drill a hole the same diameter as the tubing through a cork that fits into the neck of a 'whistling' kettle. Push one of the brass tubes through the hole in the cork – leaving 2.5cm of tube protruding.
3 Take 2m of silicone tubing, with the same diameter as the brass tubing, and push one end of it over the brass tube in the cork and the other end over the second brass tube, and bind it with string or rag.
4 Half-fill the kettle with water and secure the cork in the neck. Put the kettle on the stove. While it is coming to a boil, drill a hole slightly larger than the brass tube into a corner of the joint you wish to dismantle.
5 When steam emerges from the tube, insert the end into the joint. After two minutes, the glue will soften, and you can knock and pull the joint apart.

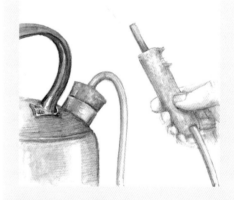

Using a steam generator
Steam will dissolve the glue in a joint.

Reassembling chairs

The method that you use to reassemble a chair will depend on whether it is frame (including balloon-back), stick, or bentwood. In all cases you must first remove the old glue from the joints. To do this, soften the glue with steam (see left), then scrape and wipe it off with a steel spatula and a rag.

Frame chairs

Reassemble a frame chair by following this sequence of steps.

1 Glue together any side and central stretcher rails.

2 Glue the front legs to the front and side rails, and glue the fronts of the side stretcher rails into the front legs.

3 Glue the back rail into the sides of the back legs. Then glue the side rails and the side stretcher rails into the back legs.

Note: Use sash clamps to secure the seat and back frames while the glue dries (below, left). Check that the frame is square before leaving the glue to set. On a balloon-back chair, use wooden blocks and tourniquets (below, right).

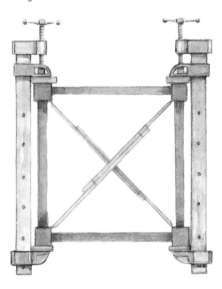

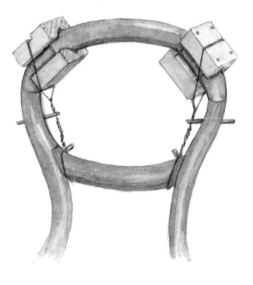

1 Squaring the seat and back frames

● Take two straight battens of wood and plane one end of both of them to a 45-degree angle.

● Secure the battens one on top of the other with two rubber bands. Slide them into position so that the two ends fit into two diagonally opposite corners of the frame.

● Keep the battens to this length, and check to see if they fit exactly into the other diagonal. If they do, the frame is square. If they don't, loosen the sash clamps, and press the frame across the longer of the two diagonals to square it up. Then retighten the sash clamps, check that the frame is still square and let the glue dry for 24 hours before removing the clamps.

1 Securing a balloon-back

● Because of the curved shape of a balloon-back, you will not be able to secure it with sash clamps. Instead, make two pairs of special wooden blocks. Cut a V-shaped notch and drill screw holes in the four corners of each block (as in the illustration).

● Glue the cresting rail onto the dowels at the top of the back legs.

● Screw two V-blocks together around the cresting rail, as shown.

● Tie loops of strong cord around the blocks and the mid rail. Insert a small stick into each cord and turn it enough times to tighten the loop like a tourniquet.

Bentwood chairs

Reassemble a bentwood chair by following this sequence of steps.

● Bolt the seat frame to the back legs with a wrench.

● Glue the front legs into their sockets in the seat frame, twisting them into place with your hands. Put the chair on a flat surface and, if necessary, push or pull the assembly with your hands to square it up.

● If the chair has retaining screws, insert these through the seat frame into the tops of the legs where they locate in their sockets, and tighten them with a screwdriver.

● Slide the hooped stretcher rail into position, and screw it to the inside of the legs.

● If the chair has hooped arm rails, screw these to the seat frame and the back legs.

● If the screws are countersunk, cut new facing plugs from matching wood. Glue the plugs into the holes above the screw heads. Leave to dry for 24 hours.

● Trim the plugs level with a chisel and medium- and fine-grade sandpaper. Stain and polish to match.

Stick chairs

Reassemble a stick chair using the following sequence of steps. Note that you may be able to twist and push the components into their sockets with your hands, but where this proves impossible, use a carpenter's mallet to tap them into position.

● Glue the stretcher rails together, then glue them to the legs. Stand the entire leg assembly on a level surface, and gently push and pull it to make sure that it is level.

● Glue the leg assembly to the underside of the seat and adjust it until the seat is level. Let the glue harden for 24 hours.

● Glue the back spindles into the top of the seat.

● If the chair has arms, glue the arm spindles to the top of the seat, and the arms themselves to the tops of their spindles.

● Glue the back rail to the tops of the back spindles. Check that the assembly is level, and let the glue dry for 24 hours.

Repairing and tightening tenons

Mortise-and-tenon joints often become loose as a result of wear and tear, shrinkage of the wood, and drying out and loss of adhesion of the glue. Two methods are recommended for tightening them, and the one you use will depend on whether the joint has been made with a 'through' tenon or a 'blind' tenon (see p.244). If a tenon has been left loose for too long, it will eventually break – either partly or completely – as a result of excessive pressure. In either case, it must be rebuilt.

Broken tenons

If a tenon has broken off from the end of its rail, you must dismantle the joint, make a replacement tenon from a new piece of wood, cut a housing in the end of the rail, glue the new tenon into it and reinforce the joint with a dowel. The new tenon is then glued into the original mortise in the leg. To do this, proceed as follows.

1 Marking and cutting the housing

● Dismantle the joint (see p.42). If a small piece of the tenon is still protruding from the end of the rail, use a tenon saw to cut off the projection and square the end of the rail.

● Set a mortise gauge to the width of the mortise in the leg, and mark an angled housing for the new tenon along the end and underside of the rail. As a general rule, the maximum depth of the angled housing that you cut in the rail should be three times the length of the original tenon.

● Cut along the outline of the housing with a tenon saw, and pare out the surplus wood with a chisel that matches the width of the housing.

2 Cutting and fitting the tenon

● Cut a new tenon from hardwood that matches the original wood. Cut the new tenon so that the grain of the wood runs in the same direction as that of the rail. Cut it over-size, so that it protrudes slightly from the top of the rail. However, cut one end of the tenon (it doesn't matter which) to match the angled housing exactly; the other end should protrude from the housing to the same length as the depth of the mortise into which it is to be fitted.

● Glue the new tenon into the angled housing. Secure it in place with a G-clamp, and leave this in place for 24 hours while the glue dries.

3 Fitting a dowel and planing flush

● Remove the G-clamp and drill a hole from one side of the rail, through the tenon, and out through the other side of the rail.

● Apply glue to a pre-cut wooden dowel, and tap it through the hole with a carpenter's mallet. The dowel should be the same diameter as the hole to give a snug fit. Let the glue dry for 24 hours.

● Use a panel saw to cut the ends of the dowel flush with the sides of rail.

● Use a wood plane to shave down the top of the new tenon so that it is level with the top of the rail.

● Reglue the tenon into its mortise, and restain and renew the finish as necessary (see pp.30–3).

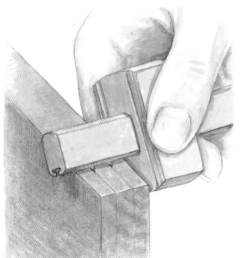

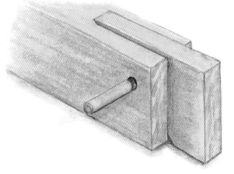

Partly broken tenons

If only part of a tenon has broken off, you need not replace the entire tenon. However, you must remove the damaged section and insert a new piece of wood.

1 Cutting out the damage

● Use a chisel the same width as the tenon to cut off the damage down to the shoulder.
● Cut a small angled housing into the shoulder with the chisel. The housing should be about 12mm deep.

2 Making and fitting the repair

● To fit the end of the tenon, cut a piece of hardwood as thick as the tenon, wide enough to be flush with the rail's edge, and long enough so that, when cut on an angle, it seats fully in the housing.
● Glue the new piece in position, secure with a G-clamp, and let the glue dry for 24 hours.

Loose through tenons

If a through tenon has become loose in its mortise, you can tighten it. However, you will have to dismantle the joint before making the repair.

1 Fitting wedges

● Dismantle the joint (see p.42). Make two cuts across the tenon with a tenon saw. The cuts should reach almost to the shoulder of the tenon.
● Using a tenon saw, cut two tapered hardwood wedges. At their thinnest point, these should be the same thickness as the width of the saw cuts in the tenon. Smooth the sides and edges of the tenons with medium- and fine-grade sandpaper.
● Glue the tenon back into its mortise.
● Apply glue to the hardwood wedges and tap them into the saw cuts in the tenon using a carpenter's mallet. The wedges will spread the tenon, making a tight fit in the mortise.
Note: Proceed cautiously when tapping in the wedges. If you have cut them too thick and then drive them too far in, they may split the tenon and the surrounding wood.
● Leave the glue to harden for 24 hours.
● Saw off the protruding ends of the wedges with a panel saw so that they are flush with the leg.
● Finish by smoothing the end of the wedges with medium- and fine-grade sandpaper. Restain and renew the finish (see pp.30–3).

Loose blind tenons

Tightening a blind tenon in its mortise is more difficult than tightening a through tenon. This is because you must pre-cut the wedges to the right length and thickness.

1 Fitting hidden wedges

● Dismantle the joint. Use a tenon saw to make two cuts across the tenon, almost down to its shoulder, as shown.
● Cut two hardwood wedges, as in stage 2 of 'Loose through tenons', left. As a general guide, the wedges should be half the depth of the saw cuts.
● Tap the tenons halfway into the saw cuts with a carpenter's mallet.
● Apply glue to the tenon and tap it into the mortise with a carpenter's mallet. As the wedges make contact with the blind end of the mortise, they will be forced deeper into the saw cuts and start to spread the tenon, thus making it fit tightly in the mortise.
Note: Proceed cautiously when tapping the tenon into its mortise. If you have cut the wedges too thick or too long, they could split the tenon or the mortise. If it proves impossible to seat the tenon fully in the mortise, you have no option but to pull the tenon out of the mortise before the glue dries, and pull the wedges out of the tenon with pliers. You must then either shorten and thin the wedges with a saw and sandpaper, or make new ones, and repeat stages 3–4 above.

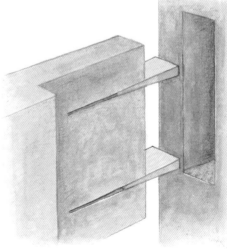

Repairing dowels and elbows

The damage seen on the 18th-century upholstered open-arm chair shown here occurs quite commonly in furniture of this kind. This chair has two particularly vulnerable points: where the backs of the arms are dowel-jointed to the sides of the back frame, and at the elbow joints where the horizontal and the vertical sections of the arms meet. Over time, downward pressure from sitters' arms can crack the dowels and force the chair's elbows apart. In this chair, the horizontal section of the left arm had cracked off. Note that although the chair was gutted for reupholstery, it would have been possible to make both of these repairs with the upholstery in place.

1 Inspecting the damage

● Hold the broken section of the arm against the back frame of the chair and the vertical section of undamaged arm, to check how clean the breaks are. In nearly all cases, the dowel that secures the back of the arm to the back of the frame will have snapped cleanly in two, leaving one half embedded in the arm and the other in the frame. A break at the elbow is more likely to have splintered or cracked the wood. Also, slivers or chips of wood may be missing from the elbow.

● If fairly large slivers or chips are missing from the elbow, you won't be able to fill these with wax; you will have to insert a new piece of wood (see step 5). Therefore you must identify the type of wood (in this case, mahogany), then purchase from a timber merchant a small scrap of seasoned wood that matches as closely as possible the figuring and grain of the chair.

2 Drilling out the old dowel

● Insert the drill bit in the electric drill, making sure that it is held securely.

● Secure the chair in an upright position by pressing one knee down onto the side of the seat frame. Working on the back of the chair, align the drill bit over the broken dowel end. Keeping the drill perfectly horizontal, bore completely through the dowel and the back frame, as shown below.

● Secure the broken arm section in a bench vice. Drill out just the old dowel. To make sure that the bit doesn't pass right through the curve at the rear of the arm, you must monitor its progress carefully. To do this, withdraw the bit from time to time and clear the wood dust by blowing hard on the hole.

● Sand or scrape old glue from the surfaces of the chair frame. Smooth the ends of the arm with medium-grade sandpaper.

3 Fitting a new dowel

● Mix a small quantity of animal glue (see p.246) and brush a generous coating over one half of the dowel.

● With a carpenter's mallet, tap the glued half of the dowel into the hole in the back of the chair. With a damp cloth, wipe off the excess glue and leave it to set for about 8 hours.

● Brush glue onto the other half of the dowel and the end of the back of the arm. Push the arm over the dowel until it lies flush against the back of the chair frame (you may need to lightly tap the arm home with the carpenter's mallet). With a damp cloth, wipe off any excess glue that has squeezed out of the joint.

4 Clamping the repair

● Brush some animal glue onto both halves of the elbow joint, then align the horizontal part of the arm with the vertical and push them together. With a water-dampened rag, wipe off any excess glue that is squeezed onto the surface of the surrounding wood.

● Clamp the repairs at both ends of the arm with G-clamps. In each case, apply firm but not excessive pressure, and place wads of cotton rag between the clamps and the wood to protect the latter from damage. When you tighten the G-clamp around the elbow joint you may find that a little more excess glue is squeezed out onto the surface of the wood. As before, remove this with a damp rag.

● Attach a sash clamp between the back of the chair frame and the vertical front of the arm, as shown. As with the G-clamps, apply firm but not excessive pressure, and insert wads of cotton rag to protect the wood. Leave the glue to set for a minimum of 24 hours before removing the clamps.

5 Restoring the elbow

● Place the scrap of matching wood in the bench vice and, using a tenon saw, cut off a thin, wedge-shaped sliver. This should be wide enough to fit snugly into the crack in the elbow, but its length is unimportant at this stage.

● Brush some glue into the crack in the elbow and onto one side of the sliver of new wood.

● Clamp the repair with a G-clamp, applying firm but not excessive pressure. Leave the glue to set for at least 24 hours.

6 Filling the gaps

● Remove all the clamps, then carefully saw off most of the excess new wood around the repair at the elbow. Don't try to saw the wood flush with the repair. You will almost certainly make it harder to file the repair smooth and may damage it.

● With a wood file, shape the new wood to follow the original contours of the elbow. Smooth it with medium-grade, then fine-grade, sandpaper.

● Fill the very small cracks around the new piece of wood by forcing tinted wax into them with a table knife. (For technique see p.64.) Leave the wax to dry for 24 hours.

7 Staining and waxing

● Restain the wood around the elbow repair to blend in with the colour of the surrounding area (see pp.30–1). Let the wood stain dry thoroughly.

● Brush a thin coat of shellac onto the restained area to seal it.

● Using a soft, lint-free cotton rag, apply a tinted beeswax furniture polish to the elbow repair (see pp.32–3), then buff it to a soft, lustrous shine with another piece of soft rag.

Note: In this case, the chair was reupholstered after being restained and waxed.

Repairing straight or curved legs

The repair technique illustrated here on an early 20th-century mahogany dining chair can be used to mend broken, woodworm-infested or rotted ends of straight or slightly curved chair legs. You must cut out the damaged section and replace it with a new piece of wood, which you bond to the original leg with a scarf joint. Finally, you reinforce the joint with a pair of dowels. The result is a strong repair which, provided that the chair is treated with respect (and not rocked on two legs by a sitter), will support as heavy a load as the original.

1 Assessing the damage

- Inspect the leg to assess the extent of the damage. To make a strong scarf joint, there must be a long enough section of leg above the top of the damaged area and below any adjacent stretcher rail through which you can make a 1-in-3 angled cut (see step 2 below). If there isn't enough undamaged leg, you will not be able to use this repair, and will have to replace the entire leg.

2 Marking and making the cut

- Using a T-square and a pencil, mark a line across the back of the leg just above the damaged section.
- Mark a pencil line across the front of the leg a minimum of 7.5cm above the top of the damaged section. (If there is room, mark the line 10cm above the top of the damage.)
- Using a ruler and a pencil, connect the ends of the lines drawn in stages 1–2 with a diagonal line on each side of the leg.
- Support the chair in a bench vice. Use a panel saw to remove the bottom of the leg by cutting across the pencil line on the back of the leg and down through the lines on the sides of the leg, to emerge across the line on the front of the leg.
- Smooth and level the face of the cut with a bench or block plane.

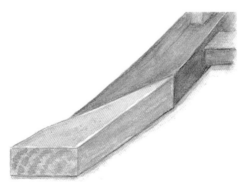

3 Cutting the new section

- Buy some seasoned wood to match the original leg (in this case, mahogany). It should be slightly wider and thicker, and 7.5–10cm longer, than the damaged section.
- Make a 1-in-3 (or 1-in-4) angled cut on the new piece (as in step 1) and plane the cut face level.
- Check that the angled cuts meet level, and make minor adjustments with a plane if necessary.

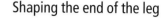

5 Shaping the end of the leg

● With a pencil and a utility knife, mark and cut out a cardboard template the same shape as the end of the matching leg.

● Remove the clamps and position the template over the new section of leg, as shown. Using a pencil, draw around the template to transfer the shape of the original leg onto the new section.

● Support the chair in a bench vice. Saw and plane the new section to shape.

6 Inserting the dowels

● Using an electric drill and drill bit, bore two diagonal holes parallel to each other into the leg. One should start 2.5cm below the repair on the back of the leg, and travel up through the scarf joint at 45 degrees; the other should start 2.5cm above the repair on the front of the leg, and travel down through the scarf joint at 45 degrees. Both holes should be 'blind' – that is, they should not be visible on the opposite side.

● Coat two pre-cut dowels with animal glue and tap them into the holes with a carpenter's mallet. The dowels should be the same diameter as the holes, and so form a tight fit.

4 Gluing and clamping the joint

● Mix some animal glue, as described on p.246, and apply a thin coat to both cut and planed surfaces with a 2.5cm standard paint brush.

● Push the two glued surfaces together. Secure them with a sash clamp fixed from the bottom of the leg to the top of the chair seat, and with two G-clamps, as shown. (To avoid denting the surface of the wood, place thin pads of wood between the leg and the clamps.)

● With a damp, lint-free rag, wipe off any excess glue that squeezes onto the surface of the leg. Leave the glue to harden for at least 24 hours.

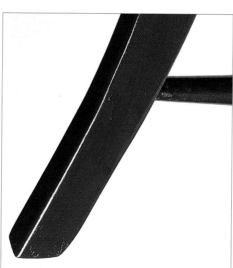

7 Finishing the repair

● Leave the glue to dry for 24 hours, then use a panel saw to cut the dowels flush with the front and back of the leg.

● Smooth the sides of the new section with medium- and then fine-grade sandpaper.

● Stain the new section to colour-match and blend in with the original leg (see pp.30–1), then fill the grain of the wood if necessary (see p.31).

● Apply an oil or wax finish to the new section. As with colour-matching with wood stains in the previous stage, the type of finish used on the new section must be the same as the type on the original leg. For advice on applying oil and wax finishes, see pp.32–3.

Repairing turned legs and rails

Turned chair legs and their supporting horizontal rails are vulnerable to breaking or cracking under pressure, particularly if the wood's grain is at a right angle to the force. Such damage most often occurs to the back legs, usually as a result of the sitter leaning back, raising the front legs off the floor and shifting his or her entire weight to the back legs alone. (However, in the case of the early 20th-century wheel-back chair shown here a front leg was broken.)

If a leg breaks below the horizontal rails, you can make the repair without dismantling the bottom half of the chair. When a break occurs above the rails you must remove at least one of the legs and the adjacent rails before making the repair (see pp.40–1 and 42). And if a rail snaps, you must remove all the adjacent legs before repairing or replacing it.

YOU WILL NEED:
Sandpaper Fine- and medium-grade
Bench vice
Fine-toothed dovetail or tenon saw
Electric drill and 6mm diameter bit
Animal glue
Pre-cut wooden dowel 6mm diameter and 7.5cm long.
Hammer or carpenter's mallet
Soft, lint-free cotton rag
Heavy-duty string or cord
Sash clamp
Utility or craft knife
Wire wool Grades 0 and 00.
Tinted wood filler In a colour to match the wood of the chair.
Table knife
Wood stain In a colour to match the wood and original finish of the chair.
Clear shellac
Disposable paint brush 2.5cm wide.
Tinted beeswax polish

1 Assessing the damage

- Inspect the broken leg or rail and decide whether it will be necessary to temporarily remove one leg or two of the rails. If it is, refer to pp.40–1 and 42. If it is not, proceed with the work with the leg in place, as here.
- Scuff the surface finish with medium- and fine-grade sandpaper in readiness for restoring the finish.

2 Cutting and drilling

- Secure the chair in a bench vice and cut through the leg with a fine-toothed dovetail or tenon saw. Cut in the middle of the broken section.
- Reposition the chair in the vice so that the truncated leg is vertical, with the cut edge uppermost.
- Insert the bit in the electric drill. Drill straight into the leg to a depth of 4cm.
- Secure the other piece of the leg in the bench vice, cut edge uppermost, and drill it as above.

3 Fitting the dowel

- Make a small amount of animal glue (see p.246) and brush generously onto half of a 7.5cm piece of 6mm diameter wooden dowel.
- With a hammer or carpenter's mallet, tap the dowel into the hole in the leg piece still in the vice. With a damp cotton rag, wipe off any excess glue. Leave the glue to dry for 24 hours.

4 Rejointing the leg

● Remove the smaller section of leg from the vice and re-secure the chair with the cut and drilled leg facing upwards.

● Brush animal glue across the cut and onto both the protruding section of dowel and the cut on the other part of the leg.

● Push the dowel into the hole in the leg secured in the vice and tap it with a hammer or carpenter's mallet until the two halves of the leg meet. With a damp cotton rag, wipe off excess glue that has squeezed from the joint.

● Before clamping the repair, wind heavy-duty string or cord around it to reinforce it while the glue dries.

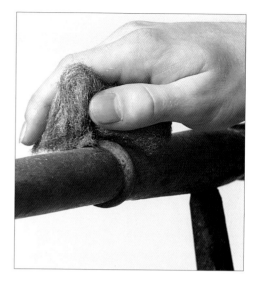

5 Clamping the repair

● Remove the chair from the vice and apply a sash clamp, as shown. Tighten the clamp to apply firm but not excessive pressure.

● Prop up the chair against a wall so that it leans back at a slight angle. In this way, no extraneous pressure will be exerted on the repair while the glue is drying.

● Leave the glue to set for at least 24 hours.

6 Smoothing the repair

● Remove the clamp and carefully cut the string with a utility knife.

● Using either medium- and fine-grade sandpaper or grade-0 and 00 wire wool, smooth the area around the repair.

● If you need to fill in any minute chips or gaps in the wood surrounding the joint, use an old table knife to press in wood filler tinted to match the wood of the chair (in this case, oak). Once the putty has dried, use medium- then fine-grade sandpaper to make it level with the surrounding area.

7 Renewing the surface finish

● To blend the repair with the surrounding wood, you may need to brush on one or more coats of wood stain of the appropriate colour (see pp.30–1). If so, leave each coat to dry for 24 hours.

● Brush on a coat of clear shellac to seal the stain.

● Rub in one or two coats of tinted beeswax polish with a lint-free cotton rag. Leave about half an hour between coats and buff to a shine, using a clean, soft rag each time.

Structural repairs to tables

Tables are made in a wide range of styles. Four of the most popular types are shown opposite: a plank-top frame table, a pedestal table with a tilt-top, a gate-leg table and a drop-leaf table (another example of which is shown right). As with seat and case furniture, most wear and tear and damage that occurs on tables results from everyday use or shrinkage and expansion of the wood caused by humidity changes.

The most vulnerable parts of a table are the joints that hold the components together. If you wish to repair mortise-and-tenoned table joints, refer to the section dealing with them in chairs, on pp.40–5. If you plan to repair a dowelled table joint, see pp.46–7. Turn to pp.50–1 if you need to mend turned table legs, and pp.60–3 for table drawers. Techniques for repairing split plank tops, pedestal bases, tilt-top mechanisms and drop-leaf rule joints are described on the following pages. The different ways in which tables are constructed are described below.

Mahogany drop-leaf table
Made c.1740, this drop-leaf table features the elegant cabriole legs and simple pad feet typical of the style.

Frame tables

Of relatively simple construction, frame tables (illustrated opposite, top left) have a leg at each corner, although long tables also have a central leg on each side. The legs are usually turned, but can be square, and may be fitted with castors. The top of the legs are either mortise-and-tenoned to side rails and end rails or are dowelled to them. On some examples of longer tables, side and end stretchers are tenoned or dowelled into the base of the legs.

The rails and the legs form a frame on which the table top sits. On long tables the frame can be augmented with a central rail blind-tenoned into the side rails. The top itself usually consists of several planks. The way in which the top is assembled and secured to the frame is described on pp.54–5, as are methods of repairing the top.

Some tables also have a drawer inserted into the frame at the end(s). If there is a drawer, the end rail is turned on its side and dovetailed to the top of the legs and side rails. Another end rail is added below the drawer, and is tenoned or dowelled to the legs. The drawer slides on runners screwed or glued to the inside of the side rails.

Pedestal tables

The circular or rectangular top of a pedestal table (shown opposite, top right) is secured to a turned column (a pedestal). The bottom of the column is supported on a tripod (a three-legged) base. On all pedestal tables the ends of the curved legs are slotted into the side of the base of the column. This part of the table is prone to wear. Methods of repair are described on p.57.

Some small pedestal tables have a fixed top. This is screwed or glued to a circular wooden block which threads onto a taper pin on top of the column. However, most pedestal tables have a 'tilt-top', which can be raised to a vertical position. Tilt-tops are fixed to the pedestal via a rigid block or a rotating gallery. These are described on p.56, as are methods of repair.

Drop-leaf tables

The frame of a drop-leaf table (illustrated opposite, bottom right) is similar to that of a frame table (see left for description and opposite top left for illustration). However, while the size of the top of a frame table is restricted to slightly larger than the size of the frame, the top of a drop-leaf can be much larger than its base. This is because the top consists of a fixed central section glued or screwed to the frame, and two side or end sections (drop-leaves) secured to the central section with hinged rule joints. The latter allow the leaves to be raised or lowered. When raised, the leaves rest on fly brackets, which swing out from the rails on knuckle joints. The rule joints are very prone to wear – see p.55 for methods of repair.

Gate-leg tables

The frame of a gate-leg table (illustrated opposite, bottom left) is constructed like that of a frame table (see left for description and opposite top left for illustration). The top of a gate-leg table is similar to the top of a drop-leaf table (see left for description and opposite bottom right for illustration). However, instead of resting on fly brackets, the leaves rest on legs that swing out from the side of the table like gates. They are fixed to posts that pivot on dowels in the side rails and stretcher rails. If the dowels fracture, see 'Repairing dowels and elbows', pp.46–7.

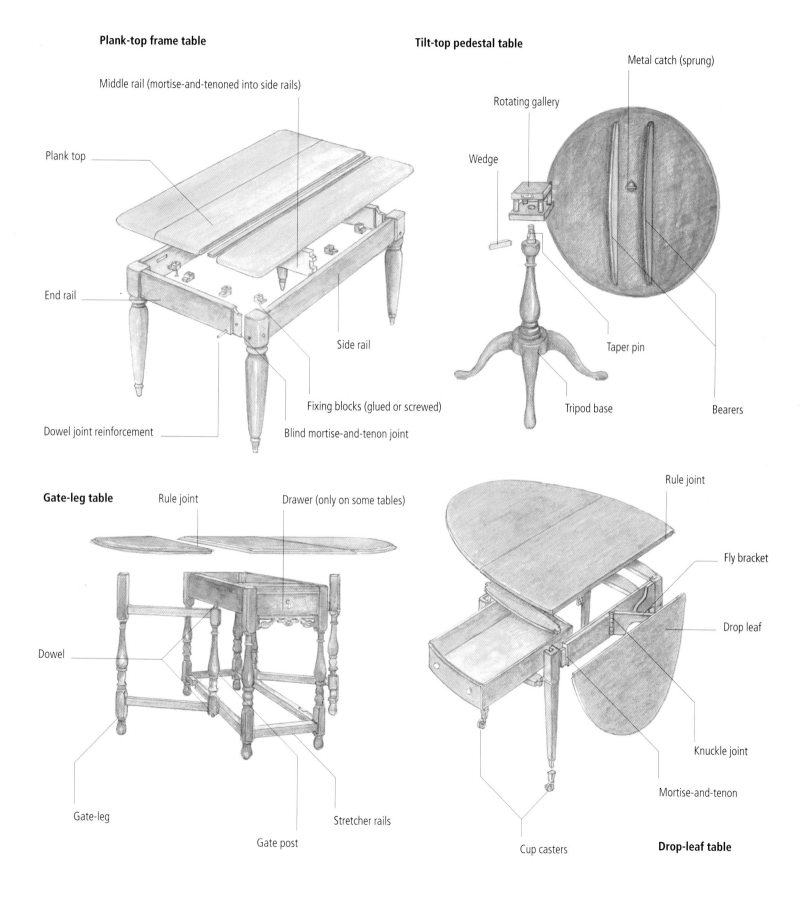

Plank-top frame table

Middle rail (mortise-and-tenoned into side rails)

Plank top

End rail

Side rail

Fixing blocks (glued or screwed)

Dowel joint reinforcement

Blind mortise-and-tenon joint

Tilt-top pedestal table

Metal catch (sprung)

Rotating gallery

Wedge

Taper pin

Tripod base

Bearers

Gate-leg table

Rule joint

Drawer (only on some tables)

Dowel

Gate-leg

Gate post

Stretcher rails

Rule joint

Fly bracket

Drop leaf

Knuckle joint

Mortise-and-tenon

Cup casters

Drop-leaf table

Repairing plank table tops

Prolonged exposure to a very dry atmosphere can cause plank table tops to split apart, either along the grain of the wood or along the glued joints between the individual planks. To make the necessary repairs, you must first remove the top from the underlying frame, then separate the individual planks from one another.

Removing the top

To separate the top from its underlying frame, proceed as follows.
• Turn the table upside down. If the top is screwed to the wooden blocks on the rails, remove the screws and lift off the frame.
• If the top is glued to the blocks, soften the glue with steam (see p.42) and prise off the blocks with a chisel.

Separating the planks

The planks can be jointed in one of four ways: butt-joined, tongue-and-grooved, dowelled or screwed. To determine the method of joining, run a hacksaw blade along the joints, and proceed as follows.

• If the blade meets no resistance, the planks are butt-joined. Direct steam along the joints to soften the glue, then pull the planks apart with your hands.
• If the blade meets resistance all along the joints, the planks are tongue-and-grooved. Direct steam along the joints to soften the glue. Place a softwood block against the end of one of the planks and strike it with a mallet. Repeat with the other planks to jolt the joints loose, then pull the planks apart with your hands.
• If the blade meets intermittent resistance, the planks are dowelled or screwed. Direct steam along the joints to soften the glue. If dowelled, you can pull the planks apart by hand; if not, see below.
• Screw hardware consists of a row of screws inserted into one side of a plank, their heads in slots in the side of the next plank. To separate planks, tap one end with a mallet. If the screws slide in their sockets, pull the planks apart: if they don't slide, tap the planks at the other end and pull apart.

Reassembling the top

Before reassembling the top, direct steam along the edges of the planks to soften any remaining deposits of old glue. Remove the softened glue with a steel spatula and a damp rag. Next, carry out a 'dry' assembly of the top (in other words, without using glue). If you discover that butt-joined planks will not butt evenly to one another, clamp the two affected planks on edge and side by side in a bench vice, with their joining edges flush to each other. Using a wood plane, carefully shave off any raised areas, so that the edges of the planks are level. To reassemble the table top with glue, proceed as follows.

Securing with clamps

• Apply wood glue to the edges of the planks.
• Align butted, dowelled, and tongue-and-grooved planks, and push them together. With screwed planks, locate the screw heads in the holes, then slide the planks to align with the screws.
• Attach two sash clamps below and near the top's ends; attach one clamp over its middle. (Place blocks of wood between the clamps and the table's sides.)
• Lightly tighten the clamps, and use a damp rag to wipe excess glue squeezed from the joints.
• Place a straight edge across the top to check for small ridges along the joints. Flatten these by placing a wooden block on top and tapping with a hammer.
• Fully tighten the clamps, leave the glue to dry for 24 hours, then remove the clamps and refit the top.

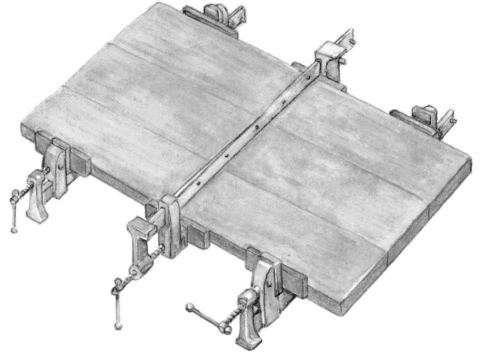

Repairing drop-leaf table tops

The drop leaves on a drop-leaf table are secured to the fixed, central section of the table top with hinged rule joints (see illustration below). These joints allow the leaves to be raised and lowered, help to support them when they are in the raised position and provide neat moulded edges for the sides of the fixed central section when the leaves are lowered. Factors such as shrinkage or expansion of the wood, caused by changing levels of humidity in the atmosphere, plus regular raising and lowering of the leaves, often cause the joints to seize or bind. You may be able to remedy this problem by rubbing candle wax over the surface of the quadrant moulding. Note also that if a table has been kept in a damp atmosphere and the wood has swollen, transferring it to a drier location for a few weeks or months will shrink the wood and may cause the joint to operate freely again. However, if neither of these remedies works, you should proceed as follows.

1 Freeing the joint

● Check to see if the short side of the hinge is set too deeply in its housing on the underside of the central section of the table top. If it is, the knuckle of the hinge will be set too high, and the leaf will bind on the lower part of the quadrant. To remedy this problem, unscrew the hinge, pack out the housing with a sliver of veneer and refit the hinge.

● If the short side of the hinge stands slightly higher than its housing, the hinge knuckle will be set too low and the leaf will bind on the quadrant's upper part. To remedy this, remove the hinge, cut the housing slightly deeper with a chisel and replace the hinge.

● If the hinge has moved towards the middle of the table, the knuckle will be set too far back from the joint (it must lie directly under the square shoulder of the joint). As a result, the leaf will bind all the way along the quadrant. If the screws have worked loose on the short half of the hinge, you may be able to remedy the problem by tightening them. However, in most cases, you must undo the long side of the hinge on the leaf, plug the holes with wood filler and, when the putty has dried, drill new screw holes nearer the end of the leaf. To complete, refit the hinge and insert a sliver of veneer between the bottom of the hinge and the bottom of the original housing.

Replacing casters

Many tables and sofas, and some chairs and pieces of case furniture, have casters on their legs or feet to make them easier to move. Because casters bear a considerable weight, the small axle that runs through the wheel will eventually distort and may even snap. The only solution is to replace the damaged caster with a replica – either a reproduction or a restored original purchased from a dealer in antique hardware.

In terms of method of attachment, there are three basic types of caster: cup, toe and screw-fitting. To remove the latter, simply unscrew the three or four screws that secure them to the underside of the leg or foot. To remove cup and toe casters, unscrew the two or three retaining screws that secure them to the sides of the leg or foot, and pull them off (tapping the edges of the cup or toe with a wooden block and a hammer, if necessary). To replace them, reverse the sequence.

Reproduction antique casters
Clockwise, from top right: standard toe; round cup; screwed claw; toe claw; standard screwed; tapered square cup.

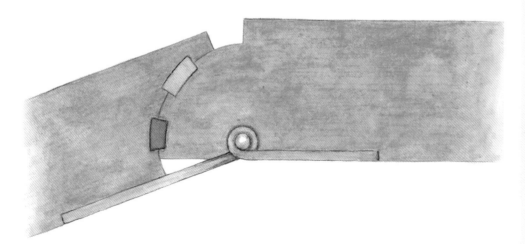

Repairing pedestal tables

Excessive loading on the top of a pedestal table causes wear in the components that anchor it to the central column supporting it. Moreover, if a tilt top is fitted, such pressure can damage the mechanism that controls the action of the top. Excessive loading can also cause the feet of the tripod base to splay and even start to break off. Remedies for these problems are described below and opposite.

Tightening loose tops

With a screwed fixed-top table, tighten or replace the screws that secure the top to the block. If a glued fixed top is loose, reglue it. Before trying the remedies given here for loose tilt-top table tops, check the screws that hold the bearers to the top. If they are loose or missing, tighten or replace them. Before strengthening pivots and tightening loose blocks and galleries, remove the tilt top as follows. Unscrew one of the bearers and slide it off its pivot. Then slide the other bearer and the top off the other pivot.

1 Tightening screw bolt pivots

• Many larger tilt-tops pivot on metal screw bolts, which pass through the bearers and into a threaded plate which is screwed to the block on the top of the central column. Check to see if the bolt has worked loose. If it has, tighten it either by hand or with a pair of pliers.

Note: If the thread on the bolt has become damaged, replace the bolt with a new one. If the thread in the plate has become damaged, unscrew the plate and fit a new one. Make sure that the plate lies level in its housing, or it will snag on the bearers.

1 Strengthening peg pivots

• Smaller tilt-tops, and some larger ones, pivot on round wooden pegs glued into the sides of the block on the top of the central column. Check if these pegs have become worn or if the holes in the bearers have enlarged. In either case, file the pegs' circumference smooth. Purchase two pieces of brass tubing of the pegs' diameter and length, and glue them over the pegs.

Note: You may also need to adjust the diameter of the bearer holes either by filing to enlarge them, or by inserting brass collars to fill them out.

1 Tightening a loose gallery

• Some tilt-tops pivot and rotate on a gallery attached to the top of the column. If the short columns that connect the halves of the gallery work loose, pull the halves apart, clean the joints and reglue.

1 Tightening a loose block

• On some tables the central column is through-tenoned into the block. If the tenon is loose in its mortise, tighten it by inserting two hardwood wedges (see 'Loose through tenons', on p.45).

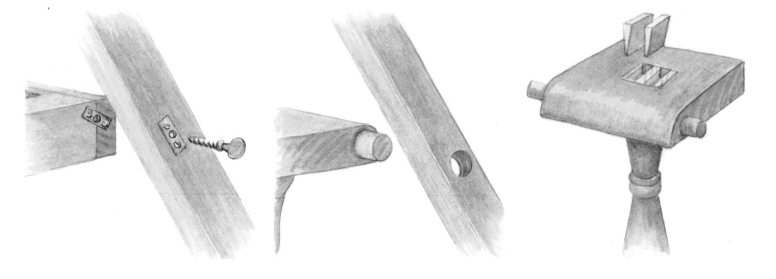

Split columns

In many cases, a split that occurs in the base of the central column of a pedestal table with tripod legs looks difficult to remedy. However, usually it is not. To repair such a split, proceed as follows.

1 Applying a tourniquet

● Using a fret saw, cut three softwood or plywood blocks to fit over the splayed legs and cut a V-notch in the outer face of each block (as in the illustration, right).

● Use the blunt edge of a table knife to push some wood glue into the split, and push the legs in towards the middle of the column.

● Wrap cord two or three times around the blocks, locating it in the V-notches. Insert a small stick between the strands of cord, and twist the stick to tighten the cord.

● With a damp rag, wipe off any excess glue that has squeezed out of the split. Leave the glue to harden for 24 hours, then remove the tourniquet.

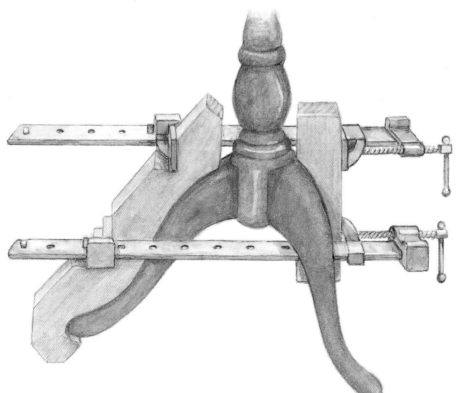

Split legs and columns

The strength of large pedestal tables is often overestimated, so that excessive pressure is applied to the top. This can cause the feet to splay, in extreme cases pulling away part of the base of the column. To remedy the problem, proceed as follows.

1 Clamping the break

● Using a fret saw, cut a softwood block to fit the outer profile of the damaged leg. Cut two V-notches in the block – one level with the top of the leg where it is inserted in the column, the other just below the level of the bottom of the column.

● Cut a rectangular-shaped block to fit between the other two legs, against the side of the column.

● Insert wood glue into the break, position the blocks as in the illustration, and secure them with sash clamps. As you tighten the clamps, excess glue will squeeze out of the joint. Wipe the glue off with a damp rag.

● Leave the glue to dry for 24 hours – after this time you can remove the clamps and wooden blocks.

Structural repairs to case furniture

Case furniture is made in numerous forms, of which the best-known are chests of drawers, tallboys, lowboys, wardrobes, armoires, clothes presses, chiffoniers, cupboards, dressers, secretaires and bureaux. Although these pieces have different functions, they are all essentially boxes or cabinets with a storage capacity, and are fitted with doors or drawers, or both.

In addition to woodworm infestation (for method of treatment, see p.244), the problems you are most likely to encounter in case furniture are splits in end-panels and doors, worn drawer runners, broken or missing dustboards, broken or missing drawer stops, worn drawer sides and bottoms, sagging or sticking doors, and damaged veneers. Apart from veneers (see pp.22–7), remedies for these typical problems are described over the following pages.

You should note that the vast majority of case furniture is very sturdily built. Consequently, you are unlikely to encounter loose joints – as you often do on antique chairs. Fortunately, this means that it is seldom necessary to completely dismantle a piece of case furniture. However, if it is, you are advised to entrust the work to a professional restorer.

Mahogany chest of drawers
Made c.1760, this solid mahogany chest of drawers has its original bracket feet and swan-neck handles.

Case construction

Over the centuries cabinetmakers have devised various methods of constructing case furniture. However, the two types of case you are most likely to encounter in cupboards, cabinets and chests of drawers are 'solid end-panel' cases and 'frame-and-panel' cases. Familiarization with the way in which they have been assembled will help you when it comes to making the repairs described on the following pages.

Solid end-panel

Almost all case furniture made before the middle of the 17th century and the advent of veneering has solid end-panels (see illustration, opposite page, above). After that period, case furniture with solid end-panels tends to fall into two main groups: smaller pieces (those not made excessively heavy by the use of solid, rather than veneered, wood); and cruder 'country'

pieces (of any size) made in areas where wood was plentiful and thus economical to use in solid rather than veneered form.

As their name suggests, solid end-panel cases have two end-panels, plus a top and bottom panel, made of solid wood. In many cases, all four panels are dovetailed together. Alternatively, the ends can be dovetailed to the bottom, while the top is screwed (from below) to two top rails (one front, one back) and four triangular corner fillets. In this arrangement, the top rails are dovetailed into the end-panels, while the corner fillets are butt-joined to the top rails and dovetailed to the end-panels.

The back of a solid end-panel case is made from several vertical planks of thin solid wood. These planks are either butt-joined or tongue-and-grooved, and secured in grooves or rebates in the top, end-panels and bottom of the case.

The bottom panel of the case can be raised off the floor in one of two ways: either on a rectangular frame (a plinth), or on feet or legs which are often screwed or

glued (or both) into small, square or rectangular blocks of wood. These are, in turn, glued or screwed to the bottom panel.

If the piece has doors, these can either be hinged to the insides of the end-panels and lie level with the facing edges of the panels, or they can be hinged to the facing edges and thus cover those edges when they are shut.

If the piece has drawers, these are supported on drawer rails that run across the front of the case and are tenoned into the end-panels. The drawers slide in and out on drawer runners – these are grooved into the end-panels. Shorter drawers (those that are not the full width of the case) are separated by an upright post, which is tenoned between the drawer rails. In addition to sliding on the runners that are attached to the end-panels, shorter drawers also slide on a central runner. This runner is tenoned into the drawer rail behind the upright post (at the front of the case), and into a central vertical plank that runs from the bottom panel to the top panel (at the back of the case). To stop shorter drawers from sliding sideways into each other, a drawer guide is screwed or glued on top of the central runner.

To make sure that the fronts of the drawers align with the front of the case when they are shut, small wooden blocks (drawer stops) are glued or nailed to the drawer rails. The blocks catch the back of the drawer fronts, stopping them from sliding too far back into the case. Finally, to stop dust from falling onto the contents of the drawers, thin wooden dustboards are often grooved into the backs of the drawer rails and the sides of the drawer runners.

Frame-and-panel

Frame-and-panel cases (see illustration, below) are widely used for making larger pieces of furniture, because of their lower overall weight. This design is also well suited to pieces made from cheaper, less attractive woods, which are then covered with more expensive, attractively figured and grained veneers. Also, frame-and-panel construction is considered structurally preferable to solid end-panel, because its component parts are less likely to warp.

A frame-and-panel case is built on similar lines to the solid end-panel type, but with one fundamental difference: the end-panels, rather than being solid wood, are usually thin sheets of veneered yellow pine or plywood rebated into a rectangular wooden frame. The four sides of the frame can be either butt-joined or tenoned together (usually the latter on better pieces). A second notable difference relates to the drawers: because the inner face of the end-panel is set into the frame, drawer guides are installed on top of the drawer runners. The runners are tenoned into the drawer rail behind the front post of the end frame.

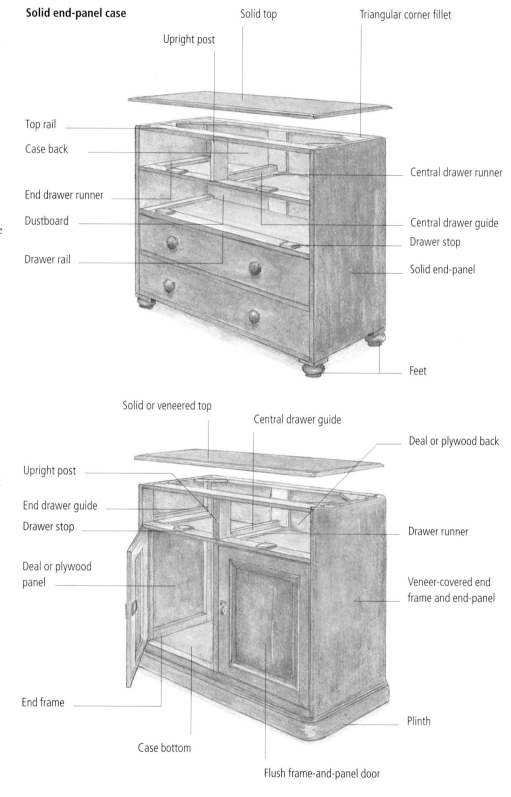

Solid end-panel case

Solid top · Triangular corner fillet · Upright post · Top rail · Case back · End drawer runner · Dustboard · Drawer rail · Central drawer runner · Central drawer guide · Drawer stop · Solid end-panel · Feet

Solid or veneered top · Central drawer guide · Deal or plywood back · Upright post · End drawer guide · Drawer stop · Deal or plywood panel · Drawer runner · Veneer-covered end frame and end-panel · End frame · Case bottom · Flush frame-and-panel door · Plinth

Frame and panel case

Repairing drawers

Drawers, and the components on which they run, are subject to considerable wear and tear. Aside from accidental knocks, most of the damage that occurs is caused by friction between surfaces as drawers are repeatedly opened and closed. Typical problems that develop on the case include worn drawer runners and drawer rails, and broken drawer stops and dustboards. Common faults with the drawers include worn sides, broken bottoms and difficulty in opening and closing them. Remedies for these problems are described on the following four pages.

YOU WILL NEED:

The tools and materials listed here are required if you wish to carry out all the repairs described on pp.60-3. You will need only some of these for individual repairs.

Workbench
T-square
Pencil
Fine-toothed tenon saw
Chisel or chisel plane
New wood To match the original component to be replaced.
Measuring tape
Wood glue
Carpenter's mallet
Cotton rag
Two G-clamps
Block plane
Large screwdriver
Hammer
Sandpaper Fine- and medium-grade.
Panel pins
Thin sheet of plywood
Panel saw
Marking gauge
Electric dehumidifier
Candle wax

Repairing drawer rails

In addition to wearing down the runners (see opposite page), the combination of the weight of the drawers and friction can also produce a shallow groove towards the front and near the ends of the drawer rails. This is usually not as pronounced as the wear that develops on the runners. However, it can interfere with the smooth running of the drawers, making it difficult to open and close them. To remedy, proceed as follows.

1 Sawing the housing

● With a T-square and a pencil, mark a horizontal line on the front of the rail just below the damage. Mark a pencil line on top of the rail, from front to back, along the side of the damage.
● Use a tenon saw to make a series of angled cuts, about 6mm apart, across the top of the damage and down to the horizontal line you drew in stage 1.

2 Chiseling the housing

● With a sharp chisel or chisel plane, pare out the waste wood. You need to work from front to back across the grain, but this leads to a risk of splintering the wood. To minimize the chances of this happening, push the chisel with your hands rather than hitting it with a hammer. Also, pare out the wood in thin slivers, rather than in thick slices.

3 Cutting and fitting a patch

● Buy wood to match the original rail. Measure the dimensions of the housing cut in steps 1–2, and mark these on the new piece.
● With a tenon saw, cut the new wood to size, making it slightly thicker and deeper than the housing.
● Apply wood glue to the housing and the underside of the patch. Tap the patch into position with a mallet, wipe off excess glue with a damp rag, and secure the patch with a G-clamp. Leave to dry for 24 hours.
● Remove the clamp and use a block plane to bring the front of the patch flush with the rail.

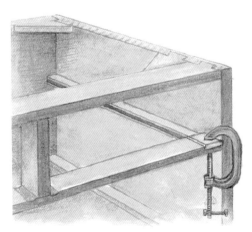

Replacing runners

The drawers in a piece of antique case furniture slide on wooden runners. Because of the weight of the drawers, and the friction that is created by use, the runners will eventually become worn in places, preventing the drawers from sliding smoothly. The only solution is to replace the runners.

There are three basic types of drawer runners: side runners in solid end-panel cabinets, side runners in frame-and-panel cabinets and central runners. In solid end-panel cabinets (see above right), the side runners are tenoned into the drawer rails at the front of the cabinet and slotted into a housing grooved across the inside of the end-panels. In antique furniture the side runners should not be glued in position – they are either held in place by a dust panel which slots into a groove along their inner edge, or secured with a single screw at the back, which is in the end-panel.

In frame-and-panel cabinets (see centre right), the side runners are behind the side frame post, tenoned into the drawer rails at the front and secured with a single screw at the back. Also, they have a thin strip of wood (known as a drawer guide) glued on top of them.

Central drawer runners are required where two drawers run side by side (see below right). These double-sided runners are tenoned into the drawer rail across the front of the cabinet, joined or screwed into the back of the cabinet, and have a drawer guide glued on top of them.

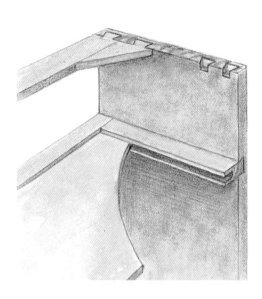

Solid end-panel runners

- If the back of the cabinet is nailed in place, carefully prise it off with a large screwdriver. If the back is screwed in place, remove the screws.
- Pull the dust panel out of its grooves in the runners.
- Ease the drawer runner out of its housing. If it is a very tight fit, a few taps with a carpenter's mallet should help to free it.
- Either use the original runner as a template to make a new runner, or have one made by a carpenter. Preferably use the same type of wood to make the new runner as was used to make the original.
- Reassemble the components in the reverse order to that in which you dismantled them.

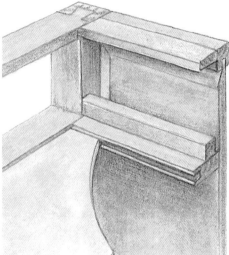

Frame-and-panel runners

- Remove the drawer runner using the method described above in stages 1–3 of 'Solid end-panel runners' above.
- Accurately record the position of the drawer guide on top of the runner. Then, using a hammer and chisel, prise off the glued drawer guide.
- Use the original runner and drawer guide as templates to make the new parts (but note that in many cases you may be able to reuse the original guide). Either do this yourself or employ a carpenter.
- Glue the guide in position on top of the new runner, and reassemble the components in the reverse order to that in which you dismantled them.

Central runners

- Remove the drawer runner using the method described in stages 1–3 of 'Solid end-panel runners' above.
- Accurately measure the position of the drawer guide on top of the runner, and prise off the guide as in stage 2 of removing 'Frame-and-panel runners' above.
- Make a new runner and guide, as described in stage 3 of 'Frame-and-panel runners', then reassemble the components in the reverse order to that in which you dismantled them.

Replacing stops

To make drawers sit flush with the front of the case, small blocks of wood called drawer stops are mounted on top of the drawer rails. For longer drawers, two stops are used – each positioned about 7.5cm from each end of the rail. For smaller drawers, a single stop is positioned in the middle of the rail. If a drawer recedes beyond the front of the case when shut, this usually means that the stop is missing. To replace a drawer stop, proceed as follows.

1 Cutting and fitting a stop

● With a tenon saw, cut a new stop from a piece of hardwood or softwood. It should be 6mm thick, 5cm wide, and about two-thirds the depth (front to back) of the rail. Remove any rough edges from the stop with fine-grade sandpaper.

● Apply wood glue to the underside of the stop, then press the stop in position on the rail – it should be about 7.5cm in from the end and flush with the back of the rail. Wipe off excess glue with a damp rag.

● Insert the drawer (while the glue is still wet) and gently push it back until the drawer front is flush with the front of the case.

● Immediately remove the drawer. If the stop is slightly too deep, the underside of the drawer front will have nudged it back on the rail. Secure the stop in this position with panel pins and a G-clamp. Leave the glue to harden fully for about 12 hours.

● Remove the G-clamp. With a saw or chisel, trim the back edge of the stop so that it is flush with the back of the rail.

Replacing dustboards

The majority of antique case furniture has thin wooden dustboards fitted between the drawers. These sit in grooves cut into the drawer rails and runners, and their main purpose is to prevent dust from entering the drawers and soiling the contents. In addition, dustboards help to secure the drawer runners in position (see 'Replacing drawer runners', on p.61). If a dustboard is badly damaged or missing, you can replace it as follows.

1 Cutting and fitting a dustboard

● If the back of the cabinet is pinned or nailed in position, prise it off with a large screwdriver. If it is secured with screws, unscrew them and lift out the back.

● If the original dustboard to be replaced is still in position, slide it out of the retaining grooves. Measure the width, depth and thickness of the board. To determine the dimensions of a missing dustboard, first measure the distance between the side runners, including the depth of the grooves. Next, measure the distance between the back of the front rail and the back, including the depth of the groove in the front rail. Finally, measure the height of the grooves to find the thickness of the board (in most instances, this will be 3mm).

● Originally the dustboard would have been made from a thin sheet of solid wood. If this proves difficult to find, use plywood. Cut the plywood to size with a panel saw. Slightly bevel the front and sides of the new panel with a wood plane, then sand them smooth with medium- or fine-grade sandpaper.

● From the back of the case, slide the new panel into the grooves in the drawer runners and push it forwards until it sits in the groove in the drawer rail. Resecure the back of the cabinet.

Replacing bottoms

The drawer bottoms on antique pieces of furniture are made from thin sheets of solid wood. These sheets are secured in grooves in the drawer sides and a groove across the inside of the front of the drawer. Over time the sheets tend to contract, leaving a gap, usually at the front of the drawer, but in some cases at the back. Traditionally, the sheets were cut to extend slightly from the back of the drawer. If shrinkage occurred, a sheet could then be pushed forward to close the gap – a remedy which you should use whenever possible. However, if the drawer bottom isn't big enough to allow this, or if it is badly split or cracked, you should proceed as follows.

1 Cutting and fitting a bottom

● Pull out the original drawer bottom and measure its length, width and thickness. If the bottom has shrunk, add the width of the gap that has opened up at the front of the drawer.

● Purchase a thin sheet of wood to match the original bottom or, if none is available, use plywood of the same thickness. Mark the measurements of the original bottom on the new sheet, and cut it to size with a panel saw. To ease fitting, slightly bevel the front and sides of the new sheet with a plane, and smooth them with medium- or fine-grade sandpaper.

● Position the front of the new sheet in the grooves in the sides of the drawers, and slide the sheet forwards to sit in the groove on the drawer front.

Repairing sides

Over time, opening and closing drawers will wear down not only the tops of the drawer runners (see p.61), but also the bottom edges of the drawer. Most of this wear usually takes place towards the rear. Eventually it will prevent the drawer from sliding smoothly in and out, and may also make it rock up and down during use. Once the latter problem develops, a vicious cycle occurs in which the damage on the sides accelerates the damage on the runners and vice versa. You should remedy this problem as soon as possible, using the following technique.

Easing sticking drawers

Expansion of the wood, caused by absorption of moisture present in the atmosphere, is the main cause of drawers sticking in the case. This problem can often be resolved by reducing the level of humidity (with an electric dehumidifier) where the piece is kept. In addition, you can rub candle wax on the drawer runners, rails and bottom edges to reduce the friction between them.

If you have tried both remedies and the drawers still stick, examine the rails, runners, bottom edges and sides for shiny spots – these indicate where components are rubbing against each other. Remedy the problem by lightly skimming over the affected areas with a wood plane set to a fine cut.
Note: Also check for protruding nails, screws or splits in the runners and guides, and treat them accordingly.

1 Sawing the housing
● Remove the drawer from the case and place it upside down on a workbench.
● Use a bench plane to shave the bottom edges to just below the level of damage. Plane from front to back, creating a shallow downwards slope along the edges. Don't remove any wood from the area above the dovetailed front corners. Also, make sure that you don't leave any bumps or depressions in the slope.

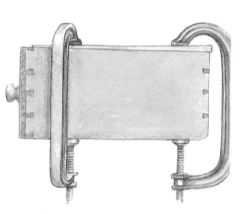

2 Cutting and fitting a wedge
● Buy wood to match the drawer sides. With a panel saw, cut two pieces the length of, and slightly wider than, the sides. Plane their undersides to the angle planed on the bottom of the sides in step 1.
● Apply wood glue to the planed sides of the wedges, and press them onto the planed drawer bottoms – flush with the sides' inner edges and slightly past the outer edges. Secure with two G-clamps. Remove excess glue with a damp rag. Allow glue to dry for 24 hours.

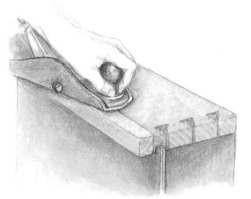

3 Planing the sides
● Once the glue has dried (after about 24 hours), remove the clamps and turn the drawer on its side.
● Use a bench plane to plane the outer edge of the wedge flush with the outer edge of the drawer. Repeat on the other side.

4 Planing the bottom
● Set a marking gauge to the true height of the drawer. You can determine this above the dovetails at the front of the drawer (where no wood was removed in step 1).
● Run the gauge along the side of the drawer to make a line along the side of the wedge and parallel to the top edge of the drawer. Repeat on the other wedge.
● Plane down to the line with a bench plane. Do this on both sides of the drawer.

Repairing split end-panels

As a result of variations in humidity, and expansion and contraction of the wood, the end-panels of case furniture often split from top to bottom. If they are made from solid wood, they split along the grain; if they are made from more than one plank of wood, they usually split along the glued butt joint between the planks. The method you use to remedy this problem will depend on the size of the split.

1 Filling with wax

● Clean the edges of the split with medium-grade sandpaper. If the split is along a glued butt joint, scrape out the glue with a wood chisel. If it is less than 6mm wide, follow the steps below; if it is more than 6mm, see 'Fitting a tapered lath', right.

● Melt coloured wax crayons in a metal container and blend them to match the colour of the end-panel.

● Scoop some of the melted wax into a teaspoon and, as it begins to harden, push it into the split with the tip of a small pointing trowel or an old table knife. Build up the wax in layers to slightly above the level of the surrounding panel, then leave it to set hard.

YOU WILL NEED:

For filling with wax:

Sandpaper Medium-grade.

Wood chisel

Coloured wax crayons

Metal container

Teaspoon

Small pointing trowel (or old table knife)

Wire wool Grade 00.

Tinted beeswax furniture polish

Lint-free rag

For filling with a tapered lath:

Wood lath

Small saw

Wood plane

Small paint brush

Animal glue

Carpenter's mallet

Sandpaper Fine-, medium- and coarse-grade.

Wood stain To match the original panel.

Linseed oil or tinted beeswax polish

Lint-free cotton rag

2 Smoothing the repair

● Using a pad of grade-00 wire wool, rub along the length of the split to remove the excess wax from the surface. Turn the pad when it becomes clogged and replace it when necessary.

3 Refinishing

● To blend the wax into the rest of the panel, apply a finish to match the original (see pp.32–3). Here a tinted beeswax furniture polish, applied with a pad of lint-free cotton rag, was used.

Fitting a tapered lath

To fill splits wider than 6mm, use a tapered lath, not wax, as follows.

● Sand the edges of the split (as in step 1, left).

● Select a strip of wood to match the damaged area. Cut it to the required length with a saw, then plane a shallow taper along its sides.

● Brush animal glue (see p.246) onto the sides of the strip, then tap the strip into the split with a carpenter's mallet until it forms a tight fit. Leave the glue to harden for 24 hours.

● Using the plane and coarse-, medium- then fine-grade sandpaper, smooth the face of the strip until it is level with the surrounding panel.

● Using a lint-free rag, apply stain and finish to match the original (see pp.30–3).

Filling a split with a lath
For splits over 6mm wide, use a tapered lath.

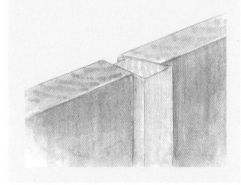

Repairing doors

Doors on case furniture are subject to various forms of wear and tear. The most common result is difficulty in opening and shutting the doors. The causes of such problems include expansion or contraction of the wood (in response to changes in humidity) and damage to the hinge housings or to the hinges themselves. Remedies are described below and opposite.

Sticking doors

If you have difficulty in opening or shutting a door, make sure that the piece of furniture is standing level on the ground. Check this by placing a spirit level on top of it. Make any adjustments by inserting pieces of cardboard of an appropriate thickness under one or more of the feet.

If the piece is standing level but the door still sticks, check the condition of the hinges and the hinge housings (see 'Sprung doors' and 'Sagging doors', right). If the hinges and their housings are in good condition, pass a piece of paper between the side of the door and the surrounding frame. If the paper sticks at some point, either the door or the frame has expanded slightly. In some cases, you can remedy this by sanding the relevant section of the door's edge; in other cases, you must shave a little off the edge with a wood plane.

With solid wood doors, you can plane at any point around their perimeter. However, with veneered doors you must plane only the bottom edge or hinge side of the door. When you are planing, you should proceed cautiously, as it is always easy to remove a little more wood, whereas if you remove too much you will have to reinstate a sliver of wood – a process that is time-consuming, difficult to disguise and may require the assistance of an expert. After sanding or planing, refinish the area and blend it into the original finish (see 'Applying traditional finishes', on pp.28–9).

Sprung doors

In addition to causing sagging (see right), a faulty hinge can also cause a door to spring open. For example, a loose screw jutting out from one side of the hinge won't allow the two sides of the hinge to close properly when the door is shut. To remedy this, tighten the screw or, if necessary, replace it with another of the correct size. Alternatively, one or both of the hinge housings may have been cut too deeply. To remedy this problem, proceed as follows.

1 Resetting the hinge

● Remove the hinge and cut a piece of veneer to fit the shape of the housing.
● Mark and drill holes in the veneer for the screws.
● Fit the veneer into the housing and position the hinge on top of it. At this stage secure the hinge with only the middle screw.
● Test the action of the door. If it still springs open slightly, cut another piece of veneer and repeat the first three stages. (It is unlikely that you will need to use more than two pieces of veneer.)
● Once you are satisfied with the action of the door, reinsert the other screws in the hinge.

Sagging doors

In addition to a cabinet being out of square or the wood expanding (see 'Sticking doors', far left), doors can stick against the bottom or sides of the frame (or an adjacent door) if they have started to sag on their hinges. Often you can remedy this problem by simply tightening existing screws or replacing missing screws in the top hinge. You may need to pack the original screw holes with a little roll of paper before you reinsert the existing or replacement screw. However, if a split has appeared in the hinge housing, you should make a repair as described and illustrated below.

Another common cause of sagging is wear in the knuckle of the top hinge. In some cases, you may be able to compensate for this by exchanging the top and bottom hinges. If this doesn't work, however, you will have no choice but to replace the hinge with a reproduction.

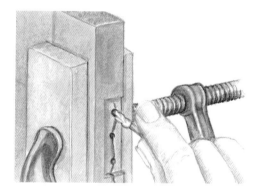

1 Mending split housings

● Remove the hinge and insert the blade of a knife into the split to open it slightly.
● Insert some wood glue into the split with the tip of a cocktail stick.
● Tightly clamp the repair with a G-clamp, placing blocks of wood between the clamp and the door to protect the wood.
● While the glue is still wet, wrap a thin piece of cotton wool round the tip of another cocktail stick and use this to remove excess glue from the screw holes.
● When the glue has dried, refit the hinge, using the original screws where possible.

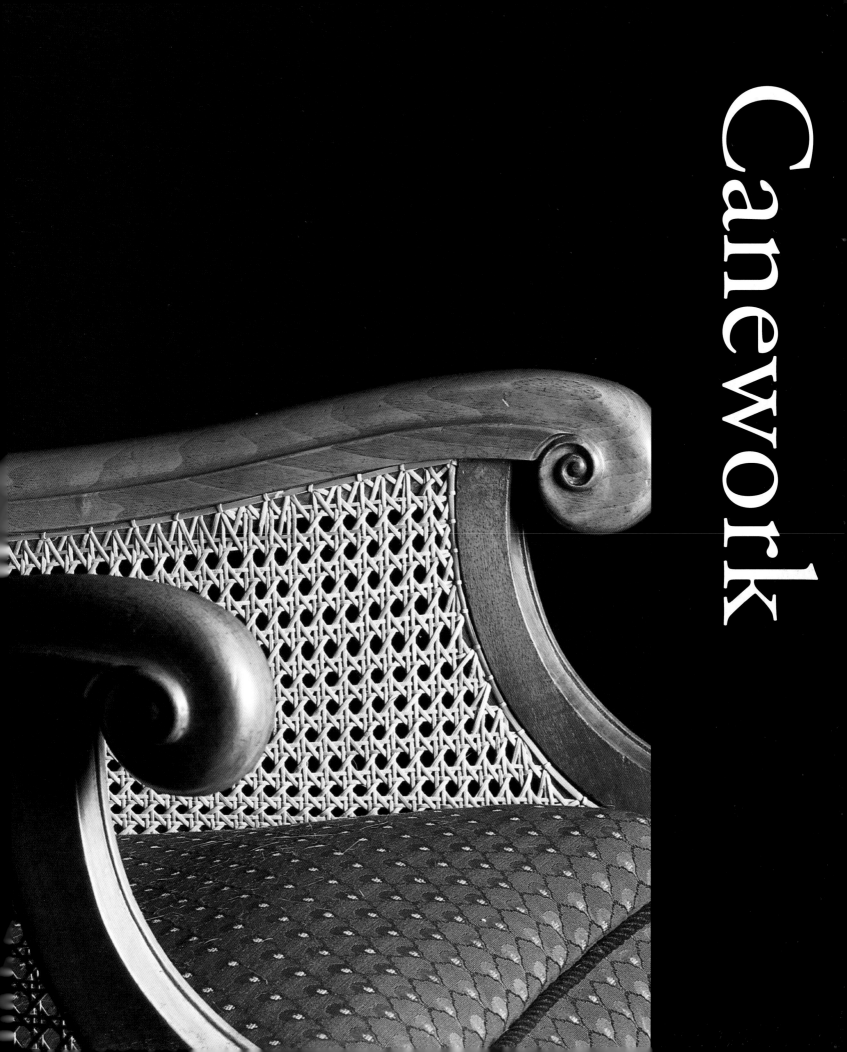

Canework

Introduction

Canework – the use of interwoven fibrous strips of rattan (a type of palm) as supportive panelling on the seats, backs and sides of chairs – originated in China. The technique was first introduced to Europe by the Dutch East India Company during the 1660s and soon afterward appeared in colonial North America. Whereas the Chinese had traditionally produced very fine-meshed, almost silky canework panels, Europeans and North Americans employed wider strips of cane to make much more open-meshed panels featuring small, octagonal holes.

17th-century canework

Between *c.*1660 and *c.*1685, the strips of cane that were imported from the Orient were often cut crudely, and the holes between the interwoven canes were large and somewhat irregular. However, by the latter years of the 17th century, finer strips, a closer mesh and more uniform and precise patterning had been introduced. At first the use of canework panels was restricted to the backs of chairs, and they were stretched between, and pegged into, oak and walnut frames in a variety of shapes, including square, rectangular and arch- and dome-topped (or bottomed). Oval panels were also in evidence at this time, mainly on Dutch chairs. Before long, cane panels were also used on seats and were usually supplemented with a squab cushion or pillow.

18th- and 19th-century trends

In both America and Europe, the popularity of canework declined after 1710, largely as a result of technical improvements in upholstered seating, which provided greater comfort. However, in both regions canework enjoyed a serious revival that began towards the end of the 18th century and ran for the first two to three decades of the 19th century. At this time canework was mainly employed on the seats of Empire-style and Regency dining chairs, side chairs, open armchairs and, notably, on chinoiserie bamboo furniture. In addition, it featured on the seats, backs and side panels of many mahogany-framed *bergères*, armchairs with deep seats which were originally made in France and later produced in large numbers in

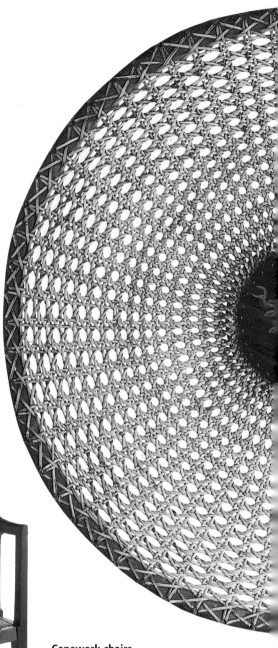

Canework chairs
The mahogany-framed, open-arm chair on the left dates from the early 20th century. It incorporates a six-way standard pattern cane back and seat. Originally both the seat and the back would have been augmented (for comfort) with a fitted squab cushion. The bentwood side chair on the right dates from the late 19th century. It features a cane-panelled shield back.

England and North America. The cane seats of most of these chairs supported a heavy upholstered squab cushion; many examples also had an upholstered squab which rested against the canework back.

19th- and early 20th-century examples

The various style revivals that proved fashionable with the Victorians during the second half of the 19th century resulted in the continued use of canework on seat furniture. Notable among these were the almost uninterrupted popularity of chinoiserie (including cane-seated bamboo furniture) and the development of an interest in the Jacobean style. In the latter case, many 17th-century-style chairs were reproduced, usually in oak, with cane seats and backs. Cane-panelled *bergère* armchairs and settees were again fashionable at the end of the 19th century – a revival that lasted into the 1930s.

Bentwood

Canework is also closely associated with bentwood furniture. Invented by an Austrian, Michael Thonet, bentwood was first shown in 1851 at the Great Exhibition in London. Thonet perfected a technique for bending solid

wood into curved and circular components which, when bolted together, formed a framework for cane seats and backs. The result – a series of lightweight, sturdy chairs with a sinuous simplicity – found favour right across the social stratum. The chairs were also easily transportable – an advantage that encouraged their distribution all over the world. By the 1860s, bentwood was being produced in vast quantities and remained fashionable well into the 20th century.

Caning patterns

Over the centuries, canework panels have been woven in various patterns. Some are so intricate that the amateur would almost certainly be defeated by them. However, most canework panels are worked in the 'six-way standard pattern' – so called because there are six basic stages. Although the six-way standard pattern looks complex, it is relatively easy for the amateur caner to reproduce (see pp.72–81).

Medallion chair back
Perhaps the most visually impressive of all caning styles, and certainly the most exacting to execute, is the medallion back, above. This consists of a circular or oval piece of wood (usually embellished with painted motifs or a wooden or metal inlay) suspended in the middle of a chair back by interwoven canes passed through holes in its circumference and holes around the internal perimeter of the back.

Tools and materials

Very few tools and materials are required for cleaning, reviving and replacing canework. The majority of them are likely to be found in the typical basic tool kit that most people have in their home. The rest can be purchased from craft shops or from suppliers of caning materials.

Tools

1 Utility or craft knife A heavy-duty model, preferably with a retractable blade, to cut off old canework.

2 Clearing tool To remove old cane pegs and small pieces of cane from the holes in the chair frame. Available from suppliers of caning materials. However, most caners use a Phillips screwdriver with a shaft of suitable diameter or a large nail, the point of which has been sawn off and filed flat.

3 Needle files One or two small round or tapered files to clear stubborn fragments of old peg from holes. These can also be used to slightly enlarge holes as needed to accommodate the new cane.

4 Hammer An upholsterer's or pin hammer to drive new pegs into the holes.

5 Pliers A pair of taper- or needle-nose pliers to pull lengths of cane through the holes and manipulate them in tight spaces.

6 Plastic golf tees To peg the cane temporarily in position while you work across the panel.

7 Cane levers (shell bodkins) These are specialist tools, each of which consists of a short metal rod that is curved and scooped out at one end. Available from most canework suppliers and many craft shops. An alternative is a bayonet-pointed spring needle.

8 Nippers A pair of end-cutting nippers, or pliers with a side-cutting facility, for cutting and trimming cane.

YOU WILL ALSO NEED:

Combing tool A metal or plastic tool used by specialist decorators to replicate the grain and figuring of hardwoods in wet paints and glazes. It can also be used to square up the lengths of cane as you work your way across the panel. Available from artist's suppliers.

Large plastic bucket To hold hot water with which to moisten the cane slightly in order to make it more flexible before you weave and peg it.

Clean hot water See above.

Large plastic bag To hold lengths of cane that have been moistened in water.

Small mixing container For mixing an optional antiquing glaze for the new canework.

Materials

9 Wood stain To revive or enhance the colour of the chair frame before caning (as in this project, although the procedure is optional).

10 French polish To rework the original finish on the chair frame (as in this project, although the procedure may not be necessary).

11 Lint-free cotton rags Use to clean, revive and polish the chair frame before recaning and to antique the cane panel after weaving and pegging. When moistened with water, a rag is also useful, just before you begin weaving and pegging, for redampening cane that has dried out.

12 Cane Available from specialist cane suppliers and many craft shops, cane is split into six standard widths, numbered, in ascending order of thickness, from 1 to 6. You must purchase the correct sizes for the chair that you wish to recane. As a general rule, use the six sizes as follows.

No. 1 This is the finest and should be used only on very small, delicate chairs.

No. 2 Use for all front-to-back and side-to-side canes where the holes in the frame are less than 12mm apart, and for looping over the beading cane.

No. 3 Use as No. 2 cane, but not on large panels where the holes are more than 12mm apart (as here). Can also be used for diagonal canes on smaller chairs where No. 2 cane was used front-to-back and side-to-side.

No. 4 Use as No. 3 cane for front-to-back and side-to-side canes on larger panels. Use for diagonal canes (as in this project), where No. 2 or No. 3 canes were used front-to-back and side-to-side.

No. 5 Use for diagonal caning on large panels where No. 3 or No. 4 cane has been used front-to-back and side-to-side.

No. 6 Use for beading the edges of the panel.

As a rule-of-thumb, for most chairs you will need about 225g of each width of cane that you use.

13 Pegging Depending on the size of the holes, cut either No. 14 or No. 16 centre basket-weaving cane (as shown here) to peg the holes, or use precut birch or ramin dowels of the appropriate diameter (available from specialist suppliers and many craft shops).

14 Van Dyke crystals This crystallized artist's pigment is dissolved in water and applied with a rag to antique new canework. Available from artist's suppliers.

YOU WILL ALSO NEED:

Mild liquid soap To clean dirty canework.

Acrylic matt medium Dilute with water to make a consolidating medium to strengthen old canework. Available from artist's suppliers.

Purified bleached beeswax polish To polish a chair frame before and after you have recaned it. Use either the clear or the tinted variety, according to preference. Dissolve the polish in benzene before use.

Benzene A solvent for beeswax. Benzene is highly flammable, so keep it away from any naked flames.

Terry towelling or an old towel To dry canework after you have cleaned it.

Restoring a caned chair seat

Canework that has become discoloured, dull and brittle can be successfully cleaned and revived by using the simple techniques described in the box 'Cleaning canework' below. However, if the canework is broken or badly frayed, it will be necessary to replace it. Renewal of individual strands of cane is not recommended because the repair will almost certainly not last very long; you must replace the entire panel.

The damaged cane seat of this late 19th-century mahogany chair was removed and then recaned in the 'six-way standard' pattern to match the original canework. The seat of this chair is gently curved along the side and front rails, but the principles of six-way standard caning apply equally to square, rectangular and tapered seats. If you need to have more complex patterns woven (two examples of which are shown on the opposite page), you should entrust the task to a professional caner.

Cleaning canework

To clean dirty or discoloured canework that is in good condition, wipe on a weak solution of mild liquid soap and warm water with a lint-free rag. Then rinse thoroughly with a clean lint-free rag soaked in clean water. (Repeat several times until all the soap and dissolved dirt has been removed.) Then gently pat dry with an old towel.

To strengthen weak areas of canework (before they start to fray or split), use a lint-free rag to wipe on one or two thin coats of a mixture of one part acrylic matt medium to one part cold clean water. Allow two hours' drying time between coats.

To revive dull canework, dissolve a small amount of purified bleached beeswax in benzene. Then rub the mixture into the canework with a lint-free rag and leave it for about an hour. Finally, buff the canework to a muted shine with a pad of soft lint-free rag.

Preparing the frame

Note that preparing a chair frame for recaning may require you to do more than remove the damaged cane and clean out the pegging holes. There is no point in replacing the canework if the frame itself is not sound. Therefore you must tighten or remake any loose joints (see pp.44–7) and repair splits as for end-panels (see p.64).

YOU WILL NEED:
All the tools and materials listed on pp.70–1, except for the following: mild liquid soap, acrylic mat medium, purified bleached beeswax and benzene.
Note: For this chair the following sizes of cane were used:
No.2 For tying in the beading
No.3 For the front-to-back and side-to-side canes
No.4 For the diagonal canes
No.6 For the beading
No.14 basket-weaving cane for making the pegs.
However, different size chairs may require different sizes of cane (as recommended on p.71).

1 Recording and cutting
● Either take some close-up pictures of the damaged cane panel or make a sketch of it: such a record will help you to replicate the original caning pattern. On chairs with curved or tapered rails (like this one), it will also help you determine which canes should go into which holes.
● With a heavy-duty utility knife, cut through the old canes around the internal perimeter of the seat and pull away the middle of the cane panel.
● If the panel has been finished around its perimeter with cane beading (as with this chair), carefully cut the beading and the cane ties that hold it in place, then pull them away.

Clearing and refinishing

2

● Pull out any loose ends of the old cane from the holes. In some instances, you will be able to do this with just your fingers. However, if the cane is stuck to the sides of the holes, you may need to tug it out firmly with a pair of pliers.

● Turn the chair upside down and punch the cane pegs out of the holes from below, using the clearing tool and hammer. You may need to strike quite firmly with the hammer. If so, make sure that the clearing tool doesn't slip and damage the chair frame.

● Closely re-examine all the holes. Some may still be partly blocked in the middle with small pieces of old

cane. To clear them, try using the clearing tool and hammer again. If that doesn't work, carefully file the sides of the hole with a round needle file. Avoid enlarging the tops and bottoms of the holes.

● Examine the chair frame itself for loose joints or cracks and splits. You must carry out any necessary repairs (see pp.44–7 and 20–1) before proceeding.

● Once the frame is sound, clean and polish it using the techniques described on pp.16–17 and 32–3.

Note: In this case the chair frame was lightly restained, then polished with button polish and, finally, beeswax-polished to a soft, lustrous shine.

Caning patterns

A variety of caning patterns have been employed over the past four centuries. Most of these developed in response to aesthetic preferences rather than as a result of functional requirements. Some patterns are simpler to weave than others. An example of a relatively easy pattern is the six-way standard pattern, which is illustrated in the step-by-step project. This was developed as a means of employment for blind people.

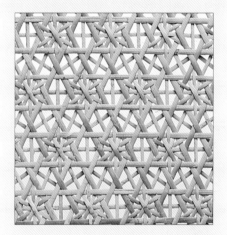

Alternative caning patterns
Complex caning patterns such as the Star of David (top) and the chevron (above) should be undertaken only by an expert caner.

Fitting the first front-to-back canes

No. 3 cane was used for the front-to-back work on this chair. (For information on other sizes of cane, see p.71.) Before starting, make a few lengths of cane more pliable by dipping them in a bucket of hot water for two minutes. Don't soak them any longer than this, or they may become discoloured. Place the soaked cane in a plastic bag to keep it moist. Have a damp, lint-free rag close at hand to remoisten the cane if it starts to dry out as you are working, and proceed as follows.

1 Locating the middle

● Count the holes along the back and the front rails of the chair. If there is an even number on each rail (as with this chair), mark the middle two, front and back, with a golf tee in each.

Note: If there is an odd number of holes, mark the middle hole on both rails with a golf tee.

● With its smooth side facing upwards, feed a long strip of No. 3 cane through each of the middle holes on the back rail. Let half the length of each strip hang down below each hole. Secure the canes by pushing a tee into each hole from above.

Note: If there is an odd number of holes on the back rail, pass one strip of cane through the middle hole.

● Position the chair so that the front rail faces you. Pull the two lengths of cane that lie above the back rail across to the holes opposite on the front rail. Feed them through your fingers with the smooth side facing up. Tension the canes fairly tightly, and pass them through the holes. Give them a half-twist as you do this so that the rough undersides face out towards the adjacent holes (see step 2 below). Retension the canes from below and secure with tees from above.

Note: If there is an odd number of holes on the back rail, repeat the above with a single cane.

● Cut the left-hand middle cane with nippers so that 7.5cm hangs below the back hole. Ignore the right-hand cane. (In the picture the free ends of both canes are obscured by the back rail.)

Note: If there is a single middle cane, leave the free end uncut.

2 Half-twisting the cane

● Of the two middle ones at the back of the chair, you have trimmed the left-hand one. For this reason you should now work on the left-hand side of the chair before you work on the right. (If your chair has only one middle cane, you can work across either side of the seat.) Proceed by pulling the left-hand cane along the underside of the front rail. Make sure that the rough side of the cane runs against the rail.

● When you reach the next hole, give the cane another half-twist and push it up through the hole; then make a final half-twist so that the smooth side emerges on top of the rail facing upwards.

3 Caning the left side

● Tension the cane and secure with the tee you used in the first hole on the front rail.

● Take the cane to the opposite hole on the back rail. Tension, half-twist and push it through as before. Secure it with the tee you used on the previous hole.

● Work across the left side, repeating the above (and transferring the same tee) until the first cane runs out.

● When the cane won't span the frame, secure it with the tee. Trim so that 7.5cm hangs below the hole.

● Anchor a new cane with a new tee in the next available hole on the opposite rail. Leave 7.5cm below the hole. Repeat steps 2–3, filling all the holes on the left of the back rail, except for the corner one.

4 Filling the left edge

● Where the seat is wider at the front than at the back, some of the holes on the front rail will still be unfilled and there will be a gap at the side of the panel. Fill this gap by running lengths of cane between the remaining holes on the front rail and some of the holes on the side of the frame, pegging with tees where necessary. You may be able to do most of this with a continuous length of cane (as before), or you may have to use single strips of cane between opposite holes. In either case it is important to select holes in the side rail that will force the cane to run as nearly parallel as possible with the rest of the panel.

5 Completing the right side

● Move to the right-hand side of the chair. Pick up the length of cane hanging below the back middle hole, and repeat steps 2–4 to complete the front-to-back canes across the right half of the panel. You must take care to leave the right-hand rear corner hole open. As you use new strips of cane, remoisten them with a damp rag if they have started to dry out.

Fitting the first side-to-side canes

Before starting to fit the side-to-side canes, dampen a few strips of cane in the bucket of hot water and transfer them to a plastic bag (as you did before fitting the first front-to-back canes). Then proceed as follows.

1 Working from the front rail

● Take a new strip of cane. If the seat has a curved front rail (as here), peg the cane into the hole on the side or front rail that will allow you to pull the cane across the front of the seat so that it crosses the front-to-back canes at a right angle and runs just inside the inner edge of the front rail. If the seat has a straight front rail, peg the end of the cane into the hole on one of the side rails that lies next to the corner hole. (In this way you will leave the corner hole free.)

● Trim the cane so that a length of 7.5cm hangs below the first hole. Then pull it across the tops of the front-to-back canes towards the hole directly opposite. As you do this, make sure that the smooth side of the cane faces up.

● Tension, half-twist, retension and peg the cane in the hole, as you did in step 1 of 'Fitting the first front-to-back canes'.

● Work your way to the back of the seat, using the same method of caning as described in steps 2–4 of 'Fitting the first front-to-back canes'. Take care to leave the two rear corner holes open.

Second front-to-backs

This stage basically repeats the fitting of the first front-to-back canes. Just as the first side-to-side canes were simply laid on top of the first front-to-back canes, so these second front-to-back canes are laid on top of the first side-to-side canes. In other words, there is no weaving at this stage. Make sure that the cane is slightly damp, then proceed as follows.

1 Working across from the side

● To fit the second set of front-to-back canes, repeat steps 1–5 of 'Fitting the first set of front-to-back canes'. However, this time start at one side of the seat, rather than in the middle. As you work your way across the seat, use the same holes as you did for the first set of canes (keeping the rear corner holes open). However, you must make sure that when the second front-to-back canes are threaded through their holes, they all lie slightly to the right of the first front-to-back canes. You may need to pull some of the first canes a little to the left. You can do this with either your fingers or, if you find it easier, the shaft of the clearing tool.

Note: Whenever you come to a hole that has already been pegged, simply remove the tee, insert the new strip of cane, tension both the original and the new cane by pulling firmly from underneath the hole, and replace the tee.

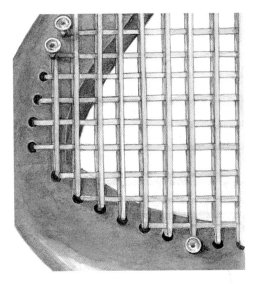

Weaving the second side-to-side canes

Now you must weave a second set of side-to-side canes to run alternately over and under the two sets of front-to-back canes. Dampen the canes in hot water, then proceed as follows.

1 Starting from the front
● Begin by pegging the first length of cane into the hole you used to start the first set of side-to-side canes. Leave 7.5cm of cane hanging below the hole.
● Working parallel to the first set of side-by-side canes, thread the end of the cane over the first front-to-back cane that you come to and then pass it beneath the one that lies immediately next to it. Repeat this over-under pattern of weaving across the pairs of front-to-back canes.
● When you have woven through three or four pairs of canes, pull the rest of the cane through and tension it slightly.
● Continue in this manner until you reach the other side (and the opposite hole). Then tension and half-twist the cane down through the hole and back up through the adjacent hole, as you did with the first set of side-to-side canes.
● Work your way back to the other side, but this time reverse the weaving sequence to under-over. Continue in this manner towards the back of the chair, pegging with tees where necessary.

2 Adjusting with a comb
● When you have completed three or four rows, moisten all the cane with a damp rag.
● Insert the teeth of a combing tool into the gaps between the cane and adjust it to square the pattern. Repeat this process throughout the weaving.

3 Finishing at the back
● When you reach the back of the seat, leave the corner holes on the rear rail free.
● Moisten the canes once again with a damp rag and, if necessary, square the pattern with the comb.
● Trim canes that hang more than 7.5cm below the holes.

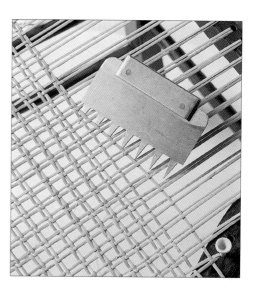

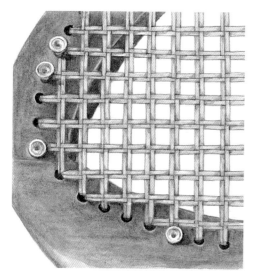

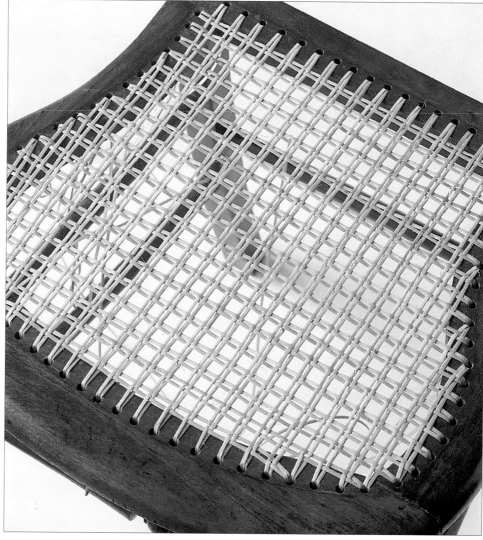

Weaving the first set of diagonals

Select slightly larger cane for the diagonals than that which you used for the front-to-backs and side-to-sides. (In this case, No. 4 cane was used.) Moisten it in hot water, then proceed as follows.

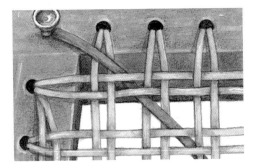

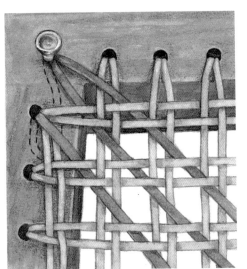

1 Starting at the back left corner

● For the first time, use the rear left-hand corner hole. Push a strip of cane through this hole so that 7.5cm hangs down, and peg it.

● Run the cane through your fingers to make sure that it isn't twisted, and pass the end over the first pair of front-to-back canes, to the right, and under the first pair of side-to-side canes, as shown.

● Continue over the next pair of front-to-back canes, and repeat this over-under weaving for three or four pairs. Pull the cane through, tensioning it slightly.

● Continue until you reach the front rail. On square seats, you will end at the point diagonally opposite. On tapered and curved seats, the cane reaches the front rail just left of where this rail meets the side rail.

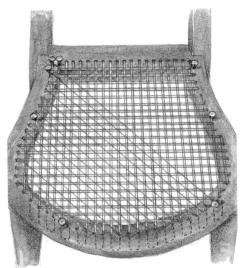

2 Completing the left triangle

● Push the cane through the appropriate hole in the front rail. Half-twist and tension it, as before, then push it up through the adjacent hole on the left.

● Weave the cane back to the rear corner hole, keeping it parallel to the first cane. The over-under weaving pattern should match that of the first cane.

● Push the end of the cane into the corner hole where you started and peg it to secure it.

● Half-twist and tension the cane, then push it up through the adjacent hole in the side rail.

● Weave towards the front rail to form a triangle of parallel diagonal canes on the left half of the seat.

Note: The first cane starts at and returns to the rear corner hole. Others usually finish on a hole adjacent to the one where they started. However, to keep diagonal canes parallel on tapered or curved seats you may have to use some holes on the side rail twice (which holes are a matter of choice). After doing this, always skip the hole directly opposite on the other side rail. This allows you to put two canes into it when fitting the second set of diagonals and so keep the symmetry.

3 Completing the right triangle

● Weave the right-hand triangle in the same way. If there is an even number of holes left on the front rail, start the weaving from the hole on the back rail adjacent to the long side of the triangle. If there is an odd number of holes left on the front rail, start on the adjacent hole on the front rail.

● When you reach the right-hand corner hole on the front rail, pass the cane through it twice (as you did on the left-hand rear corner hole in step 2). This will keep the pattern symmetrical.

Weaving the second set of diagonals

You must now weave a second series of diagonal canes, in the opposite direction to the first set. Moisten some strips of No. 4 cane, as before, and proceed as follows.

1 Starting at the back right corner
● Repeat the previous stage, but starting at the back right corner. Note that this time the cane must be woven under the first pair of front-to-back canes, to the left, and then over the side-to-side canes. In other words, this is an under-over weaving pattern rather than an over-under sequence (as with the first set of diagonals).

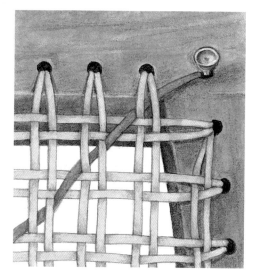

2 Completing the right triangle
● As you work your way across the right triangle of canes, you must insert two canes into the holes on the side rails that were missed out with the first set of diagonals. Also, you must miss out the holes on the side rails that already have two diagonal canes (from the first set) in them. You may find at this stage that the holes are becoming crowded and that it is therefore proving increasingly difficult to insert new strips of cane into them. If this is the case, you will find it helpful to enlarge the holes with the end of a cross-head screwdriver. However, you must do this carefully so you do not gouge the strips of cane already in the hole.

3 Completing the left triangle
● Weave the second set of diagonals in the left triangle in the same way as you did for the right triangle. When you reach the corner hole on the front rail, you must pass two canes through it (as you did with the front left-hand corner) to keep the pattern symmetrical.

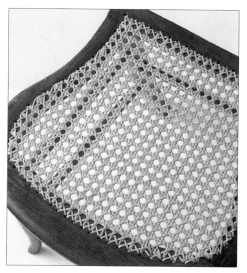

Pegging the holes

There are two traditional methods of finishing off the edge of a cane panel. On furniture made before 1850, most panels are secured with a permanent peg in every hole. On later pieces (such as this chair), only alternate holes are pegged, and a strip of cane beading is secured around the seat's edge and over the top of the holes.

If you are finishing the edge just with pegs, complete this stage and move to 'Antiquing the cane', on p.81. If you are finishing with beading, simply note the pegging technique described here and go to 'Beading the edge', on p.80.

1 Cutting and fitting the pegs
● With a heavy-duty utility knife, cut some strips of No. 14 or No. 16 centre basket-weaving cane into a sufficient number of pegs to fill all the holes. The pegs should fit tightly in the holes and be slightly shorter than the thickness of the seat rails. To make fitting easier, taper the pegs' ends slightly with a utility knife. (An alternative to cane pegs is pre-cut birch or ramin dowels of the appropriate diameter.)
● Tap the pegs part of the way into the holes with a hammer. Punch them just below the surface of the rails with the clearing tool and a hammer.
● Whenever you come to a golf tee, remove it and tension the loose ends of the cane below the hole as you drive in the permanent peg.
● When you have finished pegging, use a pair of nippers or end-cutting pliers to cut all the loose ends of cane flush with the bottom of the seat rails.

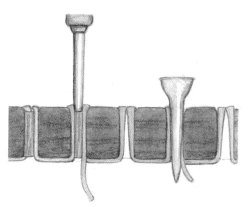

Beading the edge

To bead the edge of the panel, use No. 6 cane, plus No. 2 cane and pegs cut from centre basket-weaving cane to secure it. Moisten all these in hot water first.

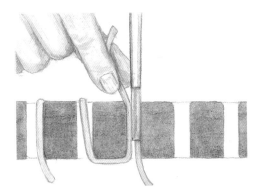

1 Pegging alternate holes

● Leave the four corner holes of the seat unpegged. Working on one rail at a time, and using the technique described in 'Pegging the holes', on p.79, peg alternate holes. On rails which have an even number of holes, the two middle holes can either be pegged or unpegged.

● If you reach a hole you don't wish to peg, but which has a loose end of cane in it, turn the end up through the nearest hole that is to be pegged. Pull the end up above the rail, and hold it taut between your fingers as you hammer the peg in place. Carefully cut away the excess with a heavy-duty utility knife.

2 Starting the beading

Note: If you are working on a frame with straight rails, follow steps 2–4. If the frame is curved, just note the techniques described in steps 2–4, then move to 'Beading curved rails', opposite.

● Using a pair of side-cutting pliers, cut four strips of No. 6 cane. Each strip should be approximately 5cm longer than the length of a side rail. Then taper 2.5cm of one end of each strip so that it will fit into a corner hole.

● Take a long strip of No. 2 cane and push one end up through the bottom of one of the rear corner holes. When it emerges at the top of the side rail, bend it over so that it lies about 3.5cm along the rail.

● Push the tapered end of one strip of beading cane into the corner hole from above. Temporarily secure it with a tee peg.

● Fold the beading cane so that it lies flat along the length of the side rail and covers the holes.

● Push the other end of the No. 2 cane up through the first open hole on the side rail. Loop it over the beading and push it back down through the same hole. Pull from below to tighten and trap the beading. Repeat along the length of the side rail through all the unpegged holes.

3 Turning the corner

● Just before you tighten the last loop at the other end of the side rail, trim and taper the end of the beading, then push it into the front corner hole.

● Pull the loop in the No. 2 cane tight and pull the loose end diagonally under the front corner. Push it up through the first unpegged hole in the front rail.

● Push the tapered end of the second strip of beading cane into the corner hole and hammer in a permanent peg.

● Bend the beading cane to lie over the holes along the front rail, and repeat the looping and tying in with the No. 2 cane.

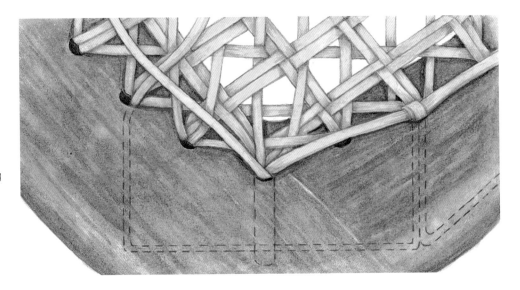

Finishing off

When you have completed the beading, you have two options for finishing the panel: you can leave the cane as it is or you can artificially age it. You may prefer to leave the new cane as it is (as shown right). However, many professional caners consider that new, untreated cane presents a rather stark contrast with an antique chair frame. The amateur can remedy this by ageing the new cane so that it looks more in keeping with an antique chair. If you wish to do this, refer to 'Antiquing the cane', below.

Before recaning the chair, you will have cleaned and polished it (see p.73, step 2). Nevertheless, handling the chair during recaning will have left finger marks on it. To restore the finish, apply a thin coat of either clear or tinted beeswax polish with a soft, lint-free cotton rag. Leave the polish for approximately 20 minutes, then buff it to a shine with another clean soft cloth.

4 Finishing the beading
● Work round the perimeter of the frame until you arrive back at the starting point.
● Remove the temporary tee peg from the first corner hole. Push in the trimmed, tapered end of the beading cane and hammer in a permanent peg.
● Trim any loose ends of cane with a pair of nippers.

1 Beading curved rails
● On seats with curved front or side rails, cut one strip of beading cane for the back rail and one for the front and sides. (Work No. 2 binding cane as in steps 1–4.)
● When working on the front and side rails, dampen the beading cane with hot water and gently bend it to follow the curves. To achieve a smooth curve, you may have to miss out a hole, running the beading cane over the top without binding it in with the No. 2 cane.

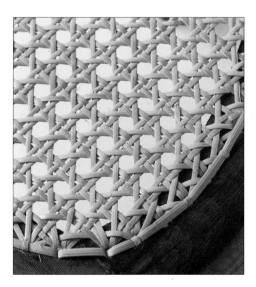

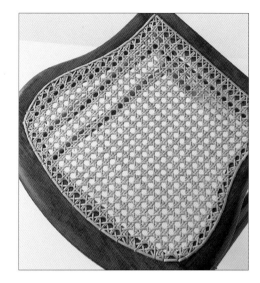

1 Antiquing the cane
● Mix a small quantity of Van Dyke crystals with cold water to make a thin, watery glaze.
● Wipe the glaze over the cane with a lint-free cotton rag and leave to dry for at least 8 hours.
● Gently buff the panel with a lint-free polishing cloth.

Upholstery

Introduction

Before the beginning of the 17th century, most chairs and benches had wooden seats, the hardness of which was relieved by cushions or squabs (seat or bench pads). From about 1620, velvet or tapestry (known as turkey work) was used to cover the arms, legs and stretchers of some chairs in England, and in this way the concept of fully upholstered seating was introduced.

Central arrangement

Until the beginning of the 17th century, seating was usually lined up along the walls of a room. But by the end of the century it was starting to be placed towards the centre of the room, and arranged in small, free-standing groupings that made conversation easier. Because they were now more on show than they had been previously, chairs and sofas required upholstery both front and back. It also became fashionable to decorate rooms en suite – that is, in smarter rooms the fabric for upholstery was selected to match the curtains, wall-hangings and other accessories.

Early upholsterers

The techniques employed by early upholsterers, particularly stitching and quilting, were derived from the craft of saddlery. Many of the tools and materials used then – for example, cord, hessian, webbing, chisels, hammers and tacks – have remained part of the upholsterer's basic kit to this day. Similarly, horsehair stuffing and woolen wadding are still used, although straw and seaweed are not.

Springs

Apart from the development of different styles of furniture and the development of mass-produced, machine-woven and printed fabrics, there have been only two major innovations in the craft of upholstery since the early 18th century. The first of these was the 'hourglass' or double-cone upholstery spring, which was perfected and patented in the 1820s. The simple result was more comfortable seating.

Buttons

The second innovation was the button and, more specifically, deep-buttoning, which evolved from the 18th-century technique of tufting. Essentially a form of quilting, tufting was designed to secure the stuffing inside squabs. The technique

Left: Rococo-revival armchair
This deep-buttoned armchair is part of a 19th-century Rococo-revival parlour suite made in Philadelphia. The suite was covered in the 1940s with a reproduction fabric (see p.98) similar to the original.

Below: Restored chaise longue
Dating from c.1815, this English Regency faux-rosewood chaise-longue has sabre legs and painted ormolu decoration. It has been restored authentically, using only webbing to support all the upholstery above it. During the late 19th and 20th centuries many similar examples were reupholstered with springs, which gave them an inappropriate 'overstuffed' look.

involved looping a series of linen threads through the upholstery and around a small bunch of silk fibres or unspun filaments of linen.

In the second half of the 18th century, tufting was used on chairs, benches and day-beds that had fixed upholstery. However, in the first half of the 19th century the development of sprung upholstery, together with the fashion for using progressively thicker layers of stuffing, rendered tufting inadequate; something stronger was required to deal with the greater strain; buttons provided the means.

In fact, so effective was the technique of deep-buttoning (see pp.99–119) that it changed the shape of seating. Not only did it allow the use of ever-thicker padding, but it also accentuated both the thickness and curvaceousness of upholstery.

Tools and materials

The comprehensive selection of tools and materials specified here has been assembled to enable you to not only tackle the projects described in this chapter, but also to deal with most of the upholstery tasks you are likely to encounter.

Tools

1 Upholsterer's hammer Has a small, magnetized head to hammer in tacks in tight spaces, and a claw end to remove tacks.

2 Carpenter's mallet A large wooden hammer.

3 Ripping chisel Has a bevelled, blunt and hardened end, plus a straight or bent shaft (the latter allows greater leverage to be applied). Used with a carpenter's mallet to remove old tacks and upholstery (see p.93).

4 Tack-lifter Features a small claw for removing stubborn old tacks, or for use where a ripping chisel might damage show wood (see p.93).

5 Webbing stretcher Designed to pull webbing taut across the frame before tacking (see p.95).

6 Mattress needles Large, double-ended, single-eyed needles, mainly used for blind- and top-stitching stuffing into shape. Also used for buttoning. 25cm, 20cm and 15cm lengths should cover most needs.

7 Spring needle This is curved with a flattened bayonet point; used for stitching the springs to the webbing and hessian, and for inserting bridle ties.

8 Small curved needles Available in various sizes, from 2.5 to 15cm. The smaller ones are used for slip-stitching seams and piping. Larger ones are useful where a straight needle is too big.

9 Straight needles Sewing needles, in a range of sizes. Mainly used to repair splits and tears.

10 Regulators Long needles with paddle-shaped ends, used to reposition stuffing once covered and to shape pleating. Available in a range of lengths and gauges, but 25cm medium-light gauge is the most useful.

11 Scissors Good-quality 20–22cm upholsterer's scissors are best for cutting fabrics.

12 Upholsterer's skewers Available in a range of sizes and used to temporarily hold hessian, scrim and top covers in place before stitching.

13 Utility or craft knife Safety-handled version for cutting and trimming the edges of tacked fabric.

14 Steel ruler Useful for measuring fabric and as a safe straight edge when cutting fabric with a utility knife.

15 Face mask and goggles Wear both to protect lungs and eyes when ripping off (see p.93).

16 Brushes Use a small paint brush to apply wood glue under hessian when making simple repairs to frames before tacking. Use a small artist's brush to apply latex glue when attaching braid.

YOU WILL ALSO NEED:
Dressmaker's tape measure
Tailor's chalk
Pencil
Screwdriver Straight or Phillips-head pattern, used to tighten screwed corner blocks or part-screwed frames.

Materials

17 Webbing Plain, woven-jute webbing is roughly 5cm wide, and used to support the upholstery on the underframe. Twill-woven cotton and flax webbing is a stronger alternative.

18 Springs Available in varying heights, from 7.5 to 35cm, and gauges, SWG Nos. 8 to 15. Gauges 9 and 10 are best for seats, 11 to 13 for backs, and 14 and 15 for arms. You may be able to re-use existing springs.

19 Laid cord Made of hemp and used to tie springs.

20 Hessian A coarse brown fabric woven from jute. Use 350g or 500g over webbing or springs, 285g for a chair's back and arms, and 225g as an alternative to scrim.

21 Scrim A fine-spun jute (or sometimes linen) used to enclose the first stuffing.

22 Curled hair Originally horsehair, but now a mixture of horsehair and hog's hair, it is used for a second or 'top' stuffing. You may be able to reuse the original.

23 Fibre A cheaper alternative to curled hair and available in a number of forms. The most popular are palm fibre and coco fibre (slightly finer than palm fibre).

24 Wadding Thick felt padding made from cotton fibres and applied between a calico undercover and a top cover. Gives additional padding and prevents strands of stuffing working their way through the top cover.

25 Skin Wadding A thinner type of wadding, usually white, and used on smaller chairs or where the top cover is a very thin, pale fabric.

26 Calico A thin, unbleached cotton fabric applied under the top cover to enclose the upholstery. Use a medium-weight or lightweight version.

27 Upholsterer's linen Made from cotton. Acts as a dust cover on the underside of chairs.

28 Twine Use stout No. 1 twine for sewing in springs and for through-ties, medium No. 2 for stitching edge rolls and finer No. 3 for buttoning and bridle ties.

29 Piping cord Soft cotton cord wrapped in the top-cover fabric and used to finish seamed edges (see p.91). Sizes – 00, 0, 1, 2, etc – denote the diameter.

30 Threads Slipping, or 'buttoning', thread is made from linen and used to hand-stitch top covers, close pleats and attach piping.

31 Upholstery tacks Improved tacks have large heads and thick shanks; fine tacks have small heads and thin shanks. Tacks come in three basic sizes. Use 15mm improved to fix webbing on thicker frames (or same-sized fine tacks on thinner frames). Use 12mm improved to fix webbing on light frames such as drop-in seat pads. Use 12mm fine to temporary tack (see p.97) hessian and scrim, and to fix the base hessian. Use 10mm improved to fix hessian and scrim, and 10mm fine to fix calico and top covers.

32 Trimmings Woven braids and gimps are available in a huge range of colours and styles, and are used to cover exposed rows of tacks.

33 Gimp pins Small coloured pins, mainly used to fix trimmings of braid and gimp to the frame, but also to fix top covers to chairs with fragile frames.

34 Adhesives White latex glue can be used as an alternative to gimp pins to fix braid. White glue (PVA) is used to bond hessian to wooden frames when making basic repairs before reupholstering (see p.93).

YOU WILL ALSO NEED:
A small block of beeswax To lightly wax twine.
Material for the top cover It is usually best to choose strong, closely woven fabrics such as damask, velvet or tapestry, in a style to suit the period of your chair.
Metal buttons To cover with the top material when button-backing.
Care and cleaning substances Distilled water, potato flour, white spirit, borax, hydrogen peroxide, detergents, talcum powder, glycerine, French chalk (see pp.88–9).
Dust sheets To protect the floor and other furnishings in the room while you are working.

General care and cleaning

From the late 17th century to the end of the 19th, upholstered chairs were supplied with two covers: fixed and loose. For example, a set of Chippendale or Sheraton dining chairs would have had their seats permanently upholstered in a fabric such as a finely woven silk damask, which was intended for use on formal occasions or when guests were in the house.

However, the chairs would have also had a set of plain cotton or linen loose covers, which were temporarily tied to the frames with small tabs. These 'slip' covers would have been used when guests were not present, or when formality was not required, and, often, during the hot summer months.

Protecting from sunlight

The main purpose of loose covers was to protect expensive upholstery from wear and tear and the fading produced by prolonged exposure to strong sunlight. Although these covers had become generally unfashionable by the 20th century, the need to protect upholstery remains the same. Therefore, if you find slip covers aesthetically unacceptable, you should, where possible, screen furniture from, or move it out of, direct sunlight. Using sheer undercurtains or drawing the main curtains during the day in summer are two simple solutions.

Adjusting humidity

In addition to reducing the effects of sunlight on upholstery, it is important to keep humidity within a room down to acceptable levels. It is surprising how quickly excessive moisture in the air can wreak havoc with upholstery fabrics. If your furniture is in a warm, humid climate for much or even part of the year, an electric dehumidifier will prove a sensible investment.

General cleaning

However well protected, upholstery in daily use will eventually become dirty and require cleaning. Apart from regular vacuuming to remove abrasive dust and grit, the simple rule of thumb for any upholstered antique chair or settee is: call in a reputable cleaning company that specializes in antiques. Its staff will decide whether a particular fabric should be washed or dry-cleaned (depending on the colourfastness of the dyes used), and will use a method that ensures any residue of the cleaning agent is completely removed. There have been too many unfortunate instances where an owner has spoilt, or even ruined, a valuable antique top cover by inexpertly applying a chemical cleaning agent.

Testing for colourfastness

Although you should always call in professionals to deal with valuable antique top covers, it is feasible to clean less valuable pieces, and to remove certain specific stains. However, you should always first test the fabric for colourfastness.

● Test for colourfastness by carefully applying the cleaning agent specified to a small patch of the fabric (preferably at the back of the piece). If the colour starts to run, call in a professional.
● If water is specified as part of the cleaning process, use only distilled water (available from chemists).
● Always start with a weak solution of the cleaning agent, and work inwards in a circle. This will minimize the risk of leaving a ring-shaped mark on the fabric.

Removing stains

There follows a list of typical stains you are likely to encounter on upholstery (together with their specified treatments). If you come across a stain that does not appear here, you will find a further list of fabric stains and their treatments in the chapter on Textiles (see pp. 144–5).

Alcohol (spirits)

Remove damp alcohol with clean water. If it has dried, gently rub in a weak solution of warm water and wool detergent with your fingertips. Then rinse and allow to dry naturally.

Beer

This can be a difficult stain to treat, and is usually best left to a professional cleaner. However, if the stain is recent and the top cover is white or an off-white colour you can apply a weak solution of 1 part 20 per cent hydrogen peroxide to 6 parts water, then rinse and allow to dry naturally.

Candle wax

Cover the area with brown wrapping paper (matt side facing the wax), and apply a medium-hot iron. Keep replacing the paper and reapplying the iron until the worst of the wax has been drawn into the paper. Carefully remove any remaining traces of wax with a clean rag moistened with a little white spirit.

Coffee

If the stain is still damp, remove it with a weak solution of 30g of borax to 500ml of water. If the stain has dried, gently rub it with a clean rag moistened with glycerine. Leave it for about an hour, then rinse it with water. Finally, gently wash it with warm, soapy water before rinsing it once again. Allow the fabric to dry naturally.

Fat and oils

Remove light stains with a clean rag moistened with a little white spirit. For heavier stains use the same method as for candle wax.

Mildew

You will not be able to do any better than apply a commercial mildew cleaner, in accordance with the manufacturer's instructions.

Milk

Wash with warm, soapy water, then rinse. You may have to add a little borax to the water if the stain proves particularly stubborn.

Shoe polish

Very gently rub the affected area with cotton wool moistened with a little white spirit.

Soot

Vacuum off as much of the soot as possible, taking care not to rub it further into the fabric with the vacuum cleaner attachment. Sprinkle a thick layer of potato flour, talcum powder or French chalk over the area. Work this in with your fingers until it becomes dirty. Vacuum it off, and repeat as many times as necessary. Next wipe the area with a cloth dipped in warm, soapy water before rinsing with a cloth dipped in plain water. Allow to dry naturally.

Tea

If still wet, simply try to rinse it out with moderately hot water. If the stain has dried, apply a solution of 1 part borax to 30 parts hot water, then rinse as above and allow to dry naturally.

Wine

Dab the stain as quickly as possible with cotton wool to remove as much wine as you can from the surface of the fabric. Then sprinkle a liberal quantity of potato flour, talcum powder or French chalk over the area. Knead this in with your fingers, and when it becomes tacky, remove and repeat the procedure. Next gently dab the area with cotton wool dipped in glycerine, leave for a few minutes, and then sponge with warm, soapy water. Finally, rinse with water by gently rubbing with some wrung-out cloths. Allow the fabric to dry naturally.

Cleaning trimmings

Many pieces of antique upholstered furniture are embellished with lengths of trimming along seams and edges. Collectively known as passementerie, trimmings come in a variety of forms, notably tassels, fringe and braid. Although often made of the same, or a similar, fabric to the top-cover material, they are also often worked in alternative fibres, including silver and gold threads. Their intricate construction can make them very difficult to clean, particularly if they are tackled in situ and at the same time as the rest of the upholstery. It is, therefore, a good idea to temporarily detach them from the item of furniture, and clean them separately. Because they are usually secured with stitching, it is a reasonably easy task to unpick them with scissors or a dressmaker's seam ripper, and then sew them back on later.

Victorian side chair

A mid 19th-century side chair, upholstered in red silk velvet and embellished with tassels on the skirt and shoulders.

Making minor repairs

Original fabrics uphold the value of a piece. If a chair's covering is basically sound, it is better to repair the original fabric than to replace it. Apart from restitching seams and replacing tacks, the two commonest repairs are mending small tears or splits and replacing worn or damaged piping.

Repairing small tears and splits

Small tears and splits in top covers can be repaired if the fabric is in fair condition. But if it is thin or worn it may not support the stitching required to close the hole. The damage illustrated here is a rip in a delicate top cover – the silk seat cover of an early 19th-century chair. The tear occurred when the chair's back brushed against a nail head, and it has begun to fray and open under pressure from the stuffing inside the seat.

YOU WILL NEED:
Small scissors 2.5–7.5cm blades.
Upholsterer's tack-lifter
Upholsterer's scissors 20–22cm blades.
Fabric Lightweight calico, or a remnant of the top-cover fabric.
Straight needle
Thread Strong thread to match top cover.
Upholsterer's tacks As used on the chair.

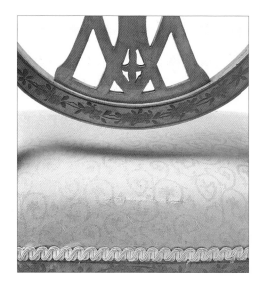

Above: Finishing off the repair
When you have mended the tear, secure the top cover with upholsterer's tacks and then stitch the decorative braid back in place.

1 Preparing for the repair
● The tacks securing the top cover are under the decorative braid. With a small pair of scissors, cut and unpick the stitches holding the braid in the area of the damage. Unstitch only enough braid to allow access to the tacks.
● Using a tack-lifter, gently prise up the upholstery tacks that secure the top cover. Work carefully, to avoid causing any further damage to the fabric.

2 Inserting backing fabric
● If you have any spare top-cover fabric available, cut out a piece 2.5cm bigger all around than the tear, and feed it under the top cover to lie flat on the calico undercover behind the tear. If you have no top-cover fabric, use lightweight calico.

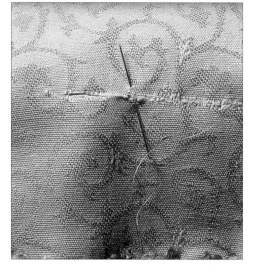

3 Stitching the repair
● Thread a straight needle with a fine, strong slipping thread in a colour as close as possible to the background colour of the top cover.
● Start at one end of the tear with a slip-knot. Insert the needle as near as possible to the edges of the fabric and pull both sides together with an under-and-over running stitch. Finish with a double-hitch. (For upholstery knots and stitches, see pp.248–9.)

Making replacement piping

Because it sticks out, the piping that runs along the seams of some upholstery suffers considerable wear and tear. It is fairly easy to replace, and this is worth doing if the rest of the top-cover fabric is in good condition. If the piping cord is covered in the same material as the rest of the piece it may be hard to find more of the material. However, many fabric manufacturers make an extensive range of period fabrics – known as reproduction fabrics (see p.98) – so a match may be possible. The alternative is to make the piping from a material of a complementary colour and pattern.

YOU WILL NEED:
Upholsterer's skewers
Small scissors 2.5–7.5cm blades.
Craft knife
Piping cord Three-strand, soft cotton cord.
Fabric If possible, an exact match.
Straight edge
Tailor's chalk
Upholsterer's scissors 20–22cm blades.
Pins
Sewing machine With piping or zipper foot.
Domestic iron
Straight needle
Thread Cotton, linen or silk to match the predominant fibre (and colour) of the piping material.

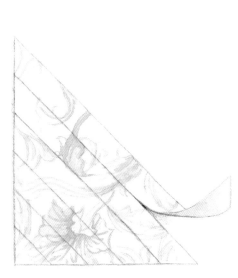

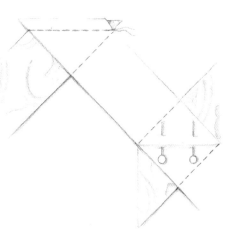

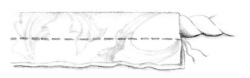

1 Removing the worn piping

● Before removing the piping, pin the surrounding fabric to the underlying stuffing with a run of regularly spaced upholsterer's skewers.
● Carefully cut the stitching that holds the old piping in place. Open a length of the old piping and remove a sample of the cord; buy replacement cord of identical weight. Cord is sold by numbers – 00, 0, 1, 2, 3, etc – that indicate its thickness. The higher the number, the thicker the cord.

2 Cutting the piping cord

● The fabric for piping is cut on the bias, to give it the necessary stretch and flexibility when running around curves and corners. To establish the bias, fold a straight raw edge down to meet the selvedge, forming a triangle. The side of the triangle opposite the right angle forms the bias line. Mark along this with a straight edge and tailor's chalk.
● Mark a series of parallel lines of the width you need (the circumference of the piping cord plus 12mm for seam allowances). Use the original piping fabric as a template.
● Cut out the strips of fabric with scissors, mark the bottom end of each, and stack them in order.

3 Sewing the new fabric

● With their right, or patterned, sides together, lay the bottom end of one strip at a right angle across the top end of the next strip to form two sides of a triangle.
● Pin, then machine-stitch the pieces together across their overlapped ends, leaving a seam allowance of 6mm. Repeat this process with additional strips until you have achieved the required length.
● Press open each seam. Trim corners that protrude past edges of strips.

4 Positioning the piping cord

● Place the joined strips of fabric right side down, then position the piping along the centre and wrap the fabric around it. Tack together just underneath the cord to make a flange.
● Using a piping foot, machine-stitch the tacked seam. On material with a slightly loose weave, sew a double or treble seam at the seams between the cut strips to prevent fraying. If you are hand-sewing, use a back stitch (see p.248). Remove the tacking stitches.
● To attach the new piping, place the flange inside the original upholstery's seams. Close the seams with a slip stitch, passing the thread through the flange and near the piping. Remove upholsterer's skewers.

Preparing for reupholstering

If you decide that the upholstery on a piece of furniture is beyond repair, you will have to strip it down to the wooden frame before reupholstering. But do not do this without first consulting an antiques expert on the value and quality of the piece, and on whether or not it should be restored by a professional upholsterer.

Before you begin you should take photographs and make sketches from all sides of the piece; although you might think you will remember dimensions and proportions, almost certainly you will not. Make notes on items such as the width of the tops of the arms, the position of any buttoning, the style of pleating, and the height of the seat in relation to the sides of the chair – they will prove invaluable throughout the process of reupholstering.

When you start removing the old upholstery, work systematically through the layers rather than just hacking them off. You will learn a lot about the construction and how sections relate to one another. Make notes and sketches as you progress.

Below: Unsprung and sprung chair seats
The illustration on the left below shows a cross section of a typical unsprung seat pad. It gives a good idea of what you can expect when you remove the old upholstery, and will act as a checklist for the sequence of reupholstering (see also the drop-in seat pad project on pp.94–8). The illustration below shows a cross section of a typical sprung seat (see also the project 'Reupholstering a button-back chair' on pp.99–119).

Cross section of an unsprung drop-in seat pad

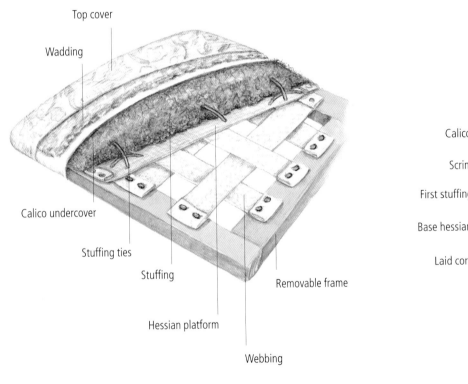

Top cover
Wadding
Calico undercover
Stuffing ties
Stuffing
Hessian platform
Webbing
Removable frame

Cross section of a sprung seat

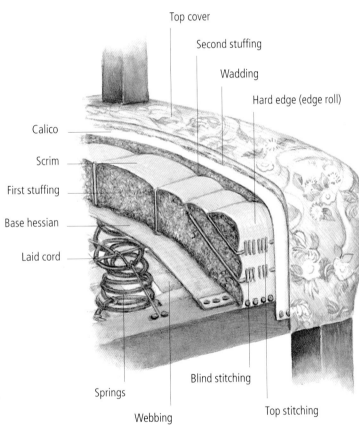

Top cover
Second stuffing
Wadding
Hard edge (edge roll)
Calico
Scrim
First stuffing
Base hessian
Laid cord
Springs
Webbing
Blind stitching
Top stitching

Ripping off

The upholsterer's term for removing old upholstery is 'ripping off'. This can be an extremely messy job. Therefore you are advised to work in a well-ventilated area (leave windows open) and to use dust sheets to protect the underlying floor covering and any other furnishings in the vicinity.

Because you will raise dust you should wear old clothes or overalls, a face mask to protect your lungs, and a pair of plastic goggles. You might wish to wear old leather gloves to protect your hands from any flying upholsterer's tacks, which can be extremely sharp and often rusty.

REVIVING OLD HORSEHAIR

Original horsehair furniture stuffing is expensive to replace. However, you can revive it for reuse:

1 Removing dust Carefully tease the strands of hair apart between your fingers to remove the dust.

2 Hand-washing Gently hand-wash it in a bucket of lukewarm, soapy water.

3 Rinsing Rinse thoroughly in clean water.

4 Drying Tease it apart again, and allow to dry naturally in a warm room.

1 Using a ripping chisel

● Begin by removing the dust cover (also known as 'bottoming') from the underside of the chair. Use a ripping chisel and a carpenter's wooden mallet to remove the upholsterer's tacks. Work along the grain of the wood, in order not to split it, and work away from the corners of the frame so that you do not put excessive pressure on the joints.

● If you are working on a drop-in seat pad this should be removed from the chair and held in a vice. When you are removing particularly stubborn tacks, or tacks that are close to any show wood, prise them out with a tack-lifter (see step 2).

2 Removing tacks

● Whether you are using a ripping chisel or a tack-lifter (above), the removal sequence from a drop-in seat pad is, after the dust cover: top cover, wadding, calico undercover, second stuffing, scrim, top stitching and blind stitching, bridle ties (cut with a utility knife), first stuffing, hessian, webbing.

● The sequence is the same for a sprung seat, except for cutting the laid cord and removing the springs before the webbing. With an armchair, the sequence is: outside back; inside arms; button ties and buttons; inside back; insides and fronts of arms, tops of arms; seat. Dismantle the sprung seat as before.

Repairing the frame

Before beginning to reupholster, any damage to the frame should be rectified. For basic repairs to doweled and mortise-and-tenon joints (such as regluing) see pp.44–7. If there is evidence of woodworm, treat this as described on p.244. If the chair on which you are working has been reupholstered many times over the years, its rails may well be splintered as a result of the repeated use of upholstery tacks. If this is the case you will need to reinforce the frame, as explained right.

1 Reinforcing the frame

● Push commercial or homemade wood filler into the holes and splits with the blade of an old knife. (Make your own filler by mixing sawdust with wood glue to form a thick paste.) Brush some more glue on top and, before it dries, place a strip of hessian over the rail.

● Apply more glue to saturate the hessian and then press the hessian firmly around the shape of the rail using a wooden block. When using this method to repair the frame of a drop-in seat pad, make sure that the hessian does not bulk up the rails so much that they will not fit back into the chair frame.

Upholstering a drop-in seat pad

Drop-in, or slip-in, seats can be found on occasional and dining chairs dating from the 17th century onwards. While some drop-in seats are sprung, most take the form of a pad without springs in which the upholstery is supported by a lattice of webbing attached to a hardwood subframe. Usually made of beech (although other woods such as pine, oak and mahogany have also been used), the subframe is commonly rectangular in shape, although some examples feature a curved or serpentine front edge. In each case the method of upholstering is broadly the same.

   The seat pad usually sits on rebates or corner blocks within the rails of the chair. This is common in 18th-century examples. Alternatively, as in early 19th-century chairs, the pad rests on rebates within the side rails and on top of the front and back rails and is held in place with a locating lug in the centre of the front rail.

YOU WILL NEED:
Ripping chisel
Carpenter's wooden mallet
Tack-lifter
Roll of 5cm cotton upholstery webbing
Upholsterer's scissors
Webbing stretcher
10mm improved upholsterer's tacks
Or fine tacks of the same size if the wood is hard and liable to split.
Upholsterer's hammer Magnetized.
500g heavyweight hessian
12mm improved upholsterer's tacks
Or fine tacks the same size as above.
No. 1 twine
Curved (half-circle) needle
Mattress needle
Horsehair About 250g of coco fibre, palm grass stuffing or revived horsehair.
Calico About 70cm.
Regulator
Wadding 60g/70cm.
Top covering About 70cm of closely woven fabric such as brocade, damask or velvet.
Marker pen

Traditional reupholstery
The mahogany occasional chair shown here dates from c.1830 and features an attractive curved front edge. Because it involves many of the basic techniques of upholstery, restoring a drop-in seat pad on a chair such as this makes a suitable project for the beginner. Reupholstering the seat will not lower the value of the chair, provided that traditional rather than modern methods and materials are used.

Preparation

When reupholstering a period chair, use traditional methods and materials wherever possible so as not to lower its value. However, because traditional wadding – a thin sheet of cotton faced with paper laid over calico – is difficult to tear accurately, professional upholsterers sometimes use a modern substitute. Similarly, horsehair, long used for stuffing upholstery, is still the most comfortable and durable choice. But its cost has led upholsterers to use less expensive palm or coco fibre as a substitute for the main stuffing and then weave in and pile up a thin layer of horsehair on top.

1 Attaching the webbing

● Strip the old upholstery and repair the frame as needed (see p.93).

●To avoid waste, use the webbing straight from the roll, cutting it as you progress.

● Fold over the end of the webbing approximately 2.5cm. Position this, with the cut edge uppermost, over the centre of the front rail and secure it with three improved 12mm tacks along the outer edge of the rail and two tacks toward the inner edge of the rail to make a W-shape.

● Hold the webbing stretcher with the handle away from you, insert the webbing in a loop through the slit from the underside, then insert the peg into the loop.

2 Stretching the webbing

● Turning the stretcher over with the handle towards you, stretch the webbing across the centre of the back rail of the frame by levering down on the stretcher. The webbing should be pulled sufficiently taut so that it 'rings' when tapped.

● Secure the single thickness of webbing at the centre of the rail with three evenly spaced tacks.

● Cut away the webbing, leaving a 2.5cm overlap. Fold this back and then hammer in two more tacks. If the tacks were all visible you would see that they form another W-shape.

3 Interweaving

● Complete all the front-to-back rows of webbing by repeating steps 1 and 2. Work from the centre of the frame outwards and use the number of rows in the original upholstery as your guide. If you are in any doubt about the right position for the strips of webbing, space them approximately 12mm apart.

● Use the same technique to apply the side-to-side strips of webbing, interweaving them as shown.

4 Positioning the hessian

● Cut a piece of heavyweight hessian about 5cm larger than the seat frame. Centre it over the webbing with the straight of the grain square to the seat.

● Tack the hessian to the centre of the back rail with two or three 10mm temporary tacks. Stretch it to the centre of the front rail and do the same. Then do the same at each side.

● Add temporary tacks at the back and front rails and sides, about 5cm apart, and tighten the hessian. Once the entire frame has been tacked, and the hessian is straight and taut, hammer home the tacks.

● Fold over the excess hessian and secure with tacks.

Adding the stuffing

1 Stuffing the front of the frame

● Drop-in seat pads require a stuffed roll at the front edge of the frame to stop the upholstery from compressing over the front edge of the seat when the chair is in use.

● Using No. 1 twine and a curved needle, sew a single bridle tie across the hessian just inside the back of the front rail of the subframe.

● Cut a strip of hessian 15cm deep and 10cm wider than the front rail. Fold over one edge of the hessian strip 2.5cm and, using the twine, curved needle, and a running stitch (see p.248), attach it to the main hessian panel 10cm back from the front rail.

● Tease out a handful of stuffing, taking care to remove any lumpy pieces, and then push it under the bridle tie to a height of 5cm.

● Stretch the hessian strip over the stuffing; tack the folded front edge to the underside of the front rail, no more than 1.5cm back from the front of the rail.

● Fold under the side edges and secure with three or four tacks along the underside of the frame.

● Use a mattress needle to blind-stitch (see pp.104–5) around both sides and the front of the roll.

2 Making the bridle ties

● To make the bridle ties which secure the stuffing to the main hessian panel, thread a curved needle with a length of No. 1 twine.

● Secure the twine with a slip knot in a corner of the panel and then make loose looped running stitches about 7.5cm long around the perimeter of the seat. The height of the loops depends on the amount of stuffing required; for most drop-in seat pads, you should be able to slide two fingers under them. Finish with a double-hitch (see p.249).

● The final bridle ties go from side to side across the seat. If it is a small seat, make one loop; larger seats need two or more.

3 Stuffing the sides

● Before you use any stuffing, tease apart the fibres to remove any lumps. If any is available, it is better to use revived and teased horsehair stuffing (see p.93).

● Tuck handfuls of the stuffing under the bridle ties. Make sure that the stuffing does not form any clumps and that the fibres are blended and fully interwoven.

● The height of the stuffing at the sides of the seat should be about 5cm.

4 Stuffing the centre

● When you have finished the sides, fill in the centre of the seat in the same way.

● Then add extra stuffing between the centre bridle tie and the side, teasing out the fibres as before.

● The height of the stuffing in the centre of the seat should be approximately 10cm. The shape of the stuffing should be domed and balanced on each side.

Fixing the calico

1 Securing the calico
● Cut the calico so that it is approximately 7.5cm larger all around than the frame.
● Lay the calico on a flat work surface and place the frame, stuffing side down, on top.
● Pull the calico over the stuffing and secure it with four temporary tacks, one in the centre of the underside of each rail. Use 10mm fine tacks.
● Insert temporary tacks about 3.5cm apart along the length of the back rail.

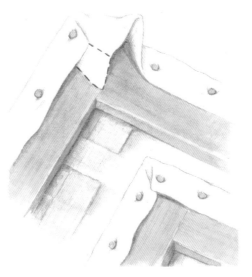

2 Temporary tacking
● Remove the single temporary tack from the front rail. Rest the seat on its back rail. Smooth the calico over the stuffing to the front edge and then over the frame to the underside. Re-apply temporary tacks so that the calico is taut.
● Repeat the same procedure at the sides, then pull the calico over all four corners and secure with a tack at each corner.
● If it proves necessary, remove the tacks, smooth the calico over the stuffing with the flat of your hand, and then adjust the tension of the fabric, working from back to front and from side to side, prior to driving the tacks fully home.

3 Finishing corners neatly
● Work the two front corners first. Fold the fabric into two pleats. Secure the first pleat with a tack, then cut away the excess fabric as shown by the dotted line in the diagram.
● Next fold the second pleat over the first one and again tack to secure.
● Finally finish the two back corners, using the same method as above.
● The undercover should be firmly and evenly tensioned across the entire frame and have a smooth, wrinkle-free surface. If you need to adjust the shape of the pad you should use a regulator to manoeuvre the stuffing (see p.103).

4 Adding the wadding
● Cut a layer of wadding approximately 2.5cm larger all around than the seat pad and position it squarely on top of the pad.
● Holding the wadding firmly in place with one hand, carefully pinch off the excess to produce a feathered edge. (A cut edge would show up as a ridge under the top cover.) The seat pad must fit comfortably into the chair frame, so make sure that the wadding does not extend over the sides of the frame.

Fixing the top cover

1 Making the top cover

- Cut the top cover 5cm larger all around than the seat pad, making a notch in the edge of the fabric to mark the centre of each side.
- Use a marker pen to mark the centre point on the underside of each rail. Secure the top cover in place, using the same method that you used to fit the calico cover. Make sure that the notches in the fabric and the marks on the frame align and that any pattern remains centred on the seat.

2 Adding a dust cover

- It is advisable to attach a dust cover of either upholsterer's linen or cambric to the base of the frame. Employ the same method that you used to attach the hessian cover (see p.95, step 4).
- Finally, gently ease the seat pad into the chair frame. Do not use excessive force or you will put undue stress on the joints of the frame.

Regency-inspired silk
The top cover used for this seat pad is a modern silk fabric, inspired by the pattern and colours of an English Regency stripe.

Choosing a seat fabric

Usage should be a major factor in choosing a chair-seat fabric. For a dining chair that will sustain heavy wear, choose a fairly heavyweight fabric; for an occasional chair that will be used less often, buy a lighter-weight fabric.

To comply with safety regulations, all upholstery fabrics today, whether synthetic, natural, or a mixture of fibres, are treated with a fire-retardant chemical. This treatment makes the fabric stiffer and therefore a little more difficult to work, but the added safety more than compensates for the extra work.

Three main types of fabric design are suitable for period furnishings, and examples are shown below. You can buy screen-printed 'reproduction' patterns copied from the archives held by fabric manufacturers and museums, or more costly authentic versions hand-blocked from the original blocks. Otherwise you can choose modern fabrics inspired by period designs and patterns.

Regency stripe
A modern, heavy-gauge woven cotton inspired by the Regency stripe.

Woven silk
This reproduction of an early 19th-century fabric features a classical lyre and foliage.

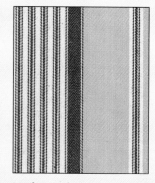

Modern stripe
A lightweight striped cotton fabric loosely inspired by Regency upholstery.

Silk canvas
This silk canvas is based on an upholstery pattern popular in the 19th century.

Cotton damask
A reproduction of a cotton damask with traditional floral motifs.

Woven linen
Two Napoleonic motifs are seen on this reproduction of an early 19th-century fabric.

Reupholstering a button-back chair

The velvet Dralon top cover of this 19th-century, button-back upholstered armchair is deeply ingrained with dust and dirt and is torn in places. The underlying stuffing has become over-compressed and misshapen in places, and the springs in the seat have lost their resilience. In short, it needs reupholstering completely. Reupholstering a sprung, button-back armchair is the most ambitious project in this book. However, by the time you have worked through all the stages, you will have covered most of the techniques required to reupholster most kinds of sprung and stuffed seating. When tackling a project such as this for the first time, you should restrict yourself to a relatively inexpensive chair; a more valuable piece should come later, when you have developed both confidence and ability.

Ripping off and preparing the frame

1 Ripping off the upholstery

- Remove the upholstery back to the frame (see pp.92–3). Take photographs or make sketches of the chair before and during this, and note the height of the seat pad in relation to the sides of the chair and the positions of the buttons.
- Lay aside the old top cover and calico undercover for use as rough templates for the new coverings.
- If the hair stuffing is horsehair or horsehair and hog's hair, you may be able to reuse it (see p.93).
- Test the springs. If the centre of one moves to one side when moderate pressure is applied to the top with the palm, you should replace it. Usually, if one spring needs replacing it is best to replace them all.

2 Sanding down the frame

- If it proves necessary, strengthen the tacking rails using the technique shown on page 93. With medium-grade sandpaper, smooth down any chips or splinters that have been raised by the ripping-off process.
- If there are any mortise-and-tenon joints that need tightening or repairing, now is the time to do this work (see pp.44–5 and pp.58–9).
- This is also the time to repolish and, if necessary, restain any show wood – in this case the mahogany legs of the frame (see pp.28–37).
- It is also advisable to replace any damaged casters (see p.55) at this stage.

YOU WILL NEED:
Face mask, goggles and leather gloves
Ripping chisel and tack-lifter
Carpenter's mallet
Dressmaker's tape measure
White glue (PVA)
Small standard decorator's brush
Sandpaper Medium-grade.
Screwdriver
Webbing One roll plain jute 5cm wide.
Upholsterer's hammer
Upholstery tacks One box each of improved and fine 15mm; one box 12mm fine; one box each of 10mm improved and fine.
Webbing stretcher
Scissors 20–22cm upholsterer's and 2.5–7.5cm needlework.
Craft knife
Springs Nine 8 or 9 gauge.
Tailor's chalk
Spring needle
Upholsterer's twine Nos. 1, 2, 3, and 6.
Laid cord Approx. 6m.
Hessian 2 square metres of 350g fabric and 3 square metres of 285g fabric.
Horsehair and hog's hair 9–10kg.
Regulator 25cm medium-light.
Mattress needle 25cm, double-pointed.
Small curved needles 5cm and 10cm.
Cotton felt wadding Approx. 5 square metres, grey or white.
Calico 5 square metres.
Sheet of paper Larger than chair back.
Wooden ruler and pencil
Material for top cover Red damask: 5m.
Metal upholstery buttons 14 or as needed.
Steel ruler
Back-tacking or cardboard strips
Skin wadding 5 square metres.
Thread One reel of strong cotton or linen 'slipping' thread to match top cover.
Straight sewing needles Regular pack.
Upholsterer's skewers 20, 10cm.
Upholsterer's linen 1.75 square metres.

Webbing and springing the seat

1 Attaching the side-to-side webbing

Note: Aim to leave a gap of approximately 5cm between each length of webbing.

● Turn the chair frame upside down.

● Turn over 2.5cm of the end of a roll of 5cm-wide woven jute webbing. Working front to back, position folded webbing about 5cm away from chair leg and no more than halfway across width of side rail. Secure it using an upholsterer's hammer and five 15mm improved tacks. The tacks should be staggered in a W-formation, with the three tops of the W facing the chair's outer edge and the two bottoms of the W facing inwards (see also 'Upholstering a drop-in seat pad', pp.94–8).

● Using a webbing stretcher, tension the webbing across to the opposite rail (see p.95). Secure with a row of three tacks (these form the tops of the W).

● Remove the webbing stretcher and cut the webbing approximately 5cm beyond the tacks.

● Fold the excess back over and secure with two more tacks (the two bottoms of the W). Then repeat the procedure until you have completed the side-to-side webbing on the underneath of the chair frame.

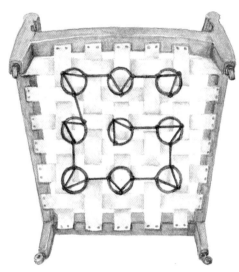

2 Attaching front-to-back webbing

● Use the same techniques as above to secure the front-to-back webbing on the underside of the chair frame. However, as in the picture, each length should be interwoven with the side-to-side webbing. Make the first length 'under, over, under, etc', the second 'over, under, over, etc' and so on, alternating them across the frame. As before, leave approximately 5cm between each length of webbing.

3 Positioning the springs

Note: Both illustrations above show a bottom view of the chair to more clearly represent the knotting pattern. You will work on the chair from the top.

● Turn the chair frame the right way up and place the springs on the webbing. (In seats of this type, the springs' gauge will be 8 or 9 SWG.) There will be three or four across in each row. They will be evenly spaced, but not too close to the back rail or sides (or they will be covered by the stuffing in the back and arms). Refer to the sketch you made of the springs' positions when you ripped off the old upholstery. Mark the springs' positions on the webbing with a piece of tailor's chalk.

● Use a single length of No. 1 upholsterer's twine to tie the springs. Thread a spring needle with the twine. (If you find that you have not threaded enough twine, knot on an extra length.)

● Keep the chair upright. Remove all the springs except for the one at the front right-hand corner. Be sure that the metal 'knot' (not shown) at the spring's top faces the centre of the chair. Starting with a slip-knot (above, right, top), sew the base of the spring to the webbing in three places (above, right, bottom).

● Working right to left, add and secure springs in a 'spiral' as shown (above, left), making sure that all the metal knots face the centre of the seat.

Lashing the springs and covering with hessian

1 Securing the springs front to back

● Hammer a 1.5cm improved tack halfway into the top edge of the back rail and in line with the centre of one of the front-to-back rows of springs.

● Cut a piece of laid cord approximately 30cm longer than the depth of the seat. Using a slip-knot, tie one end of the cord around the shaft of the tack and hammer in the tack. Hammer another tack halfway into the top of the front rail, opposite the tack in the back rail.

● Working back to front, pull the laid cord diagonally from the back tack to the first spring. Compress the spring by about one inch and secure it with a locked loop (see p.249) tied to a second loop from the spring's top.

● Pull the cord diagonally to the third coil down on the opposite side of the spring. Secure it with a half-hitch (see p.249). The spring should remain vertical. If it leans, undo the cord and start again.

● Repeat the procedure through the row: compress the next spring, tie a loop lock on the second coil, then a half-hitch on the opposite side's third coil. Keep the tension even through the row.

● When you reach the front rail, tie the cord around the shaft of the tack and hammer down. Do not cut the cord; there should be at least 20cm hanging.

● Lash the last two front-to-back rows of springs in place. Keep the tension even throughout the rows.

2 Securing the springs side to side

● To secure the springs from side to side, repeat the procedure in step 1, making sure that the springs stay vertical and are lashed securely.

3 Forming the springs into a dome

● To create a gently domed profile across the top of the springs, place each 20cm length of cord over the outer rim of the top coil of the nearest spring. Tie the spring with a double-hitch (see p.249), pulling it outwards in a slight incline as you tighten the knot. Cut off excess twine.

4 Covering springs with hessian

● Drape a piece of 350g hessian over the springs and tacking rails, and cut it 5cm larger all around than the area to be covered.

● After making sure the hessian is centred over the springs, fold back the edges by about 2.5–5cm as shown, and temporary-tack them to the top of all four rails, cutting/mitring the hessian into the corners as you go. (Temporary-tacking is hammering the tacks partway into the wood.) Use 10mm tacks and space them about 4cm apart. Slightly tension the hessian evenly all the way round, keeping the weave square to the seat. During this and the next stage, do not compress the springs any more.

● Having temporary-tacked the hessian, hammer home the tacks along the front rail.

● Move to the back rail, remove the tacks, retension the hessian (adjusting the folded edge if necessary), and then re-tack (working from the centre outwards). Repeat with the side rails, again taking care to keep the weave square.

● Finally, with a spring needle and No. 1 upholsterer's twine, sew the tops of the springs to the hessian, employing the same technique you used earlier to secure the base of the springs to the webbing.

Webbing the arms and back

1 Attaching webbing to the back

- Secure the webbing to the inside back of the chair, using the same tools, materials and techniques as you did for the seat, and follow the webbing pattern shown above. A mistake often made by amateur upholsterers is to attach the webbing to the outside back, rather than the inside back, of the chair. This has two undesirable results. First, attempts to bring the inside back of the seat forward to its correct position by adding extra stuffing invariably fail. Second, over time an unsightly bulge or 'humpback' begins to appear at the back of the finished chair.

2 Attaching hessian to the back

- Cut a panel of 285g hessian about 5cm larger all round than the back of the chair. As with the seat (see p.101, step 4), fold over the edges, slightly tension it and temporary-tack into the centre of the frame, using 15mm improved tacks. Trim the hessian neatly around the points where the tops of the arms and the ends of the stuffing rails meet the inside back of the chair.
- Having temporary-tacked the hessian, repeat the tensioning technique used on the seat, then hammer home the tacks.

3 Attaching webbing to the arms

- Secure a simple cross of two pieces of webbing to the inside of each arm, this time using 10mm improved tacks. Make sure that the vertical length of webbing lies at a right angle to the horizontal length, rather than at a slight diagonal to it.

4 Attaching hessian to the arms

- Secure a shaped panel of 285g hessian over the webbing on the inside of the arms, again using 10mm tacks. As with the back of the chair, fold over the edges of the hessian and temporary-tack it in position all round before fully tensioning it and driving the tacks home.

First-stuffing the arms

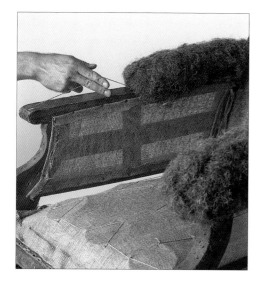

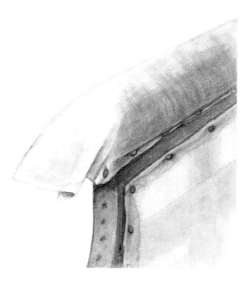

1 Attaching bridle ties

- To secure the stuffing on the tops of the arms you must first attach two simple bridle ties. Hammer three 15mm improved tacks into the top of each arm, leaving about half of the shaft exposed (as if you were temporary-tacking). Two of the tacks should be positioned about 2.5cm in from either end of the arm, and the third should be equidistant between them.
- Loop a length of No. 3 twine between the tacks, secure it around each of them with a simple slip-knot and then hammer home the tacks. The resulting two loops of twine on each arm should be about two fingers high.
- Having teased apart the fibres, insert a large handful of horsehair and hog's hair stuffing under the bridle tie near the back of one of the arms. Keep adding more handfuls, partly under and partly over the ties, teasing and meshing the fibres into the previous handfuls as you work. Move down each arm from back to front until you have constructed an even, slightly rounded roll of stuffing about 15cm high.

2 Attaching the hessian

- Measure from the back, along the top and over the front of the stuffing on the arms. Then measure from side to side.
- Transfer the measurements onto a piece of 285g hessian, add on approximately 2.5cm all round and cut one piece for each arm.
- Position the hessian pieces over the arms, and temporary-tack with two 10mm improved tacks to the front of the arms. Make any necessary cuts to the hessian so that it fits neatly around the backs of the arms, and fold back the excess. Apply an even, tight tension throughout so that the underlying stuffing is compressed to a height of about 7.5cm. Temporary-tack at a slight angle to the inside and outside edges of the tops of the arms. The tacks should be spaced at intervals of about 5cm.
- Adjust the tension of the hessian as necessary, keeping the weave square. Hammer home the tacks (apart from the two applied to the front edge).

3 Tacking down the hessian

- Return to the fronts of the arms and remove the temporary tacks from each.
- Pleat the hessian as above, before tacking to the undersides of the front edges.

4 Using a regulator

- Before proceeding, it is important to make any necessary adjustments to the position of the underlying stuffing. Using a 25cm regulator, probe through the hessian and push and tease the stuffing to remove any lumps and to ensure that the edges of the arms are sufficiently rounded.

Blind-stitching and top-stitching the arms

Blind-stitching pulls the stuffing tight to the arms' inside and outside edges, stopping it from collapsing. Use No. 3 twine and a 25cm double-pointed mattress needle, and follow the instructions carefully. Work all your stitches from left to right, so that the knots lie flat. When working on the right-hand arm (your right as you face the chair) start at the back on the inside, work forward and around the front, then work along the outside to the back. On the left-hand arm, start at the back on the outside, work forward, continue around the front and then work along the inside to the back.

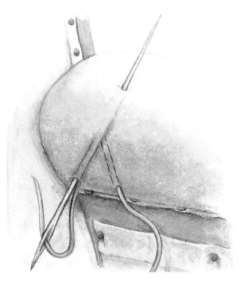

1 Blind-stitching

- Thread the needle with 1m of twine. Insert the non-threaded end of the needle into the hessian and stuffing about 5cm in from the back of the arm, just above the tacks. Push it up at an angle as shown until it emerges just short of the centre of the top of the arm and 2.5cm back from where it entered. Using both hands, ease the needle through until the eye just shows through the hessian's top (but has not emerged with the twine).
- Re-angle the needle and push it back down through the stuffing at about 45 degrees to its path of entry. The threaded end should re-emerge about 5cm back from the point of entry and just above the tacks.

2 Compacting the stuffing

- Pull the twine tight through, to draw down and compact the stuffing, and secure with a slip-knot (see p.249). In effect you will have just formed a triangle, with the two sides invisible inside the stuffing and the base visible and parallel to the tack line and the side of the arm.

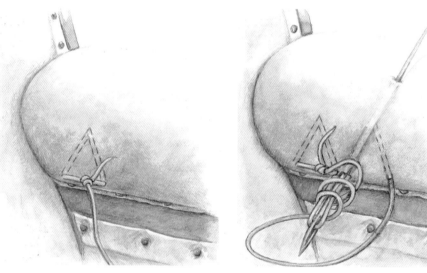

3 Stitching the stuffing

- Reinsert the needle about 5cm to the right of the original point of entry. Push the needle up to form the peak of the triangle; re-angle the needle as in step 1 and push the threaded end out until about 5cm of it has emerged. The exit point should align close to the original entry point in step 1.
- Wrap the standing end of the twine around the needle, anticlockwise, three times.
- Hold the loops close to the stuffing with one thumb. Pull the needle out of the stuffing, drawing it and the running end of the twine through the loops. Stick the needle in the stuffing to your right. (This is done simply to keep it temporarily out of your way.)

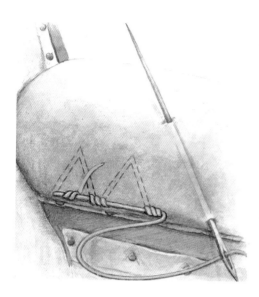

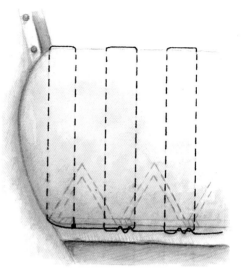

4 Forming a hard edge

● Grasp the twine with your fingers and pull it down through the stuffing to remove any slack. Then tug it firmly to your right (you might want to wear a pair of old leather gloves for this). This latter movement will draw the stuffing into a firm, compact edge and pull the loops in the twine into a neat rolled stitch.

● Work your way around the entire arm, by repeating steps 2, 3 and the above procedure. As you do so, a rolled edge will begin to form. This should be even along its whole length. If any bulges or depressions appear in it, use your regulator to redistribute the stuffing (see p.103).

● When you come to the end of your first length of twine, simply tie on another length with a reef knot. Make sure that the knot falls between two stitches, has no superfluous loop and is as close to the hessian as possible.

● When you come to the last stitch at the back of the arm, instead of working the needle back to your left, turn it the opposite way so that it emerges as close to the end as possible. Then tie off the twine with a double-hitch (see p.249).

5 Top-stitching the arms

● This technique is very similar to blind-stitching. It flattens the top of the stuffing and squares off the sides, to form a solid platform for the secondary stuffing and wadding. In effect three rolls are formed: two smaller outer ones and a larger one in the centre. Again work from left to right, using a 25cm mattress needle and No. 3 twine.

6 Forming a rectangle

● Insert the needle into the bottom of the stuffing about 2.5cm from the back of the arm, and about 6mm above the base of the blind-stitching. Push it up at an angle to emerge about 2.5cm in from the edge of the top of the stuffing. Pull it all the way through. Move the threaded end 2cm back along the top of the arm, and push it down at an angle to emerge 2cm back from the point of entry and 3mm in front of the back of the arm.

● As you did with the blind-stitching, tie off with a slip-knot (see p.249). You will have formed an elongated rectangle, with the two long sides invisible in the stuffing and the two short sides visible at the top and bottom of the stuffing.

● Re-insert the needle 5cm to the right of the first point of entry and push through to the top of the stuffing. Move the threaded end back 12mm along the top, and reinsert to emerge 12mm back from the second entry point. As you did with the blind-stitching, loop the twine three times anticlockwise around the needle's threaded end. Pull the rest of the needle out of the stuffing and down through the loops, then insert it firmly into the stuffing to your right. Seize the twine with your fingers and pull it down to take up any slack. Then tug it to your right to pull the loops into a neat rolled stitch.

● As before, repeat all the way around the arm, adjusting the stuffing with the regulator as you go.

Second-stuffing, wadding and calico

1 Attaching bridle ties

• Make simple two-loop bridle ties along the centre of the arms of the chair, as you did earlier for the first stuffing (see p.103). However, this time you should use a 10cm semicircular needle with the No. 3 twine (see step 1 of 'Stuffing the seat' on the opposite page). Again you should be able to get two fingers under the centre of each loop.

• When you have the secured bridle ties in position, build up a thin, even layer of horsehair and hog's hair stuffing to a height of no more than 2.5cm along the tops of the arms.

2 Adding wadding

• Place a thin layer of cotton felt wadding on top of the stuffing. Tear the wadding to size with your hands – do not use scissors as they will leave too sharp an edge and you will end up with a ridge showing under the top cover. Tear the wadding so that it hangs level with the bottom edges of the outer rolls on top of the arm.

Note: If you intend to apply a light, pale-coloured top cover, you are advised to use white wadding. The grey wadding used here can 'ghost' through the calico undercover and a pale top cover.

3 Covering the tops of the arms

• Using upholsterer's scissors, cut two pieces of medium-heavy calico to roughly cover the tops of the arms. The ends of each piece should overhang the front of the arms by approximately 2.5cm and be about 5cm longer at the backs. The sides of the pieces should be cut long enough so that they can be tacked near the top of the sides of the arms.

• Position one piece of calico on each chair arm. It should overhang the front and back as described above and be centred side-to-side. Mitre the back of the fabric so that it hangs over the sides of the vertical rail at the chair's back (see illustration below left).

• Using 10mm fine tacks, temporary-tack the calico, at intervals of approximately 2.5cm, near the top of the side of the arm (use this spacing for all tacking). Tension it fully and evenly, then tack it in place.

• Pleat, trim and tack over the front of the arms as you did with the hessian. At the back of the arms, ease the excess hessian down behind the stuffing and pull it through to the vertical rail of the chair back.

• Secure the calico by driving in the tacks fully.

4 Trimming off excess calico

• Having pulled the calico back and down from the arm, trim any excess folds and tack it to the sides and back of the vertical back rail.

Stuffing the seat

1 Attaching bridle ties

● Before beginning the stuffing, stitch a series of bridle ties to the top of the hessian, as described under 'First-stuffing the arms' (see p.103, step 1). Tease apart the fibres of a large quantity of horsehair and hog's hair stuffing, and insert handfuls of it under and over the bridle ties.

2 Inserting the stuffing

● Build up the stuffing in stages, teasing and meshing together the fibres. Create a slightly domed centre reaching just below the height of the arms. Produce a gradual drop-off of about 7.5cm to the front, back, and sides. Ensure that along the front edge the stuffing forms a gently curving roll that juts out about 7.5cm at the centre of the curve and about 2.5cm just above the front rail. It should also come over the curved rails between the tops of the arms and the felt, and follow their curved profile.

● Redistribute the stuffing thoroughly to remove any lumps – this may take up to 20 minutes – otherwise you will feel these through the top cover later on.

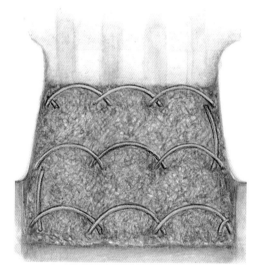

3 Attaching looped ties

● Thread a 10cm semicircular needle with a length of No. 3 twine. Make a slip-knot (see p.249) near one of the back corners of the seat. Sew three or four rows of looped ties, as shown in the illustration, finishing off with a double-hitch (see p.249).

● If you are using looser coco or palm fibre rather than horsehair and hog's-hair stuffing, you will need to insert a few extra rows of ties.

4 Attaching the hessian

● Measure the seat from front to back and side to side, taking the dressmaker's tape down to the tacking rails.

● Cut a panel of 285g hessian, allowing 5cm extra all round. Centre the hessian on the seat and mitre-cut the back corners to fit round the vertical rails of the chair back. Temporary-tack along the tops of the side rails first, then the front rail and finally the back rail, using 10mm fine tacks in each case.

● Starting with one side, remove the temporary tacking, tension the hessian and tack it in place, using five tacks in a W-formation (see p.100, step 1) and folding over the edge of the fabric by about 2.5cm.

Repeat the procedure on the other side, then the front, making sure that you keep the weave of the hessian square to the seat.

● Finish by tacking the hessian in place along the back rail, trimming and pleating the corners around the vertical rails the same way you did with the calico on the tops of the arms.

● When you have finished, use the regulator (see p.103) to redistribute the stuffing where necessary.

Blind-stitching and top-stitching the seat

1 Creating a fabric roll
● To prevent the front edge of the seat sagging during use you must create a firm roll along the top edge. Begin by blind-stitching the stuffed edge, using the same tools, materials and techniques as you did when blind-stitching the tops of the arms (see p.104). However, there are four important changes. First, use No. 2 twine. Second, the mattress needle should emerge from the top of the seat about 12.5cm back from the front edge. Third, when you pull the needle down it should emerge about 2.5cm left of the original point of entry (if you are working left to right). Fourth, make not one but three or four parallel rows of stitching. The bottom row should run as close to the bottom of the hessian on the front edge as possible. Each subsequent row should be 12mm further up the front edge. (The more rows, the higher the seat's front.) When you finish each row, use the regulator to make any necessary adjustments to the stuffing.

2 Top-stitching the fabric roll
● To further firm up the roll along the front edge, top-stitch it the same way you did the arms (see p.105). The needle should enter the front edge about 6cm below the top and emerge at the top roughly the same distance back. The distance between stitches should be about 2.5cm.

Second-stuffing, wadding and calico

1 Using through ties
● To anchor the stuffing and hessian to the base of the seat and prevent wrinkles in the top cover, sew a series of through ties. Using tailor's chalk, draw a rectangle on the seat top about 10cm in from the sides, front and back. Then turn the chair on its back, to reveal the webbing underneath.
● Thread a 25cm mattress needle with 1.5m of No. 1 twine. Starting at any corner of the rectangle, push the needle down through the top hessian, fibre and base hessian. Pull it through so that 15cm of

twine is left above the seat top. Do not snag the twine on the springs. Move 6mm along the rectangle and push the needle back up to emerge by the entry point. Secure with a slip-knot (see p.249) and tighten.
● Move 7.5–10cm along the rectangle and push the needle down again. When it has fully emerged, reinsert it about 6mm back from the point of exit. Push the needle through to the top, pull the twine tight, move 7.5–10cm along the line, reinsert the needle and continue like this around the perimeter.

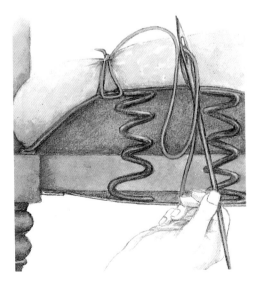

2 Finishing the through ties

- When you have tied the whole perimeter of the chalk rectangle, if the seat is of small to medium size add a further single through tie in the centre. However, if the seat is particularly large, add a separate small rectangle of ties in the centre.

3 Adding second stuffing

- Sew bridle ties to the top of the hessian, using the same method and materials as before (see p.106).
- Build up a second layer of horsehair and hog's-hair stuffing. Slightly dome the stuffing to a height of approximately 7.5cm above the centre of the seat. Make the front edge of the stuffing level with the front edge of the top-stitched roll.

4 Adding felt wadding

- Having torn it to size with your hands rather than cutting it with scissors, lay a blanket of cotton felt wadding over the seat. Make sure that it extends just over the roll at the front and tuck at least 2.5cm of it under the rails at the sides and back. If you tuck in less than this amount, small depressions may occur in the seat, particularly at the sides, when the chair has been in use for some time.

5 Cutting calico for the seat

- Measure the seat lengthwise, from the bottom of the front rail to the bottom of the back rail. Then measure across the seat from the top of one side rail to the top of the other.
- Cut a panel of medium-heavy calico, adding about 2.5cm all around. Lay the calico over the seat and, using the same method and the same sequence as for the hessian (see p.107), temporary-tack all the way around with 10mm improved or fine tacks. Tension the calico fairly tightly to compress the stuffing, and tack fully down. Cut off any excess calico.

Note: At the front of the seat, tack along the facing edge of the rail as near to the top as possible. At the sides and back of the seat, tack along the tops of the rails (as you did with the hessian). At the back of the side rails, mitre-cut the calico (again as you did with the hessian) and trim any excess material before inserting tacks. At the sides of the front of the seat, trim the calico so that you can pull it tightly and evenly down between the hessian and the curved rails that run between the bottom of the arms and the tops of the legs.

Stuffing the back

1 Building up the stuffing

● Secure bridle ties into the hessian over the inside back of the chair. Use the same materials and method as you used for attaching ties to the seat (see pp.103 and 107).

● Gradually build up the horsehair and hog's-hair stuffing to a height of about 15cm; in the area that aligns with the small of the back, gradually dome the stuffing up to about 25cm.

2 Attaching hessian to the back

● Measure the inside back of the chair. Add 12.5cm at each side to allow for tensioning and tacking. Add enough to the height so that the hessian can be inserted between the seat and the back and will pass under the upper bottom rail and then wrap over its top. (Here there are two bottom rails; some chairs have only one.) Cut a panel of 285g hessian to these dimensions.

● Using the tips of upholsterer's scissors, make mitred cuts in the hessian where the ends of the arms join the vertical back rails.

● Position the hessian over the stuffing. Temporary-tack it to the frame using 10mm fine tacks. Tack as near as possible to the top edge of the forward-facing side of the top rail; cut and pleat at the corners. Tack as near as possible to the front of the outside of the side rails. Pass the hessian between the seat and back, then under and around the bottom rail, and tack along the top of the bottom rail.

● After temporary-tacking, fully tension the hessian – from side to side first, then from top to bottom – and tack it fully home. Make sure that you keep the lengthways weave of the hessian square to the vertical.

● Once you are satisfied with the tension of the hessian and have tacked it in position all round, step back and assess the appearance of the chair. You may find that there are some small bumps and indents showing up across the surface. It is essential to get rid of these at this stage, or they will spoil both the appearance and the comfort of the chair. To remove them, pierce the hessian with a regulator (see p.103), then redistribute and even out the underlying stuffing.

Blind-stitching and top-stitching the back

1 Blind-stitching the back

● Insert three rows of blind-stitching around the back's top and sides. Use No. 3 twine and the method used for the seat front (see p.108). Put the first row very close to the edge, the second 2.5cm up, and the third a further 2.5cm up. Work from left to right. Regulate the stuffing as you go and after each row.

2 Top-stitching the back

● Add one row of top-stitching to form a tight roll around the top and sides. As before, use No. 3 twine and the same method employed on the arms and the front of the seat.

Second-stuffing, wadding and calico

1 Adding more stuffing

• Apply more bridle ties to the back (see p.103) and build up a second layer of horsehair and hog's-hair stuffing. This should be about 3–5cm deep around the top and sides, and gradually dome up to about 7.5cm over the area that aligns with the small of the back.

2 Adding cotton felt wadding

• Measure the height and width of the chair's back, including the thickness of the sides and top. Tear a panel of cotton felt wadding slightly larger than these dimensions. Lay it over the back to fully cover the top and sides. Tear off excess.

3 Cutting calico for the back

• Measure the length of the back of the chair from the rear edge of the top rail down and around to the rear side of the upper bottom rail. Measure the width from the back edge of the outer side of one of the vertical rails to the same point on the vertical rail on the opposite side.

• Cut a panel of medium-heavy calico to size, adding about 12.5cm all round. Place this in position on the back of the chair, and temporary-tack it with 10mm improved tacks. Tension the calico as before, tacking it down from side to side and then from top to bottom, and cut off the excess fabric.

Note: At the corners of the top rail, cut and pleat the calico, as you did with the hessian. Tack along the back edges of the top, side and upper bottom rails. The exception is where the calico is cut and pulled under the tops, and behind the sides, of the arms; in this case, tack it to the front of the vertical back rails.

Preparing the back for buttoning

To mark the positions for deep-buttoning you will need a ruler, a dressmaker's tape, a pencil, tailor's chalk, about 20 upholstery tacks, and a sheet of paper larger than the chair back. Here two horizontal lines of four buttons alternate with two horizontal lines of three buttons. On a larger chair you might see more lines and more buttons. If your chair is smaller, expect to reduce the spacing between buttons. Use this method for chairs with square or rectangular backs. **Note:** Accurate drafting of the buttoning pattern is critical to this project's success. Practise working out the buttons' positions on paper before marking the chair. Any error in cutting the buttonholes will mean stripping the chair's back and starting over.

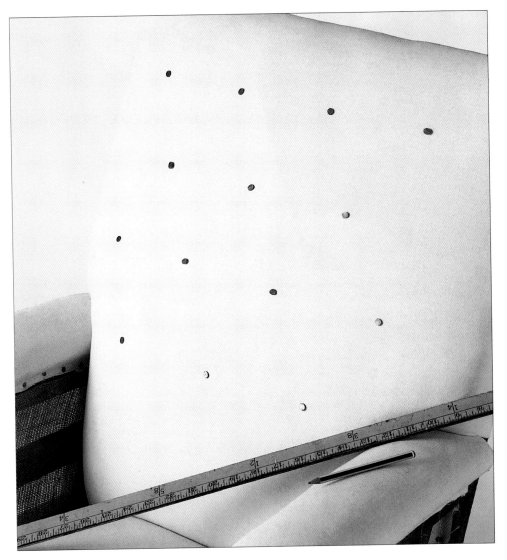

1 Calculating the number of buttons

- Measure the inside back of the chair, noting the height of the tops of the arms, and draw an outline of the back on the paper. With the ruler and pencil, draw line D, which corresponds to the height of the centre of the tops of the arms.
- Draw line A, 10cm below the top of the back. (For chairs with a curved profile, see opposite page.) Measure 10cm in from each side of the chair and mark each point with a dot on the line. Divide the segment between the dots into thirds, marking the divisions with additional dots. (The resulting spaces on this chair each measured 12.5cm.)
- Measure the space between line A and line D (in this case 34cm). Divide it into thirds and draw lines B and C at these divisions. You now have four lines evenly spaced from top to bottom on the paper.
- Mark line C with four dots as you did for line A.
- Lay the ruler across the paper to intersect A1 and C3. Join the dots with a pencil line, and where this passes through lines B and D, mark two more dots (B2 and D4). Repeat this process until you have joined diagonally all the dots on lines A and C and marked all the points where the lines intersect lines B and D.
- Complete the grid by drawing opposing diagonal lines. Begin by connecting A7 and C5.

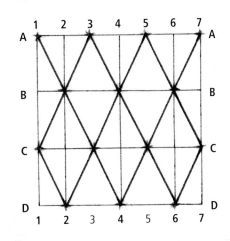

2 Marking the buttons' positions

- The diagonal lines you have drawn form a diamond-shaped grid. Each point of each diamond represents the position of a button. Note that, on this chair, each side of each diamond is 12.5cm long and that each diamond measures 23cm from top to bottom. Having worked out the pattern of the buttons on paper, replicate the grid on the chair back itself using a dressmaker's tape, a ruler and tailor's chalk. Mark the lines faintly, then mark the buttons' positions by pushing tacks into the calico.

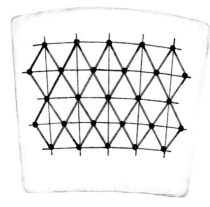

Flared buttoning

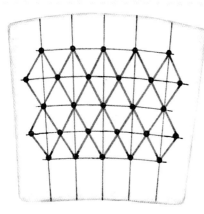

Flared buttoning with pleats

Other buttoning patterns

The deep-buttoning pattern described in the project is best suited to chairs with square or rectangular backs. For backs that are wider at the top, you need a buttoning pattern that better accommodates the shape of the chair. Two common patterns – flared and vertical – are shown here, each with a pleated variation. (Pleating accentuates the basic shape of the pattern.)

Note: These buttoning patterns are more challenging to draft than the one described for the project. You should always perfect these patterns on paper before marking and cutting the chair.

Flared patterns

In the two examples of the flared pattern (left), the top and bottom rows have the same number of buttons. The vertical lines form a slight fan.

Vertical patterns

The vertical patterns (right) have buttons set in strict parallel lines. The width at the top is accommodated by adding a button to each end of the row.

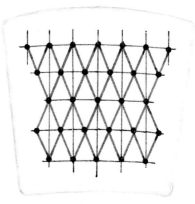

Vertical buttoning

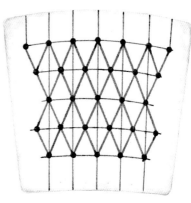

Vertical buttoning with pleats

3 Preparing the button holes

● Using the tips of a pair of upholsterer's scissors, make 2.5cm crossed cuts in the calico. The centre of each cross should be exactly over the mark for each button.

● Gently push a finger and the flat end of a regulator into the holes, moving aside the wadding and the stuffing. Insert the tips of the scissors to make another cross cut through the top layer of hessian. Carefully continue until you reach the layer of hessian over the webbing. Under no circumstances must you pierce this layer of hessian. If you do, you will be unable to secure the buttons properly later on.

Top-covering the seat and tops and insides of the arms

Most people new to upholstery feel quite intimidated when it comes to cutting out and putting on the top cover. But the only difference between attaching the top cover and the calico undercover is that you have to line up any prominent pattern with the centre of a panel. With asymmetrical or irregular patterns, such as florals, it is helpful to mark a central motif by tacking lines side-to-side and top-to-bottom.

1 Cutting the seat's top cover

● Measure the seat from front to back and side to side. Add 7.5cm all round and transfer these measurements to the top cover fabric. Cut the top cover. Place the fabric over the seat and check the pattern's alignment. As you did with the calico (see p.106), mitre-cut the back corners to fit either side of the vertical rear rails. Cut and pleat the front corners as you did with the calico at the top of the back.

● Using 10mm improved tacks, temporary-tack the fabric at intervals of about 2.5cm along the tops of the side rails, on the top of the bottom back rail and on the underside of the front rail.

● Tension fully, from side to side first, then from front to back, and tack home. Keep the pattern centred and the weave square to the seat. When you have finished, trim any excess fabric.

2 Cutting the tops of the arms

● Measure and cut the fabric for the tops of the arms, allowing extra for pleating and tacking. Cut, pleat and tack as you did with the calico (see p.106). The 10mm improved or fine tacks should be spaced at intervals of about 2.5cm. First tack along the sides of the inside of the arms. Tack along the bottom of the outside of the arms.

● At the back end of the arms, pull the fabric down, through and around to the back of the vertical back rails. Partly secure it with one tack on the outside of these, and then fully secure it with tacks along the back of them. At the fronts of the arms, pleat and tack as far back on the underside of the rail as possible.

3 Stuffing inside the arms

● Before starting to introduce the wadding, insert two equally spaced parallel bridle ties from front to back on the inside of the arms.

● Gradually introduce a layer of wadding beneath the bridle ties. The wadding should run level with the bottom of the tops of the arms, feed under the upper tacking rails at the sides and turn over the front of the curved vertical rail between the bottom of the fronts of the arms and the tops of the front legs.

● Apply a second layer of wadding, but do not carry it over the curved front rail. If you do, later on it will cause the top cover to bulk up too much and give it an 'overstuffed' appearance.

Back-tacking

Inserting a flexible stiffener under the top cover along the top of the inside of the chair's arm creates a straight edge and covers all the tacks. Use buckram back-tacking strips or strips of cardboard 1.5cm wide and as long as the arm of the chair. (Upholstery suppliers sell buckram back-tacking strip in various widths.)

● Lay the chair on its side. Lay the fabric face down outside it and pull the leading edge over the side of the top of the arm until it lines up with the inside bottom edge of the arm rail.

● Cut a piece of buckram back-tacking strip or cardboard to the length of the chair's arm. Position it on top of the face-down fabric and along the bottom edge of the tops of the arms. Tack through the strip and fabric at intervals of 2.5cm.

● Stand the chair back on its feet, then fold over the rest of the fabric to the inside of the chair and pull it through the gap between the seat and the inside of the arm.

4 Covering the inside arms

● Measure and cut panels for the inside of the arms, allowing extra for folding and tacking. Temporary-tack with 10mm fine or improved tacks, then fully tension and tack as follows.

● Back-tack along the bottom edge of the tops of the arms as described above.

● Tack the bottom edge of the fabric along the edge of the lower side rails.

● At the back, pull the fabric through the calicoed chair back and the small vertical rail that runs between the arm and the upper bottom rail. Cut, pleat and tack the fabric to the rear of the vertical back rail.

● At the front of the panel cut the fabric into a series of strips that terminate close to the outer edge of the curved rail. Make a series of mini-pleats, cutting excess fabric and tacking on the outside of the rail as you go. You may need to remove small amounts of wadding on the outside edges to give a clean profile. Cut and tack the fabric as close to the edge of the wood as possible: if you pull it too far it will pucker. In the front, where the side fabric meets the seat's leading edge, fold back the seat fabric. Push in the side fabric and tack it on the inside of the rails, then turn back the folded front edge.

Measuring and marking the top cover for buttoning

You cannot simply transfer your button pattern from the calico to the top cover, although you will use the same process (see p.112) to draft the new grid. As the top cover is partly drawn into the button holes and pleated around them, the size of the diamonds on the buttoning grid must be proportionately larger. Establish the measurements as described below.

Note: Covering buttons by hand can be laborious, so professional upholsterers use a machine. Save time and money by having buttons covered by an upholsterer or a department store with a buttoning service.

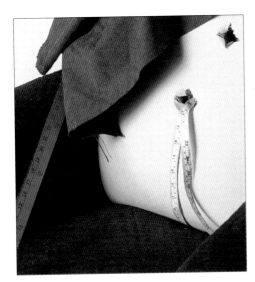

1 Finding the total measurement

● Working front to back, push a dressmaker's tape between the seat and the back of the chair. Pull the tape through until the end is 5cm below the centre of the bottom-most rear rail. Hold the tape on the front of the chair and push its running end 5cm into the hole cut at D4. Leave the tape in position and note the total measurement. This is measurement A.

● Extend the tape's running end up the back, push it 5cm into the hole at B4, then run it up and over the top of the back to a point 5cm below the bottom of the top rail. Note the total measurement. This is measurement B.

2 Marking the buttons' positions

● Use the fabric's full width for the chair back's width. Cut the length to equal measurement B. Fold selvedge to selvedge and mark the centre line on the wrong side with tailor's chalk.

● Working on the wrong side of the fabric, measure up the centre line from the cut edge for a distance equal to measurement A. Mark a dot at that point with tailor's chalk. This dot corresponds to D4 on the calico.

● Mark the positions that correspond to D2 and D6. On the calico they are 12.5cm apart, but on the top cover it is 12.5cm plus 6mm for every 2.5cm (i.e. 16cm), to allow for buttoning and pleating.

● Establish the position of B4. On the calico it was 23cm above D4. On the top cover the gap is 23cm plus 6mm for every 2.5cm: i.e. 28.5cm. Mark B2 and B6 with same spacing (16cm) as on line D.

● To mark the position of lines A and C, line up the ruler diagonally across the button marks already established on lines B and D. Draw right-to-left and left-to-right diagonals, extending the lines to form the outermost corners on lines A and C. Mark the position of the buttons on the back with tailor's chalk.

● The diamond grid on the top cover will mirror the grid on the calico back, but with diamonds large enough to accommodate buttoning and pleating.

Fitting the inside back top cover

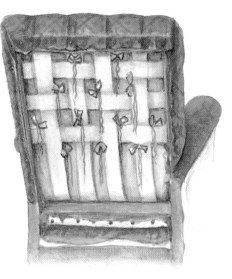

1 Attaching the buttons

● Place the top cover over the chair's back. Fold it back to look at the grid on the reverse side and line up the button marks with the cross-cuts in the calico. Start in the centre, locating C3 and C5, D4 and B4. The holes form a diamond pattern.

● Using your finger, push the fabric about 4cm into the holes and start to form the pleats.

Note: So that they do not become dust traps, pleats should always turn either sideways or downwards.

● Having had the metal upholstery buttons covered with the top-cover fabric (see opposite), thread a length of No. 6 upholsterer's twine through the loop at the back of the button.

● Thread the ends of the upholsterer's twine through the eye of a 25cm mattress needle. Push the needle through the centre hole on line D and straight back until it emerges through the hessian on the outside back of the chair. Make a slip-knot (see p.249) in the ends of the twine.

2 Securing the buttons

● Cut a piece of webbing 5 x 5cm and roll it into a toggle. Insert this through the centre of the slip-knot and pull fairly tight to draw the button firmly into its recess in the chair back. Repeat with the other three buttons of the first diamond. You will tighten the buttons fully later.

3 Pleating the back

● Repeat steps 1 and 2 for the rest of the back. Work out and up, roughly pleating. Use the regulator's blunt end to neaten the pleats before and after the first tightening of the buttons.

4 Attaching the back cover

● Using 10mm improved tacks, fasten the top cover to the back of the frame, cutting and pleating where necessary around the top, the arms and the bottom of the seat, as you did with the calico. Note, however, that the vertical pleats at the top of the back extend from the top line of buttons and continue right over to the back of the frame, where the fabric is tacked down.

● The same applies to the bottom and sides. At the bottom, the three vertical pleats continue down the back of the seat, and the fabric is tacked to the top of the bottom-most back rail (not the rail above it). At the sides, the pleats are taken around to the back of the rails and tacked down.

● When you have tensioned and secured the inside back cover, pull hard on the slip-knots on the toggles to fully tighten the fabric and buttons. Tie off the slip-knots. This will ensure that each button is firmly embedded in its hole. You must pull each button back to the same depth in its respective hole.

Padding and covering the outer arms and back

The main purpose of the wadding is to provide a cushion over the wooden rails and upholstery tacks. If it was not there, these would slightly protrude through the top cover. Tearing wadding by hand avoids the straight edge that cutting with scissors produces – such an edge often shows up through the top cover.

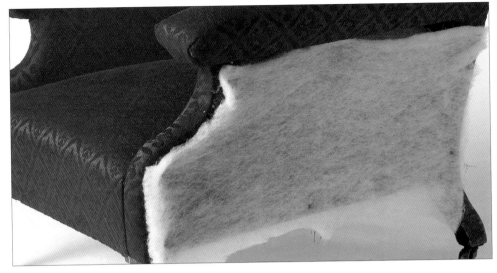

1 Adding skin wadding to the arms

● Using your hands rather than scissors, tear a piece of skin wadding to the shape of the outside of the arms and lay it in position.

2 Attaching the side panels

● Cut two pieces of top-cover fabric to the shape of the side panels, allowing 5cm extra all round. Back-tack (see p.115), using 10mm tacks, below the tops of the arms. Tack the back of the panel to the rear of the vertical rail of the chair back. Fold under the fabric and skewer it in place along the curved leading edges of the arms. Tension the fabric's bottom edge and tack it to the underside of the side rails.

● Using a 5cm semicircular needle and cotton or linen slipping thread, sew together the adjacent pieces of fabric along the curved front edges of the arms. Use a very tight slip stitch (see p.248).

3 Adding skin wadding to the back

● Using upholsterer's scissors, cut a panel of skin wadding to a size very slightly *smaller* than the overall dimensions of the outside of the back of the chair.

● Secure the skin wadding in place on the chair's back with 10mm improved tacks, spacing them at intervals of about 5cm around the perimeter of the back.

4 Attaching the back panel

● Measure and cut a panel of top-cover fabric for the back, allowing 5cm extra all round. Try to match the pattern on the back to that on the sides of the back.

● Turn the chair on its front and back-tack the fabric neatly along the top edge with 10mm improved tacks.

● Position the panel, cutting and pleating the corner as needed. Tension and temporarily fix with skewers.

● Adjust the side-to-side tension by moving the skewers. Keep the pattern and weave square.

● Tension the bottom of the fabric and tack it under the bottom rail. Tightly slip-stitch the sides to the adjacent fabric on the back, removing the skewers as you go.

Fitting the dust cover and finishing off

1 Attaching upholsterer's linen

• Turn the chair upside down. Measure the base and cut a panel of upholsterer's black linen to serve as a dust cover. (Fabric used for this purpose is also called 'bottoming'.) Allow about 5cm extra all round.

• Turn the edges under, cutting and folding them around the base of the legs.

• Secure the edges all round with 10mm improved tacks spaced at intervals of approximately 5cm.

2 Adjusting joins and seams

• Using a small, curved sewing needle, slip stitch the folded edges at the front of the seat to the fabric on the adjacent section of the curved arm fronts.

• Spend ten minutes looking at all the joins and seams on the chair. If any of them need closing up or re-tightening, make the necessary adjustments with some tight slip stitching. Use a 5cm curved needle or a small straight needle, depending on which is more convenient.

Right: Protecting the chair
When the chair's restoration is complete, it is wise to spray the new upholstery with a commercial stain guard. This will make it easier to clean the fabric if it becomes soiled.

Leatherwork

Introduction

People have used animal skin for some 75,000 years. Originally adapted for clothing, it has subsequently served a wide variety of purposes in the form of leather. In the field of antiques and collectibles, leather goods include bottles, drinking vessels, armour, gloves, bags and cases, bookbindings, chest covers, wall hangings, fire-screens and room dividers, tabletops and desktops, and upholstery.

Types of skin

Almost any type of skin can be tanned to produce leather, but those most often found in antiques are calfskin, cow hide, goatskin, sheepskin and various exotics, including shark skin, snake, lizard or alligator and chamois.

Calfskin, a smooth fine-grained leather produced in natural or coloured finishes and various thicknesses, is primarily used in bookbinding. Cow hide is smooth-grained, has a natural or coloured finish, and is generally thicker than calfskin. Although used in upholstery, it is best suited to tooling and carving.

Leathers made from goatskins include Morocco, a fine-quality leather tanned with sumac and dyed on the grain side. It is mainly found in bookbindings, desktops and tabletops (since the 18th century), and small accessories such as purses. Levant, a Morocco with bold, irregular-shaped graining, is often turned into high-quality book covers, while Roan, an imitation Morocco made from sheepskin, is employed for books and upholstery. Skiver, a thin leather made from the grain side of sheepskin, comes in many colours and is mostly seen in desktops and tabletops.

Shagreen, made from shark or ray skin and often dyed green, is one of the most exotic leathers. It has covered all manner of items, but particularly jewellery boxes, telescope barrels, tea caddies, musical instruments and cutlery boxes. (Imitation shagreen is sometimes made from horse-skin, embossed with small seeds while still wet to simulate the characteristic graining of shark skin.)

Chamois, originally made from the skin of an Alpine and Pyrenean antelope but now more often made from sheep, goat or deer skin, is used in upholstery.

Extravagantly grained and textured reptile skins, notably from snakes, lizards and alligators, have been widely used in accessories such as luxury shoes and purses.

Tanning

One of the earliest tanning techniques was to dry skins in the sun and then rub them with animal fat to make them supple. Stiffer, or 'tawed', leathers were produced by the Ancient Egyptians, who rubbed salt or alum into hides. However, until the second half of the 19th century the preferred tanning method was to place alternate layers of skin and pieces of plant or tree into a pit, cover them with water,

Above: A pleasing patina

An eclectic collection of 19th- and early 20th-century leather goods, including items of luggage, sporting goods and an upholstered armchair. The attractive patination on most of the pieces is a result of regular feeding and polishing of the leather.

and then leave them for several months. The tannic acids produced by the plants combined with proteins in the hides and protected them from decay. Materials favoured by tanners include bark from oak, black alder, Douglas fir and hemlock spruce, as well as dwarf sumac leaves, Iceland moss and tanner's dock root.

From about 1860 tanning by chemical means provided an alternative (and less malodorous) option. The use of chromium salts produced resilient leather with a good resistance to heat and water and the whole process took only about half a day.

Dyeing and lubricating

After tanning, the skins or hides can be either shaved or split to make thinner grades of leather. The splits are smooth and show no grain, while the outer skin retains the graining. At this stage the leather can, if required, be dyed in a variety of colours. Traditionally, vegetable dyes were used, but since the late 19th century synthetic aniline dyes have virtually replaced these.

Before the leather is lacquered, glazed, polished and, if desired, tooled and embossed, it must be lubricated to stop it drying out. A wide range of lubricants have been used for this, including animal and vegetable fats; fish, vegetable and mineral oils; kerosene wax; and soap (all often with the addition of either sulphur, colloidal graphite or mineral salts). In Renaissance Italy the search for ever-softer and suppler leather even led some shoemakers to immerse it in poultry droppings or warm dog dung.

Care and repair

Most of the problems associated with antique leather result from poor maintenance. The various lubricants mentioned above soon evaporate if the leather is not regularly 'fed' and 'dressed', and the leather dries, cracks and eventually disintegrates. While the restoration of high-quality leather should be entrusted to a professional, a good deal of remedial work and general maintenance (see pp.126–7) can be done by the amateur.

Right: Original calf-leather boards
This first edition of Poems, by John Keats (published by C. & J. Ollier in 1817), retains its original calf-bound boards. Rebinding, even if it was carried out by a professional restorer, would approximately halve the value of this volume.

Tools and materials

A professional leather restorer employs a variety of special tools which can be very pricey. For example, incised metal wheels for tooling or embossing decorative motifs on hides and skivers laid on desktops and tabletops can cost hundreds of pounds each. Some professionals have well over a hundred of these tools in their workshops: a daunting expenditure for the amateur restorer. Therefore, if you intend to replace a hide or skiver, buy it cut to size, and pre-tooled or embossed, from a specialist supplier. The tools and materials described here are not expensive and form a basic kit that will suffice for all amateur maintenance and repair tasks.

Tools

1 Brass-wire suede brush To clean and finish suede leather.
2 Old toothbrush To apply cleaning, reviving and polishing fluids, pastes and creams.
3 Shoe-cleaning brushes For polishing and buffing leather.
4 Straight edge A steel metrestick for measuring and as a guide in cutting new pieces of leather.
5 Paring knife To skive, or pare, leather patches.
6 Utility or craft knife A heavy-duty version with a safety handle to cut leather.
7 Spokeshave Can be used instead of a paring knife to skive leather patches.
8 Scissors Large, heavy-duty scissors to cut leather and a smaller, lighter pair to cut threads.
9 Hammer A small-headed upholsterer's hammer to flatten new stitching and compress glued repairs.
10 Glover's needles Sizes 00–6 to stitch repairs.
11 Curved upholsterer's needles Sizes 2.5–10cm to stitch repairs to areas that cannot be reached with straight needles.
12 Brushes A small standard paint brush and a small artist's brush to apply dyes and stains when recolouring leather.

YOU MAY ALSO NEED:
Upholsterer's skewers To temporarily hold seams in position before stitching.
A flat chisel To remove old hides and skivers from desktops and tabletops.
Fine-grade sandpaper To smooth rough patches of leather before refinishing.
A sponge To apply wet saddle soap.
Glass jars To mix cleaning fluids.

Materials

13 Strong threads Available in various colours and thicknesses for stitching repairs (pre-waxed varieties are available).
14 Beeswax To wax threads before stitching.
15 Adhesives To bond repairs and new patches: either white glue (PVA) or an acrylic leather adhesive (the latter has greater flexibility and is better with thinner leathers).
16 Aniline dyes Powder pigments which, when mixed with methylated spirits, can recolour leather.
17 Saddle soap To clean, soften and protect leather.
18 White spirit To remove grease and various types of stain.
19 Methylated spirits To remove various types of stain.
20 Lighter fuel To remove grease and various types of stain.
21 Fuller's earth A grey-white powder that absorbs grease and fats.
22 Hide food A cream that cleans leather as well as restoring its natural oils (and therefore its suppleness).
23 Leather reviver A dressing, containing a fungicide and an insecticide, that restores dried-out leather.
24 Microcrystalline wax A specialist wax that enhances colour and polishes and protects leather.
25 Shoe polishes Creams and waxes for consolidating and adjusting the colour of leather and for polishing.
26 Lint-free cotton rag To apply cleaning fluids and creams and for polishing.
27 Cotton buds To clean small, recessed areas.

YOU MAY ALSO NEED:
Cotton wool For cleaning.
Wallpaper paste (with fungicide) To stick down new hides and skivers on desktops and tabletops.

Polyacrylate resin A clear resin which is available from some artist's suppliers and leather restorers, and which consolidates dried-out and fraying leather.
Distilled water To reduce wet ink stains and sluice off some cleaning agents.
Trichloroethane 1.1.1. A solvent, available from some chemists and from industrial suppliers, which removes various types of stain.
Dichlorobenzene crystals To fumigate small leather objects infested with moth grubs and other parasites.
Thymol Derived from oil of thyme; when mixed in solution with alcohol, it acts as a mild fungicide and insect repellent.
Eucalyptus oil To remove various stains and marks of indeterminate origin.

General care and cleaning

Leather that is well maintained will develop a pleasingly rich patina over time. The patination of leather may include various stains, scuffs and abrasions from heavy use. Sustained exposure to sunlight may have lightened the item's original colour; while certain chemicals and cleaning agents may have darkened it. As with antique upholstery and woodwork, you should think seriously before undertaking a major restoration of an item that is entirely made of, or contains, leather. These marks and stains will have become an integral part of the patina and over-zealous cleaning will not only destroy the aesthetic appeal that time has lent the piece but also almost certainly reduce its value.

Avoiding the effects of humidity

Leather is a relatively tough material that stands up well to everyday wear and tear. Nevertheless, it is vulnerable to adverse atmospheric conditions. For example, the combination of humid air or damp surroundings with inadequate ventilation encourages the growth of unsightly mould, while excessively dry, hot air causes evaporation of the leather's natural oils. In both cases a rapid deterioration of structural fibres occurs, leading to eventual disintegration.

If a piece is basically sound, the best way to avoid such problems is to keep it in an atmosphere of around 65 per cent relative humidity. If you own any valuable leather goods, there is a strong case, as with antique furniture, for investing in an electric humidifier to maintain their condition and value.

Countering damage from air pollution

The high levels of sulphuric acid and sulphur dioxide in the atmosphere in some cities and industrial areas pose a threat to leather. These air-borne pollutants, when they are combined with excessive humidity, can initiate a process of corrosion that causes leather to decompose and eventually crumble into a fine red powder. This condition is known as 'red rot', and once it has set in it is incurable. The best way to avoid it is to regularly 'feed' and polish the leather, as described on pp.132–3.

Treating insect infestation

Before carrying out any remedial work, check for insect infestation. If necessary, you should first treat the wooden sub-frames of screens and trunks and cases for woodworm (for technique, see p.244). Leather showing early signs of moth grubs and other parasites can be fumigated as follows:
● Find a can large enough to take the object(s) and line it with white paper.
● Place the object(s) inside the can, together with a small, open-mouthed glass jar filled with crystals of dichlorobenzene. Put bigger pieces in a polythene bag (available in large sizes from industrial suppliers). Add 150g of crystals per cubic metre of container.
Note: Wear a face mask and protective gloves when handling crystals.
● Seal the lid of the container or bag with adhesive tape and leave the object(s) in place for about a week.

Discourage future infestation by polishing the leather from time to time with a leather wax that contains an insect-repellent.

Dealing with fungus

The best protection against fungus is to store and display leather objects in a damp-free, well-ventilated environment. In very damp climates a traditional supplementary deterrent is to get a chemist to make up a mild fungicide solution of thymol saturated in alcohol and, using an old perfume atomizer, spray it over the leather. This solution also serves as a mild insect deterrent, and where leather-bound books are at risk you should also spray it over the shelves and backs of bookcases. Always wear protective goggles, gloves and a face mask when using the solution.

Removing stains

You are likely to come across various types of stain on antique leather. The following common stains usually respond well to the specified treatments.

Recent grease and fat
Remove recent grease and fat stains by gently rubbing the affected area with Fuller's earth.

Old grease and fat
Remove old grease and fat stains by dabbing them very gently with cotton wool or a cotton bud lightly moistened with white spirit.

Indeterminate stains
You can also remove many stains of indeterminate origin by gently rubbing them with cotton wool moistened with either a solution of Trichloroethane 1.1.1. or eucalyptus oil.

Candle wax
Remove candle wax by first carefully scraping off the excess with the blunt edge of a piece of wood (do not gouge the surface of the leather). Place a piece of blotting paper over the remaining wax and apply very gentle heat with an iron on a low setting. The wax will slowly melt and be absorbed into the paper.

Ink
It is usually a mistake to try to remove ink stains from leather with a strong bleaching agent such as oxalic acid. The bleach may well cause damage to the structure of the leather. Indeed, there is a strong case for leaving most ink stains on desktops well alone, for over time they tend to blend into the overall patination of the leather and acquire a certain appeal. However,

you can reduce the visual impact of fountain-pen ink by gently dabbing it with a soft cloth moistened with warm distilled water. If that proves unsuccessful:

● Make a paste of lemon juice and salt.
● Spread the paste over the stain and leave it in position for 5–10 minutes.
● Wipe the paste off with a clean rag and warm distilled water. Repeat if necessary.

To remove marks caused by ballpoint pen ink, gently rub them with a rag moistened with methylated spirits or, if this does not work, lighter fuel.

Consolidating dry leather

Excessively dried-out leather starts to desiccate and become fragile. To stop it disintegrating completely you may need to consolidate or support it as follows.

● With a soft-bristled paint brush, gently apply one or more coats of clear polyacrylate resin to both sides of the leather.
● If you cannot gain access to one of the sides, slowly inject the liquid with a hypodermic syringe.

Note: Before you start, test a small area of the item for colourfastness. If the dyes run, take the piece to a professional cleaner-restorer.

Cleaning suede

Take large suede items to a professional cleaner. Clean smaller suede items as follows:

● Remove any dust that has built up in the pile of the suede by gently brushing with a brass-wire brush.
● Spray on an aerosol suede cleaner (following the manufacturer's instructions), and work the foam into the pile with an old toothbrush. Allow the foam to dry thoroughly, and then brush the pile with a suede brush.

Note: For Recolouring and restoring gilding, see p.131; for General cleaning, reviving, and polishing, see pp.132–3.

Cleaning leather upholstery

Badly torn or frayed leather upholstery almost always needs to be replaced, and a professional restorer should carry out the work. But if the leather is basically sound, just rather dirty and dried out, you can clean it and revive it yourself. Begin by removing any dust from the surface with a soft-bristled brush. Next, thoroughly clean the surface with saddle soap (as described on p.133). If the colour of the leather has not faded, stop the cleaning process at this point, making sure that the leather has dried before putting the chair back into use. However, if the colour has faded slightly you should apply, very sparingly, a commercial leather dressing (following the manufacturer's instructions). After applying the dressing, it is important that no one sits on the chair for between one and two weeks, to avoid the risk of soiling clothing.

Below: Mission-style armchair
Red calfskin was used for the upholstered seat and pillow back of this armchair.

Restitching

Rotten or frayed stitching along leather seams should be reworked before you revive and polish the surface of the piece. While you are unpicking the old stitching with scissors, a utility knife or a dressmaker's seam ripper, closely examine the type of stitching used. Try to reproduce the original stitching so that the new blends into the old and, wherever possible, use the original holes.

Typical stitches used for leather include the back stitch and the slip-stitch (also known as the 'ladder-stitch'). These, and other stitches, are also employed in upholstery and textiles, and you should refer to p.248 for illustrations and explanations of how to reproduce them.

In addition to the above stitches, the most common means of stitching and restitching leather seams (particularly with thicker varieties of leather) is the saddle stitch. Proceed as described below.

YOU WILL NEED:

Small scissors or utility knife

Dressmaker's seam ripper

Thread Of strong linen, to match the original stitching. Pre-waxed or unwaxed varieties.

Beeswax Available at haberdashery counters and quilting shops.

Harness needles Choose needles that are thin enough so that, when threaded, both can pass through the existing stitch holes simultaneously without stretching or damaging the leather.

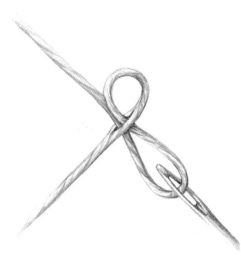

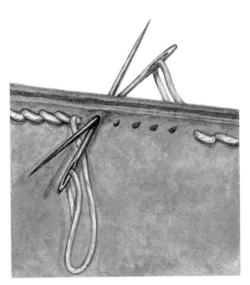

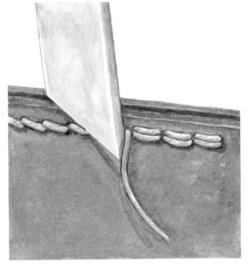

1 Attaching harness needles

● Lightly lubricate a piece of stout linen thread approximately one metre long by pulling it across a small block of beeswax.

● Obtain two harness needles whose diameter is such that they will pass through the existing stitch holes at the same time without difficulty.

● Attach a needle to each end of the length of thread. To secure the ends in place, push the point of each needle through the thread close to the needle and pull the threaded ends through to form a tight knot.

2 Working along the seam

● Lubricate the needles with beeswax. Insert one of them three or four stitches before the seam opens up (this will tie in the new stitching with the old).

● Pull the needle through so that you have an equal length of thread on either side of the seam.

● Working towards you, insert both needles through the next hole and cross them over, with the right-hand needle on top of the left.

● Work your way along the seam, using the same technique as described above and pulling the stitches tight as you go. Rewaxing the needles from time to time makes the work easier.

3 Finishing off

● When you reach the other end of the seam, continue sewing over the original stitching for two or three stitches.

● Work back through the stitch holes by approximately four or five stitches into the repair.

● With small scissors (or a utility knife), carefully cut the new thread as close to the seam as possible. Take care not to damage the leather.

Repairing tears

If it is not polished or fed with a suitable restorer such as hide food, leather dries out and becomes brittle, and then it can easily split or become torn. However, it can be repaired or reinforced by using the following techniques.

Fixing tears on backed leather

- To repair items such as book covers where the leather is glued to a cardboard or wooden backing, clean the underlying surface with a cotton bud moistened with soapy water or, for grease, white spirit. Apply wallpaper paste with a clean cotton bud; smooth the leather over the pasted surface.
- After wiping off the excess paste with a damp rag, place a piece of tissue paper over the repair and weight it down while the glue dries.

Repairing unbacked leather

- When leather has no stout cardboard or wooden backing directly below it, as with leather-upholstered sofas, make the repair on the non-grain side. With upholstered items, remove panel by unpicking stitches and pulling out upholsterer's tacks.
- Place the panel grain side up on a flat surface. If it is fairly thick leather, and the tear is clean and more or less intact, reposition the torn leather to fit and brush glue over the tear and around it.

- Cut a piece of thin canvas larger than the torn area, and stick it down, applying more glue over and around the canvas. Allow to dry before re-attaching the panel.
- When dealing with a thin leather covering, follow the above procedure but use nylon gossamer fabric (available from specialist suppliers) instead of canvas to support the repair. Use an acrylic leather adhesive rather than white glue (PVA); when dry it has more flexibility, and is better suited to lightweight leathers.

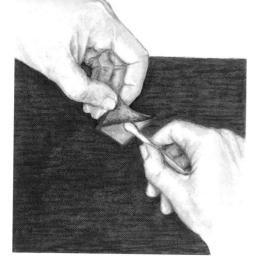

YOU WILL NEED:
Wallpaper paste
Cotton buds
Damp rag
Tissue paper
Small scissors
White glue (PVA)
Small brush
Small piece of thin canvas
Nylon gossamer fabric
Acrylic leather adhesive
Utility knife
Spokeshave or paring knife

Patching unbacked leather

- If a tear on unbacked leather has frayed, cut it out of the damaged area with a utility knife so that you can insert a new patch from behind.
- Cut a patch of similar leather larger than the hole. Skive or taper its edges before fixing, so that no ridges will show through the finished repair.
- To shape the patch, clamp it to a workbench and taper it with a spokeshave (as shown right) or skive it with a paring knife (see p.130). There is no need to skive the edges of the original leather.
- Glue the patch with either white glue (PVA) or acrylic leather adhesive. White glue (PVA) is best for thick leather, acrylic adhesive for thin leather. (If the

leather is thin, support the repair with nylon gossamer netting. Cut a patch of netting slightly larger than the leather patch. Stick it over the patch and the surrounding material with acrylic adhesive.
- Remove excess glue or acrylic adhesive with a damp rag, cover the patch with tissue paper and weight it down while the glue or adhesive dries.
- When the glue or adhesive is dry, colour and polish the leather using the techniques on pp.131–3.

Patching repairs

If you have a leather desktop or tabletop that is in basically sound condition apart from one or two damaged or missing fragments, it is possible to make effective patch repairs before reviving and polishing it. Note that, regardless of how well you do it, this type of repair is rarely, if ever, invisible to the eye.

The technique you will employ is similar to the one used to patch small sections of wooden veneer in the chapter on furniture (see pp.24–5). You will need to purchase a small piece of leather of similar thickness and, preferably, colour to the original. It is worth making an effort to find a close colour match; it is always easier to make minor rather than major adjustments to the basic hue of the leather. A specialist leather supplier (or even a friendly leather restorer or upholsterer) should be able to provide this, as long as you supply a small sliver of the original leather removed during step 1 below.

YOU WILL NEED:
Steel ruler
Heavy-duty utility knife and scalpel
Warm water
Wood filler
Medium-grade sandpaper
New leather patch
Paring knife
Acrylic leather adhesive
Lint-free rag
Aniline dyes/tinted polish (see p.131).
Leather reviver (see p.133).

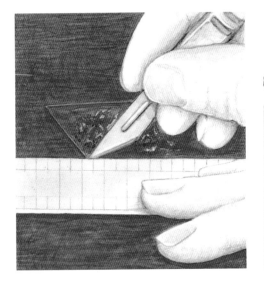

1 Preparing the damaged area

● Cut out the damaged area with a utility knife. Use a steel ruler and make the cut-out a diamond shape slightly larger than the damaged section.
● Carefully scrape off any residue of old glue from the underlying wood with a scalpel blade. A little warm water will help to soften the glue, but use it sparingly, or it will impede the drying of the wood filler you might need to apply.
● If necessary, repair any gouges or splits in the wood with wood filler. When the filler has dried thoroughly, smooth the surface with medium-grade sandpaper. (Wrapping the sandpaper around a piece of flat wood before sanding will help ensure a flat surface.)

2 Preparing the patch

● Cut the new leather to fit the diamond-shaped recess. If necessary, sand or pare the new leather to bring it to the same thickness as the existing leather.
● If you are using a fairly thick hide, you should also very slightly taper the edges of the patch to ensure that they are not higher than the surrounding area. Work on the non-grain side and make very fine cuts with a sharp paring knife.

3 Applying the patch

● Stick the patch in position with an acrylic leather adhesive. This should contain a plasticizer that will compensate for slight expansion and contraction of the leather during variations in atmospheric conditions. Do not leave any adhesive on the surrounding leather; remove any excess as directed by the manufacturer.
● If necessary, adjust the colour of the patch to match the rest of the leather, using either tinted shoe polishes (see p.131) or, if a more radical colour change is required, aniline dyes (see p.131).
● Finally, revive and polish the entire surface of the leather (see pp.132–3).

Recolouring and regilding

Two relatively simple techniques – recolouring with shoe polish or aniline dye, and regilding with gold transfer tape – can be employed to restore the colour and the gilded tooling to leather that has become scuffed or looks tired.

Recolouring

Where the colour of a leather piece has been lightened by small scratches and scuffs, you can recolour the damaged sections and blend them into the surrounding area with tinted shoe polishes. Minor fading or bleaching caused by excessive exposure to sunlight can be treated the same way. To achieve a good colour match, start with the lightest-coloured polish that you think might work and apply progressively darker tints: it is easier to darken an overly light repair than it is to lighten one that is too dark. Shoe polishes may prove inadequate for recolouring deep scratches and extreme fading. Where this proves to be a problem, use an aniline dye. Aniline dyes are available from art supply shops. They come in a wide range of colours and penetrate deep into the leather. Some are fairly toxic, so you must work in a well-ventilated area when you are mixing and applying them and wear protection for your eyes, lungs and hands. Aniline dyes are concentrated, so when you mix them with methyldated spirits start by adding only a small amount: it is easier to darken the solution than to lighten it.

1 Cleaning
● Remove surface grease or oil with Fuller's earth or white spirit (see p.126).

2 Colour matching
● Dissolve a little aniline dye in methylated spirits. Test on an inconspicuous area. Add dye until you achieve a colour match.
● Treat thin, deep scratches by applying dye with a small artist's brush. Use a lambswool pad for larger scratches. Work fairly quickly, and do not overbrush or wipe the area, or you may produce an uneven finish.
● Allow the dye to dry – it will lighten as it does so. Then apply a further coat if necessary.
● Leave at least 48 hours before polishing the repair and the surrounding area.

YOU WILL NEED:
Cotton wool and cotton buds
White spirit
Methylated spirits
Gold transfer tape
Scissors
Leather tooling wheel (smooth-faced)
Steel ruler
Soft-bristled dusting brush
Leather polishes (see p.133).
Lint-free rag

Regilding

Decorative gilded tooling on leather is often dimmed by dirt and wax polish. To restore some of its original brilliance, dip a cotton bud in white spirit and gently rub it over a small section of the gilding. As soon as the dirt and wax begin to dissolve, dry the area with cotton wool. Then move to the adjacent section. Make sure that the white spirit does not stray onto the surrounding leather. If part or all of the original gilding has worn away, you can replace it fairly inexpensively.

1 Applying gold transfer tape
● Remove dust, dirt and polish from the tooling. Lay a strip of gold transfer tape over the top, with the backing paper uppermost.
● Gently heat the tooling wheel and, using a steel rule as a straight edge, run the wheel back and forth along the top of the tape, applying moderate pressure.
● Peel the backing paper from the transfer tape. If small sections of gilding are missing, repeat step 1.

2 Finishing off
● Remove excess gold with the dusting brush. Leave the repair to harden for 48 hours, then polish the entire surface (see p.133).

Reviving and polishing a leather case

The leather case used in this project dates from the early part of the 20th century and has clearly received some heavy use during the intervening years. It encloses a black leather-bound traveller's writing box, containing compartments for paper, envelopes, pens, inks and stamps. At one time it had a protective canvas cover which, sadly, is now missing. The absence of this cover has contributed to the fact that, although the case is basically intact, some sections of the leather have dried out and are flaking, while some of the stitching has rotted and the surface has become stained and discoloured. In addition to the restitching, it was decided that general cleaning, reviving and polishing would be required if a comprehensive and sympathetic restoration was to be carried out. However, it was also felt that most of the stains should not be specifically treated as they made a pleasing contribution to the age, authenticity and patina of the piece.

YOU WILL NEED:
Soft cotton rags
Cotton wool and cotton buds
Distilled water
Old towelling
Utility or craft knife and small pair of scissors or dressmaker's seam ripper
Strong linen thread
Beeswax
Glover's needle
Upholsterer's skewers
White glue (PVA) or acrylic leather adhesive
Fine-grade sandpaper
Sponge
Saddle soap
Hide food
Leather reviver
Aniline dyes (see p.131).
Shoe polish Dark and mid tan.
Shoe-cleaning brushes You can use these instead of a cloth when applying polish to thick, sound leather, but not to thin or fragile leather.
Old toothbrush This is optional, but it can prove useful for working polish into crevices.
Microcrystalline wax
Wire wool Grade 000.
Brass polish

1 Preparatory cleaning
● Remove any loose dust and dirt by wiping down the surface with a dry soft cloth. Wipe down again with cotton wool dipped in distilled water and thoroughly wrung out. Do not make the leather wet or damp; remove moisture by drying it instantly with a piece of clean old towel.

2 Removing damaged stitching
● Where the old stitching has frayed, cut it free with a small pair of scissors, a utility knife or a dressmaker's seam ripper. Without damaging the leather, carefully open the seam.

3 Restitching the seam
● Match the colour and thickness of the new linen thread to the old. Cut a piece no longer than your arm. Lightly wax it with beeswax to reduce friction on the leather; thread it through the eye of a glover's needle.
● Restitch the seam, using the technique shown on p.128. Start about three stitches in front of the open seam and continue the same distance beyond at the other end. This will secure the ends of the old stitching in place. You may also find it helpful while stitching to hold the sides of the seam together with one or two upholsterer's skewers, but do this only if there is no risk of tearing or splitting the leather.

4 Repairing dry patches
● Where small patches of the leather have dried so much that they have begun to flake, you can stick them down by applying a small amount of white glue (PVA) on the end of a cotton bud. (Alternatively, use an acrylic leather adhesive.) Make sure that you do not get any glue or adhesive on the surrounding areas and immediately remove any excess with a slightly damp cloth.
● Once the glue has dried thoroughly, very lightly rub down any rough areas with fine-grade sandpaper to produce a smooth, level surface over the entire case. (Apply only moderate pressure when sanding as even fine sandpaper can cause damage.)

5 Cleaning the leather

- The next part of the process depends on the condition of the leather. If the piece is not too dirty, proceed to step 6.
- To remove ingrained dirt, first rub a slightly damp sponge over some saddle soap to work up a lather.
- Work the lathered sponge over the surface of the leather in a circular motion (rinsing, wringing out and re-lathering the sponge when necessary).
- When you have finished a section of the piece (such as one side or the top), remove the lather with a clean, rinsed and nearly dry sponge.
- Finally, pat dry the section with a piece of clean towelling before moving on to the next area.

6 Feeding the leather

- If the dirt is not too bad, omit the saddle soap and apply hide food. This will remove the dirt, feed the leather (restoring suppleness) and to some extent revive the original colouring.
- However, if you had to use saddle soap and/or the leather is particularly dry, apply a leather reviver. In addition to containing a fungicide and an insecticide, this provides deep nourishment, brings out colour, and gives a good base for polishing. Apply it sparingly with cotton wool (dabbing it on if the leather is brittle), and leave to dry for about 48 hours.
- Gently buff the surface with cotton wool or a very soft cloth.

7 Recolouring

- Leather reviver or hide food will have, to varying degrees, enriched the colour of the leather. However, it may be patchy or not as dark as you would wish. In extreme cases you may need to recolour sections using aniline dyes (for technique, see p.131). However, in this and most cases, you can improve the colour by applying a suitably tinted shoe polish. (A mix of mid and dark tan was effective here.) Apply the polish sparingly with a soft cloth; on thick, sound leather you can use a shoe brush. An old toothbrush is helpful for reaching recessed areas.
- Leave to dry for a minimum of half an hour before buffing to a shine with a soft cloth.

8 Applying wax polish

- For additional protection and further colour enhancement, finish off with an application of microcrystalline wax polish. Apply it sparingly, using a soft cloth on thinner leathers and a shoe brush on thicker ones.
- Buff to a shine with a soft cloth as the wax starts to dry, but before it dries completely.
- Finally, clean and polish any brass fittings with fine-grade (000) wire wool and a brass polish. Buff with a soft cloth.

Replacing a leather desktop

This early 20th-century piece is a copy of an 18th-century mahogany pedestal desk. (We also did some minor repairs to one of the pedestals and revived and polished the mahogany; see p.64 and pp.16–17.) The tooled leather top was in very poor condition and beyond salvaging. A replacement leather – cut to size and pre-tooled – was purchased by mail order from a specialist supplier and restorer. Traditionally the leather used on desktops and tabletops is Morocco, cow hide or a skiver. (A skiver is made from sheepskin. It is a thinner and less expensive type of leather, and is available in virtually any colour.) On a better-quality desk or table, you are advised to fit a hide or Morocco. When doing your own restoring, take a piece of the old leather to the supplier to identify the correct thickness. If the leather is missing from the piece, measure the depth of the recess in which the new leather will sit before you place your order. A leather that either sits low in the recess or is raised will not be satisfactory.

YOU WILL NEED:
Paring chisel
Carpenter's wooden mallet
Warm water 100ml; to be used sparingly.
Wood filler
Sandpaper Coarse and medium grades.
Sanding block
Tape measure
Pre-cut and pre-tooled hide or skiver
Masking tape
Heavy-duty wallpaper paste Containing fungicide.
Mixing bucket
Standard paint brush 5cm.
Lambswool
Steel ruler
Heavy-duty utility or craft knife
Neutral leather polish
Furniture polish

Repairing the wood

3
● Treat any woodworm (see p.244) in the recessed wooden panel.
● Repair splits or gouges with wood filler.
● Once the filler has dried, sand down the surface, using first coarse- and then medium-grade sandpaper. Aim to produce a perfectly flat bed with clean edges, but a slight surface roughness will aid adhesion.

Preparing the piece

1
● Make any repairs to the desk, and revive and polish the wood (see pp.16–17). Polish the desktop surround again once the new leather is fitted.

Removing the leather top

2
● To remove the old leather top, carefully scrape it off with a sharp paring chisel. If the original glue is very old and brittle, the leather will come away quite easily.
● For areas where it is stuck fast you may need to tap the end of the chisel with a carpenter's mallet (but make sure you do not damage the underlying wood). Old glue can also be softened with a little warm water to ease removal. However, be careful not to over-wet or dampen the wood as this can cause problems of contraction and expansion later on.

Repairing curled edges

Salvage the original leather if you can. If the edges are curling, fold them over thin cardboard and scrape off old glue with a utility knife or a scalpel. Stick them down with white glue (PVA) (or leather adhesive) on a small artist's brush.

4 Applying the new leather top

● Measure carefully the dimensions of the panel and purchase a pre-cut and pre-tooled hide or skiver from a specialist supplier. The leather will arrive slightly oversize, so you must trim it *in situ.*

● Protect the surrounding area with masking tape.

● Mix up some heavy-duty wallpaper paste (with fungicide) and, using a small standard paint brush, quickly apply two or three even coats over the panel. The paste should not be runny, but sticky to the touch, when you fit the leather. Lay the leather over the panel. Align it along the front edge of the recessed panel and one of the adjacent sides.

5 Removing air

● Make up a fist-sized pad of lambswool and, working out from the centre, press down and smooth out the leather, making sure you do not leave any pockets of trapped air. If you are fitting a skiver (which is thinner than a hide) do not press too hard or you might stretch the leather.

● To ensure that the leather adheres round the edges of the recess, wrap cloth over the rounded end of your brush handle and press the edges of the leather firmly down. If excess adhesive squeezes out from under the edges, remove it with a slightly damp cloth. Let the leather dry for one hour.

6 Trimming excess leather

● Using either a steel ruler or straight edge, and a heavy-duty utility or craft knife, trim the excess leather.

● Hold both the steel ruler and the knife firmly, and apply a steady, even pressure. If you are not careful, the blade can slip and cut through the masking tape protecting the surrounding wood.

● As soon as you have finished cutting, run the cloth-covered brush handle around the perimeter once again to consolidate the fixing and the clean edge.

● Once you are satisfied with the fit and the adhesion of the leather, remove the masking tape.

7 Applying leather polish

● The pre-cut hide or skiver will already have been polished by the maker (and you can also request an 'antiqued' finish). However, an additional coat of neutral leather polish will usually make it look even better (see pp.132–3).

8 Repolishing

● Finally, although you repaired and polished the desk before fitting the new leather, you should lightly repolish the top, particularly if the masking tape has left a slight residue on the surface of the wood.

Textiles

Introduction

The term 'textiles' embraces many household and personal items, notably curtains, bedclothes and wall-hangings; decorative panels and samplers; table and cushion covers; costumes (for people and dolls); and accessories, including purses and decorative trims. Almost all of these items are made from fabrics spun, woven, knitted or stitched from one of four natural fibres: silk, wool, linen or cotton.

Colour

Textiles are either coloured by dyeing the fibres before they are worked or by dyeing the fabric after it has been made up from natural fibres. Tapestries and damasks are examples of textiles patterned in the weave—their colored warp and weft threads are manipulated to form patterns and motifs while the fabric is on the loom. (Warp threads run lengthwise in the fabric; weft threads run crosswise, at a right angle to the warp.) These weavings also contribute to the material's texture. Processes that add colour to finished fabric include hand painting and, more often, hand blocking or machine printing.

Before the mid-19th century vegetable dyes were the main agents used to colour textiles. Subsequently man-made aniline dyes, synthesized from coal tar, were increasingly used. Colour, especially colour derived from vegetable dyes, will run when the fabric is washed unless it has been fixed with a mordant (metal salts). Before washing or removing stains from any textile, it is vital to determine if it is colourfast (for methods of testing see p.142). If the item is not colourfast, professional cleaning or dry-cleaning with potato starch are then the only options (see p.142).

Decorative techniques

Over the centuries hand and machine stitching techniques have also been used to create intricate decorative effects. The stitching may either be embroidered on an existing fabric or it may comprise the fabric itself. (Lace and knitwear are examples of fabrics made by stitching.) Popular types of applied embroidery are: couching, crewel work, cutwork, drawn thread work, smocking and whitework. Needlepoint (canvaswork), Berlin woolwork, beadwork, lace and quilting are among the other decorative treatments of textiles you may encounter.

Examining fibres and stitches

The following pages give advice on cleaning and making minor repairs to antique textiles. Before you work on any piece you must not only test it for colourfastness as described above, but also inspect the fibres and stitches (with a magnifying glass

Above: Quilts in storage
Some fine examples of late 19th-century American patchwork and appliqué quilts are stored in an old pie safe. The punched-tin panels in the sides and doors of the safe provide ventilation, while layers of acid-free tissue paper placed on the shelves protect the quilts from the acidity of the wood.

if necessary) to assess their condition. Time and wear and tear may have weakened them so much that cleaning must be left to a professional restorer.

It is also important to establish which of the four natural fibres has been used to make the textile and any trim or stitching used on it. The answer will determine the appropriate cleaning method. If you are in doubt about the identity of the fibre, seek the advice of an antique dealer or a professional cleaner-restorer. (The textile division of a museum may recommend one of the latter.) If this is not possible, carry out the following test. Pull a thread or fibre from an unobtrusive and non-structural part of the textile. Burn this sample and look out for any of the following effects. Burning silk gives off a fishy smell and shrivels to a gooey mess. Linen burns with a yellow flame, smells of burning grass and leaves a residue of grey ash. Cotton burns with a yellow flame, smells of burning paper and also leaves a residue of grey ash. Wool usually burns without a flame, gives off the distinctive smell of burning hair, and reduces to small, bead-like fragments that can easily be crushed.

Below: A collection of antique textiles

A silk embroidered shawl dating from around 1900 is draped over the bedside table. The bed is dressed with a floral Mercella bedspread from the 1850s and a late 19th-century appliquéd satin pillow. Two 19th-century linen nightgowns sit on top. The garment on the left is decorated with lace, the other with crocheted lace.

Tools and materials

The tools and materials that you will need to maintain and make minor repairs to textiles are not particularly expensive. A few, although by no means all, of the chemicals used to remove various stains from fabrics require great care during handling. Therefore it is important that you adhere to the advice on safety wherever it appears on the following pages.

Tools

1 Embroidery frame Used to stretch needlepoint taut before making repairs. For larger pieces, stand-mounted frames are available.
2 Embroidery scissors Small-bladed scissors used to cut fine threads.
3 Dressmaker's scissors Larger-bladed scissors, also known as dressmaker's shears, used to cut fabrics and backing materials such as canvas and linen.
4 Needles A selection of curved needles and standard embroidery needles to carry out various repairs.
5 Brass pins Non-rusting pins used to pin out textiles when washing and drying.
6 Lace pins Very fine pins used to pin out delicate textiles. They can be inserted between the threads of fabrics without causing damage.
7 Magnifying glass To inspect damage and when making small, fine repairs.
8 Domestic iron Used on a low or cool setting to press some heavier fabrics.

YOU WILL ALSO NEED:
Hair dryer Used on a low or medium heat setting to dry various textiles after cleaning.
Vacuum cleaner To remove dust particles.
Hardboard After cleaning, various textiles can be pressed between two sheets of hardboard weighted down with heavy weights or piles of books.
Plastic buckets and trays To wash small textiles. Trays should be about 45cm long and 30cm wide.
Bathtub To wash larger textiles.
Sponge For cleaning textiles a natural sponge is preferable to a synthetic one.
Plastic spatula or knife To remove candle wax.

Materials

9 Thread Silk, cotton and linen threads are used to make repairs.
10 Crewel wool Available in a wide range of colours, and used to repair damaged sections of needlepoint.
11 Lambswool To apply various cleaning fluids.
12 Towelling To dry various textiles after washing.
13 Nylon-monofilament screening To protect some textiles when washing and cleaning.
14 Acid-free tissue paper To pad out and store textiles.
15 Mothballs To prevent moth attack during storage.
16 Blotting paper To absorb various stains.

THE FOLLOWING ARE ALL USED TO EITHER CLEAN TEXTILES OR REMOVE SPECIFIC STAINS:
17 Wool detergent
18 Potato starch Available from chemists, health-food shops and supermarkets.
19 Ammonia Available in solution from chemists.
20 Rust-stain remover To remove rust stains and iron mould.
21 Baking soda
22 Salt
23 Lemon juice
24 White spirit
25 Methylated spirits
26 Candle wax or beeswax

YOU WILL ALSO NEED:
Cotton wool and cotton buds For cleaning.
Saponaria A mild natural detergent extracted from plants; available from herbalists and used to wash particularly delicate fabrics.
Chloramine T A mild bleaching agent available in solution (usually 2 per cent) from chemists. Protect hands, eyes and lungs when handling it and use only in a well-ventilated space.
Acetone
Petroleum jelly
Glycerine
Insect repellents
Lavender
Eucalyptus oil
Washing soda
White vinegar
Hydrogen peroxide A bleaching agent available in solution (usually 20 per cent volume) from chemists. Take precautions when handling as for Chloramine T.
Oxalic acid A highly poisonous acid that should be purchased ready diluted from chemists (not as crystals for dilution at home). Dilutions are specified in the text. Take the same handling precautions as for Chloramine T.
Egg white
Distilled water For all cleaning or rinsing tasks except those for which a bathtub is recommended (for which you should use water from the tap). Professional textile cleaner-restorers prefer distilled water to tap water because it has fewer chemicals and impurities.

General cleaning and storage

Dusty or dirty textiles can usually be hand-washed (but not machine-washed) or dry-cleaned. However, tapestries, most silks and other pieces that are particularly valuable or fragile should be entrusted to a professional cleaner-restorer of antique textiles. Never take such pieces to non-specialist dry-cleaners, because the strong chemicals that they employ may well damage the fibres.

Testing colours

To check whether you should wash or dry-clean a piece, first test it for colourfastness.

1 Wetting the sample

● Dab a small, unobtrusive area of the textile (preferably on the back) with cotton wool that has been moistened with warm, soapy water. To avoid damaging the textile, you should always use a soap or detergent designed for washing wool by hand rather than machine.

2 Using blotting paper

● Leave for five minutes, then apply a small swatch of white blotting paper to the treated area. If the paper remains unmarked, the area tested is colourfast. If it absorbs colour or dye, the fabric is not colourfast and should be dry-cleaned with potato starch (see opposite page).

3 Testing each colour

● If there is more than one colour in the textile, you must test each one in turn, using the above method. Each dye must be colourfast if the piece is to be washed.

4 Removing trimming

● If you are testing a textile with decorative trimming and you establish that the main body of the textile is colourfast but that the trimming is not, unstitch the latter before washing the main part. It is best to have the trimming dry-cleaned by a professional cleaner specializing in antique textiles. Afterwards, reattach it with the same type of stitching as was used originally.

Dry-cleaning

Textiles that are not colourfast should be dry-cleaned using this traditional method.

YOU WILL NEED:
One sheet of plastic
One sheet of nylon monofilament screening
Vacuum cleaner
Potato starch
Saucepan to heat potato starch
Spoon
Soft-bristled dusting brush

1 Removing dust

● Place the textile on a sheet of plastic and cover it with nylon filament screening.
● Pass the nozzle of a vacuum cleaner 2.5 to 5cm above the surface to remove any dust.

2 Using potato starch

● Lay the textile on the screening. Heat dry potato starch in a saucepan until hand-hot. Cover the textile with flour to a depth of about 2.5cm, and work in the flour with the back of a spoon.
● Leave for 10 minutes, during which time the flour will absorb the dirt, then brush it off.

3 Finishing the cleaning process

● Repeat step 2, using fresh starch each time, as many times as necessary, until all the dirt has been removed.

Hand-washing

The following technique is suitable for small textiles (for washing larger pieces, see 'Washing larger textiles', right). Note that textiles in sound condition require a different treatment than frayed pieces.

YOU WILL NEED:
One sheet of nylon monofilament screening
Shallow plastic tray or a piece of clean
white towelling
Distilled water
Mild wool detergent or saponaria
Brass pins
Hair-drier or white blotting paper

1 Sponging

● Remove dust (see 'Dry-cleaning', opposite). If the textile is frayed, put screening on clean white towelling and place the textile flat on screening. Dab with a clean, damp sponge. If the piece is sound, place on screening and immerse in a tray of cold water.
● If using the tray, drain the water and replace with hand-hot, soapy water. Use a mild wool detergent or, if the piece is fragile, saponaria. Dab with a sponge, and keep replacing the water until no more dirt dissolves. If using towelling, dab with the sponge moistened with the soapy solution. Rinse by dabbing: use a wet sponge in the tray, or a moist sponge on the towelling.

2 Drying

● Gently remove the textile and pin it flat with brass pins, on a table covered with plastic or towelling. The piece is then ready to be dried using either one of two methods.
● Gently play a hair-drier (as shown top) on a low heat setting back and forth about a foot above the surface of the textile.
● An equally effective but slower method for removing moisture from a textile is to gently dab it with clean white towelling or white blotting paper (as shown above) and then allow it to air-dry.

Washing larger textiles

To hand-wash larger textiles, use the following method.

● Fill a bath with cold water to a depth that fully covers the textile.

● Place the textile flat on a sheet of nylon filament screening and carefully lower it into the bottom of the bath.

● Work the water gently into the fabric with your fingers, then leave the piece to soak for 10 minutes.

● Drain the water, then refill the bath with cold water. Immerse the piece for 10 minutes. Drain water. Refill bath.

● Remove the textile and nylon screening, drain and refill the bath with hand-hot water.

● Mix in a wool detergent (for hand, not machine, washing) or saponaria. Use saponaria for delicate textiles.

● Re-submerge the textile on the screening and gently knead it in the soapy water.

● Remove the textile and screening once again, and drain off the dirty water. Refill with clean, hand-hot water, re-submerge, and rinse (again kneading with your fingertips).

● Rinse the piece with fresh hand-hot water at least twice more.

● Remove the textile, drain off most of the water and slide it off the screening onto a clean, flat surface.

● Dab off the excess water with a piece of clean white towelling.

● Allow the textile to dry naturally or play a hair-drier on a low heat over it.

143

Removing stains

It is feasible to remove a wide range of identifiable stains yourself, provided you combine the advice given in the general rules for cleaning textiles on pp.142–3, and that on cleaning upholstery on pp.88–9, with the treatments prescribed below for specific stains.

If the textile is particularly valuable or fragile, never attempt to clean it yourself, but take it to a professional textile cleaner-restorer. You should also bear in mind that the older the stain is, the harder it will be to remove without damaging the fabric – some deeply ingrained stains defy treatment by the amateur and even pose a serious problem for the professional.

The stains that are most commonly found on textiles are caused by the following substances. Remember to check for colourfastness (see p.142) before attempting to remove any stain.

Adhesives (traditional)
Remove animal and fish glues by very gently rubbing in warm distilled water. Be patient as it may take a while for the glues to dissolve.

Adhesives (modern)
Gently rub in a little warm water with a cloth. If this does not work, add a few drops of acetone to the damp cloth and rub gently.

Alcohol See p.88.

Beer See p.88.

Beetroot
Place the affected area flat over the top of a jug (or similar open-mouthed container). Mix a solution of 30g of washing soda to every 500ml of warm distilled water; pour this through the stain. Rinse until the stain is gone, then rinse with warm distilled water.

Blood
Leave well alone if it is an old stain or a valuable textile as the cleaning process required will create more problems than it solves. However, you can achieve some success with relatively recent stains.

Begin by gently sponging the affected area with a weak solution of cold distilled water and salt. Rinse thoroughly, and repeat once more. If additional treatment is required first apply a weak 2 per cent solution of Chloramine T, then rinse thoroughly with distilled water. Apply a 2 per cent solution of oxalic acid. Rinse several times with distilled water.
Note: When using Chloramine T and oxalic acid (the latter is highly poisonous), you must wear protection for eyes, lungs and skin, work in a well-ventilated area, and keep children and animals well away.

Candle wax See p.88.

Chewing gum
There are two treatments for this. Work egg white into the gum to soften it, then carefully pick off as much as possible. Sponge away the remaining gum with a mild solution of warm distilled water and soap, before rinsing with distilled water. Alternatively, pack ice cubes around the gum to make it brittle. Carefully pick off as much as possible. Wash and rinse as above.

Chocolate
Gently scrape off as much as possible with a plastic spatula. Then wash with a mild solution of distilled water and soap, before rinsing. If this proves unsatisfactory, treat as for beetroot. Finally, with white textiles only, remove any remaining stain by applying either a weak solution (2 per cent) of Chloramine T or a weak solution (maximum 20 per cent volume) of hydrogen peroxide, before rinsing thoroughly with distilled water.
Note: When handling Chloramine T and hydrogen peroxide take the same precautions as specified under blood.

Coffee See p.88.

Cosmetics
Remove foundation creams and moisturizers with heated potato starch, using the dry-cleaning technique shown on p.142.

To remove lipstick, try gently rubbing with warm, soapy water, then rinsing. If this does not work, rub a dab of petroleum jelly into the stain, add a drop of ammonia to the warm, soapy water and gently rub the stain. Rinse thoroughly. If the fabric is not colourfast, dry-clean with heated potato starch (see p.142).

Remove nail polish with methylated spirits. If that does not work, gently rub the stain with a small quantity of undiluted acetone.

Egg
First remove the worst of it by gently scraping with a plastic spatula. Remove egg white with a solution of salt and water; rinse with water. To remove egg yolk, work a dilute solution of wool detergent into the stain, then rinse with clear distilled water. Repeat washing and rinsing until stain is gone. Rinse thoroughly.

Fat and oils See p.88.

Fruit juice
On washable textiles remove still-wet stains by placing them over the top of an open container and pouring hot water through the stain. If that proves insufficient, gently rub with lemon juice before rinsing. If it is an old stain, either treat as for beetroot, or apply warm, soapy water with a drop of ammonia in it. Then rinse.

On fabrics that cannot be washed, rub in a small quantity of glycerine. Leave for about 45 minutes, then partly remove with a moistened sponge. Follow up by gently dabbing with white vinegar, then 'rinse' by dabbing with a slightly moistened sponge.

Grass

First try hand-washing with warm water mixed with wool detergent. Then try gently dabbing with a little methylated spirits. If neither of these methods works, try dabbing with a little eucalyptus oil.

Ink

Remove Indian ink with methylated spirits. Remove fountain-pen ink by first dabbing with warm distilled water. Then apply a paste of salt and lemon juice and leave for 10–15 minutes before rinsing thoroughly. Repeat the procedure if necessary. If there is still a problem, try a 2 per cent solution of Chloramine T, then rinse thoroughly.

Remove felt-tip-pen ink with methylated spirits. Then wash with warm, soapy water and rinse thoroughly. If necessary, lightly bleach white textiles afterwards with a 2 per cent solution of Chloramine T and then rinse thoroughly.

Ballpoint-pen ink can be very difficult to remove. Apply a little methylated spirits, then rinse thoroughly. If that does not work, take the piece to a professional restorer-cleaner.

Iron mould

This orange-brown stain can be very difficult to remove, but may respond to a paste of salt and lemon juice. Apply the paste to the affected area and let it sit for about an hour. Rinse thoroughly. If that does not work, try a commercial rust-stain remover, following the manufacturer's instructions.

Lead (graphite) pencil

Try a gum eraser first, then sponge with warm, soapy water and rinse thoroughly. On white textiles, lightly sponge off any remaining marks with a 2 per cent solution of Chloramine T, then rinse.

Metal polish

Take old stains to a professional cleaner. To remove new stains, sponge as soon as possible with warm, soapy water and rinse by dabbing with wet towelling.

Mildew See p.89.

Milk and cream For milk, see p.89; for cream, see Cosmetics, above.

Perspiration

Try these methods in the following order. Gently dab with cotton wool moistened with a solution of 1 part white vinegar to 15 parts warm distilled water, then rinse. If this proves ineffective, dab with cotton wool moistened with a solution of ammonia (15 per cent volume) then rinse. If that does not work, lightly sponge the stain with a little methylated spirits.

Rust

Gently brush out the worst of the rust with a weak solution (20 per cent volume) of hydrogen peroxide, and then rinse thoroughly. Alternatively, try a commercial rust remover intended for use on fabrics.

Scorching

Wash with a warm solution of 500g of washing soda to 500ml of distilled water, then rinse. If this proves ineffective, mix up a thick paste of washing soda and glycerine, spread it on the mark, and leave for 12 hours. Then wash with warm, soapy water and rinse thoroughly. You may be able to bleach out any remaining marks on white textiles with a 2 per cent solution of Chloramine T.

Shoe polish See p.89.

Soot See p.89

Tar To remove soft tar, scrape off the worst with a plastic spatula. Wipe the rest with a cotton bud dampened with white spirit. To remove hardened tar, soften with a cotton bud dampened with olive oil. Treat with white spirit, as above. In both cases, wash with a mild wool detergent solution, then rinse by dabbing with a cotton bud dampened with water.

Tea See p.89.

Wine See p.89.

Ironing and pressing

Never iron a fragile or damaged textile. Lay it flat on white blotting paper or acid-free tissue paper and put this on a sheet of hardboard (smooth side up). Put another sheet of blotting or tissue paper on the textile, and another sheet of hardboard (smooth side down) on top of that. Apply pressure with heavy weights and leave for an hour.

If the textile is sound and fairly strong, use a domestic iron, with its temperature at one setting below that recommended for the fabric. Never iron or press dirty or stained textiles, as this will further fix the discoloration.

Below: Machine lace

An early 20th-century machine-made lace tablecloth covers a 19th-century mahogany table. After cleaning, lace should be pressed only very lightly, to avoid crushing the fibres.

Repairing textiles

Damaged textiles should be restored as closely as possible to their original condition. Frayed or torn areas should never be darned. This places undue strain on the surrounding fabric and spoils the look of the piece. Damaged areas must be patched with a supportive lining as in the following projects. When renewing stitching along seams or in worn sections of needlepoint, you must replicate the original thread, both in fibre and colour, and the type of stitch (see pp.148–9).

Attaching a supportive lining

The top cover of this late 19th-century quilted bed cover has become very fragile, and small areas are starting to tear and fray.

To prevent further deterioration of this kind, you should insert a supportive lining between the top cover and the wadding.

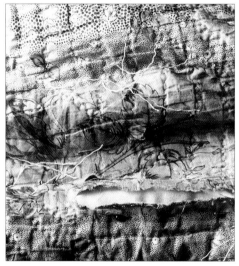

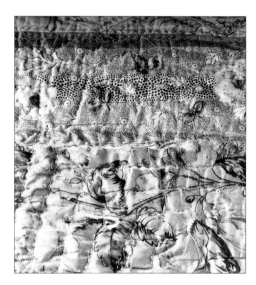

1 Replacing wadding

• If, as here, some of the original wadding has crept on to the surface of the piece, push it back in and gently tease it apart with your fingers or, if it is too difficult to work in this way, a small crochet hook. Redistribute it evenly under the top cover. If some of the wadding is missing, replace it with either more of the original type, or, if that is not available, blend in a modern polyester wadding of similar weight.

2 Inserting lining material

• Cut a patch of lining material about 2.5cm larger than the tear or split. On heavier textiles use a linen lining; on lighter ones use silk. In both cases try to match the colour of the lining material to the main colour in the top-cover fabric.

• Carefully insert the lining through the split or tear, and position it flat on top of the wadding and centred under the split or tear.

3 Stitching the split

• Choose a thread of the same weight and colour as the original stitching, and match the gauge of the needle to the weight of the thread. Carefully stitch both sides of the split or tear together and, at the same time, stitch the fabric to the lining. Use the same number of stitches per inch as the original quilter. Finish with a back stitch (see p.248) to lock the thread in position.

Supporting with fine-meshed net

The damage seen on this 19th-century patchwork quilt is typical of that found on such textiles. It would be impossible to insert a supportive lining beneath the top cover because of the way the piece is stitched and because the torn and frayed areas would not support further stitching. Replacing the damaged patches with pieces of modern fabric would compromise the integrity of the original work and reduce its value. Therefore it is necessary to protect the damaged areas with fine-meshed net (available from specialist textile and fabric suppliers, and some department stores).

YOU WILL NEED:

Polyester wadding If the underlying stuffing of your quilt is intact you will not need to buy this. However, if it is missing or damaged, choose a replacement of the same or similar thickness and weight as the original stuffing.

Fine-meshed net

Small embroidery scissors

Lace pins These have very thin shafts and so will not damage fine or frail fabrics. If the quilt is covered with a strong fabric in sound condition you can substitute ordinary brass pins.

Fine needle

Thread To match original stitching.

1 Cutting the net

● If any underlying wadding is out of position or missing, reseat or replace it as in step 1 of 'Attaching a supportive lining' (see opposite).

● Cut a piece of fine-meshed net the same shape as the damaged area; include a narrow seam allowance. (Netting should be 3–6mm larger than the damage.) In this case, because of their close proximity, one piece was cut to cover both the hexagon and the six-pointed star. Non-adjoining patches should be repaired with separate pieces of net.

2 Stitching the net in place

● Lay the quilt flat on a tabletop and position the net over the damaged patches, temporarily securing it with lace pins.

● Thread a fine needle with thread that closely matches that used for the original stitching. Using a simple running stitch (see p.248), sew around the perimeter of the net, folding its edges under as you go. Stitch over the original stitches along the edges of the patches wherever possible. Take care to avoid stitching through to the underlying layers.

Left: Displaying the result

The finished repair reveals the various advantages of this type of restoration. First, even when it is viewed reasonably close up, the net is fine enough to be virtually invisible. Looking at it from a metre or so away, you would not notice it at all. Second, it places little or no strain on the original fabrics. This is vital if further damage is to be avoided. Third, it makes it possible to display the quilt with its original fabrics, pattern and colourways intact – which a substitute patch would not allow you to do. Finally, careful restoration of this kind will not adversely affect the value of the piece.

Repairing damaged needlepoint

This 20th-century needlepoint is based on a 19th-century pattern. The frayed stitches are typical of the damage, due to age and wear and tear, found on old needlepoint.

To make an acceptable repair, you must spend some time matching as closely as possible the colours and weight of the replacement threads to the original ones. Note also that if the backing canvas behind the missing or frayed threads is damaged you will have to buy a new piece, cut out a patch slightly larger all round than the hole and glue it to the back of the canvas before making the repair.

YOU WILL NEED:

Scissors Small embroidery scissors and dressmaker's shears.

Magnifying glass

Pre-shrunk linen A piece at least 5cm larger all round than the textile to be repaired.

Embroidery frame Use an adjustable stretcher frame, large enough to support the textile mounted on a temporary linen backing.

Standard sewing machine

Threads Buy crewel wools of the same colour and weight as the damaged or missing originals. (The same applies if silk or cotton threads were used.) You will also need button thread to temporarily attach the backing fabric to the embroidery frame.

Embroidery needles Usually sold in packets of four to six needles, at least one of which will be of a suitable size for the thread used and the width of the holes in the backing canvas.

Brass pins

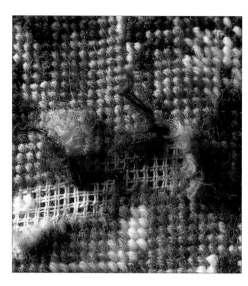

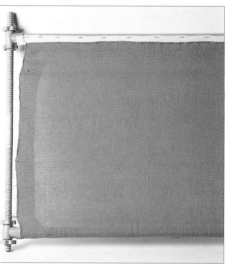

1 Assessing the task

● If the needlepoint has been mounted, either on a display panel or as a cushion cover, unstitch it from the backing fabric and lay it out flat on a work surface. Inspect the damaged area, using a magnifying glass if necessary, and assess how the frayed coloured threads made up the original pattern. If the threads are missing altogether, you will need to look to the surrounding areas to approximate the right colours.

● Cut off the frayed threads, taking great care not to damage the canvas backing.

2 Attaching the linen to the frame

● Cut a piece of strong, pre-shrunk linen at least 5cm larger all round than the needlepoint. Adjust the embroidery frame so that it accommodates the linen. Tack the linen to the webbing on the roller ends of the frame. Readjust the frame to evenly tension the linen lengthways.

● Attach the sides of the linen to the stretcher sides of the frame with lengths of button thread and a medium-gauge embroidery needle. Make another adjustment to the frame, creating an even but not overly tight tension all around.

3 Securing the panel to the linen

● Centre the needlepoint on top of the linen. Using button thread and a simple running stitch (see p.248), sew either the top edge or the bottom edge of the panel parallel to the corresponding edge of the linen. Secure the sides and the other end of the panel to the linen with brass pins, making adjustments to the pins as you go, to make sure that the panel is evenly tensioned. Then secure the pinned sides with a running stitch as you did before (removing the brass pins as you work your way around the perimeter).

● Once you have finished, make another adjustment to the frame to slightly and evenly tension the panel.

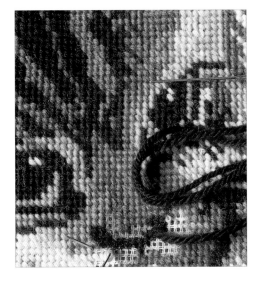

4 Matching the original stitch

- Thread the needle with the first of your coloured threads. In most cases you should work from the perimeter to the centre of the hole. If this is impracticable, plan the sequence of threads that best suits the repair.
- Begin to fill in the bare patch of canvas using a stitch that matches the original. (The most common types of traditional needlepoint stitch are shown on the right.) Pull your stitches through the linen backing.

5 Finishing off the threads

- When you have finished stitching the first coloured thread into the pattern, knot it off on the back of the linen before starting the next thread. Repeat the process with each thread.
- Once you have finished knotting off all of the threads, carefully trim the excess thread from the knots with a pair of small embroidery scissors. .

6 Reattaching the repaired piece

- When you have completed the repair, remove the piece from the embroidery frame and restitch it to its original display panel or cushion, trimming the linen backing to size if necessary.
- If you repaired a cushion cover and would prefer to display it, refer to page 150, where techniques for mounting and displaying textiles are described.

Needlepoint stitches

The diagrams below illustrate the stitches most commonly used for needlepoint. Each diagram shows the stitches as they appear on the show side of the piece. In each case, 1 is the starting point – where the needle is brought through from the back of the canvas to the front.

Half cross stitch

Cross stitch

Tent stitch

Cross stitch over three holes square

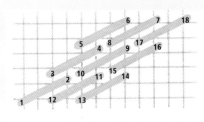

Oblique Slav stitch

Displaying and storing textiles

Textiles are particularly vulnerable to deterioration. Their colours and fibres may degrade as a result of mishandling, improper storage, exposure to sunlight, heat, moisture or humidity, atmospheric pollution and incorrect methods of display. To maintain them in the best possible condition, especially if they are already fragile, follow the procedures described below.

Storing textiles

Sticking to the following rules will keep stored textiles in good condition.

- **Avoid direct sunlight** To prevent fading, never store (or display) textiles in direct sunlight.

- **Ideal temperature** If possible, store textiles in the dark at a temperature of around 12°C and a relative humidity of around 55 per cent. Avoid damp surroundings, which encourage mould.

- **Storage methods** Never fold or crease textiles. Roll large textiles, right side out, around a cardboard tube covered with acid-free tissue paper. Cover with a clean dust sheet. Roll small textiles around pads or tubes of acid-free tissue paper.

- **Using calico bags** Never store textiles in or under plastic bags or sheets, which encourage mould. Calico bags will protect them from dust.

- **Discouraging pests** Regularly dust cupboards and other storage areas and insert mothballs. Make sure that the mothballs do not come into direct contact with the surface of the textiles.

- **Period costume** Store flat. Pad out the shoulders, sleeves, and any unavoidable folds with acid-free tissue paper. Insert slivers of tissue paper between the material and any metal buttons. Remove any pinned jewellery.

Mounting small textiles

Small textiles should be mounted on a fabric-covered board before framing. Proceed as follows.

1 Preparing a cardboard mount

- Cut a piece of thick cardboard 2.5cm bigger all round than the textile. Smooth its edges and corners with fine sandpaper.

2 Attaching the backing fabric

- Cut a piece of cotton, linen or silk (matched to the fibres used in the textiles) at least 7.5cm larger all round than the cardboard.
- Place the cardboard on top of the backing fabric. Turn the edges of the material over the back of the cardboard and glue it in place. (You will need to miter the corners of the fabric before sticking it down.) Allow to dry.

3 Stitching the textile in place

- Turn the cardboard over and centre the textile on the fabric-covered mount. Tack it in position with brass pins, squaring it up as you work around the perimeter. Permanently secure the textile to the mount with a running stitch (see p.248), using a thread of suitable weight and colour.

4 Framing the textile

- It is wise to have the mounted textile professionally framed under glass. You will be offered a choice of regular or non-reflective glass. If, as is recommended here, you exclude strong natural or artificial light sources from the room, non-reflective glass should prove unnecessary.

Hanging large textiles

Never fix a large, heavy textile to wooden battens or walls by passing tacks or nails through the fibres. Instead, stitch it to a backing panel (see step 3 of 'Mounting small textiles', left) then attach the panel to the battens or wall. There are three basic methods that you can use:

Hook-and-loop tape method

This gives an even distribution of weight along the length of a supporting batten. The batten can either be attached to a wall or hung on chains from the ceiling. When the batten is in position, glue the rough side of the hook-and-loop tape to it. Then glue the smooth side of the hook-and-loop tape to a strip of fabric. Sew the fabric strip along the top edge of the panel's back (as in the first drawing below). Press the two sides of the hook-and-loop tape together to secure the textile in position.

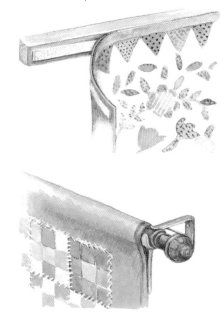

Sleeve method

Turn over the top of the backing material and machine-stitch it to form a tube or sleeve. A wall- or ceiling-mounted pole can then be inserted through the sleeve (as in the drawing above). This method is best suited to hanging heavy textiles.

Tab method

Use this method only for lighter hangings, because it does not produce as effective a distribution of weight as the hook-and-loop tape method or the sleeve method.

YOU WILL NEED:

Calico or canvas backing material Or any other suitable strong fabric.

Cylindrical curtain rod

Sewing machine

Scissors

Sewing needle

Thread Silk, cotton or linen to match the predominant fibre in the textile.

Cylindrical curtain rod Metal or stained, painted or gilt wood.

Wall brackets Of a size and style to match the curtain rod.

1 Making the tabs

● Take a strip of fabric 10cm wide and long enough to make the required number of 12.5cm tabs. Fold it in half lengthways and machine-stitch the open side. Cut the tabs and turn them right side out.

2 Spacing the tabs

● Pin the tabs to the back of the panel, spacing them approximately 15cm apart along the top edge. Machine-stitch to secure them.

3 Hanging the textile

● If you have not already done so, stitch the textile to the face of the backing panel. Use the method recommended for mending damaged needlepoint (see p.148, step 3).

● Slide the curtain rod through the tabs of the backing material. Then hang the rod from brackets attached to the wall. Alternatively, the rod can be hung from chains either secured on a picture rail or attached to hooks inserted in the ceiling. However, note that this alternative method is best suited to large textiles and looks out of scale with small ones.

Rugs & Carpets

Introduction

The antique rugs covered in this section fall into two main categories: flat-woven, or tapestry-type, and knotted pile. Flat-woven rugs are mentioned by the writers of ancient Greece and Rome. Knotted-pile rugs originated in Mongolia around 1000 B.C. and were brought to the Middle East, notably Persia and Turkey, by migrating tribes. The export of pile rugs westward into Europe followed the arrival of the Moors in Spain, the Crusades of the 11th–13th centuries, the travels of Marco Polo and Venetian trade with the East from the 13th century on.

The production of pile rugs in Europe began in Spain in the 12th century, but remained small in scale until the 17th century, when Poland, Romania, Italy, Sweden, England and France developed industries. France's main rug-making centers were at Savonnerie and Aubusson, England's at Wilton and Axminster. In North America, flat-woven ethnic rugs were made by Native Americans from the 16th century on (and later by European settlers). Industrial production of pile-woven rugs began in the United States during the second half of the 19th century.

The loom

Both flat-weave and knotted-pile rugs are made on a loom whose basic principle of operation has changed little over the centuries. Most looms are upright wooden frames which hold the vertical warp threads of the rug under tension. This allows the weaver to sit on a plank in front of the loom and pass the horizontal weft threads over and under the warp threads, and to knot any pile fabric to them. Working from the bottom up, the weaver raises the plank as the work progresses.

An alternative is the horizontal loom. Held by stakes driven into the ground, it is easy to move and therefore favoured by nomadic tribes. The weavers (usually in pairs) sit on top of the completed weave or pile as they work along the warps.

During the Industrial Revolution, the traditional methods of making rugs on hand looms were initially augmented, and eventually supplanted, in many major weaving centres, by devices powered at first by steam and later by electricity.

Traditional flat weaving

There are two basic types of flat-woven rug: the Kelim and the Soumak. Kelim weaves originate from Turkey and Persia, and are made by weaving horizontal weft threads in front of and behind alternate vertical warp threads, then beating them down with a comb hammer. Soumak weaves originate from northeastern Iran and the Caucasus, and have weft threads which are passed over two warp threads and looped back around them before being passed forward to the next pair of warps. With both, motifs and patterns are created by the weaving method and the use of

Oriental and Persian rugs
A collection of rugs from the Orient and Persia (now Iran),
with a Kelim-covered cushion from the Balkans.

different-coloured warp and weft threads. The majority of Kelims and Soumaks are made of wool. However, silk and cotton ones are also produced.

Traditional pile knotting

Knotted-pile rugs are produced by tensioning parallel warp threads vertically on the loom. Short lengths of yarn are then knotted to pairs of warp threads across the width of the rug. After a row of knots is completed, a continuous weft thread is passed over and under alternate warps, then beaten down with a heavy comb hammer before the next row of pile is woven. The length of the pile is usually trimmed after each knot has been tied and then again when a row is finished.

In knotted-pile carpets, motifs and patterns are created by using weft threads made up of one or more strands of coloured yarn and by arranging the different-coloured knots in various positions. The three basic knots are Turkish (Ghiordes), Persian (Senneh) and Jufti. Descriptions are given on p.166.

Kelim ends, fringe and side cords

The ends of both flat-woven and knotted-pile rugs are commonly known as Kelim ends. These are basically an extension of the flat-weaving process, in which the warp extends beyond the weft to form fringe or tassels, or is woven into braid. Not only are they decorative, they also protect the weave and pile of the rug.

The edges of rugs are secured and decorated with side cords. These usually consist of one or more warp threads bound by weft threads. (If there is more than one warp thread, they are twisted together.) An alternative arrangement involves weaving the wefts in a figure-of-eight through several pairs of warps.

Dyes

Until the mid-19th century, all yarns were dyed with vegetable or animal extracts. Typical examples include cochineal red, weld-plant green, oak-bark brown, indigo blue and vine-leaf yellow. All could be combined to produce a wide range of colours. The main advantages of these dyes were their aesthetically pleasing soft tones, colourfastness (in most cases) and resistance to fading. However, they were superseded by the invention in 1856 of cheaper aniline dyes, synthesized from coal tar. Many aniline dyes proved unstable and changed radically in colour over time. They were also harsher in appearance than their vegetable and animal counterparts. Aniline dyes were in turn superseded, in the 1920s, by stable synthetic chromatic dyes. However, recently there has been a revival in the use of vegetable dyes, largely because of their unequalled softness and subtlety of colour.

Tools and materials

You need relatively few tools to make minor repairs to old rugs and carpets, and they are all readily available from haberdashery departments and hardware stores. The quantity of materials you need depends largely on the sort of repair and cleaning problems you face. The basic cleaning fluids and chemicals are included here. For more information on the wide choice of substances that can be employed for stain removal, also see pp.86–9 and 144–5.

Tools

1 Iron In combination with blotting paper, this removes various stains.

2 Pliers Slip-joint or long-nose pliers to pull threaded needles through thick pile rugs when making repairs.

3 Scissors Trim fringe with a small pair of straight-bladed scissors. Trim pile with nail scissors with curved blades (alternatively, buy a pair of pile scissors with a flat edge specifically designed for the purpose). A pair of 20cm dressmaker's scissors are useful for various tasks.

4 Needles You will need a selection of straight and curved needles to make various repairs to rugs and carpets. To work with thick gauges of yarn, select needles with large eyes. You will need tapestry needles (sizes 20 and 22), and sewing needles (sizes 2, 6 and 8).

5 Thimble This is essential when repairing most rugs and carpets. It sometimes requires considerable force to push a needle through the backing or pile of a rug, and it is easy to hurt your fingers on the eye end of the needle.

YOU WILL ALSO NEED:

Carpet beater Beating small rugs and carpets removes particles of grit and dust. Carpet beaters are available from some hardware stores and importers of Middle Eastern basketwork products.

Vacuum cleaner Must have an attachment for cleaning carpets and upholstery. Use to remove dust and other dirt before repairing or cleaning and treating stains. To avoid damaging the fibres, select a low-suction setting.

Dustpan and brush For removing dust and other dirt. Use instead of a vacuum cleaner if one with variable suction isn't available.

Soft-bristle scrubbing brush For specified cleaning and stain-removal tasks.

Hair-drier In specified circumstances, and when set to low heat, this speeds the drying process after general cleaning and stain removal.

Utility or craft knife To cut old and new threads and yarns.

Large wooden clothes pegs To secure small rugs on a clothesline for dusting.

Heavy-duty clothesline To hold small rugs during dusting with a carpet beater.

Bradawl or blunt needle To unpick frayed weft threads and loose knots.

Tweezers To help pull finer threads through when making repairs.

Hammer For hammering in carpet tacks when attaching rugs to wooden frames during reweaving.

Carpet tacks Use the thinnest tacks available.

Heavy-duty cardboard tube A 50cm length to give support when repairing the edges or ends of rugs.

Tailor's chalk To mark a cutting line when repairing splits and tears.

Materials

6 Wool or silk thread For repairing the pile and mending the fringe of most rugs and carpets. Try to match the colour and weight of the new thread as closely as possible to the original. The two basic types of yarn required are known as tapestry wool and crewel wool.

7 Cotton and linen sewing thread Strong cotton and linen thread are required when making various kinds of structural repairs. These threads are available in a wide choice of colours and thicknesses, and should be matched as closely as possible to the original in the rug.

8 Beeswax To lubricate needles and cotton and linen threads. Sold in small blocks or, as an alternative, you can use a beeswax candle.

9 White blotting paper Use when testing for colour-fastness, mopping up spills and, in combination with an iron, to remove grease and wax.

10 Carpet shampoo Buy a shampoo specifically designed for cleaning rugs and carpets. Refer to the advice on testing for colourfastness, and the limitations on its use, on pp.158–9.

11 Wool detergent In specified situations, use a good-quality detergent for cleaning and stain removal.

12 Potato flour For dry-cleaning, but use only in specified situations.

13 Salt For stain removal.

14 White vinegar For stain removal.

YOU WILL ALSO NEED:

Cotton wool For cleaning.

Nylon monofilament screen To support small rugs during immersion and washing in a bathtub.

Mothballs These and other specified insect-repellents should be used when storing rugs and carpets.

Brown paper Thick paper on which to lay a large rug or carpet when dusting it on the floor.

Planed wood Approximately 1.2–3m of 1.25 x 7.5cm planed softwood to make a tensioning frame.

Nails To make a tensioning frame.

General cleaning and displaying

To maximize the life of rugs and carpets and to protect their fibres from damage, you must clean them regularly. How often you have to do this depends on various factors. For example, if the piece is displayed hung from a pole or wooden batten, or covers a tabletop, it will attract less dirt and highly damaging grit than if it is used as a floor covering. Also, rugs and carpets housed in rural environments tend to remain cleaner for longer than their urban counterparts, as there is nearly always more atmospheric pollution in built-up areas than in the countryside.

In addition to cleaning rugs and carpets regularly, you should deal with any accidental stains as soon as possible. Numerous substances in general use around the home can disfigure colour and pattern, as well as damage fibres. The latter can also be caused by incorrect methods of display: rugs and carpets hung from poles and battens will suffer if the method of attachment doesn't spread the load evenly across their length.

Before you wash or remove stains from a rug or carpet, no matter what type it is, you must first test it for colourfastness. If any of the colours run, you should have the piece cleaned professionally by a specialist in antique rugs. Avoid regular carpet-cleaning companies; the powerful chemicals they use to clean modern carpets will, over time, cause further harm to an antique rug. Apart from dusting it regularly, never attempt to clean a very rare or valuable rug or carpet yourself. Instead, find a specialist cleaner to carry out the task.

Dusting a small, sturdy rug

Rugs should be dusted regularly, and always before washing and removing stains, to remove small pieces of grit and dirt that gradually erode the fibres if left to accumulate. Regular dusting will also remove any moth eggs that might be incubating in the fibres.

1 To dust a small rug or carpet, hang it outdoors on a high, heavy-duty clothesline. Choose a dry, windless day and hang the piece with as little of it overlapping as possible, so that as much as posssible of the back is exposed for beating.

2 Beat quite vigorously across the back of the rug with an old-fashioned carpet beater. Never use a thin cane or stick for beating: the force of each blow won't spread over a large enough area and you might damage the fibres. Don't beat the front of the rug: you will only succeed in driving the dirt and grit deeper into the pile or weave.

3 Once the dust has stopped rising, pull the rug over the line and attach it near to the other end, again with as little turned over as possible. Beat the newly exposed back as before.

4 Attach a curtain and upholstery cleaning accessory to the hose of a vacuum cleaner. Vacuum the back of the rug, using a light suction setting for finer rugs and medium suction for coarser ones.

5 Vacuum the front of the rug. With flat-woven rugs, work the accessory up and down the length of the rug. With knotted-pile rugs, always work in the direction of the pile: working against it may loosen the threads.

Dusting a large or fragile rug

If a rug is too fragile to be beaten vigorously, or too large to be hung from a clothesline, you must clean it flat on the floor. Proceed as follows:

1 Roll up the rug and vacuum up any dust or dirt from the floor underneath it.

2 Put sheets of thick brown paper on the floor, and unroll the rug pile side down on top of the paper. Do not use old newspaper: the ink may be unstable and stain the surface of the rug.

3 If the rug is fairly sturdy, beat it vigorously with a carpet beater. If it is fragile, beat it very gently. Every now and then, give the rug a shake to help dislodge the dirt.

4 Carefully lift the rug and pull out the sheets of paper. Fold them over so that the dirt doesn't fall onto the floor (or the back of the rug) and dispose of them.

5 Carefully vacuum the back of the rug. Use the lightest possible suction on fragile rugs. Use a mid-strength suction on sturdier ones.

6 Turn the rug over. If it is flat-woven, work up and down its length with the vacuum cleaner. If it has pile, work in the direction of the pile.

Testing for colourfastness

After dusting you can wash an antique rug or carpet with a good-quality carpet shampoo. However, if the piece is rare, valuable, fragile or made of silk, you should take it to a cleaner specializing in antique rugs. You should also have a rug or carpet professionally cleaned if the dyes used are not colourfast. Test for colourfastness first, as follows.

1 Dab a small, unobtrusive area of the rug or carpet with a piece of cotton wool, or a white cotton rag, moistened with the carpet shampoo (diluted to the manufacturer's specifications).

2 Leave for about five minutes, then press a piece of white blotting paper onto the treated area. If the blotting paper remains unmarked, the area tested is colourfast. If it absorbs dye, the piece is not colourfast and must be cleaned professionally.

3 You must test each and every colour in the piece in the same way. Don't proceed with the washing unless you have established that all of them are colourfast.

Washing on a countertop or floor

After testing the rug or carpet for colourfastness, inspect it for damage. If any repairs are necessary, you could do them before washing (see pp.160–71). However, at this stage it is preferable to secure temporarily any loose or damaged pieces, so that a permanent repair can be matched to the clean rug or carpet after washing. To make such temporary repairs, use an ordinary sewing needle, cotton thread and a simple tacking stitch (see p.248).

To wash a rug or carpet either on the floor or on a work surface, proceed as follows.

1 In a plastic bucket or mixing container, dilute some carpet shampoo with warm (not hot) water. Mix the shampoo and water in the ratio and to the volume recommended by the manufacturer.

2 Tackling no more than a quarter of a square metre at a time, gently work the cleaning solution into the fibres with a large, soft-bristled scrubbing brush. With a pile carpet, first gently brush against the direction of the pile, then with the pile.

3 Rinse off the shampoo by gently dabbing with pieces of clean, white cotton rag dampened with clean, lukewarm water. Work against any pile and then with it. Repeat this procedure, changing the rag and water when necessary until all the shampoo has been removed. Then move onto an adjacent, slightly overlapping area. Repeat the shampooing and rinsing until you have covered the entire surface of the rug.

4 Clean fringes, Kelim ends and side cords in the same way as you cleaned the main body of the rug.

5 Leave the rug to dry flat on the work surface or floor. Never hang it to dry from a clothesline, because when it is damp, the additional weight of the water may cause it to stretch and distort. Make the room as warm and dry as possible. You can slightly accelerate the drying process by moving a hair-drier on a cool or low-heat setting about 15cm above the surface. Don't walk on the rug, or place furniture on top of it, until it is completely dry.

Removing stains

Always remove as quickly as possible any substance accidentally spilled on or rubbed into a rug or carpet. If you are dealing with a liquid, very lightly dab some white blotting paper or white cotton rag over the affected area to mop up as much as possible. Then, if the rug is rare, delicate or valuable, entrust it to a specialist cleaner as soon as possible. The longer you leave the stain, the more difficult it will become to remove it satisfactorily.

With less valuable and sturdier rugs, you may be able to treat the stained area yourself. Refer to pp.88–9 and 144–5 for a comprehensive list of stains and their treatments. Always test for colourfastness before proceeding.

Using, displaying and storing

There are various simple precautions you can take to maximize the life of a rug or carpet when it is in use, on display or in storage.

● Make sure that underlying floorboards are clean, dry and close-fitting. Fibres are easily damaged by exposure to moisture or if trodden down into hard-edged recesses. Also, dust can rise through gaps in the floor and discolour the back of the rug. Laying rugs on non-slip underlay, or on top of a wall-to-wall carpet, will help to alleviate this problem.

● Avoid placing rugs on stone or ceramic-tiled floors that have protruding sharp edges, as these will soon cut underlying fibres.

● Place protective cups underneath the castors and legs of furniture. This distributes the weight over a larger area and avoids crushing and denting the pile of a rug or carpet. For the same reason, it is also a good idea from time to time to move heavier pieces of furniture to different positions in a room.

● Rugs placed in front of open fires are always vulnerable to flying sparks. You can minimize the risk of damage by installing a fine-meshed metal fireguard around the hearth.

● Never lay antique rugs and carpets in bathrooms and kitchens, because of the high levels of moisture and the constant risk of accidental spillage.

● If you place a dining table on an antique rug, it is a good idea to lay a protective cloth over the rug during mealtimes. In previous centuries it was common practice to protect better-quality carpets from falling food and drink by employing a 'crumb cloth' made from heavy linen or cotton; this covering could be easily removed for washing.

● Whether a rug or carpet is laid on the floor, placed on a table or hung from a pole or batten, avoid placing it in direct sunlight or too close to radiators. Regular exposure to heat and strong light will make it brittle and cause colours to fade.

● If you wish to hang a rug or carpet, use one of the three methods described under 'Hanging large textiles' on pp.150–1. Make sure that it is always hung from one of the ends (rather than the sides), so that the stronger warp threads (rather than the more vulnerable weft ones) take the strain.

● If you need to store a rug or carpet, it is best to roll it round a stout tube or pole. Folding it flat places considerable strain on the creased or folded fibres.

Mending fringes and Kelim ends

Although basically hard-wearing, rugs are susceptible to considerable wear and tear, particularly if they are constantly under foot. Typical damage to fringes and Kelim ends takes the form of untwisting and weakening of the end-to-end warp threads, and breaking of the side-to-side weft threads. When the latter happens, the weave and the knots in the main body of the rug are left unprotected and soon start to fray and break. Various methods are used to repair fringes and Kelim ends. One of the four shown here will prove suitable if the original fringe or end is basically intact, but needs strengthening. However, if part of the fringe is missing, and new warp threads need to be inserted, turn to p.162.

However, if part of the fringe is missing, and new warp threads need to be inserted, turn to p.162.

YOU WILL NEED:
Bradawl or blunt needle
Small pair of straight or curved scissors
Tweezers
Beeswax (block or candle)
Standard straight sewing needle
Tapestry needle Size 20 or 22.
Thimble
Pair of slip-joint or long-nose pliers
Strong cotton or linen thread Size 18 in a colour to match either the fringe or pile.
Strong wool yarn In a colour to match side cords.
Strong silk thread In a colour to match either the fringe or the pile.

Preparation

All the following methods of repair begin with removing any frayed weft back to the point where there is a complete, unbroken line of weft across the end of the rug. In addition, you must remove any broken knots attached to broken lines of weft. Do this as follows.

1 Unpicking the weft

● Working from the back of the rug, use a blunt needle or a small bradawl to carefully unpick the first line of loose or frayed weft thread and any knots that are attached to it.

2 Cutting the weft

● If the line of weft is still attached to either end of the rug, cut it free with a pair of small straight- or curved-bladed scissors. When you are doing this, it is particularly important that you don't cut through any of the warp threads.

3 Unpicking the knots

● Repeat steps 1 and 2 until you come to the last row of damaged knots. Unpick these carefully, one by one, with a blunt needle and a pair of tweezers. Continue until you have a continuous, unbroken line of weft across the end of the rug. You can now proceed with one of the four methods (illustrated right and opposite) designed to safeguard the original weft.

Simple knotting

This is the simplest of all the methods for securing the weft, but it is only suitable if the fringe is more than 5cm long. Note also that it is not the most secure of the methods illustrated and that over time further movement or loosening of the weft may take place.

1 Looping the knot

● Lay the rug face up on a work surface, with the fringe facing you.
● Starting at one side, twist four or five warp threads together.
● Fold the threads into a loop and pull the ends through the loop to make a simple overhand knot. Don't tighten the knot fully at this stage.

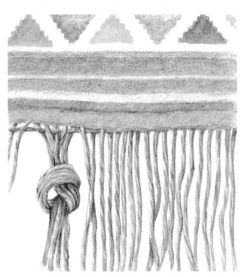

2 Tightening the knot

● You must now decide how close to the outer weft thread you wish to tighten the knot. The closer the knot is to the weft, the less vulnerable the weft is to further damage.
● Tighten the knot by pulling it with your thumb and finger towards the weft. Repeat steps 1 and 2 for the rest of the warps, making sure that all the knots align.

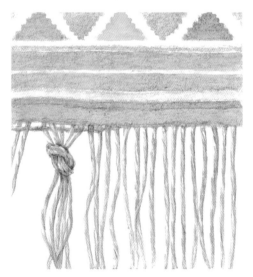

Overcasting (thread)

Although overcasting is not the most attractive repair method, it is very strong and easy to execute.

1 Sewing with linen or cotton

• Lay the rug face down on a work surface, with the fringe facing away from you.

• Thread a straight needle with strong prewaxed linen or cotton thread (or wax the thread yourself by rubbing it with a block of beeswax or a beeswax candle). The thread must be of a diameter appropriate to the fineness or coarseness of the rug.

• Hold the fringe out with your free hand, so that you will be able to see the needle coming out of the body of the rug. Then, working from right to left, push the needle into the rug. The depth to which the needle penetrates should be such that you will be able to catch the last line of weft on each stitch, and also such that it doesn't show above the height of the pile on the front, or show, side. The stitches should slope backwards and be spaced approximately 12mm below the weft and between every four warp threads. As you work your way along, pull the thread down tightly enough to slightly depress the line of weft.

• When you reach the other side of the rug, fasten off the thread with a simple knot.

Note: On some coarser rugs, you may need to use a pair of slip-joint or long-nose pliers to work the needle in and out of the weave and pile.

Overcasting (yarn)

This method is particularly suitable for damaged fringes where some of the end border has been damaged and is missing and a new contrasting-coloured line is required to finish the edge of the original design. It is a very strong method of repair, especially when used on short-pile rugs.

1 Sewing with yarn

• It is usually best to choose a woollen yarn that matches the colour of the side cord. The yarn should also be of a diameter proportionate to the thickness of the rug and should be threaded through a tapestry needle also of appropriate size (usually either size 20 or 22).

• Lay the rug face up on a work surface, with the fringe pointing away from you.

• Insert the yarn into and out of the right-hand side cord to secure the end.

• Lay the yarn in one continuous strand on top of the fringe and across the complete width of the rug.

• Wax a new strand of yarn by rubbing it with beeswax, and rethread the needle.

• Secure to the right-hand side cord as before.

• Use a simple overcast stitch to secure pairs of warp threads together along the new overlaid weft wool. Pull the stitches reasonably tight throughout, then finish off in the left-hand side cord in the same way that you started on the right.

Chain stitching

This method is better suited to fringes made of cotton or silk than those made of wool. This is because the threads must be pulled tighter than is generally advisable for wool thread in order to stop them from slipping off later.

1 Making the chain

• Lay the rug face up on a work surface, with the fringe pointing away from you.

• Thread a cotton or silk thread through a straight sewing needle. The needle and thread should be of a diameter proportionate to the thickness of the fringe.

• Starting on the right-hand side, run the first stitch towards you, underneath the overcast yarn on the side cord, for about 5cm, and then back again at a slight angle. Do not fasten off with a knot, but pull the thread tight enough so that it can't be seen on the surface of the rug.

• Pass the thread across the front of the first pair of warp threads and hold it with your free thumb about 6mm above the weft. Then pass the needle behind the pair of warp threads, from right to left and through the loop held by your thumb. To tighten, pull to the left and parallel to the weft.

• Repeat with each pair of warps across the rug. Make sure all the stitches are even and equally tensioned.

• To finish off, secure the thread as tightly as possible within the left-hand side cord, as you did on the right.

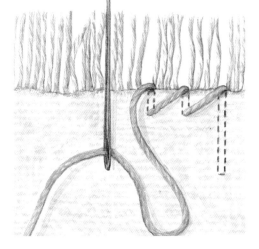
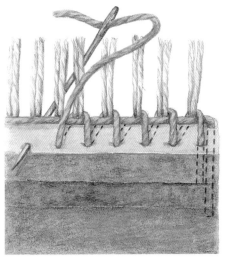
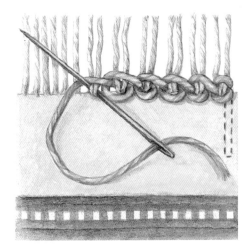

Weaving new warp threads and fringes

1 Beginning the stitching

- Lay the rug face down on a work surface, with the fringe facing you. Thread a straight needle with linen or cotton cord that closely matches the warp. Starting to the right of the damage, insert the needle and thread into the rug in line with the first broken warp, and through the side of the first knot.
- Push the needle in to emerge approximately 12mm from the edge of the rug. Leave an end of thread that is longer than the intended length of the new fringe.

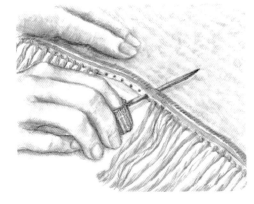

2 Making the first loop

- Loop the needle around to the right and push it back into the rug about 12mm from the edge.
- Pass the needle back through the other side of the knot that you went through in step 1.
- Pull the needle and thread through so that they emerge parallel with the first warp thread. Make sure that you don't pull through the length of extended thread you left at the end of step 1.

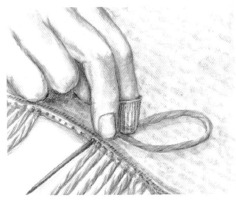

3 Continuing the loops

- Repeat steps 1 and 2 across the missing section of fringe, to produce a series of equal-length loops extending from the end of the rug. Throughout the process, make absolutely sure that none of the stitches is visible on the pile (or 'show') side of the rug.
- When you reach the other side of the repair, fasten off the last loop with a simple knot.

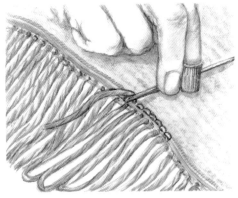

4 Trimming the fringe

- Adjust the position of the rug so that the fringe hangs down over the edge of the work surface.
- Using long-bladed scissors, cut the loops to run parallel with the rest of the fringe.
- Secure the new fringe with one of the stitches shown on p.161.

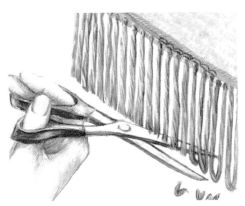

Man- or machine-made

Many machine-made pile rugs are so well made it can be quite hard to distinguish them from hand-woven originals. However, examination of the fringe at the ends of the rug should enable you to establish the method of manufacture. As in the example shown below, the fringe on hand-woven pile rugs is a natural continuation of the warp threads. On most machine-woven pile rugs, the fringe is a trimming, secured to the ends of the rug by oversewing (often with a machined chain stitch).

Detail of a hand-woven rug

This 19th-century hand-woven Caucasian pile rug has a short fringe that is a continuation of the warp threads, rather than an oversewn trim (as can be found on many 20th-century, machine-made copies).

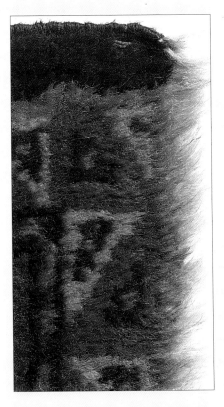

Repairing splits and tears

The repair technique demonstrated below is an accepted method for mending a split or tear in the edge or end of a rug. Its use should be limited to coarsely woven rugs, and it should certainly not be applied to rare or valuable rugs. One of the main advantages of the technique is that it allows you to make good small areas in which a few rows of pile have come adrift and are now missing, without having to resort to reweaving. If done well, the repair will be difficult to spot, particularly at a glance. However, note that this type of repair is not an example of invisible mending. Because it requires you to cut a thin sliver of pile and backing from the rug, it leaves a small amount of distortion in the pattern.

YOU WILL NEED:
Dressmaker's scissors With 20cm blades.
Tailor's chalk
Cardboard tube 50cm long.
Stout cotton or linen thread Quilting thread is best, or, wax the thread yourself.
Beeswax in block or candle form
Straight sewing needle
Thimble

1 Cutting along the weft

● Place the rug face down on a work surface, with the tear next to you.

● Take a pair of long-bladed dressmaker's scissors and make a straight cut, parallel with the weft, along one edge of the tear and towards the middle of the rug. You should extend the cut to just beyond the point where the pile is missing (which may be further in than the end of the tear).

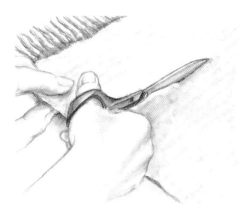

2 Overlapping the sides

● Grip the two sides of the tear and pull them together so that the straight edge you cut in step 1 lies on top of the uncut side of the tear and completely covers any fraying.

● If a small bump forms in the rug around the end of the tear, get rid of it by slightly extending the length of the cut you made in step 1.

3 Marking and cutting

● Overlap the sides again and, using a piece of tailor's chalk, mark on the back of the rug a line that runs parallel to and against the overlapping side of the cut edge.

● Cut along this line, with the dressmaker's scissors, towards the middle of the rug to the point where it meets the end of the edge cut in step 1.

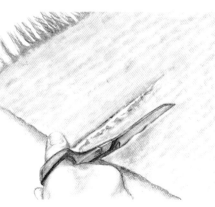

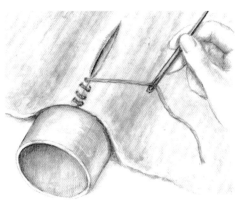

4 Stitching the repair

● Support the torn section, face down as before, on a length of cardboard tube. Take great care when handling the cut edges of the rug. Because some of the knots will have been cut in step 3, it will be all too easy to fray the edges.

● Thread a straight sewing needle with heavy cotton or linen thread. (If the thread isn't pre-waxed, wax it yourself with a small beeswax block or candle.)

● Working from the outside of the tear towards the centre of the rug, secure the two sides with a simple zigzag stitch.

● When you reach the end of the tear, repeat the stitching in the reverse direction, and fasten off with a double-hitch knot (see p.249).

Repairing side cords

Side cords, like fringes and Kelim ends, are designed both to be decorative and give protection to the main body of a rug. Because they are usually the thickest part of a rug – standing slightly above the main body – they wear fastest if the rug is laid on the floor. Side cords are formed by binding several warp threads together with the weft threads as each row of knots is completed during the weaving process. In many cases, the cord is then built up and strengthened with an additional outer binding. However, there are regional variations on the style of binding, and the most typical examples are illustrated below. Wear and tear invariably takes the form of erosion of the outer binding first, followed by a gradual breakdown of the core – the warp and weft threads.

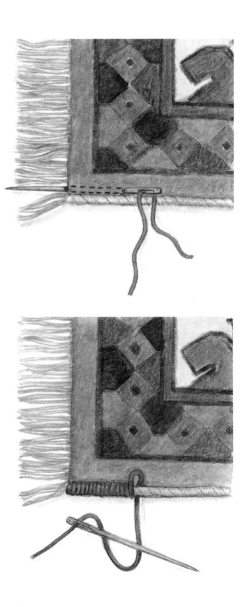

YOU WILL NEED:

Tapestry needle Size 20 or 22, depending on the thickness of the rug.
Tapestry or crewel wool In colours to match the original binding.
Small straight-bladed scissors
Thimble
Cotton thread In the same thickness and colour as the original warp and weft threads.
Cotton, wool or silk thread In thicknesses and colours to match the original binding.

Typical side cords

Methods of binding vary from region to region. For example, Isfahan (Iranian) rugs have a single binding, many Caucasian rugs have a double binding, and some Kurdish rugs have three (or more) bindings.

Top *Side cord held with a single binding.*
Middle *Side cord held with a double binding.*
Bottom *Side cord held with a triple binding.*

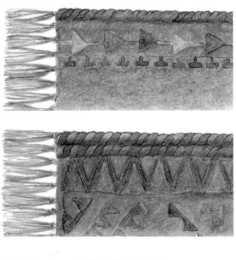

Overcasting

Most rugs have an outer binding of wool, although in some cases silk is used. If the binding is wearing thin, but is unbroken and the core threads are intact, you can make a simple repair to minimize further damage. You will need a tapestry needle, size 20 or 22, depending on the thickness of the rug, and coloured yarn (or silk or cotton) that matches the original binding.

1 Securing the end of the thread
● Lay the rug face up, with the damaged edge facing you. Thread the needle. If repairing a fine rug, use one strand of yarn or thread. If repairing a thicker, coarser rug, use a double strand.
● Attach the yarn or thread by running the needle for approximately 5cm through the side cord until it emerges through the fringe at the left end of the rug.
● Pull the yarn or thread through so that its other end lies just below the surface of the side cord.

2 Stitching the roll
● Working from left to right, overcast the yarn or thread in a continuous, slightly diagonal roll until you reach the rug's other end. Keep the stitches as tight and as close as possible. If you reach the end of the yarn or thread before finishing the job, add another length (see 'Joining threads', p.248).
● Finish by running the yarn or thread through the side cord, as you did when starting in step 1.

Repairing the core

If the binding has worn through and the core threads have begun to fray or are broken, you must repair them before you overcast the outer binding. If you do not repair the binding and core threads, the weave and pile of the main body of the rug will remain vulnerable to damage.

While this repair is more demanding than the relatively straightforward process of overcasting, it is a feasible project for the amateur restorer. However, don't use it on a rug that is either rare or valuable.

1 Trimming loose ends

- Lay the rug face up on a work surface, with the damaged edge facing you.
- Using tweezers and a pair of small, straight-bladed scissors, carefully cut and pull away any damaged pieces of the outer binding that remain wound round the damaged or partly missing section of the core.
- Very carefully snip off any broken warp threads, again using a pair of small, straight-bladed scissors. It is important that you make a clean, even cut on each side of the damaged section. Don't cut into the original binding, and leave about 3mm of warp extending past the outer binding.

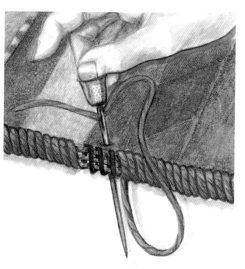

2 Sewing the new warps

- Thread a sewing needle with thread that matches the original cotton or linen warps.
- Insert the needle and thread into the side cord about 2.5cm from the end of one side of the missing section.
- Push the needle so that it emerges with the new thread in line with one of the original warp threads.
- Then push the needle into the end of the original side cord opposite, so that it lines up with the counterpart of the warp thread on the first side.
- Push the needle up through the side cord about 2.5cm. Push it back through, repeating the previous sequence in reverse. Continue to replace all the warps.

3 Sewing the new wefts

- To add the new wefts to a single cord binding, loop them around the new warps and into the body of the rug, as in the illustration. Each loop should be taken approximately 12mm into the body of the rug before emerging and re-entering. Start and finish with a double-hitch, and trim the excess.
- Don't pull the loops (stitches) too tight, or they will alter the tension of the new warps. Also, make sure that they don't show through the pile.

Note: When repairing a double or treble cord binding, weave the new weft threads alternately over and under each band in a figure-of-eight movement.

4 Overcasting

- Once you have completed the new wefts, bind the new section of core using the overcasting technique shown on the opposite page.
- As before, you should choose a yarn or thread that matches that of the original binding as closely as possible. Also, closely inspect the original binding to see if a single or double strand of yarn or thread was used. On coarser rugs, a double strand is typical.

Repairing the pile

The knotted pile of rugs can be damaged in various ways. Common causes range from the passage of feet over the years, to cigarette burns, sparks and hot coals from open fires, and consumption by moths. In most cases the amateur restorer can repile the affected area, provided it isn't larger than a few square centimetres and if the warp and weft threads are intact. Larger areas of damage should be entrusted to a professional restorer, as should all damage to rare or valuable rugs. If the warp and weft threads of the rug are not in good condition, they must first be rewoven (for technique, see pp.168–71).

Before repiling, clean the rug (see pp.158–9). This will allow you to colour-match the new yarn or thread to the originals. It is also important to match the texture of the new threads, plus the type of knot used, to the original ones so that the repair sits relatively unnoticed among the adjacent areas of the rug.

YOU WILL NEED:

Tweezers

Tapestry needle Size 20 or 22.

Yarn or thread Of the same colour, weight and texture as the original ones that make up the pile.

Scissors With curved blades.

Fine-bristled wire brush

Knots

There are three basic types of knot used in hand-made oriental rugs: the Turkish (Ghiordes), the Persian (Senneh) and the Jufti. The Turkish knot (below) is symmetrical, while the Persian (above right) is asymmetrical and tends to be used for closely woven and denser piles. The Jufti (below right) is used for the coarsest rugs. It can be in either Turkish or Persian form, but is tied around four warp threads instead of two.

Persian (Senneh) knot

Turkish or Persian?

Before you can begin repiling, you must first be able to recognize the type of knot you will be replacing. To do this, locate a row of knots running parallel to the warp threads (i.e. along the length, not the width, of the rug). As in the illustrations below, use your fingers and thumbs to bend back the rug on each side of the knots.

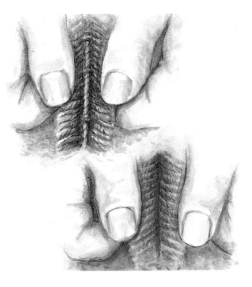

Turkish knots (above)
You can't part the two end threads of Turkish knots, but you can see the bases of the knots on the warps.

Persian knots (top)
You can part the two end threads of Persian knots to reveal the underlying warps.

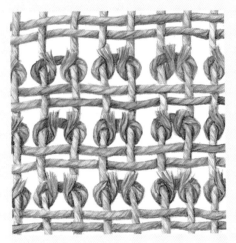

Turkish (Ghiordes) knot

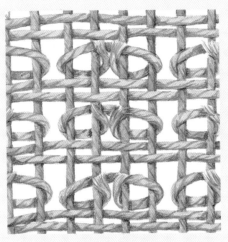

Jufti knot (in Turkish form)

Turkish repiling

Before repiling with Turkish knots, first unpick the damaged original pile by pulling out the threads with tweezers. This will leave the underlying warp and weft threads clear. Don't try to make the bare patch into a rectangular or square shape; a ragged-edged repair is invariably less visible than a straight-edged one.

1 Starting the knot

● Lay the rug face up on a work surface, with the pile running towards you.
● Thread a tapestry needle with 45–60cm of yarn. Starting bottom left, pass the needle's point down between the first and second strands of warp threads.
● Push the needle under and around the left-hand warp thread and pull it through to leave 4cm of yarn sticking up above the height of the original pile.
● Hold down the 4cm of yarn with your free thumb. Pass the needle from right to left under and around the right-hand warp thread.
● Pull the needle and thread up tightly between the first and second warps. Then move to your right to repeat with the next pair of warps. Depending on the pattern of the rug, you may need to change the colour of the yarn at this point.
● Repeat the above, leaving the loops of the pile 4cm long and uncut, until you have completed the repiling. Then refer to 'Trimming the pile', top right.

Persian repiling

Persian knots are slightly more difficult to execute than Turkish knots, because you must repeatedly pass the needle from one hand to the other. This may feel awkward at first if you aren't ambidextrous.

You must also establish whether your rug has a right- or a left-hand lay, as this determines the method of knotting. To establish the direction of the lay, smooth down the carpet with your hand so that the pile runs towards you rather than away from you. You will notice immediately that the pile lies either slightly to the left or to the right of dead centre.

1 Repiling a right-hand lay

● Begin in the same position as for the Turkish knot (see left) and pass the needle and yarn under and around the left-hand warp.
● Then pass the needle to your other hand and, as in the illustration, pass the needle back over the first warp and under the second (right-hand) one.
● Then pass the needle up again between second and third warps.
● Pull the yarn tight and, as with the Turkish knot, leave the loops 4cm long.
● Repeat the knotting sequence until you have completed the repiling. Then refer to 'Trimming the pile', above.

2 Repiling a left-hand lay

● Starting at the bottom right-hand corner, pass the needle and yarn under the first warp thread from left to right, and pull them up between the knotted row to the right of the first warp thread.
● Transfer the needle to your other hand, and pass it back over the first warp, under the second one, and up once more through the second and third warps.
● Pull the yarn tight, again leaving loops 4cm long, and continue with the knotting sequence until you have completed the repiling. Then refer to 'Trimming the pile', above.

Trimming the pile

Whether you are using Turkish or Persian knots, you must trim the pile once you have finished knotting. Do this with curved scissors, making sure that you don't trim the new pile to below the height of the original.

To finish off, gently wire-brush the tips of the yarn in the direction of the pile. You can also gently hammer down the pile with the brush to compress and 'age' it.

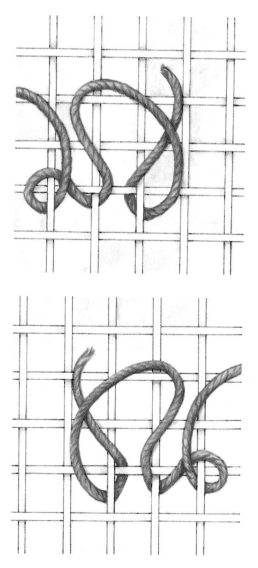

Reweaving

It is only possible to repile a section of rug if the damage to the knots and pile has not extended to the underlying warp and weft threads. If these have been damaged (or if they are missing, along with the pile) it will be necessary to replace them. However, this task is only practical for an amateur to undertake if the damage or hole isn't particularly extensive: you should entrust any repair that is larger than 7–10 square centimetres to a professional restorer. Also, you should not attempt this sort of repair if the rug is particularly rare or valuable. Generally speaking, coarser wool rugs are the easiest type to deal with.

Before starting the repair work, you must inspect the old warp and weft threads to see which fibre(s) they are made of. Most are made from cotton or wool, or a combination of the two. Sometimes the warp threads will be cotton and the wefts wool (or vice versa). If you are not sure about the nature of the fibre you are dealing with, clip a short strand of warp and weft from the damaged area and try the fibre test described on p.139. If that doesn't resolve the problem, take the rug to a rug or fabric specialist for identification.

YOU WILL NEED
Utility or craft knife
Tweezers
Cotton thread To match the original warp or weft threads.
Wool yarn To match warps or wefts.
Beeswax in block or candle form
Tapestry needle Size 20 or 22.
Small, straight-bladed scissors
Small bradawl (or blunt needle)
Small wooden frame See p.170, step 1.
12mm fine carpet tacks
Hammer
Straight sewing needles Of a size suitable for the thickness of the warp and weft threads.
Thimble

Preparation

1 Cutting the back
- Lay the rug face down on a work surface, with the weft running from side to side.
- Using a utility knife, make a series of cuts through the back of the damaged section. The cuts should each be in a straight line between the knots and parallel with the warp threads. Make sure that you don't cut into the surrounding areas.

2 Clearing the debris
- Use a small pair of tweezers to carefully pick out the loose warp and weft threads (and any remaining knots).
- Once you have cleared the debris, inspect the shape of the hole. It must be square or rectangular. If one or more of the sides is slightly curved, repeat steps 1 and 2 to straighten it.

Stitching new warps

1 Starting off
- Lubricate the thread with beeswax, and thread it through the needle.
- Start at the bottom right-hand corner, with the rug face down. Push the needle through the back of the right-hand loop of the knot that lies three rows below the hole, and push it out just below the first row of knots that lie just below the hole's edge.

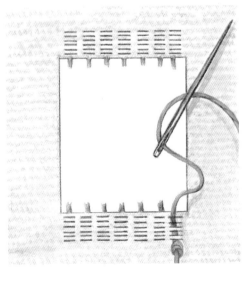

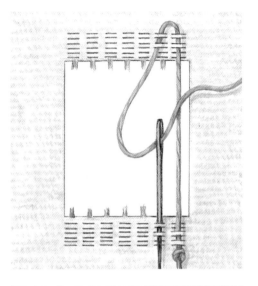

Trimming

Before proceeding to the new wefts and knots, you must remove the first row of original knots and wefts that lie next to the edges of the top and bottom of the hole.

2 Spanning the hole
● Pass the needle and thread over to the other side of the hole. Make sure that the thread runs parallel with the original warps.
● Push the needle through the right-hand loop of the opposite knot that lies in the second row of knots beyond the edge of the hole. (You must make sure that the needle and thread pass over the first row of knots that lie just beyond the hole's edge.)
● Keep the needle below the surface of the rug until it reaches the fourth row of knots back from the hole. Push it through the right-hand loop of the knot, as before. Then loop it around, and push it back in again to return through the left-hand loops of the knots.

1 Picking out knots
● Using a bradawl (or a blunt needle) and a small pair of tweezers, very carefully pick out the first row of knots that lie close to the edge at each end of the hole.
● Then, with a small pair of scissors, cut the exposed weft threads at each end of the hole. Make sure that you don't cut into the next row of knots.

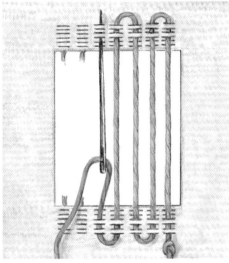

3 Completing the warps
● Pull the thread reasonably tight, and then pass the needle back over the hole to the other side. Again, the thread must run parallel to the first warp.
● Push in the needle as before, and repeat the stitching process until you have established the new warp threads right across the hole.
Note: Throughout this process you should establish a reasonably firm tension for the warps. However, do not pull the thread too tight. This can distort the weave of the rug and stop it from lying flat.

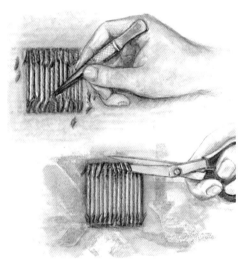

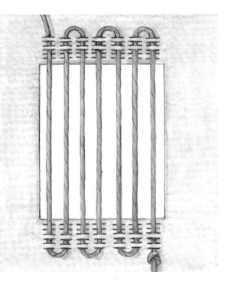

4 Knotting off
● Once you have covered the hole, secure the thread behind the last knot that you passed it through. Use a double-hitch knot to do this (see p.249), and cut off the excess thread with a small pair of scissors.

2 Trimming the warps
● Turn over the rug, so that it lies face up on the work surface.
● With a pair of straight-bladed scissors, carefully cut off the ends of the original warp threads that are slightly protruding over the hole. Cut as close to the row of knots as possible, making sure that you don't accidentally damage the knots or cut into the new warp threads.

Framing the rug

Before you can weave in the new weft threads and tie in the knots, you must first tension the warp threads. The best way to do this is to secure the rug to a simple wooden frame. It is extremely unlikely that you will have a wooden frame of the right dimensions simply waiting to be used for the purpose. However, it doesn't require any advanced carpentry skills to make a suitable frame: to form the four corners simply butt-join them with screws or nails.

1 Nailing to the frame

● Screw or nail four lengths of planed 1 x 7.5cm softwood to forrm a simple square-shaped frame. The internal width of the frame doesn't have to be much bigger than the damaged area, so a 30 x 30cm frame should suffice.

● Lay the rug face up over the frame, with the hole in the middle. The new warps should run exactly parallel with the sides of the frame.

● Using 12mm fine carpet tacks and a hammer, secure one end of the rug to the frame. Space the tacks about 12mm apart.

● Gently stretch the other end of the rug over the other end of the frame, to create an even, firm tension along all of the new warp threads. Then tack down with carpet tacks as before.

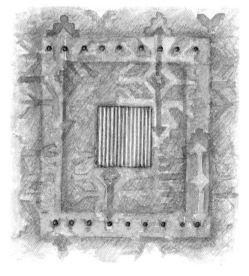

Rewefting, repiling and finishing

Having temporarily secured the rug to the wooden frame, you are now ready to begin the process of replacing the weft threads, tying in the new knots and trimming the pile to the correct height.

If you have not already done so, you must now choose a cotton thread or wool yarn that matches as closely as possible the fibre and size of the original weft threads (see 'Preparation', p.168). Having threaded the yarn or thread through a tapestry needle of a suitable diameter (either size 20 or 22), proceed as follows.

1 Positioning the wefts

● Starting with the end of the repair that is nearest to you, and working from left to right, slide the threaded needle alternately over and under the warp threads.

● When you reach the last warp on the right-hand edge of the repair, loop the weft thread around it and work your way back to the left side of the repair, passing the thread alternately over and under the warps as before.

Note: You should not cut the weft thread at this stage, nor should you attach it to the main body of the rug. Both of these tasks will be carried out at a later stage of the project.

2 Knotting

● Knot in the first row of pile to the warp threads (see 'Repairing the pile', pp.166–7).

Note: The type of knot you use – Turkish, Persian or Jufti – must not only match the original knots in the rug, but also align with them.

3 Packing the weft

● After you complete each row of knots, pack down the weft thread immediately above them with the side of a needle. Squeeze them down so that they align as closely as possible with the original wefts on each side of the repair.

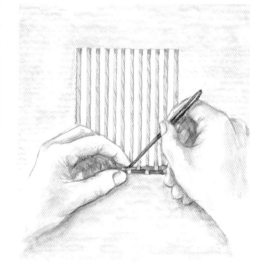

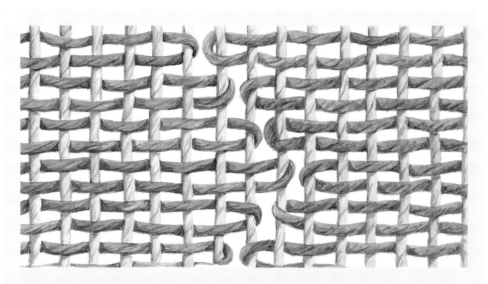

4 Completing the knots and weft
• Knot in the pile and pack down the weft alternately, until the patch is complete.

5 Stitching the sides and trimming
• Pull out the carpet tacks and lift the rug off the wooden frame.
• Wax strong cotton thread with beeswax and thread it through a straight sewing needle.
• With the rug face down, sew up the splits at the sides between the repair and the main body of the rug. Use a zigzag running stitch (see p.248).
• With the rug face up, trim the new pile as described on p.167.

Repairing Kelim and Soumak rugs

Repairs to the flatweave of both Kelim and Soumak rugs are carried out by replacing warp threads first and weft threads second. You should note that the design of Kelim rugs (above) is created by winding different-coloured weft threads back and forth across the warps – not from one side of the rug to the other as a continuous thread, but only as far across the warps as the pattern demands. Where different-coloured weft threads meet, a small gap is formed between the two warps.

The method of weaving Soumak rugs (below) differs slightly from that employed for Kelims. With Soumaks, the weft is passed over and under two (or sometimes four) warp threads, and then looped back over two warps before being carried forward again to the next pair of warps. The result is a continuous chain-like weave across the rug.

Flat-weave rugs
An example of traditional Kelim flat-weaving is shown above and of Soumak flat-weaving below.

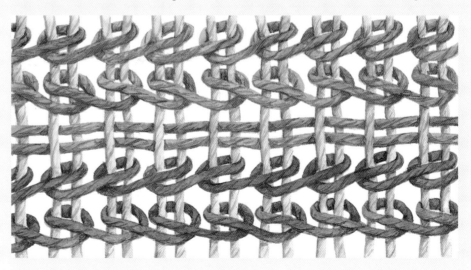

Ceramics

Introduction

The following pages include a variety of techniques for maintaining and repairing ceramics. Some of these are suitable for pottery and some for porcelain. To avoid using an inappropriate technique, you must be able to distinguish between the different types of pottery and porcelain. The following advice will help you to do this, but if you are in doubt about a piece, consult a ceramics specialist.

Types of pottery and glaze

The two basic types of pottery are earthenware and stoneware. Earthenware is made from clays fired at low temperatures. The colour of the clay body, which needs a glaze to waterproof it, ranges from white to beige, brown, red or grey. Stoneware, which is very hardwearing and waterproof in its own right, is made by adding flint or stone dust to clay, and then firing at high temperatures.

There are three basic pottery glazes: tin, lead and salt. Tin glaze produces an opaque white finish, which is either matt or, if coated with a lead glaze, brilliant and lustrous. Tin glaze is applied to Italian majolica, French and German faience, and Dutch and British delft. Lead glaze is glassy in appearance and can be either transparent or coloured, as well as crazed or iridescent. Notable examples include creamware and pearlware. Salt glaze is thick and glass-like, and is made by throwing salt into the kiln while stoneware is being fired. Salt-glaze wares range in colour from white to pale beige, grey or brown.

Decorating pottery

There are three basic methods of decorating pottery with patterns and motifs: underglazing, overglazing and slipping. Underglazing involves painting on various metal oxides or minerals before firing. The best-known examples – blue-and-white Chinese pottery and European delftware – are made by painting black cobalt oxide onto the body. The oxide turns blue during firing. Other colours are produced with iron (brown), manganese (purple), copper (green) and antimony (yellow).

Overglazing involves adding metallic oxides to molten glass, reducing the cooled mixture to powder pigment and mixing it with an oil to make enamel paint which is applied before firing. In slipping, a creamy coat of liquid clay is applied over the object. Before firing, patterns can be cut through the slip with a sharp tool (sgraffito). Alternatively, two contrasting-coloured slips can be combed over the object, or one coloured slip trailed over the contrasting ground colour of the object. Other notable methods of decoration include sprigging (applying slip mouldings to the surface before firing) and sponging or spattering (in which the object is daubed with a sponge after firing to produce a mottled effect).

Hard and soft paste porcelain

Porcelain is fired, glazed and decorated in a similar manner to pottery, but there are differences, notably in the ingredients mixed with the clay. The two basic types of porcelain are hard paste and soft paste. Hard paste, developed in China between A.D. 618 and 906, was not produced in Europe until the early 18th century at Meissen, in Germany. Its main ingredients are kaolin (china clay) and petuntse (china stone). Fired at 900°C, the object is then glazed and fired again at 1300°C. Hard paste is waterproof, semitranslucent, feels cool, and has a hard, glittery glaze. Soft paste was developed in Italy in the late 16th century. Made from white clay and frit (powdered glass) or soapstone, it is fired at a lower temperature than hard paste and is softer, more prone to discolour and feels warmer. Subcategories of porcelain include bone china, biscuit and Parian. Bone china, invented *c.*1820 in England, is a hard paste made of petuntse, kaolin and bone. Biscuit is porcelain fired once or white porcelain unglazed and undecorated. Parian is a semi-matt biscuit porcelain made from petuntse and china clay, and resembles white marble.

Pottery or porcelain?

There are additional characteristics that will help you distinguish between pottery and porcelain. First, provided it isn't cracked, porcelain gives a clear ringing tone when tapped; pottery makes a duller sound. Second, porcelain is lighter than pottery. Third, most porcelain is fairly translucent if held to the light, whereas pottery is opaque. Fourth, a broken edge in pottery reveals a coarse granular body and a distinct line between the glaze and the body, whereas the body of porcelain is much finer and smoother and has an almost glassy appearance where the glaze is fused to the body.

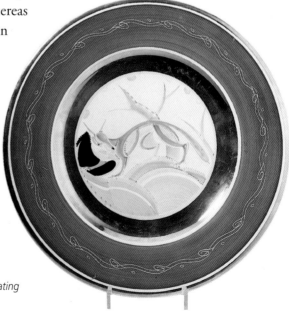

Pottery and porcelain
Flambé-glazed pots and vases (left), dated to c. 1939, by William Moorcroft (1872–1945). An Art Deco bone-china plate (right), incorporating a stylized fox motif, by Susie Cooper.

Tools and materials

In addition to the tools and materials listed below, you will also need a solid work surface and good lighting when repairing ceramics. Daylight is preferable for matching colours and mixing paints and glazes; a powerful artificial light is better for locating hairline cracks. You should also pay attention to health and safety. Always work in a well-ventilated area to prevent a build-up of fumes from some of the recommended solvents and cleaning fluids, and wear a face mask to minimize the risk of inhaling them. Also, protect your eyes and hands from sharp fragments and caustic fluids by wearing plastic goggles and chemical-resistant rubber gloves.

Tools

1 Bench vice To secure pieces during repair. Take great care as ceramics are easily cracked.

2 Magnifying glass For close inspection of damage.

3 Utility or craft knife To open old repairs before remending and to scrape off old adhesives.

4 Scalpel (plus spare blades) Can be used instead of, or in addition to, a utility or craft knife.

5 Razor blades These can be bent slightly for cutting back adhesives and fillers around curved surfaces.

6 Palette knife To mix and apply fillers.

7 Boxwood modelling tools Small wooden tools, available in sets from artist's suppliers. They come in a choice of shapes and sizes, and are ideal for shaping and smoothing fillers while these are still wet.

8 Needle files You will need round-, square- and bevel-ended needle files to shape fillers when dry. Available from hardware and hobby shops.

9 Tweezers To hold small swabs of cotton wool when applying various bleaches and solvents.

10 Pliers A pair of taper- or needle-nosed pliers to shape supporting wires for modelling materials.

11 Toothpicks To apply adhesives and fillers.

12 Rubber gloves Use a chemical-resistant type when applying various solvents and cleaning fluids.

13 Plastic safety goggles

14 Face mask

15 Artist's brushes Various sizes (00–3 are the most useful) for repainting and touching-in gilding.

16 Dusting brush Use a soft-bristled artist's dusting brush, or a make-up brush, for regular cleaning and to prepare objects for repair.

17 Toothbrush A medium- or soft-bristled toothbrush to clean broken edges before repair.

18 Small natural sponge To apply various cleaning fluids and to rinse surfaces.

19 Cotton buds To clean recessed areas.

20 Hard pencil To simulate crazing.

21 Eraser To erase errors in simulated crazing.

YOU WILL ALSO NEED:

Two plastic basins To wash and rinse ceramics.

Small containers To mix paints and glazes.

Paint tray Fill with fine sand to support repairs while the adhesive dries.

White ceramic tile To test colours when repainting.

Thin laminated cardboard

Large plastic bag

Small pin

Teaspoon

Materials

22 Epoxy-resin adhesive The standard version of this two-part adhesive sets in about 6 hours, while the quick-setting type sets in about 10 minutes.

23 White glue For repairing terracotta and pottery.

24 Cyanoacrylate adhesive To repair breaks in delicate, hard-paste porcelain. Also known as superglue.

25 Household bleach Use diluted to remove stains from tea and coffee pots.

26 Spirit of salts (hydrochloric acid) To remove mineral build-up. Available from chemists. This substance is corrosive, so take great care when handling it.

27 Rust remover

28 Paint stripper A solvent that breaks down various specified adhesives.

29 Epoxy putty Use to repair porcelain.

30 Cellulose filler Use to fill cracks in pottery.

31 Titanium dioxide Add to epoxy-resin adhesives to stop them from yellowing with age.

32 Silicone-carbide paper Fine- and medium-grade.

33 Chrome polish To buff and polish filler and glaze.

34 Talcum powder Can be mixed with epoxy-resin adhesive to make filler.

35 Fine sand Use to support various types of repair while the adhesive dries.

36 Masking tape To secure repairs and to protect surrounding areas while painting or gilding.

37 Modelling clay To support repairs and to take impressions of component parts.

38 Latex emulsion To make castings.

39 Methylated spirits For specified cleaning tasks.

40 White spirit As above.

41 Ammonia To bleach various stains.

42 Cotton wool To apply cleaning fluids.

43 Gold size A sticky, viscous fluid applied to surfaces before gilding with metallic powders.

44 Gold metallic powders To regild damaged or worn areas. Available in various shades.

45 Cold-cure lacquer Provides an easier alternative to reglazing in an oven. Available from artist's suppliers.

46 Artist's powder pigments Available in a wide choice of colours. Use to colour repairs and for repainting.

47 Acrylic paints These water-based paints are the easiest to control when repainting ceramics.

48 Rubber bands

49 Lint-free rag

50 Terry towelling or old towels

YOU WILL ALSO NEED:

Distilled water Purer than tap water and therefore better for mixing with cellulose and plaster of Paris fillers and for rinsing after cleaning.

Acetone To degrease pieces before rejointing.

Kaolin Mix with epoxy-resin adhesive to make filler.

Plaster of Paris To repair chips and cracks in pottery.

Sheet of foam To line the bottom of a plastic basin when washing glazed ceramics.

Mild liquid soap To wash glazed ceramics.

Whiting To remove dirt from terracotta.

Borax To remove tea and coffee stains.

Modelling wire To support epoxy-putty repairs.

Fine sawdust To strengthen latex moulds.

Wire wool Grade 0000.

General care and cleaning

To preserve their appearance, condition and value, ceramics must be regularly dusted and cleaned. How often you will need to do this depends on whether the pieces are used or displayed. Pieces displayed behind glass will become dirty more slowly than those exposed to the atmosphere or used to store food or liquids.

Various methods of cleaning are described below. Choose one that is suitable for the composition and condition of the piece in question, as well as for the type of dirt or stain that you wish to remove. Using an inappropriate method can result in irreversible damage that spoils the appearance of the piece and devalues it.

Regardless of its composition, condition, age and value, there is one inflexible rule that you must always stick to when cleaning an antique ceramic piece: never put it in a dishwasher. The combination of high water temperatures, turbulence and abrasive cleaning agents will damage glazes, fade colours and even cause chips and cracks. There is no acceptable alternative to careful cleaning by hand.

Dusting

All ceramics should be dusted regularly, and always before washing and removing stains. Do this by supporting the piece with your free hand and lightly flicking a soft-bristled artist's dusting brush or make-up brush back and forth across the surface. Also, gently work the bristles into crevices to remove the dust that builds up in them.

Cleaning glazed ceramics

Before washing any glazed ceramics, inspect them for signs of damage. If a piece has been repaired with adhesives, if there are any chips or cracks present, or if the glaze has worn away in places, use the cleaning technique recommended for unglazed or partly glazed ceramics (see below). However, if the piece is in good condition, proceed as follows.
● Line the bottom of a plastic basin with a sheet of foam about 2.5cm thick.
● Fill the bowl with hand-hot water and mix in a few drops of mild liquid soap.
● Take the first piece and thoroughly dust it before proceeding. To minimize the risk of breakage, wash only one piece at a time. If a piece has more than one component, wash each separately.
● Lower the piece into the soapy water and gently wipe it with a soft, lint-free rag. To loosen dirt from crevices, use the bristles of a dusting brush. Wipe and brush until you can remove no more dirt.
● Line the bottom of a second plastic sink bowl with a 2.5cm-thick sheet of foam and fill it with hand-hot water. Transfer the piece from the soapy water to the clean water, and gently move it around to rinse off the soap and remnants of the dirt.
● Remove the piece from the rinsing bowl and dry it carefully with terry towelling. To remove any remaining grease, employ the technique described below.

Removing grease from glazed ceramics

To remove stubborn greasy marks from the surface of a piece, try one or more of the following methods.
● Gently rub the marked area with soft, lint-free rag moistened with mild liquid soap. Then repeat the general washing technique described above.
● If soap fails to remove the mark, moisten a cotton bud with either white spirit or methylated spirits and lightly rub it over the mark.
● If either of the above solvents fails to work, rub the mark with a cotton bud moistened with acetone.
● After successful removal, wash with liquid soap, as described above, and pat dry with a soft, lint-free rag. Lightly buff the surface with a soft, dry, lint-free cloth.

Cleaning partly glazed ceramics

Partly glazed ceramics include various types of tin- or lead-glazed pottery and earthenware. The glaze covers the sides and top (or rim) of the outside of the body, but not the outside of the base or the inside of the body. Because of the porosity of the unglazed areas, don't immerse such pieces in water for any length of time. The safest way to clean such pieces is to use the method prescribed for unglazed ceramics (see below).

Cleaning unglazed ceramics

Bisque (unglazed porcelain) and various types of unglazed pottery and earthenware, notably unglazed terracotta, are highly porous and so can be damaged by regular or lengthy immersion in water. You may have to immerse them in water to remove certain types of stain (see below), but don't use this method for general cleaning. Instead, proceed as follows.
● When possible, restrict surface cleaning to dusting with an artist's dusting brush or make-up brush.
● Try to remove accumulations of dirt in crevices by working a little whiting into them with the tips of the bristles of a dusting or make-up brush. Then brush out the whiting and the dirt with another brush.
● If the dirt proves very stubborn, and the above method is not strong enough to remove it, wipe the surface with cotton wool moistened with lukewarm water. Work lukewarm water into the crevices with a brush. Then, using terry towelling, pat the piece completely dry as quickly as possible.
● If the piece is still dirty, add a little mild liquid soap to the water before applying. Immediately follow this

by 'rinsing' several times using cotton wool moistened with clean, lukewarm water. Finish by patting the surface completely dry with terry towelling.

Removing stains from glazed ceramics

Glazed ceramics are not very vulnerable to staining because glazing limits their porosity. However, staining can occur, particularly on the inside surfaces of vessels that are in regular use. Before you attempt to treat the stains listed below always inspect the piece for damaged glaze. If the glaze is worn or chipped, don't immerse the piece in any of the prescribed cleaning or rinsing fluids. Instead, apply the appropriate fluid sparingly on a moistened cotton bud.

Note: The glaze on many pre-19th-century pieces is unstable. Entrust the removal of stains from such pieces to a professional restorer.

Tea and coffee stains

It is inevitable that teapots and coffee pots that are in constant use will eventually become badly stained inside. To remove such stains, proceed as follows.
● Pour clean, lukewarm water into the pot and let it stand for about an hour before emptying the pot.
● Put on plastic goggles and rubber gloves to protect your eyes and hands.
● Mix a solution consisting of 50g of borax to 500ml of lukewarm water, and pour it into the pot. Let the solution stand for an hour, occasionally stirring it and brushing it against the inside of the pot with a soft-bristled brush. Pour away the solution.
● Mix a solution of one part household bleach to three parts lukewarm water, and pour it into the pot. Let it stand for an hour. During this time stir it occasionally with a brush.
● Pour away the solution and rinse out the pot four or five times with running cold water. Dry thoroughly with terry towelling.

Mildew and mould

Glazed vessels that have been stored without being dried thoroughly may develop an internal grey-brown stain caused by the growth of mildew and mould. To remove this, use the method prescribed for removing tea and coffee stains (see above).

Metallic stains

Copper and iron rivets or staples were once used to repair breaks in glazed ceramics. Over time they can stain the surrounding area. Remove them as follows.
● Rub off copper stains with a cotton bud moistened with ammonia.
● Rub off rust stains with a cotton bud moistened with a rust remover designed for use on ceramics. Immediately afterwards, rinse the treated area with distilled water.
Note: Rust remover contains phosphoric acid, so wear plastic goggles and rubber gloves when using it.

Removing stains from unglazed pottery

Stains on rare and valuable pieces of pottery should be treated by a professional restorer. However, you can remove stains from lesser pieces yourself. The treatments require you to immerse the piece in water. Because of the porosity of unglazed pieces, and the damage that can result from absorption of water, you should use these treatments as infrequently as possible.

Stains of indeterminate origin

To remove most stains from unglazed pottery, even if you are not sure of their origin, proceed as follows.
● Immerse the piece in clean lukewarm water for one to two hours.
● Put on plastic goggles and rubber gloves.
● Position the piece so that cotton wool dampened with a solution of one part household bleach to three parts lukewarm water can be pressed onto the stain. If the stains are on more than one side of the piece, treat them in turn.
● Wrap a plastic bag around the object to keep the cotton wool moist and leave for three or four hours.
● Remove the bag and cotton wool and rinse thoroughly with clean water.

● Repeat the above procedure, soaking the piece in water each time before you apply fresh cotton wool, until the stain has gone.

Lime scale

A thin white layer of lime scale (calcium carbonate) often builds up on the inside of unglazed ceramic pots and bowls used to display houseplants. To remove it, proceed as follows.
● Put on plastic goggles and rubber gloves.
● Pour enough cold, clean water into the vessel to cover the lime scale.
● Very slowly add spirit of salts (hydrochloric acid) to the water until the lime scale begins to bubble. Leave the acid solution to stand until you can see that the scale has dissolved. You may have to add a little more spirit of salts to the water to achieve this.
Note: Always add spirit of salts to water. Never add water to spirit of salts. If you do the latter, the solution will boil and you could be seriously burned.
● Pour away the acid solution and the dissolved lime scale, then rinse the piece thoroughly with copious amounts of clean, lukewarm water.
● Dry the piece thoroughly with terry towelling.

Salts

Powdery white salts can accumulate on unglazed pottery and earthenware as a result of exposure to moisture. If the piece is rare or valuable, or its surface is friable, ask a professional restorer to remove the salts. If the piece is sound, proceed as follows.
● Place the object in a plastic basin and pour in distilled water. Do not completely cover the piece: leave about 2.5cm of the top exposed to the air.
● Let the piece stand for 24 hours, then change the water. Repeat this procedure at least three or four times.
● To test if all the salts have been removed, remove a teaspoonful of the distilled water and hold it over a flame until the water has evaporated. If there is any residue of salts in the spoon, repeat the soaking technique and test again until no salts are left.

Bonding simple breaks

The technique used here for mending a simple break in a late 19th-century plate is not difficult to master and can be tackled with confidence by a patient amateur restorer. Note that this method of bonding can also be employed to repair breaks in cups, saucers and bowls.

This plate is made of porcelain, but earthenware, terracotta and pottery can be repaired in a similar way. (The different adhesives required, and the variations in preparing and bonding the piece, are described at appropriate points in the text.) However, whatever the type of ceramic needing repair, if it is rare or valuable, you should entrust the task to a professional restorer.

If a piece has multiple breaks, you will need to adopt a slightly different approach to the one that is demonstrated in the project. First you should lay out the components on a work surface and plan the required sequence of assembly. Practise assembling the pieces by securing them together temporarily with masking tape. When you are completely sure about the sequence, tag each piece with a numbered strip of tape. The rules of assembly are: fit one piece at a time (letting the adhesive set before moving to the next piece). Work from the middle out, so you don't lock out any pieces and have to dismantle the repair in order to include them. Finally make sure that each piece is perfectly aligned with and bonded to the adjacent ones, because the result of errors of alignment will be that the final pieces to be positioned will not sit correctly.

1 Preparing the surfaces

● Clean the porcelain thoroughly with soapy water, as described on pp.178–9. Rinse with clean water and dry with a piece of terry towelling.
● To make sure no soap or grease is left on the broken edges after the initial cleaning, wipe the edges and immediate surrounding areas with a piece of lint-free rag moistened with acetone. If you don't remove the residue, the adhesive will not bond.
● If you are repairing earthenware, terracotta or pottery, use a lint-free rag and clean water to dampen the edges that are to be bonded. This will stop the adhesive from being absorbed into the body of the piece before it sets, which would severely weaken the joint.
● Cut several 7.5cm-long strips of masking tape and stick them to both sides of one half of the plate at right angles to the line of repair. Half of each strip should be stuck down, while the other half should hang over the edge and then be temporarily folded back on itself.

YOU WILL NEED:
Warm water
Liquid soap
Lint-free rag
Terry towelling
A medium- or stiff-bristled toothbrush
Acetone
Masking tape
Two-part epoxy-resin adhesive Use if you are mending porcelain.
Titanium dioxide To minimize the yellowing of epoxy-resin adhesive.
Artist's powder pigments In appropriate colours to tint epoxy-resin adhesive when you are mending coloured pieces.
White glue (PVA) To bond earthenware, terracotta and pottery.
Cyanoacrylate adhesive Also known as superglue, this adhesive is useful for repairing multiple breaks in porcelain because of its thin consistency and fast setting time. It is also ideal for pieces that are too small to be taped.
Cocktail sticks To apply adhesive.
Cotton buds
Methylated spirits
Plastic or metal paint tray
Fine sand To support large pieces.
Modelling clay To support small pieces.

2 Applying adhesive

- If you are repairing porcelain (as here), gently warm the two tubes of two-part epoxy-resin adhesive. This will help it to flow more easily when you are mixing and applying it. If it is possible, use one of the thinner epoxy-resin adhesives specifically designed for repairing china, as this will make it easier to produce a close, clean joint.
- Mix a small quantity of the epoxy-resin adhesive, following the manufacturer's directions for the proportions.
- With a cocktail stick, carefully apply the adhesive to the broken edge of the untaped half of the piece. Apply as little adhesive as possible to produce a strong, close bond.
- If you are repairing white porcelain, add a little titanium dioxide to the adhesive to compensate for the yellowing that takes place over time.
- If you are repairing coloured porcelain, add artist's powder pigments in the appropriate colour(s). For advice on tinting with pigments, see pp.192–3.
- If you are repairing earthenware, terracotta or pottery, use white glue (PVA) straight from the tube, or, if necessary, add artist's powder pigments in the appropriate colour(s) to blend in the repair better with the surrounding area.
- If you are repairing very small pieces of any porcelain (or multiple breaks), you may prefer to use a fast-setting superglue instead of epoxy-resin adhesive.

3 Bonding and taping

- Carefully align the two sections of the repair, using a firm but gentle rocking action to squeeze excess glue from the joint and produce a perfect fit.
- Holding the two halves firmly together, stretch the strips of masking tape across the joint and stick them to the other half of the piece. You must apply even tension to each strip and avoid dislodging the joint.
- Wipe off excess adhesive with a cotton buds moistened with an appropriate solvent: methylated spirits if you are using epoxy resin, acetone for superglue and water for white glue. (Adhesive under the tapes can be removed later.)

4 Adjusting the fit

- Scrape a fingernail along and across the exposed sections of the joint to test for alignment. If this can be improved, carefully lift the strips of tape, rework the joint by applying gentle pressure, then re-tape.
- When you are satisfied with the repair, support the object in a paint tray filled with fine sand while the adhesive dries. (Small pieces can be supported on a lump of modelling clay.)

5 Finishing

- Let the adhesive dry thoroughly (following the manufacturer's advice on drying times). Carefully remove the object from the sand or clay, and peel off the strips of tape.
- Moisten a cotton bud with the proper solvent (see step 4), and rub off any excess adhesive that has collected under the tapes. You may need to scrape off stubborn pieces of adhesive very carefully with the edge of a scalpel or razor blade, but avoid this if possible.
- Closely examine the repair. If there are any small chips on any side of the joint that need to be filled, use the technique for filling chips and cracks described on pp.186–8. If any painted decoration needs to be touched up, see pp.192–3.

Remaking old repairs

One of the problems that you are most likely to encounter in previously repaired ceramics is the breakdown or discoloration of bonded breaks. In this example the adhesive that was used to bond the cracked rim of a porcelain cup had yellowed with age and begun to give way. The only solution in such cases is to undo the old repair and remake it. However, if the piece in question is rare or valuable, you should employ a professional restorer to carry out the whole procedure.

The technique recommended for bonding a simple break is described on pp.180–1. The method used to first dismantle and clean the repair is shown here. Note that the type of solvent required to dissolve the old adhesive depends on the type of adhesive that was used. In this example it was necessary to use paint stripper to dissolve the old two-part epoxy-resin glue. The solvents for alternative adhesives, together with their methods of application, are specified in steps 1 and 2.

YOU WILL NEED:
Rubber gloves
Plastic goggles
Small artist's brush
Paint stripper A water-based type with the consistency of jelly to dissolve epoxy-resin and rubber-based adhesives.
Hot water
Plastic basin
Methylated spirits To dissolve shellac.
Acetone To dissolve cellulose-based adhesive and white glue.
Cotton wool or cotton buds
Scalpel (or small utility or craft knife)
Stiff-bristled toothbrush
Lint-free rag
Terry towelling

1 Examining the old repair

• Look closely at the previous repair to try to discover the type of adhesive that was used. This will determine both the type of solvent that you will need to dissolve it and the method of application. The following information will help you to identify the adhesive, but if you still can't decide which type was used, consult a professional ceramics restorer.

• Epoxy-resin adhesives (as used here) set extremely hard and tend to yellow with age, particularly if they were not whitened with titanium dioxide when applied. They can be dissolved only with paint stripper.

• Old rubber-based adhesives are much softer than epoxy-resin adhesives, and most gradually turn from white to yellow-white over time. They can be dissolved with paint stripper.

• Old animal adhesives (such as rabbit-skin glue) are brown and can usually be dissolved with hot water or exposure to steam.

• Shellac, which was occasionally used in the past, is brown and tends to become brittle with age. It can sometimes be dissolved with hot water. If that doesn't work, try methylated spirits, and if that fails, use paint stripper.

• PVA is white and most commonly used to repair earthenware, terracotta and pottery. In some cases it is possible to dissolve it with hot water. If this method proves unsuccessful, apply a little acetone, which always works.

2 Applying the solvent

• If the adhesive is epoxy-resin or rubber-based, or shellac that hasn't responded to either hot water or methylated spirits, use a small artist's brush to apply a thin coat of water-based paint stripper so that it slightly overlaps both sides of the joint. Move to step 3 as the adhesive begins to soften.
Note: Before applying paint stripper, put on protective rubber gloves and plastic goggles.

• If you are dealing with animal glue, shellac or white glue, immerse the object in a plastic basin of lukewarm water. Then very slowly add hot water. As the adhesive begins to soften, use an old stiff-bristled toothbrush and, if it proves necessary, a scalpel blade or utility knife to rub it off. Then proceed to step 5.

• If shellac doesn't respond to hot water, wipe several applications of methylated spirits along the joint with cotton wool or cotton buds, then proceed to step 3. If that doesn't work, apply water-based paint stripper with a small artist's brush, then proceed to step 3.

• If white glue doesn't respond to hot water, soak cotton wool or cotton buds with acetone and wipe them back and forth along the joint several times, until the glue softens.

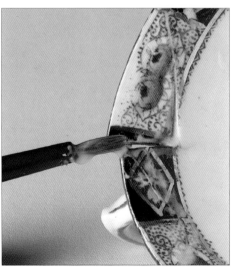

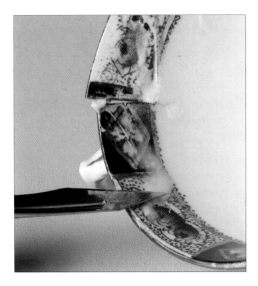

3 Removing excess adhesive

● Regardless of the type of adhesive used, as soon as it softens, use a scalpel blade or utility knife to very gently scrape off excess adhesive and solvent from the surface surrounding the joint. Keep the blade clean during this process by wiping it with lint-free rag.

Note: In some cases a second application of solvent will now be needed to soften the adhesive more.

4 Separating the broken pieces

● Once you have carried out steps 2 and 3 for a second time, you may be able gently to pry off the broken section from the main body of the object with your fingers and thumbs. However, you will probably need first to insert the tip of a scalpel blade or a utility knife into the joint carefully and cut through the softened strands of glue. Make sure that the blade doesn't slip and cut your fingers.

5 Cleaning the joint

● Moisten a stiff-bristled toothbrush with the appropriate solvent, and rub off any traces of the old adhesive.

● Clean the broken edges well with a toothbrush moistened with lukewarm water. Then dry the object thoroughly with a piece of terry towelling.

Note: If the surface of the piece is stained, treat it now. For the appropriate method, see pp.178–9.

Supporting handles

When rebonding a broken handle to a cup, tureen, or similar vessel, support the handle with masking tape while the adhesive is drying, to make a tight, accurate joint.

Support the main body of the piece in fine sand or on modelling clay. After applying the adhesive and refitting the handle, place one piece of tape lengthways over the handle and secure each end to the body of the piece. Stretch two pieces of tape diagonally across the handle, securing as before. Tension the three tapes equally. Avoid dislodging the joint while taping.

6 Remaking the repair

● When you have cleaned and dried the joint thoroughly, rebond it with epoxy-resin adhesive for porcelain, or white glue for earthenware, terracotta and pottery. For illustrated instructions on how to rebond simple or multiple breaks, refer to 'Bonding simple breaks' on pp.180–1.

Note: You must add white titanium dioxide to the epoxy-resin adhesive if you are repairing a white or predominantly white piece. This will counteract the tendency of the adhesive to yellow with age and thereby emphasize the presence of the repair.

However, if you are repairing a coloured piece, you should mix small quantities of artist's powder pigments, in the appropriate colours, into the adhesive to help the repair blend in with the surrounding area. For advice on tinting adhesive with powder pigments, see pp.192–3.

Remodelling a broken spout

Because of their hollow, elongated shape, the spouts of teapots and coffee pots are easily broken. The restoration technique demonstrated here on a late 19th-century teapot is specifically designed for repairing the chips, cracks and breaks that often occur at the end of a spout. To effect the repair, you will need to model the missing section by hand directly onto the end of the existing spout, but this is easier than you might at first suppose. Nevertheless, if the damaged piece is particularly old or valuable, you should entrust the repair to a professional restorer. Note also that, once it has been repaired, the pot should be used only for display purposes. Despite the fact that modern, two-part epoxy-resin adhesives make a very strong bond between joined surfaces, regular exposure to hot liquids such as coffee and tea will eventually cause the repair to soften and break.

YOU WILL NEED:
Plastic basin
Mild liquid soap
Hot and cold water
Acetone
Lint-free rag
Cotton buds
Terry towelling
Modelling clay
Utility or craft knife
Talcum powder
Two-part epoxy-resin adhesive
Titanium dioxide If the spout is white.
Artist's powder pigments If the spout is coloured.
Cocktail sticks
White epoxy putty
Boxwood modelling tools
Needle files
Silicon-carbide paper Fine-grade.
Cold-cure lacquer White and clear types.
Artist's brushes Selection from sizes 00–3.

1 Cleaning the surfaces

• Wash the pot in a plastic basin full of warm, soapy water. Rinse it with clean, cold water and dry thoroughly with terry towelling.

• Remove any stains or discoloration from the pot's surface, using the materials and techniques described on pp.178–9. If you don't remove them at this stage, you will find it difficult to blend the repair into the surrounding areas later.

• To make sure that the adhesive to be applied in step 4 bonds properly, run the tip of a cotton bud moistened with acetone around the broken end of the spout. This will remove greasy deposits that remain after the cleaning with soapy water.

2 Plugging the spout

• Knead a small quantity of modelling clay between your fingers. The heat generated by your hands will make it more pliable and therefore much easier to shape.

• Push the clay into the end of the broken spout. Smooth it with your index finger moistened with water to the shape and contour of the inside of the spout. It is advisable to spend some time on this, because accurate modelling of the clay plug at this stage will pay dividends later.

• Cut off any clay protruding from the end of the spout with a utility knife, and smooth the end of the plug as before with a damp forefinger.

3 Dusting with talcum powder

• Dry your hands and sprinkle a fine coating of talcum powder over the surface of the clay plug. The powder will stop the epoxy putty applied in step 5 from bonding to the clay.

4 Applying epoxy putty

● Mix a small quantity of two-part epoxy-resin adhesive, adding a little titanium dioxide to counteract the yellowing of the adhesive that takes place over the course of time. Then, with a cocktail stick, apply a thin layer of the adhesive around the broken edge of the spout.

● Mix a small quantity of two-part, white epoxy putty, following the manufacturer's instructions as to the proportions of filler to hardener.

● Using your fingers, and occasionally moistening them with clean, cold water, gradually build up the putty around the modelling clay so that it stands slightly above, and roughly follows the shape of, the outside of the original spout.

● Use a selection of different-shaped modelling tools to smooth the putty into a close approximation of the contours of the spout. You should keep dipping the ends of the tools in clean, cold water to assist with the modelling of the putty and, as and when necessary, wipe the tools on a piece of lint-free rag to clean off the thin film of putty that will gradually accumulate on their surfaces. The more accurate your modelling at this stage, the less you will have to do in step 5.

● Wipe off excess putty that creeps down over the rest of the spout with a lint-free rag.

5 Filing the putty

● Let the putty dry thoroughly for the period recommended by the manufacturer.

● Using a selection of square- and bevel-ended needle files, abrade the hard putty so that it no longer stands out from, but follows the exact shape and contours of, the circumference of the original spout.

● Smooth the surface of the contoured putty by sanding it down with some small pieces of fine-grade silicon-carbide paper.

6 Applying the first glaze

● If the spout is white, apply a thin coat of white cold-cure lacquer with a fine-bristled artist's brush, using the technique recommended for glazing ceramics on pp.192–3.

● If the spout is coloured, mix some artist's pigments into white or clear cold-cure lacquer until you have achieved a good colour match. Brush on a thin coat, as described above.

● Leave the lacquer to dry for at least 12 hours.

7 Decorating and final glazing

● If the end of the spout is decorated with patterns or motifs, renew or extend them by using the materials and techniques described on pp.192–3.

● If the end of the spout is undecorated, or once any renewed painted decoration has dried thoroughly, apply one coat of clear cold-cure lacquer with a small artist's brush, as in step 6.

Repairing shell chips

The technique demonstrated here is specifically designed to repair 'shell' chips, which often occur as a result of accidental knocks against the vulnerable rims and edges of plates, bowls and saucers. You should make this type of repair as soon as possible. If the damaged area is exposed to dust, dirt and moisture for too long, it will become stained or discoloured, and thus need additional preparation work before it can be repaired. This method of repair can be adapted to fix open joints and holes in china.

1 Preparing the surface

● Wash the object in a plastic basin full of warm, mild soapy water. Rinse with clean water and dry thoroughly with a piece of terry towelling.

● Remove any staining or discoloration present on and around the damaged section, using the materials and techniques described on pp.178–9.

● To make sure that no greasy deposits remain, wipe a cotton bud dipped in acetone over the damaged and immediately surrounding area.

● If part of the rim or edge has completely broken away, bend a strip of thin cardboard to shape and secure it with tape to the back of the object. This will provide a temporary support for the filler. Apply a thin layer of talcum powder to the cardboard to make sure that no adhesive or filler sticks to it.

● Mix a small quantity of two-part epoxy-resin adhesive (in accordance with the manufacturer's directions). Add a little titanium dioxide to the mix to counteract the eventual yellowing of the adhesive.

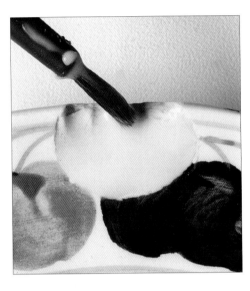

● Using a small artist's brush, apply a thin layer of adhesive to the surface of the chip. If you have had to use a cardboard backing, make sure that you apply the adhesive only to the edges of the chip – don't brush any adhesive onto the cardboard.

YOU WILL NEED:
Plastic basin
Mild liquid soap
Hot and cold water
Acetone
Lint-free rag
Cotton buds
Terry towelling
Thin cardboard Required only if you need to bridge a gap to support a section of the filler temporarily.
Talcum powder Required only if you have to use thin cardboard as a support.
Two-part epoxy-resin adhesive
Titanium dioxide
Artist's powder pigments In appropriate colours if the object is of coloured porcelain.
Cocktail sticks
White epoxy putty
Boxwood modelling tools
Needle files
Silicon-carbide paper Fine-grade.
Cold-cure lacquer The clear variety, but also the white version if the object is white.
Artist's brushes Sizes 00–3.
Acrylic paints These will be needed only if you have to touch in areas of original painted decoration (as here).

Filling joints and holes

To fill in any fine surface cracks that may develop or be left along the edges of jointed repairs (such as the bonded break shown on pp.180–1), proceed as follows.

● Press epoxy putty into the cracks with a palette knife. If you are repairing pottery, mix a cellulose filler instead of epoxy putty. If the object is coloured, you must tint the putty or filler with powder pigments, as described on pp.192–3.

● Level the putty by scraping the edge of the knife across the line of the crack. Smooth it by dampening the knife with a little water and lightly pressing it along the line of the crack.

● Let the putty dry, then give it a final smoothing with fine-grade silicone-carbide paper.

● Test the smoothness of the repair by running a finger along it to feel for any ridges or depressions, and if necessary, repeat the above procedure with more filler.

● To fully blend the repair in, you may need only to wipe a very thin coat of chrome polish over the whole object, using a lint-free rag, then buff it with another clean rag. However, you may also have to touch in any surface decoration as described in steps 5 and 6 opposite, and on pp.192–3.

Note: To fill small holes that pass right through a piece, use the technique described here. However, you will need to back the hole temporarily with tape or modelling clay. You must sprinkle talcum powder on the tape or clay to make sure that the putty or filler doesn't adhere to it. Remove the tape or clay once the repair has fully hardened.

2 Applying the filler

- Mix some two-part, white epoxy putty (following the manufacturer's instructions).
- Using your fingers, and occasionally moistening them with clean, cold water, press the putty into the shell chip, gradually building it up so that it follows the contours of the object and stands very slightly higher than the surrounding areas.

Note: While the putty is wet, you can use not only a moistened forefinger but also modelling tools to smooth the putty into shape (see p.185, step 4). Repeatedly dip the ends of the tools in cold water and wipe them clean on a lint-free rag. Also, wipe putty from the surrounding areas with a rag.

3 Smoothing the dry filler

- Once the filler has dried, carefully peel away the tape and cardboard (if you have used it) from the back of the repair.
- You may now find it necessary to use a square-ended needle file to rub the putty or filler so that it doesn't stand out from the surrounding areas. When using the needle file, take great care not to abrade or scratch the surface immediately surrounding the repaired shell chip.
- To create as smooth a surface as possible for glazing and painting, lightly sand the hard putty or filler with small pieces of fine-grade silicone carbide paper. Avoid abrading the surrounding areas.

5 Hand painting

- If you need to repaint any pattern or motif on the edge of the object, you have a choice of mediums. You can use either artist's acrylic paints, or white or clear cold-cure lacquer tinted with artist's powder pigments. Both should be applied with small artist's brushes; two or three, ranging in size from 00 to 3, should cover the largest and smallest motifs. Allow the paint or lacquer to dry thoroughly before proceeding to step 6.

Note: For advice on colour matching and applying paints and lacquers, see pp.192–3.

4 Applying background glaze

- If the background colour of the piece is white, apply a thin coating of white cold-cure lacquer with a fine-bristled artist's brush. Try not to over-brush the lacquer, or you may leave unsightly brush marks in it. Let the lacquer dry for at least 12 hours before proceeding either to step 5 or 6, or to both.
- If the background colour is off-white (as here), rather than 'pure' white, or if it is coloured, tint the white cold-cure lacquer with artist's powder pigments before applying it, using the technique described on pp.192–3. For the most effective result, spend time achieving a good colour match before applying.

6 Applying the final glaze

- Whether or not you have had to replace painted decoration, finish the repair by brushing on a coat of clear cold-cure lacquer. This will further blend in the repair and provide some protection against discoloration and wear and tear.

Modelling new handles

This project is based on a modelling technique that you can use to replace missing handles. However, you should never attempt it on rare or valuable pieces – for such pieces you must employ a professional restorer. In this case the handle of a 19th-century porcelain tea cup had snapped off and, unfortunately, been lost. There was no alternative but to fashion and attach a replacement handle. The basic principles of modelling new handles are the same as for the projects 'Remodelling a broken spout' (see pp.184–5) and 'Repairing shell chips' (see pp.186–7). Here you will once again need to shape and smooth epoxy putty by hand, but this time you will have to make the missing component in its entirety, without being able to rely on assistance from surrounding contours.

You will find it extremely helpful to have an identical cup (from a tea or coffee set) to serve as a visual reference when modelling a new handle. If the damaged cup is not part of a set, look for a reference for the handle in one of the many specialist books that include illustrations of antique ceramics from different periods.

YOU WILL NEED:
The tools and materials that you will need for this project are the same as those needed for 'Repairing shell chips' (see pp.186–7). The only additional items you will need are:
Modelling wire A short length (no longer than 7.5–10cm). Available from most craft and hardware shops and from some artist's suppliers.
Pliers A pair with a wire-cutting device.
White cardboard A thin sheet for copying or drawing freehand the outline of the handle.
Hard pencil
Bench vice Optional.

1 Cleaning and filing

● Thoroughly clean the cup, using the materials and techniques described on pp.178–9. Complete the cleaning process by degreasing the points of attachment for the new handle with a rag or cotton bud moistened with acetone.

● If the handle hasn't snapped off cleanly from the body (this was the case with this teacup), file the broken stubs with a square-faced needle file to create two smooth, flat points of attachment. This will make it much easier for you to model and to attach the replacement handle.

2 Drawing an outline

● Cut a square of white cardboard with a utility knife. It should be larger all around than the replacement handle and cut along one edge to follow the contours of the cup.

● Position the cardboard along the edge of a work surface. If you have one, hold a duplicate, unbroken cup so that its handle rests on the cardboard. Trace round the outline of the handle with a pencil.

● If you don't have a duplicate cup, draw the outline of the handle freehand, following a reference picture of an identical or very similar cup in a book.

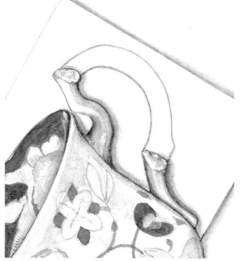

3 Shaping the wire

● Bend some modelling wire on top of the cardboard following the middle of the basic contours of the handle. Don't shape the wire into any small projections from the basic outline, as these will be dealt with in step 5. Most modelling wire can be bent easily by hand. However, if you are not strong enough, grip one end of the wire in a bench vice and bend it with pliers – test the shape from time to time against the outline on the cardboard.

● Cut off the ends of the wire with pliers so that they don't project beyond the ends of the outline.

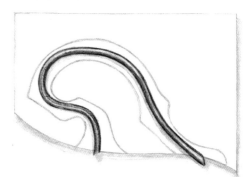

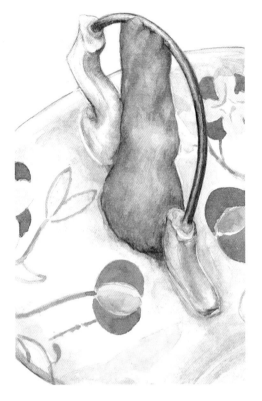

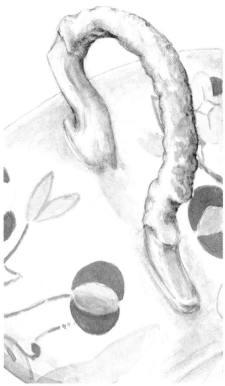

4 Adding the core

● Dust your fingers with talcum powder. Roll a pinch of white, two-part epoxy putty into a thin sausage the same length as the wire.

● Press the putty around the wire. Avoid distorting the wire. Smooth the putty with freshly dampened fingers and leave it to set hard.

● Abrade the ends of the putty core with a needle file so that they sit flush with the points of attachment.

● Support the opposite side of the cup on a lump of modelling clay and support the middle of the putty core on a small column of modelling clay. Attach the ends of the core to the cup with specks of two-part epoxy-resin adhesive and let it dry.

5 Building up the shape

● Mix some more white epoxy putty and press it around the core, building it up to the shape of the original handle. Hold the pencil outline on the cardboard close to the work so that you can check it for accuracy. Keep dampening your fingers to ease the smoothing of the putty. When making small ridges or projections, complete the basic shape and let it harden before applying additional putty.

6 Finishing

● Once you have completed the modelling by hand, let the putty fully harden.

● Adjust the handle's shape by abrading the hard putty with a combination of square-, bevel- and round-ended needle files. You will find the latter particularly useful for adjusting the curved profile of the inside of the handle.

● Once you are satisfied with the shape of the handle, smooth the surface of the putty by sanding it lightly with fine-grade silicon-carbide paper.

● Remove any surface dust with the dry bristles of an artist's brush.

● Apply a thin background glaze with another artist's brush, using cold-cure lacquer and the technique described on pp.192–3.

● Touch in painted decoration, using the materials and techniques outlined on pp.192–3.

● Finish with a coat of clear cold-cure lacquer.

Casting missing components

It is not unusual to find small pieces of applied decoration broken or missing from certain types of ceramics. Typical examples include flowers, leaves and animals grouped around the base of figurines, and pieces of bocage. The latter, made and collected in large quantities during the 19th century, are small pottery or porcelain tree-stumps covered with densely packed bouquets of flowers.

Sometimes it is possible to remodel painstakingly by hand broken or missing components, using the techniques described on pp.184–5 and 188–9. However, in many cases the intricate shapes involved preclude this approach. The alternative method of repair is to cast the component by making a mould from an identical (or near-identical) part located on the same object, or from one on a similar object. Note that you shouldn't attempt this repair on a rare or particularly valuable piece – this task should be entrusted to a professional ceramics restorer.

YOU WILL NEED:
Cotton buds and acetone
Small artist's brush
Latex emulsion Available from craft stores.
Small pin
Fine sawdust
Palette knife
Talcum powder
Two-part epoxy-resin adhesive
Titanium dioxide
Modelling clay
Needle files
Fine-grade silicon-carbide paper

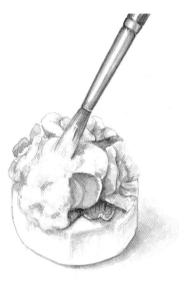

1 Making the mould

● Clean the duplicate decoration using the methods described on pp.178–9 and wipe it with a cotton bud moistened with acetone.
● With a small artist's brush apply a layer of latex emulsion over the decoration (and slightly over the surrounding area). Work the latex right into all the crevices and prick any air bubbles with a pin.
● Leave the latex to dry until it turns from white to brownish. Apply four or five additional coats in the same way. Mix a little fine sawdust into the final coat and press it in place with a palette knife.
● Leave the mould to harden fully for at least 12 hours before carefully peeling it off with your fingers.

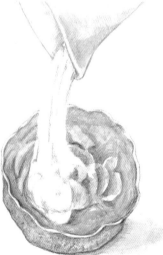

2 Filling the mould

● Lightly dust the inside of the mould with a little talcum powder.
● Mix some two-part epoxy-resin adhesive with a little titanium dioxide.
● Very slowly pour the resin into the mould, pricking any air bubbles that form on or near the surface.
Note: If it is cold, gently warm the resin near a heater (not a naked flame) before pouring. This will make it flow into the mould more smoothly.
● While the resin sets, support the mould in an upright position with pieces of modelling clay. Allow at least 24 hours for the resin to harden fully.
● Carefully peel the latex mould off the casting.

3 Attaching the casting

● Using needle files and fine-grade silicon-carbide paper, grind down any remnants of the original component to create a level surface to which the new casting can be attached.
● Test the fit of the casting. In most cases you will have to file some projections smooth around the base.
● Mix a very small quantity of two-part epoxy-resin adhesive, then add a little titanium dioxide.
● With a small artist's brush, apply the adhesive to the base of the casting and gently press it into position on the piece. Remove excess adhesive with a cotton bud.
● When the adhesive has dried, glaze and paint the new piece as described on pp.192–3.

Regilding

In addition to touching in patterns and motifs when repairing ceramics, you may also have to replace small sections of gilding. The finest pieces are usually gilded with gold leaf – a job that must be left to a professional restorer. However, lesser pieces are often gilded with metallic powders, and you can renew this type of gilding using either or both of the methods described below.

You should note that gold metallic powders are available from craft shops and artist's suppliers in various shades, one of which may well provide you with a perfect colour match with the original gilding. However, it is more likely that you will need to blend different shades of powder together to match the original.

Gilding rims and edges

- Mix small quantities of metallic powders on a white ceramic tile to match the original gold.
- Gradually add clear cold-cure lacquer to produce a glaze with a consistency similar to single cream.
- Add the hardener that comes with the lacquer, in accordance with the maker's directions.
- Place the object upright on a work surface and grip it with your free hand. Support your brush arm on a pile of books placed on the work surface. The pile should be high enough to bring the tip of the brush level with the rim or edge that you are gilding.

- Dip the bristles of a small sable-bristled artist's brush into the glaze. Don't overload the brush.
- Keep the brush tip still on the rim or edge, and steadily rotate the object to transfer the glaze in one sweep from the bristles to the surface. With practice, one coat of glaze should be enough, but at first another may be needed once the first coat has dried.
- Let the glaze dry for a minimum of 12 hours, then lightly burnish it with a soft, lint-free rag.
- Brush on a thin coat of clear cold-cure lacquer to protect the gilding.

Gilding flat surfaces

- Mix the dry metallic powders, as in stage 1 above, to match the original gilding.
- With a small artist's brush, apply a thin coat of clear cold-cure lacquer to the flat surface. At the same time brush a test strip of lacquer onto a white ceramic tile.
- As the test strip becomes tacky, dip the dry bristles of another artist's brush into the powders. Sprinkle the powders over the lacquer on the object. Repeat until you have completely covered the required area.
- Using the same brush, lightly stipple the powder into the lacquer, then let it set for two hours.
- Gently shake off any loose powder and, with the tip of a cocktail stick moistened with the recommended lacquer solvent, scrape off any powder that has crept over and stuck to the surrounding area.
- Leave it for at least 12 hours, then gently smooth and burnish the gilding with soft, lint-free rag. Gently smooth any ridges with Grade-0000 wire wool.
- Brush on a coat of clear cold-cure lacquer.

A painted and gilded sugar bowl
The gilding on the lid of this 1930s sugar bowl had been partly rubbed away over the years and was restored with a metallic powder glaze.

Simulating crazing

To blend an epoxy-putty repair fully into a piece of lead-glazed pottery, you may have to simulate the fine network of lines that sometimes appears in the glaze. Known as 'crackling', these lines develop during the cooling period after the object has been fired and removed from the kiln. They are caused by the body of the object cooling at a different rate to the glaze and thereby creating lesions in the surface of the glaze as it dries. Rather than attempt to reproduce this haphazard process in the kiln, many professional ceramics restorers employ the following simple technique.

- Using a sharp hard pencil, draw a network of lines over the dry putty repair to connect the edges of the pattern to the original lines on the surrounding areas.
- Seal the surface by lightly brushing on a coat of clear cold-cure lacquer.

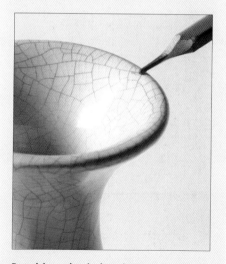

Repairing a lead-glazed vase
Once the chipped rim of this lead-glazed vase had been repaired, the 'crackling' characteristic of the glaze was touched-in with a lead pencil.

Painting and glazing

To complete the repairs to ceramics described on pp.180–90, you must renew sections of glaze. When repairing white china you may find that the original white of the ceramic matches the white of the epoxy-putty filler. If so, simply finish with a coat of clear cold-cure lacquer (or glaze). In most cases, however, the china will be off-white, and therefore the lacquer will have to be tinted slightly to match it. It will also be necessary to match the colour of the putty to the colour of the ceramic when you are repairing a coloured piece.

In addition, you may have to replace areas of painted decoration in order to complete the repair. Neither colour-matching glazes and paints, nor freehand painting of motifs and patterns, is the easiest of tasks. Nevertheless, competence normally develops rapidly with practice. It is best to begin by restoring relatively simple, boldly patterned pieces before working on more intricately decorated ones. However, you should never attempt to reglaze or repaint rare or valuable pieces. Instead, employ a professional restorer.

The information below outlines the basic tools, materials and techniques required for repainting and reglazing repaired ceramics. When it comes to mixing colours and freehand painting, it is best to experiment on cheap white ceramic tiles before using these techniques on the piece you wish to repair.

Brushes

Purchase three or four sable artist's brushes, ranging from size 00 to 3, with which to apply paints and glazes. The bristles of the smallest ones should end in a very fine point, which is necessary for detailed work.

Ceramic tiles

Buy at least six white ceramic tiles. Their glazed surface provides an ideal background for mixing and testing off-white glazes, and is also a good substitute for an artist's palette when you are mixing and colour-matching paints.

Additional tools

In addition to artist's brushes and ceramic tiles, you will also need the following: palette knife, scalpel or utility knife, lint-free rag, a cocktail stick, fine-grade silicon-carbide paper and a hard pencil.

Solvents

You will need cold water when thinning and mixing acrylic colours (see below) and for cleaning brushes afterwards. You will need the thinner specified by the manufacturer when tinting cold-cure lacquer (glaze) with artist's powder pigments (see below) and for cleaning brushes.

Glazes

Inexperienced amateur restorers should avoid glazes that have to be hardened in a kiln or oven, as there are many things that can go wrong, notably cracking, crazing, shrinkage and discoloration. Instead, use a cold-cure lacquer (available from artist's suppliers), which will dry at room temperature. The lacquer is mixed, in accordance with the manufacturer's directions, with an accompanying hardener, and the setting time is about 12 hours.

There are two types of cold-cure lacquer. The clear variety is always applied as a final protective coat, while the white version can be tinted with artist's powder pigments (see below) and used to match the original background colour of the object, or to repaint motifs and patterns.

Artist's powder pigments

Powder pigments are available in a wide choice of colours and can be mixed to make other colours. They are soluble in water and white spirit. However, when you are using them to tint glazes and paint ceramics, you must mix them with the thinner specified by the manufacturer for cold-cure lacquer. Very subtle variations in tone and colour can be produced with powder pigments. They are therefore well suited to matching the original colours of ceramics. However, they are slightly more difficult to mix and use than acrylic paints (see below).

Acrylic paints

Available in a wide selection of colours, acrylic paints can be mixed in infinite combinations to create numerous additional shades. Soluble in water, they are relatively easy to mix and apply, and they dry quickly (usually in 2–3 hours). Purchase artist's acrylics rather than standard acrylics, because they offer greater opacity and strength of colour.

Tinting and colouring a glaze

The method you use to tint white cold-cure lacquer is basically the same whether you are matching an off-white background or a coloured background, or you are mixing colours to replace painted decoration. All that differs is the amount of pigment you add. For specific advice on which colours to mix to produce other colours, you should refer to a specialist book on colour theory. The procedure for mixing and colour-matching is as follows.

● Pour a small amount of white cold-cure lacquer onto the middle of a white ceramic tile.

● If the lacquer is from a previously unopened can, it will be of the right consistency. If it is from an old one, it may be slightly too thick and sticky, in which case add a little of the thinner (solvent) specified by the manufacturer of the lacquer.

● Put about one-tenth of a teaspoon of the pigment(s) you wish to add around the perimeter of the tile and carefully chop it finely with a scalpel blade or utility knife to remove any lumps.

● Using the tip of a palette knife, gradually mix a very small quantity of the pigment into the lacquer until you have matched the colour of the original. To increase the opacity of the glaze, add more white lacquer and pigment; to increase its translucency, add more thinner.

● After matching the colour, add the hardening agent that comes with the lacquer and apply the glaze to the repaired area, as described below.

Note: The vast majority of white or slightly off-white ceramics have what professional restorers term a 'cold' or a 'warm' cast. When trying to match these colours, you should add blue or green pigment (or both) to cool a white glaze, and brown or red-brown pigment to warm it.

Mixing acrylic paints

To mix acrylic colours, you should follow roughly the same procedure as for tinting and colouring a glaze. However, because of their faster drying time, it is necessary to work more quickly. Proceed as follows.

● Place a small quantity of white acrylic paint in the middle of the white ceramic tile.

● Place very small quantities of the coloured acrylics around the perimeter of the tile and gradually mix them into the white with a brush or the tip of a palette knife until you have achieved the desired colour. Adding a little water to the mix will make it more fluid and increase its translucency.

Applying tinted and coloured glazes

When you have mixed a tinted or coloured glaze (using either cold-cure lacquer and powder pigments, or acrylic paints), touch in the ground colour of the ceramic as follows.

● Load the bristles of an artist's brush with the glaze or paint. Don't overload the brush, but apply just enough to let the glaze or paint flow smoothly onto the surface.

● Brush a thin coat of paint or glaze over the repaired area, working outwards from the middle to the perimeter. Try to use light individual brush strokes, because brushing over an area more than once can leave brush marks in the glaze.

● To blend the newly glazed or painted section into the surrounding areas, you must 'feather' around the edges. Do this as quickly as possible (particularly if you are working with quick-drying acrylics) by lightly stroking the bristles over the edges of the repair. Try to drag the colour gently from the middle outwards, but work in a slightly different direction from the one you followed in the previous stage.

● Again, while the glaze or paint is still wet, repeat the feathering technique. This time, if you are using white-tinted lacquer glaze, moisten the bristles with clear lacquer; if you are using acrylics, moisten them with water. The aim is to use the clear glaze or water to thin the colour as much as possible around the edges of the repair so that no distinct line is formed between the new and old sections.

● If you have unintentionally over-feathered any surrounding pattern or motif with the tinted glaze, moisten a cocktail stick with thinner and use the tip and edge of the pick to carefully remove the glaze to the edges of the pattern or motif. (If you have over-feathered acrylics, moisten the pick with water.)

● Let the glaze or paint dry fully, then very lightly sand it with fine-grade silicon-carbide paper. The aim is to remove any visible brush strokes and wear away any noticeable line between the reglazed or repainted section and the surrounding area.

● Wipe off any dust from the surface and repeat the previous stages to apply a second coat of glaze or paint, if necessary adjusting the colour. You may have to apply a third coat.

● When you have sanded the final ground coat, brush on a single coat of clear cold-cure lacquer, feathering the edges of the repair as before. However, if you have to repaint any sections of pattern or motif (see below), do so before applying the clear glaze.

Freehand painting

As with the ground coat, retouching motifs and patterns can be done with either white cold-cure lacquer coloured with powder pigments, or with artist's acrylics, both of which are applied with sable-bristle artist's brushes. Freehand painting is largely a matter of artistic ability, but there are some measures that you can adopt to make things easier. Among these are the following.

● With more complicated patterns, outline them first with a series of faint dots made with a sharp pencil. This will provide you with a guide for your brush strokes.

● In addition to using a fine-tipped artist's brush, in some situations you will find it helpful to touch in very fine lines by applying the glaze or paint with the tip of a cocktail stick.

● Never overload the bristles of the brush.

● Always work on only one colour of the motif or pattern at a time. Don't move on to the next colour until you are satisfied with the shape, colour and opacity of the previous one.

● When using acrylic paints, try to work as quickly as possible, because they dry relatively quickly compared with other finishes.

● Keep some thin, lint-free rags and cocktail sticks on hand, plus the appropriate solvent (water for acrylics; thinner for lacquer), so that you can immediately remove the effects of over-brushing or any accidental splashes or spillage.

Glassware

Introduction

Glassmaking can be traced back to Ancient Egypt around the 16th century B.C. Since then, typical items made from glass include drinking vessels, storage vessels for food and liquids, candelabra, chandeliers, paperweights, doorstops, bells, inlays for furniture, jewellery, and clear and coloured window panes. The basic ingredient of glass is silica, which occurs in the form of flint, quartz or sand. Silica's melting point is far above that needed to make glass, so an alkaline flux is added to reduce the melting point of the mix, as well as to bind the ingredients together. By and large, it is the composition of the flux that determines the type of glass produced.

Types of glass

There are three basic types of glass: soda, potash and lead-crystal. Soda glass is made by heating silica, sodium carbonate and calcium carbonate to 1000°C (1832°F). Despite the high temperatures required to make it, soda glass is easy to produce and has often been used to make inexpensive items such as bottles. One of the best-known examples of soda glass is *vetro di cristallo*, a clear or pale yellow glass developed by the Venetians in the 14th century.

Potash glass (sometimes known as 'forest glass') was developed in Bohemia during the Middle Ages. A compound of potassium carbonate and silica, potash glass is very hard. It is unsuitable for cutting, and is mainly used to make household vessels. The term 'potash' derives from the practice of burning wood and using the ashes as a source of potassium chloride.

Lead-crystal glass was first made by the British glass-maker George Ravenscroft in 1671. It is produced by using a high proportion of lead oxide in a mixture that usually consists of three parts silica, two parts red lead, one part potash and small amounts of saltpeter, borax and arsenic. This high-quality, soft, brilliant glass is well suited to cut and engraved decoration.

Shaping glass

Before the 1st century B.C., glass was shaped by 'core forming', a technique in which threads of molten glass were wound around a sand or clay core. Once the core was covered, the vessel was then smoothed, or 'marvered', on a flat surface to fuse the threads. During the 1st century B.C. the Romans devised a new shaping technique: blowing. Free-blown glass was made by placing a blob of molten glass, a gather, on the end of a hollow iron blowing rod. When the main body of the vessel had been formed, it was often transferred to a pontil rod for further shaping. Mould-blown glass was produced by blowing the gather into a wooden or metal mould made up of one or more parts. A third method of shaping – pressing – was developed in the

Victorian glass
A collection of 19th-century, blown and pressed, plain and coloured glass. Decorations include diamond-point engraving and acid-etching.

Rodney decanter
An early 19th-century dark green Rodney decanter. Designed by Admiral Lord Rodney, the decanter's flattened onion-shaped base provided necessary stability when used on board ship.

early 19th century. Pressed glass was made by pouring molten glass into a mould, and forcing it in with a plunger. This process was mechanized in the United States: compressed air was used to push the plunger into the mould.

Coloured glass

There are four basic methods of colouring glass. The first method involves mixing metal oxides into the basic ingredients. The second method entails partly inflating a gather to form a bubble. A second gather is then placed inside it and blown, so that the two layers fuse as they inflate, to give 'cased' or 'overlay' glass. The third method involves painting or dipping a vessel in a contrasting colour to leave a thin surface film that can be cut or engraved, to produce 'flashed' glass. The fourth method entails painting on a solution of metal oxides, to make stained glass.

Decoration of glass

There are two basic categories of glass decoration: 'in front of the kiln' and 'after making'. 'In front of the kiln' decorations are applied while the glass is still hot and soft. The best-known examples are 'trailing' and *lattimo*. 'Trailing' involves laying thin rods of molten metal or threads of hot glass over the main body of the glass to form a decorative pattern. *Lattimo*, a milky-white glass developed in Venice during the 15th century, is used in the form of lace-like threads to make decorative patterns within the body of the glass. Examples include *vetro a fili* (straight or spiral patterns) and *vetro a reticello* (a lattice effect).

'After making' decorations include: enamelling, gilding, cutting, acid-etching and engraving. Enamelling involves binding coloured powdered glass with an oily substance, painting it onto the glass object, and reheating it to fuse the decoration. Gilding involves mixing gold paint, leaf or powder with a fixative and firing it to the vessel. Cutting glass entails cutting sharp-edged patterns into the surface of the glass to maximize the refraction of light and therefore enhance its brilliance. In 'acid-etching' the vessel is covered with an acid-resistant coating, through which a design is engraved. The glass is then dipped into acid, which traces the design and creates a matt or frosted effect. There are three methods of engraving. 'Diamond-point' is achieved by inscribing patterns with a diamond nib. 'Wheel engraving' employs a copper cutting wheel to the same effect. In 'stipple engraving' a diamond needle produces a pattern of small dots.

Tools and materials

The tools and materials you will need to clean and repair glassware call for some precautionary measures. It is important to protect your eyes, lungs and any areas of exposed skin when handling various cleaning fluids and chemicals and, where specified, to work in a well-ventilated area. Also, while it is advisable to keep a first-aid kit to hand when repairing almost any object, it is particularly important when working with a fragile and potentially sharp material such as glass. In addition, you should keep children and pets out of the work area.

Tools

1 Scalpel blade (or utility or craft knife) To trim repairs made with anaerobic adhesive.
2 Razor blades As above.
3 Scalpel As above.
4 Magnifying glass To inspect surfaces of glass before you make repairs.
5 Electric drill To drive a buffing mop.
6 Buffing mop A polishing attachment for the above. A small lambswool version is best.
7 Dusting brush A medium-sized, soft, fine-bristled brush to dust glass.
8 Artist's brushes A selection of small, pointed and flat-tipped sable artist's brushes to touch up painted and gilded repairs, and to apply adhesive to jointed repairs. Sizes 00–3 should suffice.
9 Wood dowel A short length of 2cm dowelling. Used with silicon carbide paper for grinding down small chips and sharp edges.
10 Plastic goggles To protect eyes.
11 Face mask To protect face and lungs when using various cleaning fluids.

YOU WILL ALSO NEED:
Small plate or saucer Or a similar shallow vessel on which to mix paints.
Gloves Thin, tight-fitting leather gloves to protect your hands from cuts. Chemical-resistant rubber gloves are required when using chemicals to clean glass.
Flexible drive attachment A useful accessory for an electric drill. The attachment allows you greater control over buffing and polishing, improves access to recessed areas and minimizes the risk of breakages.
Soft-bristled toothbrush To clean recessed and engraved areas of glass.

First-aid kit
Hair-drier
Soft-bristled scrubbing brush
Cocktail sticks
Plastic basin

Materials

12 Silicon-carbide paper Also known as wet-and-dry paper. Medium- and fine-grade versions to grind and smooth chips and sharp edges.
13 Soft linen cloth Lint-free to clean, dry, and polish.
14 Chamois leather As above.
15 Cotton buds To clean recessed areas.
16 Masking tape To protect surrounding areas when cleaning, repainting and regilding.
17 Adhesive tape To support glued repairs while the adhesive is drying.
18 Modelling clay As above.
19 Adhesives To bond broken glass use a proprietary anaerobic clear adhesive specifically formulated for the purpose. However, to mend some pieces of opaque coloured glass you must use a cyanoacrylate adhesive (super or instant glue). Unlike anaerobic adhesive, this is not dependent for setting on exposure to ultraviolet light (which some coloured glass can filter out). For specified cases you will also need a two-part epoxy-resin adhesive.
20 Paints Specially formulated glass paints are available from most craft and art supply shops. Artist's acrylic paints can also be used, and their greater opacity makes them particularly suitable for mixing with epoxy-resin adhesives when making tinted repairs to coloured glass.
21 Liquid metal leaf Available from artist's suppliers and some craft shops, liquid metal leaf is used to touch up areas of gilding on relatively inexpensive pieces. It is available in gold, silver and a selection of other colours.
22 Metallic powders An alternative to liquid metal leaf for touching up gilded glassware. They are available in a range of colours.
23 Gold size A clear adhesive for metallic powders.

THE FOLLOWING ARE USED TO CLEAN GLASS:
24 White spirit
25 Lemon juice
26 White vinegar
27 Hydrochloric acid A solution of hydrochloric acid (available from pharmacists) will remove lime scale.
Note: Hydrochloric acid can be highly volatile. Wear protective gloves and clothing when handling it. Always add the acid to the water; if you add the water to the acid, the mixture will bubble over and may splash into your eyes or skin, causing severe burns.
28 Jeweller's rouge A fine, slightly abrasive cleaning and polishing paste available from most jewellers.

YOU WILL ALSO NEED:
Acetone
Distilled water
Washing-up liquid
Scouring powder
Ammonia
Methylated spirits
Paraffin
Eggshell
Salt
Olive oil
Coarse sand
Lead shot
Terry towelling

Cleaning glassware

The procedures employed to clean antique glassware are reasonably safe and straightforward, provided you stick to the simple precautions explained below. Some of the chemicals you will need to remove stains from glass are flammable or caustic. Always protect your eyes, lungs and skin when working with them, and make sure the work space is well ventilated and that there are no open flames around. Finally, never place antique glassware in an automatic dishwasher.

Clear and coloured glass

To avoid breakages always wash one piece at a time, using the following method.

1 Line the bottom of a plastic basin with three or four layers of thick terry towelling.

2 Fill the basin with warm water and mix in some washing-up liquid. If the glass is particularly dirty or greasy, add a few drops of ammonia.

3 Wearing rubber gloves, immerse the glass and wash it by hand. You will find a soft-bristled toothbrush is ideal for cleaning crevices and engraved areas. If it proves necessary, remove stubborn dirt and grime in these areas by dipping the toothbrush in a little methylated spirits.

Note: Never use methylated spirits on the inside of decanters and containers for potable liquids.

4 Rinse the glass thoroughly under lukewarm water, then dry as described later on this page.

Stained glass

Old and valuable stained glass that has deteriorated badly (usually from long exposure to pollution) should be entrusted to a professional restorer. Gently clean lesser pieces with a soft-bristled scrubbing brush, warm water, washing-up liquid, and a few drops of ammonia (as described above), then rinse and dry thoroughly (as described right).

Enamelled and gilt glass

Gently wipe away dirt and grime with a soft chamois leather moistened with methylated spirits. Then gently buff the piece with a dry chamois.

Mirrors

Even if the silver backing of an antique mirror has badly deteriorated, you should never attempt to repair it, for any such restoration will always substantially devalue the piece. Three traditional methods are used to clean the fronts of mirrors, and all are effective. Whichever one you choose, make sure that you don't allow any moisture to creep behind the glass, which will cause further deterioration of the silvering.

● **Cleaning with methylated spirits**
Wipe the glass with a lint-free linen cloth moistened with methylated spirits.

● **Washing with water and ammonia**
Immerse a lint-free linen cloth in a bowl of lukewarm water to which you have added a few drops of ammonia. Wring out the cloth until it is just moist, then wipe the surface of the glass.

● **Cleaning with paraffin**
Lightly moisten a lint-free rag with paraffin and wipe the glass.

Note: Although this method works very well, it leaves a smell of paraffin in the air for some time afterwards.

Cleaning chandeliers

In the past, the cut-glass pendants and drops of candle-lit chandeliers rapidly accumulated dirt and grime, mainly from tallow smoke, and so they required frequent cleaning. Dirt is much less of a problem with chandeliers lit by electric bulbs, but the heat that they generate does attract it, and cleaning their numerous components is no less labour-intensive. Moreover, if they can't be easily removed from the ceiling, the power supply must be switched off before cleaning begins. This is to prevent the risk of electrocution as a result of electricity being conducted through the liquid cleaning agents.

There are two traditional methods for cleaning the pendants and drops of a chandelier. You can wipe them with either a solution of hot water, a little washing-up liquid, and a few drops of ammonia, or with hot water and a small quantity of methylated spirits and white vinegar. In either case, start at the top of the chandelier and work down, so that drips don't fall onto the pendants and drops you have already cleaned. When you have finished cleaning, rinse with warm water and dry thoroughly (as described below).

To clean any metal mountings on chandeliers (or any other item of glassware), refer to the chapter on Metalware (see pp.210–13).

Drying glass

Prolonged exposure to moisture or dampness will produce either a dull white cloudiness, or iridescence (a rainbow-like effect), on the surface of glass. In some cases general cleaning (see left) will eliminate the problem, but failing that you must employ a more radical treatment (see Removing stains, opposite). However, it is far better to prevent the problem from arising than to have to cure it. You can do this by always drying glass thoroughly after cleaning, and by always storing or displaying it in well-ventilated, damp-free surroundings.

The best way to dry all types of glass is to wipe it gently with either a chamois leather or a soft, lint-free linen cloth. (You should not use a cotton or woollen cloth as these can deposit small flecks of material that will spoil the appearance of the glass.) If you can't pass a cloth through the neck of a vessel such as a decanter, direct a hair-drier, on a low or medium heat setting, into the opening for two or three minutes. Do not overheat the glass or you risk cracking it.

Removing stains

There are two basic causes of stains on glassware: exposure to moisture or dampness, and exposure to alcohol. The iridescence and cloudiness caused by moisture and dampness can sometimes be removed during general cleaning and drying (see opposite). More often than not, however, you will have to apply the remedy for removing the grey-white calcium carbonate deposits that can also form on glass during prolonged exposure to moisture and dampness.

Alcoholic drinks, in particular red wine, port and sherry, will leave a residue that forms dark stains on the surface of the glass. The insides of decanters are particularly prone to this. Various remedies for removing stains are outlined below, although you should note that stains that have been left untreated for a considerable length of time often prove impossible to remove completely.

Iridescence and cloudiness

To remove or reduce iridescence and cloudiness, proceed as follows.

1 Soak the glassware in distilled water for up to seven days, changing the water every day.
2 At the end of this period, remove any remaining cloudiness with a soft-bristled brush. If this proves only partly successful, try the remedy for removing deposits of lime scale (calcium carbonate) (see below).

Deposits of lime scale

To remove or reduce a build-up of grey-white deposits of lime scale (calcium carbonate) proceed as follows.

1 If the deposits are inside a container, pour enough distilled water into the container to cover the stain. If the deposits are on the outside of a piece of glassware, submerge the piece in a plastic basin filled with distilled water.
2 Make sure the work area is well ventilated, and put on protective goggles, chemical-resistant rubber gloves and a face mask. Very slowly pour hydrochloric acid into the water until the deposit starts to bubble.

3 Leave until the deposit has completely dissolved (carefully adding a little more acid if necessary). Pour out the acid solution.
4 Rinse the container with warm water. Then wash it with warm water and a little washing-up liquid before rinsing again and drying thoroughly.

Alcohol

Virtually all alcohol stains form inside decanters. Five traditional remedies are outlined below. If the first proves unsuccessful, try the next, and so on.

• Pour white vinegar into the decanter to a depth of 2.5cm. Add 5ml (1tsp) of mild scouring powder. Fill the rest of the decanter with warm distilled water. Insert the stopper, shake the decanter thoroughly and let it stand for 24 hours. Pour off the cleaning solution, rinse with warm water, and dry with a hair-drier.
• Pour white vinegar into the decanter until it is a quarter full. Add 10ml (2tsp) of table salt. Insert the stopper and shake the decanter vigorously. Leave for 24 hours, then empty, rinse and dry as before.
• Crush a handful of eggshell and drop it into the decanter. Add warm distilled water and a few drops of ammonia. Shake vigorously, then leave for 24 hours. Empty, rinse and dry as before.
• Fill the decanter with lemon juice and 10ml (2tsp) of salt. Shake, leave, empty, rinse and dry as before.
• Put a handful of coarse sand or lead shot into the decanter. Add a little water and gently shake for a few minutes. Empty, rinse and dry as before.

Freeing a glass stopper

Glass stoppers often become stuck in the neck of decanters and claret jugs, particularly if they were replaced when the neck was still wet with alcohol. You should never attempt to wrench, twist or tap out a stopper; you risk breaking the neck of the decanter.

Instead, pour a small amount of olive oil around the area where the stopper enters the vessel. Leave the vessel to stand for a few hours, during which time the oil will very gradually seep between the stopper and the neck. It should then be easy to remove the stopper. (You must then wash off all traces of the olive oil.)

French magnum decanter

An 18th-century French decanter decorated with gilding and enamelling. British decanters of this period were a standard two imperial pints – notably smaller than this French magnum.

Repairing glassware

Antique glassware is very fragile. Consequently, it is all too easy to scratch, chip or break it, and such damage almost always significantly devalues the piece. Moreover, repairing the damage hardly ever restores its full value, and the majority of repairs are impossible to disguise completely. Nevertheless, while the repair of any rare or valuable piece should always be left to a professional glass restorer, it is possible for the amateur restorer to successfully carry out various minor repairs to lesser items, such as those described below and opposite.

Grinding chipped rims and edges

Because the edges and rims of drinking glasses, bowls and decanters are relatively thin, it is very easy to chip them accidentally. Aside from aesthetically impairing the piece, such damage can easily cause cut fingers or lips if the piece is used. If the piece is rare or valuable, you should not attempt to repair it yourself; take it to a professional glass restorer. If it is not rare or valuable, and the chip isn't large, you can improve its appearance and its usability by grinding and smoothing the rim. The two basic methods for doing this are described below. The one you use will depend on the breadth and depth of the damage. You may wish to wear leather gloves for this work.

Removing scratches

The mass of fine scratches often found on the base of antique glass decanters, vases and bowls is called 'moss scratching'. It is a sign of the piece's age and is caused by everyday use (although it is sometimes faked). Never try to remove it. However, scratches on any other part of a glass item dull it and detract from its appearance. If a piece is not greatly valuable, remove or reduce scratches as follows.

● For fine scratches, moisten jeweller's rouge with methylated spirits to make a creamy paste. For deeper scratches, use undiluted rouge. Dip a piece of chamois leather into the rouge and rub out the scratches using a circular motion and moderate pressure.

Note: In both cases, finish by rinsing the piece with cold water, patting it dry with terry towelling, and buffing it to a shine with a soft, lint-free linen cloth.

1 Grinding fine chips

● Cut a strip from a sheet of fine-grade silicon-carbide paper and wrap it tightly around a piece of 2cm wooden dowelling approximately 5cm long.

● Support the glass, bowl or decanter with one hand, and press the dowelling against it with the other hand. Using moderately firm pressure, move the dowelling from side to side to grind the sharp edges smooth.

1 Grinding large or deep chips

● With epoxy-resin adhesive, glue half a sheet of fine-grade silicon-carbide paper to a flat work surface.

● Wet the rim of the piece in water and grind it by hand in a gentle, circular motion over the paper. Stop regularly to re-wet the rim and to assess whether you have reduced its height to level with the bottom of the chipped area. Change the paper as necessary.

Patching holes in glass

When glass breaks, fragments may splinter off, leaving small holes. After mending the break (see opposite), fill these with clear anaerobic adhesive (for clear glass) or tinted epoxy-resin adhesive (for coloured glass).

● With a cocktail stick, insert adhesive to fill the hole. If the hole goes right through, place adhesive tape over one side to stop the adhesive falling through. Once the adhesive has set, carefully peel off the tape.

Mending simple breaks

'Water-clear' anaerobic and epoxy-resin adhesives are both used to mend broken glass. On clear glass the former look better because they are less visible. Another advantage is that they set only when exposed to daylight. This gives you time to align and joint the repair under artificial light (with any curtains or blinds shut), and then expose it to daylight to harden the adhesive once you are ready. The setting time is 10–15 seconds in direct, bright sunlight and 2–3 minutes on overcast days.

Clear glass

To mend simple breaks in clear glass, proceed as follows, but bear in mind that completely invisible repairs are almost impossible to make.

- Remove any dirt or grease from the edges of the break with a lint-free cloth moistened with acetone.
- Attach masking tape to one side of the break.
- Block out daylight from any windows or doors and work under artificial light. Using a cocktail stick or the edge of a scalpel blade, apply a very thin layer of anaerobic adhesive along both edges of the break.
- Bring the edges together to make the joint. Apply pressure with your fingers to expel excess adhesive and air bubbles.
- Carefully stretch adhesive tape from one side of the repair to the other and press it down.
- Using a lint-free rag moistened with acetone, immediately wipe off the excess adhesive from the surrounding surface.
- Expose the repair to daylight, which will set the adhesive. Leave the repair for a further 24 hours to ensure full hardening.
- Peel off the adhesive tape, and buff the glass to a shine with a chamois leather.

Coloured glass

To mend breaks in coloured glass, employ the same method as recommended for clear glass (*see* above). However, some pieces of opaque coloured glass filter out the ultraviolet rays in daylight that set anaerobic adhesive. To mend such a piece you may have to use a two-part epoxy-resin adhesive or a cyanoacrylate adhesive, both of which set chemically rather than photochemically. If an anaerobic adhesive fails to set, remove it with the solvent specified by its maker and apply an epoxy-resin adhesive to the break instead.

You can also tint either anaerobic or epoxy-resin adhesive with proprietary glass paints or artist's acrylic paints, so that the repair blends in with the surrounding surface. Because matching the colour to the original is a matter of trial and error, tint some test batches of adhesive on a saucer or plate before you carry out the repair. Blend the paints into the adhesive while it is still wet, using a small artist's brush and adding additional colour(s) until you are happy with the mix.

Try also to match the translucency of colour of the glass that you are repairing. In general, proprietary glass paints are more translucent than artist's acrylics, but the latter can be made less opaque by thinning them with a small quantity of water before mixing them with the adhesive.

Repairing a broken wine glass stem

To repair the broken stem of a wine glass, follow the procedure described under 'Mending simple breaks', above. However, instead of supporting the repair with adhesive tape, turn the glass upside down and, on each side of the stem, attach a column of modelling clay to support the base while the adhesive hardens.

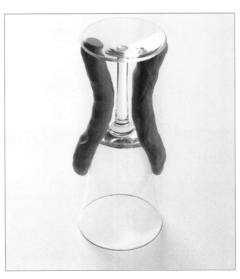

Restoring gilding

In the decorative technique of gilding the glass is painted with gold leaf, gold dust or gold paint. This is either allowed to set cold or is fired in a kiln. It is not unusual for gilding to wear away, particularly on the rims of drinking glasses, such as the blue rummer shown below. If the piece is rare or valuable, you should entrust the task of regilding to a professional restorer. However, to touch up worn gilding on lesser pieces, use liquid gold leaf paint or metallic powders and employ the method for regilding ceramics described on p.191.

Rummer with gilding

This drinking glass – known as a rummer – was made in Bristol, England, at the beginning of the 19th century. The gilding around the rim is typical of rummers made of coloured, rather than clear, glass. Many examples were further decorated with gilding on the body, which usually took the form of names or mottos.

Metalware

Introduction

An enormous variety of antiques is made either wholly or partly from metal, and the range of metals used is also considerable. Apart from any intrinsic worth, most antique metalware is highly prized for the patination that builds up on its surface over time. This can be easily damaged if an inappropriate method of cleaning is applied. Initial identification of the metal in question is therefore of paramount importance. While the following should be of some help in this respect, if you have any doubts about what the metal is you are dealing with, seek professional advice.

Gold

Pure gold is rarely used, because of cost and the fact that its relative softness makes it vulnerable to damage. Consequently, other metals are usually added to produce a tougher alloy. The proportion of gold in the mix is specified in carats. Pure gold is 24 carats, while the lesser standards are: 20, 18, 14 and 9 (12 and 15 carats became obsolete in 1932). In addition to a maker's mark, most items are stamped with an assay mark by the country of origin or import. These 'hallmarks' will help you to identify pieces, and you should refer to a specialist book for more information.

The colour of gold alloys varies, depending on the other metals present. The addition of silver lends the basic yellow a whitish hue, while copper produces a subtle, reddish patination. Rolled gold (made by fusing a thin sheet of gold onto a base metal) and gold plate (made by applying a thin coat of gold to a base metal by electrolysis) are not hallmarked, although the latter is often stamped 'gold plated'.

Silver and silver plate

Objects made of solid silver are usually assayed to determine how much silver they contain. Again, refer to a book on silver marks for help with identification. However, because in the past assaying wasn't a legal requirement in some countries, this method of identification isn't foolproof. Fortunately, the silver content of a piece can be established by a silversmith, who employs a simple chemical test.

Less expensive alternatives to 'solid' silver include Sheffield plate, which was made between 1742 and 1840 by rolling a thin sheet of silver onto a sheet of flux-covered copper. Thin grey lines of tin solder along the joints of a piece indicate plate, as opposed to solid silver, as does the absence of hallmarks and date stamps.

Electroplating, invented in 1840, uses electrolysis to cover an object made of a base metal with a very thin coat of silver. Because less silver was used, electroplated items were less costly than Sheffield plate, and rendered the latter almost obsolete. Nickel (or German) silver was also developed in the 19th century. Primarily used for jewellery and tableware, it is in fact an alloy made from copper, zinc and nickel.

A silver sauce tureen
Made in 1791, the English silver tureen shown right was designed to keep gravy hot at the dining table. One of a pair, it has an elegant two-handled shape, and restrained, classical-style reeded decoration (plus monogram), typical of the late 18th century.

Silver dressing-table set
A typical 19th-century silver dressing table set. The bottles, jars and casket are from a different set from the brushes and other paraphernalia of this Victorian lady's boudoir.

Copper, brass and bronze

Pure copper is mainly used for domestic items, notably skillets and kettles. When tarnished, it takes on a dull brownish hue; when polished, it displays a brick-red blush. Many items are made of brass, a yellow alloy originally of copper and tin, but now of copper and zinc, sometimes with one or more other metals. When tarnished, it is a greenish-black or brown. Bronze is an alloy made of copper and tin (although zinc, phosphorus and lead have also been used). It is suited to casting and is mainly found in statuary, weapons and household items. It ages to a dark brown, and corrosion can take the form of verdigris – tiny, light green spots – also found in copper and brass.

Chromium, nickel and tin

Chromium is applied as a thin plating over a base metal. Typical pieces include cocktail shakers and toys. When polished, it has a white, almost mirror-like finish. Over copper it can show a subtle reddish-yellow sheen. Nickel-plated objects have a silver-like appearance when polished, as do those plated or lined with tin. Tin is used mainly as a lining for copper cooking utensils, or as a plating for the steel panels of toys, including the mechanical kind called automata.

Iron and steel

The low carbon content of wrought iron makes it tough, malleable and suitable for forging items such as andirons and fenders. It is steel-grey when polished. Cast iron, also grey, has a high carbon content. Too brittle to forge, it is poured into moulds while molten to make pieces such as fire surrounds and garden furniture.

Steel is an alloy made up of mainly iron and carbon. Extremely tough, and capable of maintaining a sharp edge, it is well suited to the manufacture of swords and other weapons, as well as fire grates, fenders, pokers and tongs. Stainless steel, which contains 8–25 per cent chromium, is impervious to rusting.

Pewter and lead

A grey alloy largely made of tin, pewter has mostly been used to make drinking vessels and tablewares. Specific types of pewter include Ashbury metal, which is used for snuff boxes, spoons and forks. Also grey, lead is used mainly for garden ornaments and toy soldiers (and often painted). Lead pieces are either hollow-cast or solid, and when weathered outdoors develop a blue-grey-green patination.

Victoriana
The copper coffee pot, accompanied by a small bronze urn, is slightly the worse for wear. Both pieces are 19th century, the pot inspired by Middle Eastern forms and decoration, the urn by Classical Greek design.

207

Tools and materials

Some of the chemicals needed to clean metalware are caustic or toxic, or both. When using them, always work in a well-ventilated area, and wear goggles, gloves and a mask, to protect your eyes, hands, face and lungs. Children and pets should be kept out of the work area, and when not in use the chemicals should be stored safely in a secure place.

Tools

1 Hammers Use a plastic- or rubber-faced hammer to reshape metal pieces; used carefully, this will not leave hammer marks on the surface of the metal. However, you can use a metal-headed hammer, such as a ball pein, to strike the end of a wooden stake when reshaping the bases of various specified pieces.
2 Rubber mallet An alternative to a plastic- or rubber-faced hammer when reshaping larger surface areas.
3 Bench vice Also known as an engineer's vice. Use this, firmly attached to the edge of a work bench or table, to secure items to be reshaped and soldered.
4 Electric hand drills A standard-sized electric drill will drive buffing and polishing mop attachments for polishing metalware. To carry out tasks on smaller items, use a small electric drill of the type available from craft shops. These craft drills are usually supplied with a range of attachments, including sanding and buffing wheels and metal drill bits.
5 Buffing mop A lambswool buffing mop designed for use with an electric hand drill is an effective means of polishing metalware.
6 Soft-bristled brush To dust and polish metalware, use a fine-bristled sable brush.
7 Soldering iron To solder minor repairs, use an electric soldering iron with a tapered head.
8 Wooden stake Use a length of hardwood (after tapering or rounding the end) as a 'former' when beating or pressing out dents, plus a block of hardwood to support bases when knocking out dents.
9 Small, stiff-bristled artist's brush Use this or a stiff-bristled toothbrush to remove dirt from recesses.
10 Plastic goggles To protect the eyes from various caustic cleaning fluids.
11 Face mask To protect the face and lungs from dust and the noxious vapours given off by some of the specified cleaning agents.

YOU WILL ALSO NEED:
Rubber gloves Wear chemical-resistant rubber gloves to protect the hands from various caustic cleaning fluids.
Cotton gloves Wear these when handling metalware, especially silver, to protect the surface from marks caused by sweat, acids and oils in the skin.
Tweezers To hold cotton wool when cleaning small pieces, particularly those made of silver.
Wooden tongs To hold silver pieces in a chemical dip.
Plastic basin To contain the chemical dip solution mostly used to clean silver and silver plate.
Mixing vessels To mix cleaning agents, use plastic, metal or glass vessels in various sizes.
Small tenon saw To cut lengths of hardwood.
Wood file To shape hardwood 'formers'.
Heavy-duty utility or craft knife Use as above.
Household scissors
Metal tape measure or ruler
Small paint brush
Magnifying glass

Materials

12 Epoxy-resin metal adhesive
13 Adhesive tape
14 Solder and flux Use these with a soldering iron.
15 Metallic pastes and powders To disguise minor repairs. Available from artist's suppliers.

THE FOLLOWING ARE USED TO CLEAN SPECIFIED ITEMS OF METALWARE:
16 Paint stripper
17 Rust remover
18 Silver polish Available in liquid form, or as a chemical-impregnated cloth. The latter is very useful for frequent light cleaning and polishing.
19 Brass polish

20 Ammonia Available from chemists.
21 Methylated spirits
22 Washing soda
23 Jeweller's rouge Available from most jewellers and some hardware stores.
24 Emery paper To remove or disguise scratches in harder metals (but not copper or silver).
25 Wire wool Grades 000–0.
26 Aluminium foil To line a plastic basin when preparing a chemical dip.
27 Clear lacquer To seal and protect brass.
28 Chamois leather
29 Paraffin
30 Cotton wool
31 Lint-free rag

YOU WILL ALSO NEED:
Sandpaper Coarse, medium and fine grades.
Whiting Use to remove fine scratches.
White spirit
Liquid soap
Rhubarb leaves Use to remove stains from aluminium.
Note: Handle these with care, as they contain oxalic acid, which is highly poisonous.
Lemon juice
White vinegar
Distilled water
Salt
Borax
Microcrystalline wax
Chrome polish
Beeswax
Sunflower oil
Old towelling
Parcel string
Sheets of fibreglass matting

General care and cleaning

Most metalware is subject to various forms of tarnishing and discoloration caused by general use and atmospheric pollution. To protect metal pieces from these problems and to maintain their value, you must regularly dust, clean and polish them, using the techniques and materials described below.

Whatever metal you are treating, work slowly and carefully, since it is easy to overdo cleaning and remove desirable patination rather than just surface tarnish and dirt. This is particularly important if you use an electric drill and lambswool buffing mop to polish robust base metals, such as iron and steel, rather than polishing them by hand with a cloth. Bear in mind also that the treatments are suitable only for the metal for which they are specified. If a piece contains more than one metal (or another material), you may have to isolate and treat each one in turn to protect those adjacent to it from an inappropriate cleaning agent.

Finally, to protect cleaned and polished metalware that is to be stored rather than displayed, wrap it first in acid-free tissue paper and then in a proprietary impregnated anti-tarnish paper or cloth.

Aluminium

The following is a traditional method for removing stubborn stains from aluminium. Boil the tops of the stalks and the leaves of a rhubarb plant in water. Apply the liquid to the surface with a wad of cotton wool, and leave for 5–10 minutes. Remove the wad, and the stain should have gone. Rhubarb leaves contain oxalic acid, which is poisonous, so you should wear goggles, a face mask and rubber gloves when you are using it for cleaning, and keep children and pets away from where you are working.

Arms and armour

Great care is called for in cleaning arms and armour. Because different metals are often incorporated in one piece it is easy to splash a cleaning agent appropriate for one metal over another, damaging its patination. The way to avoid this problem is to take the piece apart. However, this is often impossible or beyond the abilities of the amateur restorer. You can have such items cleaned professionally. Alternatively, cover surrounding areas with masking tape and gradually apply, on a small piece of cotton wool, the appropriate

cleaning agent for the metal you are treating. This procedure is both time-consuming and labour-intensive, but it will minimize the risk of damage.

Brass

Various cleaning methods will revive tarnished brass, and the remedy you choose will depend on how unsightly the tarnishing is. In every case, wear plastic goggles and rubber gloves. If the piece is minimally tarnished, clean and polish it with a proprietary brass polish and a soft, lint-free rag. If the problem is a few obstinate marks, mix a little paraffin with jeweller's rouge to form a thick, cream-like paste. Gently apply the paste with a rag until the marks have gone. Adding two drops of ammonia to the mix often helps. To remove heavier tarnishing, mix a tablespoon each of salt and vinegar with 300ml of hot water. Gently apply this with fine-grade wire wool. When the tarnishing has been removed, wash the piece with warm, soapy water; rinse thoroughly with clean, cold water, and dry immediately with a piece of towelling. Protect and polish brass by applying very sparingly, on a soft lint-free rag, a proprietary brass polish or a

little microcrystalline wax. Alternatively, for outside brass door knockers, knobs and handles, brush on a coat of clear lacquer.

Bronze

Treat all bronze pieces with great caution, and never use abrasive powders to clean them. A considerable part of their value lies in the subtle patination that gradually accumulates over the years. You can safely dust them with a soft-bristled brush, and tease out any dirt or grease from recessed areas with a soft-bristled toothbrush moistened with white spirit. If the bronze was originally polished, it will respond well to treatment with a fine white wax polish, such as the microcrystalline wax that is used to finish leatherware (see pp.132–3).

Champlevé

A decorative form of metalwork, champlevé involves cutting small depressions into the surface of a metal, usually copper, filling them with enamel pastes, then firing the piece at high temperature to fix the enamels. Before cleaning a champlevé piece, inspect the enamels with a magnifying glass to make sure they are secure. If they are, give the piece a thorough cleaning by gently working a solution of good-quality liquid soap and lukewarm distilled water over the surface with a soft-bristled artist's brush. Finish by rinsing with clean water. Remove any spots of grease with the artist's brush moistened with white spirit. If the enamels have become loose, have them secured by a professional restorer before cleaning.

Chasing

In the surface decoration known as chasing, small punches, chisels and a chasing hammer are used to gouge out shallow grooves in the metal. To remove the dirt and grime that collects in these hollows, clean the piece gently with a soft-bristled brush or a soft-bristled toothbrush moistened with white spirit.

Chromium

Remove reddish-brown rust spots (iron oxide) from thin chromium plating by gently applying a proprietary chrome polish with a soft cloth in accordance with the manufacturer's instructions. To remove dirt, wash the piece with lukewarm, soapy water and a soft cloth. Rinse with clean water, and dry thoroughly with old towelling. If the chromium is discoloured, add a few drops of ammonia to the lukewarm, soapy water. Buff with a small quantity of chrome polish on a soft cloth.

Cloisonné

In this ancient form of decorative metalware, small fences of metal (usually silver or gold) are soldered to a metal surface, filled with enamel pastes, then fired in an oven. Use the same cleaning method as described for champlevé.

Coins and medals

The various forms of patination that build up on coins and medals are highly prized by collectors and often contribute substantially to their value. For this reason, you should entrust treatment for corrosion, and even general cleaning, to a professional.

Copper

Clean copper items using any one of the methods recommended for brass, or use the chemical dip for cleaning silver described on p.213. Remove small spots of blue-green verdigris by using a small piece of cotton wool to wipe on a paste made from white vinegar and salt, then rinse the piece with water and dry it thoroughly. To treat more extensive patches of verdigris, mix a solution consisting of approximately 15g of lemon juice to 600ml of warm distilled water, and sponge the solution over the piece. Rinse it with a weak solution of warm, soapy water, and then again with clean, warm water. Finally, dry it thoroughly with old towelling. You can protect the cleaned piece with a thin coating of microcrystalline wax.

Damascening

In damascening, metals (usually precious) are inlaid into the surface of another metal (usually base) and then hammered into position. Cleaning this type of metalwork requires the use of nitric acid, which is dangerous, so employ a professional.

Engraving and etching

The lines formed by the technique of engraving collect dirt and grime. Clean and polish them with a small artist's brush and the cleaning-polishing agent specified for the metal in question. Buff thoroughly to remove all the polish, or more dirt will be attracted. To clean etching, first examine the piece under a magnifying glass. If edges of the metal are breaking down, take the piece to a professional for cleaning; if they are not, use the method for cleaning engraving.

Gold

See p.225.

Iron and steel

Cast and wrought iron, and steel (an iron alloy), are particularly prone to rusting. You can treat it when it first appears (as a reddish-brown tinge) with a rust remover, or by wiping the piece with a brush soaked in paraffin. In both cases, rinse afterwards with white spirit, before drying thoroughly with old towelling. It is wise to protect the surface against further corrosion by heating it very slightly (with a hair-drier) and then applying a thin coating of microcrystalline wax.

If the rust has been developing for a long time, the metal will be pitted. There is nothing you can do about this except brush off the rust and treat it as described above. Never grind down the pitting, particularly on old swords and armour: you will almost certainly destroy their value. However, certain cast-iron fittings, such as fire surrounds and fenders, can be shot-blasted to remove rust and encrusted paint,

before you wipe on microcrystalline wax and then carefully polish with an electric drill and a lambswool buffing mop. Flaking paint can be removed with a paint stripper, but you must wear chemical-resistant rubber gloves to protect your hands when carrying out this task.

Lead

The blue-grey-green patina that develops on old pieces is easily destroyed. Limit cleaning to brushing the surface vigorously with a stiff-bristled artist's brush. Mould growth, which is particularly common on garden ornaments, should be allowed to dry out naturally indoors before you brush the piece.

Niello

This is a decorative effect produced by filling engraving or chasing with a black composition material. It is very easy for an amateur accidentally to rub out the composition and undo at a stroke the skilled work of the craftsman. You are advised to have niello cleaned and restored by a professional.

Pewter

The patination typical of pewter is easily destroyed by abrasive cleaning agents and overwashing. Therefore limit cleaning to dusting down with a soft-bristled brush and then gently rubbing over the surface with a clean chamois leather. Old pewter is subject to contamination by salts that form spots. You should have these treated by a professional, as the technique employs dangerous chemicals.

Platinum

See p.225.

Silver

See pp.212–13.

Washing and cleaning silver

Always wash silverware soon after use, particularly if it has been exposed to egg, salt, vinegar, fruit juice or salad dressing. Wash it in hot, soapy water, wiping it with a soft cloth and scrubbing recesses with a soft toothbrush. Rinse with clean, hot water and dry with clean, soft towelling. If the silver is not tarnished, buff with a clean, dry, soft cloth; if it is, polish as described below. Silver and silver plate are very vulnerable to tarnishing: a dull dark-brown or purple film of silver sulphide forms on the surface. This occurs when silver is exposed to sulphur dioxide in the atmosphere, and is exacerbated by salt, casein-based emulsion paints (often found on the inside of old cupboards) and the acids in your skin. Because of this last problem, always wear white cotton gloves to handle silver or to clean it by hand.

YOU WILL NEED:
White cotton gloves
Proprietary silver polish Available as an impregnated cloth, a liquid or a paste. The severity of the tarnishing will determine which is required.
Soft cloth
Soft-bristled toothbrush
Chamois leather
Fine-bristled artist's brush

Cleaning and polishing silver by hand

In the majority of cases tarnished items of silver and silver plate can be successfully cleaned and polished by hand, using a soft cloth and a proprietary silver cleaner. However, you should note that all such cleaners have a mild abrasive action which removes a minute layer of silver from the surface of a piece each time they are used.

The long-term effects of this are most noticeable on pieces made of silver plate. Eventually, enough silver is worn away to expose the base metal underneath the plate.

It is for this reason that you should use the gentlest possible buffing and polishing action when treating items of silverware with a cleaning agent (as shown opposite). However, before proceeding you should consider the alternative: cleaning them in an electrochemical dip (as described on the opposite page).

1 Assessing the piece

● Wash, rinse and dry the silver as described above, then assess the degree of tarnishing. If it is light, you can use an impregnated silver cloth. More serious tarnishing will require a liquid or paste. If it is very bad, clean the item in an electrochemical dip (see opposite page).

● With silver-plated items such as the stirrup cups shown here, assess how much silver has worn away and how much of the base metal is showing through. If a lot of the latter is visible, brief immersion in a chemical dip is the best approach, as it will minimize further erosion of the silver.

2 Cleaning and polishing

● Put on white cotton gloves. If you use an impregnated silver cloth, rub it over the piece, pressing slightly harder where the tarnishing is most marked. Turn the cloth as it becomes dirty.

● If you use a proprietary liquid or paste, apply it sparingly with a soft cloth. For recessed or engraved areas, you may need to use a soft-bristled toothbrush. Once the tarnishing has been removed, wash, rinse and dry, as above.

● Buff the surface to a deep shine with another clean, soft cloth or a chamois leather. Buff recessed areas with a fine-bristled artist's brush.

Cleaning silver in an electrochemical dip

To remove severe tarnishing, place silver in an electrochemical dip. Less abrasive than manual cleaning, it won't remove a thin layer of silver. This makes it suitable for cleaning worn silver plate, provided that you don't immerse the piece for too long. (An electrochemical dip will also clean copper and brass. However, never clean different metals in the same dip: you will simply chemically transfer a thin film from one to another. Also, never clean inlaid or enamelled pieces in this way: the chemical reaction will loosen the inlay or enamel.)

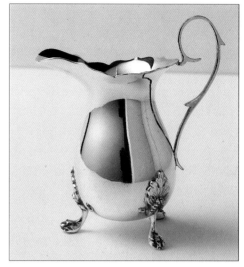

1 Determining the dipping time

- Refer to a book on hallmarks to determine if the piece is solid silver, like the 18th-century cream jug shown here, or silver plate. If it is silver plate, and particularly if some of the silver has eroded to reveal the base metal, you should not immerse it in the electrochemical dip for longer than the time specified in step 2. If you do, even more of the plate will be removed.

YOU WILL NEED:
Large plastic basin
Roll of aluminium foil
Rubber gloves
Plastic goggles
Protective face mask
Plastic mixing bucket
Packet of washing soda crystals
Hot water
A 20cm length of thin wooden dowelling
To handle silver objects. Alternatively, use a pair of wooden tongs.
Soft cloth or chamois leather
Soft-bristled toothbrush
White cotton gloves

2 Preparing and using the dip

- Line a plastic basin with a sheet of aluminium foil.
- Put the basin on a work surface in a well-ventilated area, and put on rubber gloves, plastic goggles and a protective face mask.
- Place the piece in the basin.
- In a plastic bucket, mix 142g of washing soda in 600ml of very hot water. Then slowly and carefully pour the solution over the piece in the plastic basin until it is completely immersed. Don't be alarmed when the solution begins to bubble violently: this is the chemical reaction that will transfer the tarnishing from the silverware to the aluminium foil.
- If the piece is solid silver, or silver plate in good condition, leave it in the basin for one to two minutes. If it is silver plate that has eroded in places to reveal the base metal, leave for about 20 seconds.
- Using a pair of wooden tongs or, if the piece has a handle, a length of wooden dowelling, remove the piece from the dip. The tarnishing should have disappeared. If it has not, dip the piece again.
Note: Don't use your hands to remove the piece: the rubber gloves don't guarantee full protection from the washing soda, and the interaction of the chemical and the rubber will create unsightly marks on the silver.

3 Rinsing, drying and polishing

- Hold the piece with tongs or dowelling and rinse it with hot water. Make sure that the rubber gloves don't touch the surface.
- Remove the rubber gloves, and wash, rinse and dry the piece as described on the opposite page.
- Wearing white cotton gloves, buff the piece to a deep, lustrous shine with either a soft cloth or a chamois leather.

Removing coffee and tea stains from silver

If used regularly, silver coffee pots and teapots tend to become stained inside. To remove staining caused in this way:
- Mix 5ml (1tsp) of borax with 600ml of hot water.
- Fill the pot with the solution, and let it stand for about two hours.
- Swirl the mixture around the pot with a soft-bristled artist's brush.
- Pour out the solution, and wash the pot out with warm, soapy water.
- Rinse the pot with clean, warm water, and dry thoroughly with a piece of soft towelling.

Repairing and restoring metalware

On the following pages you will find techniques suitable for use by the amateur in restoring less valuable metalware. Whenever possible, you should practise them first on everyday metal items bought inexpensively in job lots at auction. In that way, learning by your mistakes won't prove to be too costly or upsetting.

Never try to repair antique pieces made of gold, silver or any other precious metal, and this includes mending dented silverware. This work should always be given to a professional restorer, as it is easy to cause further damage if you lack either the necessary skills or access to some of the specialist tools required. Also, a botched repair will look unattractive and almost certainly reduce the value of a piece to well below what it would have been in an unrestored condition.

> **YOU WILL NEED:**
> **Bench or engineer's vice**
> **Work bench or table**
> **Length of hardwood** Approximately 30cm long and 2.5–5cm square.
> **Small tenon saw**
> **Heavy-duty utility or craft knife**
> **Wood file**
> **Sandpaper** Medium and coarse grades.
> **Large, plastic-faced hammer**
> **Block of hardwood** Of a size and shape that allow it to sit flush under the base of the piece.
> **Ball pein hammer**

Removing dents from brass and copper

As they are harder and less malleable than items made of lead and pewter, dented pieces made of brass and copper cannot be worked into shape by hand alone.

However, using some very simple and traditional smithing tools and techniques, you can repair minor dents in pieces made of these harder metals, provided that the piece is neither valuable nor dented to the point where the metal has folded or creased. You must leave such repairs to a professional restorer.

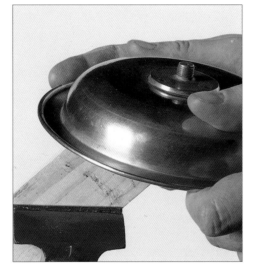

1 Removing dents in the sides

● Clamp an engineer's vice to a work bench.

● Take a piece of hardwood 30cm long and 2.5–5cm square and, using a tenon saw, a heavy-duty utility knife, a wood file, and coarse and medium-grade sandpaper, shape one end to match the vessel's internal curves or contours.

● Clamp the intact end of the stake in the vice, at an angle of roughly 45 degrees.

● Position the piece so that the stake's shaped end aligns with the inside of the dent. Apply even manual pressure to smooth out the dent. If small ripples appear in the outside of the vessel, lightly tap over the surface with a large, plastic-faced hammer.

2 Removing dents in the base

● If the piece to be repaired has a flat base, place it bottom down on a flat wooden work surface.

● If the base has a rim (as with this pewter tankard), take a hardwood block and saw, file and shape it with sandpaper to a size and shape that will fit under the rim and support the entire surface area of the base.

● Make a wooden stake, as described in step 1, and position the shaped end directly over the dent inside the bottom of the vessel.

● Using the flat face of a ball pein hammer, strike the intact end of the stake with a series of taps to push out the dent.

Removing scratches

To eliminate fine scratches that remain on brass and copper after normal cleaning and polishing, use the method described below. However, don't use it on softer metals such as silver or pewter – or on bronze – as it may remove valuable patination.

YOU WILL NEED:
Chamois leather
Household scissors
1m parcel string
5ml (1tsp) sunflower oil
Jeweller's rouge
Clean, soft rag

● Make a rubbing pad by first cutting a strip of chamois leather 7.5cm wide and long enough to be rolled into a cylinder (as in the top illustration) with a diameter of about 5cm. Bind the cylinder tight with parcel string (as in the bottom illustration). Make a second rubbing pad.
● Mix a few drops of sunflower oil or other light oil with jeweller's rouge to make a smooth creamy paste.
● Dip one end of one pad into the paste, and apply it over the scratched areas of metalware using gentle, but reasonably firm, circular strokes.
● Remove excess paste with a soft rag, then polish the piece with the second rubbing pad, again using gentle, circular strokes.

Reshaping lead and pewter

Lead and pewter are relatively soft metals. Consequently, objects made from them that have become slightly dented or distorted can often be manipulated back into their original shape by hand. Note that pewter is the easier of the two metals to fashion in this way. This is because it tends to be used in very thin, relatively malleable sheet form, to make pieces such as drinking vessels and vases.

YOU WILL NEED:
Sheets of old newspaper, or soft cloth

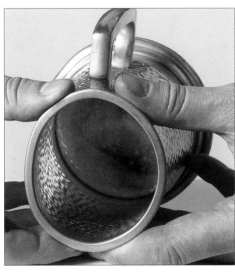

Before carrying out a repair, establish whether the piece is made of pewter or lead. If necessary, consult an antiques dealer or expert. Next, assess the degree of damage. It is possible for an amateur to reshape a buckled rim of the kind seen on this pewter tankard. However, if the metal is creased, don't try to make the repair yourself. An attempt to press the metal back into shape may make the crease even worse.

Making the repair

● Grasp the upper body of the tankard firmly with your fingers. Apply a steady, even pressure against the direction in which the rim has been elongated.
● Push in the sides of the tankard until the rim approximates its original circular shape. It is important not to push too hard; if you do, you will distort the metal in the opposite direction and may even produce a crease in it.

Finishing the repair

● Place a soft cloth or several layers of newspaper on a solid work surface. Set the piece on its side on the padded work surface. If you are working on a plate, set the rim on the pad.
● Using your thumb, rub and press around the inside of the rim of the tankard (or on top of the rim of the plate) to remove any remaining dents and distortions. Again, work cautiously, always making absolutely sure that you have moved the underside of the section you are working on around so that it is in contact with the work surface – if it is not, additional denting and distortion may take place.

Repairing crushed metal

Small items of antique metalware, such as thimbles, snuff boxes and, as shown here, matchbox holders, are frequently made of fairly thin metal. As a result they are very vulnerable to being accidentally crushed or badly distorted. This is particularly true of small items of silverware. If a damaged piece is valuable or rare, you should have it professionally repaired. If it is not, you should be able to restore it yourself using the following method.

1 Measuring and cutting

● Measure the internal length, width and height of the crushed object with a ruler or metal tape measure.

● Take the first length of wood and, using a tenon saw, heavy-duty utility or craft knife and wood file, taper one end to the above measurements so that it will just fit inside the open end of the piece.

● Using, in sequence, coarse, medium and fine-grade sandpaper, smooth down the tapered end of the wood. Take care to remove any rough edges.

2 Inserting the stake

● Apply a light coating of beeswax to the tapered end of the stake. This will make it easier to insert into the open end of the piece.

● Carefully ease the tapered end of the stake inside the piece, gently twisting it from side to side as you do so. This action will both open up the piece and begin the process of restoring it to its original shape. Don't try to complete the reshaping with the stake. This will probably cause new distortions and place stress on any unwelded joints.

3 Inserting the wooden former

● Remove the stake. Then take the second length of wood and, using a wood file and coarse- to fine-grade sandpaper, shape it to make a former that will fit snugly inside the piece.

● Apply beeswax to the former and insert it gently, tapping in with a rubber-faced hammer if necessary.

● Place the piece on a work surface and lightly tap over each side with the rubber-faced hammer to restore the original shape and remove any slight creases, bumps or depressions.

YOU WILL NEED:

Metal tape measure or ruler

First length of wood Approximately 22cm long by 2.5cm wide by 1.25cm thick (but definitely no wider or thicker than the internal dimensions of the piece to be repaired).

Tenon saw

Heavy-duty utility or craft knife

Wood file

Sandpaper Coarse, medium and fine grade.

Beeswax

Second length of wood 5–7.5cm longer than the external length of the piece to be repaired, and slightly thicker all around than its internal dimensions.

Small, rubber-faced hammer

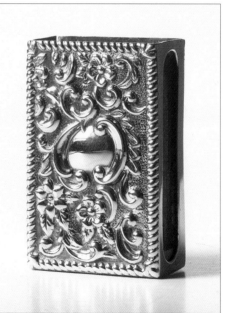

4 Finishing off

● Once you are satisfied that you have restored the shape of the piece as well as you can, carefully ease out the wooden former.

● To finish, clean and polish the piece, using the technique and materials specified for the metal in question on pp.210–11.

Mending cracks and breaks

Tiny surface cracks in metalware can sometimes be disguised by filling them with a proprietary metallic paste of suitable colour (in accordance with the manufacturer's instructions). Large cracks and breaks require a different approach. Epoxy-resin adhesives specifically formulated for mending cracks and breaks in metal make it easy for the amateur to carry out reasonably simple repairs. However, they do have their limitations. If a joint will be subject to strain, or if you want to join thin sheets of metal edge to edge, a traditional soft-soldered repair is the best option for the amateur. (For information on soldering, see p.247.)

You should use epoxy-resin metal adhesives to mend breaks in metals with a low melting point, such as lead and pewter, as these are damaged by the heat produced during soldering. These adhesives are also more suitable where other materials are in close proximity to the metal and would be damaged by heat. But, above all, if the item to be repaired is rare or valuable, and particularly if soldering is necessary, you should entrust the work to a professional restorer.

Mending cutlery

Items made of metal and another material, such as a bone or wooden handle on a piece of cutlery, are best repaired with adhesive, rather than soldering. The intense heat that is required to set the solder could damage the second material.

Repairing the break

● Scrub the tang and its socket with warm, soapy water. Rinse thoroughly with cold water and dry with clean, soft towelling.
● Wipe both sides of the areas to be joined with a clean rag moistened with methylated spirits to remove any grease.
● Mix a little two-part epoxy-resin metal adhesive in a saucer, following the manufacturer's instructions, and push a small amount into the socket of the handle.
● Push the tang into the socket, easing it from side to side until you achieve a good fit. Immediately wipe off any excess adhesive with a rag moistened with methylated spirits.
● Tightly wrap adhesive tape around the repair to support it while the adhesive dries.
● Once the adhesive has dried, remove the tape and polish as specified on pp.210–13.

Mending cast iron

Epoxy-resin metal adhesive can provide an alternative to soldering for breaks in cast iron, provided that excessive stress will not be placed on the item. A case in point are cast-iron fire surrounds; being brittle, these sometimes break when dropped or crack after exposure to variations in temperature. They are usually screwed to the wall through a pair of lugs on the outside of the vertical jambs. Remove the screws to free the fire surround, then repair it as follows.

YOU WILL NEED:
Soap
Cold water
Soft towel
Clean rag
Methylated spirits
Two-part epoxy-resin metal adhesive
Small paint brush
Adhesive tape
Fibreglass matting Cut to the repair's size
Household scissors

1 Seating the repair
● Apply adhesive along one side of the break.
● Reset the non-glued piece, applying gentle pressure to squeeze out excess adhesive. Wipe this off with a rag moistened with methylated spirits.
● Apply strips of adhesive tape to secure.

2 Reinforcing the joint
● Once the adhesive is dry, remove the tape, brush adhesive on the repair's back with a paint brush and lay fibreglass matting on it.
● Brush more adhesive on the matting. Allow to dry.
● Reattach the fire surround to the wall, and polish the exterior surface as described on p.211.

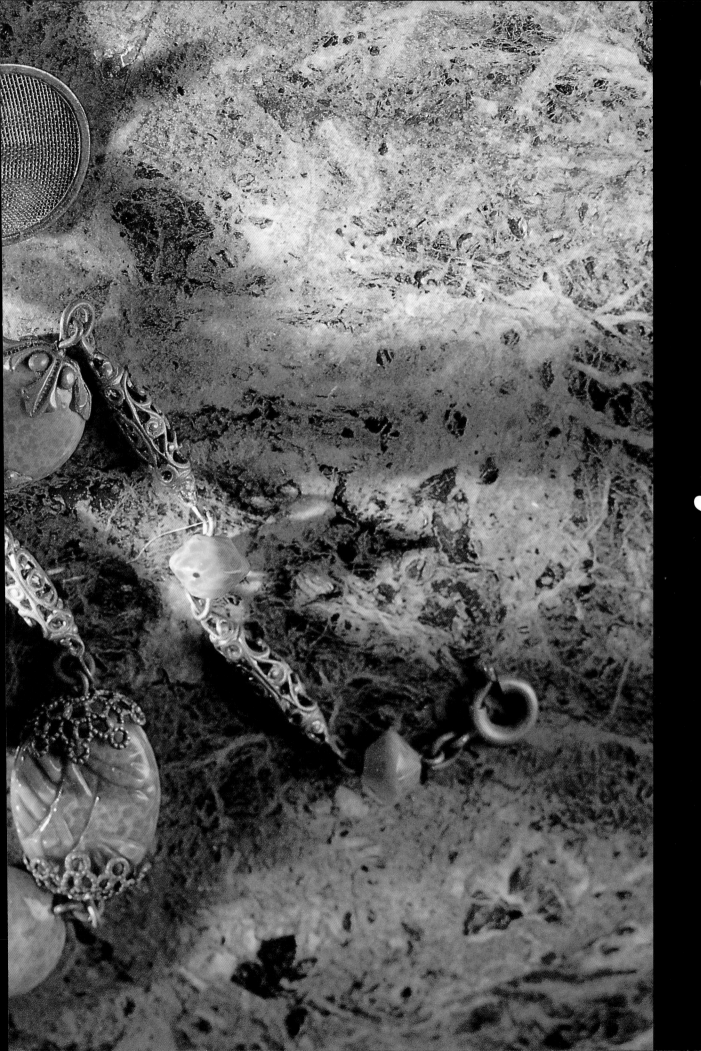

Jewellery

Introduction

Since prehistoric times, people have embellished their appearance and affirmed their status and wealth by wearing jewellery. Materials used range from the rare and valuable, such as gold, silver and precious stones, to the abundant and inexpensive, such as base metals and glass. Some items of jewellery are made from one material, but often two or more are used. Usually these materials are cut and shaped, welded, glued or strung on a support, and polished to enhance colour, pattern and lustre.

Precious and non-precious metals

Gold, rolled gold, gold plate, silver and silver plate have been used extensively in jewellery. Some pieces, such as chains, bracelets and rings, are made exclusively from these precious metals. In items such as brooches and earrings, they provide settings for precious or semi-precious stones. Platinum and non-precious metals such as copper, brass and bronze have also been employed. Settings crafted from these metals are used to anchor stones and other decorative materials. Various styles of setting exist, but the two most common types are 'open' and 'closed'. In an open setting, the metal behind the stone is cut away so that light can shine through it. In a closed setting, the stone is backed by solid metal. When a translucent or transparent stone is placed in a closed setting, metallic foil is often placed behind it. The foil reflects light back through the jewel, enhancing its colour and brilliance.

Precious stones

Precious stones – diamonds, emeralds, rubies and sapphires – are distinguished from semi-precious stones by their hardness, brilliance, colour and clarity. The intrinsic value of a stone is determined by factors including rarity, size and aesthetics. Gemologists rate hardness on a scale of 1–10, with stones rated at 9 or 10 classified as precious. Of this category, diamonds are the hardest and the most valuable. The most sought-after diamonds are flawless – free of cracks, chips and bubbles – and either pink, blue, green or colourless. They are prized for their rarity – most diamonds display a slight brown or yellow tinge. These stones are cut and ground to produce facets that refract light and flash prismatic colours.

Emeralds are rare and valuable, but often flawed and of variable quality. They range from pale to dark green, the latter being the most valuable, particularly if displaying brilliance and clarity. Rubies, like emeralds and sapphires, are a variety of the hard mineral corundum. They are

Costume earrings
A pair of earrings designed by Elsa Schiaparelli during the 1920s. Apart from their aesthetic appeal, their true worth lies in the collectability of the maker.

Art Deco brooch
A 1930s Art Deco brooch of cast bronze and hammered ironwork. The stylized woman, with bobbed hair, ringlets and an elongated face, is typical of the period. The maker is unknown and therefore the piece is not particularly valuable.

A jade and enamel pendant

Created c.1920 by the French designer Georges Fouquet, the jade and enamel pendant above is typical of his work – both in its use of colour and in its incorporation of geometric-shaped motifs inset and framed by small brilliants. Primarily because of its maker, this piece is a highly prized collectable.

A 1930s brooch pin

The orange brooch pin shown above is made of Bakelite – an early form of plastic. The demand for plastic jewellery grew during the 1920s and '30s. Pieces such as this are valued highly, despite being made from materials that have no intrinsic worth.

red, the best examples being flawless and dark blood-red with a strong fluorescence. Sapphires range from bright blue to dark blue. The best are from Kashmir.

Semi-precious stones

Semi-precious stones have a hardness rating of 8 or less. Those most commonly used in jewellery are agate, amber and aquamarine; jade and jet; opal, pearl and turquoise. Agate is a fine-grained quartz. When polished, it has variegated tones of blue, grey, green, brown and orange, often divided by irregular milky-coloured bands. Amber is the fossilized resin of the pine tree. A softish stone, it ranges from pale yellow and honey to brown, red-brown, red and black. The finest are clear, and the most prized contain embedded insects. Aquamarine ranges from blue to green; sky-blue examples are made by heating the stone.

Jade is a collective term for the minerals nephrite and jadeite. Nephrite is hard and translucent, and varies from white to shades of brown and green. It has a greasy appearance when polished. Jadeite is rarer, harder and more brittle. It can be dark green, green and lavender, emerald or variegated white and emerald; translucent emerald green is the most valuable. Jet is a type of coal (fossilized wood) with a glossy black appearance. It is most associated with 19th-century mourning jewellery.

Opals, a form of silica, are usually milky-white, although tinges of pink, blue, yellow and green are often present. Pearls are formed in the shells of molluscs such as oysters, mussels and clams when foreign particles are enveloped by nacre, also known as mother-of-pearl. Pearls range in colour from shades of pink to black and are classified according to shape and lustre. The most sought-after are spherical or drop-shaped, and have a satin sheen. Wild (or true) pearls occur naturally, while cultured pearls are made by placing a foreign object in the shell. Turquoise is a blue-green gemstone. Generally, the bluer the stone, the greater its value.

Other semi-precious materials

Various other materials are widely used in jewellery. Coral, a hard organic material formed from the skeletons of marine polyps, ranges from pinkish-white to red. Mother-of-pearl is the smooth, iridescent lining of the shell of various molluscs. Its iridescence fades over time in sunlight. Tortoiseshell is the mottled, mainly dark-brown shell of the sea turtle. It can be moulded by heating, and enlarged or thickened by joining pieces under pressure. The finest comes from the hawksbill turtle. Enamel is a smooth, glassy medium that is fused onto ceramic, glass or metal. It is usually carved and often painted. Ivory, a hard, dentine tissue from animal tusks (mainly elephant), is white or yellow-brown and is often carved.

Tools and materials

You will need to prepare a work surface on which to clean and repair jewellery. It is best to work on a large, preferably wooden, tray with raised sides. Line the tray with a piece of clean cotton or terry towelling. Choose a colour that contrasts with the main colours of the piece; terry towelling will prevent round beads, stones or pearls from rolling about. The tray's raised sides will keep them from rolling onto the floor, where they may be lost or damaged.

Clean jewellery in small containers on the tray. Never attempt to clean pieces of jewellery over a sink as precious or semi-precious components may be dislodged and washed away.

An egg carton or an assortment of small cardboard boxes will be helpful when you are dismantling pieces made up of smaller pieces, such as strings of pearls. The components can be sorted and stored in sequence for easier reassembly.

Finally, be certain that you have adequate light and, if needed, a means of magnifying the piece to be worked on. Arrange the rquired tools and materials in convenient positions on the work surface surrounding the tray.

Tools

1 Pliers and nippers Small needle-nose, taper-nose and flat-nose pliers for making various minor repairs. These should all have smooth rather than serrated jaws, to avoid damaging components made of soft metal. You will also need a pair of small end-cutting nippers for cutting wire.

2 Jewellery saw Fitted with a fine blade, it cuts soft metal as well as harder materials such as ivory and bone.

3 Needle files Available in various shapes, including round, flat, tapered and beveled, these can be bought individually or in sets.

4 Magnifying glass or jeweller's eyeglass For inspecting small pieces before and during cleaning or repair. A jeweller's eyeglass (not shown) is more suitable for some repairs as it leaves both hands free to work.

5 Utility or craft knife Choose one with disposable blades, so that a sharp cutting edge is always available.

6 Tweezers Essential for holding small components during cleaning or repairing.

7 Small electric drill plus attachments Available from specialist hardware stores and model-maker's outlets. This type of drill can be outfitted with a miniature lambswool buffing attachment for polishing sturdy pieces and components.

8 Brushes A soft-bristled dusting brush, or clean cosmetics brush, to remove surface dust and dirt. Use small, fairly stiff-bristled artist's brushes to clean small pieces and remove dirt from crevices. An old toothbrush is an alternative to a stiff-bristled artist's brush.

9 Beading needle For restringing necklaces. Available from craft shops and jewellery suppliers.

YOU WILL ALSO NEED:

Chamois nail buffer Available from cosmetic counters in chemists and department stores.

Small glass jar with lid

Small pocket knife Choose one with as thin a blade as possible.

Carpenter's nail Use a round or oval one as a former when making new links.

Nail scissors

Small plastic spatula

Materials

10 Acid-free tissue paper For wrapping and storing jewellery.

11 Wire wool Use the finest grade (0000) when removing encrusted dirt from specified base metals.

12 Methylated spirits Cleans many types of precious and semi-precious stones.

13 Jewellery dip Cleans various specified metals and stones. Available from most jewellers.

14 Powdered magnesia For dry-cleaning various stones. Available from chemists.

15 Almond oil Useful for cleaning and reviving various semi-precious stones. Available from chemists.

16 Jeweller's rouge Where specified, use to polish various metals and other materials. Use in the form of a powder-impregnated cloth or a block.

17 Adhesives Two-part epoxy resin, PVA adhesive, anaerobic adhesive, and clear cyanoacrylate adhesive (superglue) for making various specified repairs.

18 Coloured wax crayons Melt and combine these to provide filling material when carrying out specified minor repairs.

19 Cold-cure lacquer Available from artist's suppliers. Use with enamel paints when restoring enamel.

20 Silver polish

21 Thread Silk thread for restringing antique necklaces.

YOU WILL ALSO NEED:
Chamois leather
Cotton wool and cotton buds
Lint-free cotton rag
Soft terry towelling
Masking tape
Crocus powder
Soap
Mild detergent suitable for hand-washing wool
Olive oil
Milk
Bread crumbs
Potato flour
White spirit
Ammonia
Microcrystalline wax
Artist's powder pigments These can be used to tint epoxy-resin adhesive when repairing and filling cracks and breaks.

Cleaning and repairing jewellery

Antique jewellery is made from a wide variety of materials, two or more often being combined in the same piece. It is important when cleaning pieces to prevent certain cleaning agents that are suitable for one material from coming into contact with another material which could be damaged by them. In some cases, this risk makes it necessary to mask an area with tape, while in others it demands careful application of the cleaning agent with a small brush or tiny pieces of rag, chamois leather or cotton wool.

You should always examine the setting of the stones in a piece of jewellery before you begin to clean it; this is best done by using either a magnifying glass or a jeweller's eyeglass. A piece which has an open setting (see p.220) can usually be cleaned with the specified cleaning agent without loosening a stone. But if the piece has a closed setting (see p.220), make sure that no liquid creeps behind the stone, as this can loosen the glue or cement that holds it in place. With a closed setting, carry out only a very careful surface cleaning with a cotton bud moistened with the specified cleaning agent. Alternatively, use a specified dry-cleaning agent. You should also dry-clean strung necklaces, because silk or cotton thread should not be dampened.

If you are in any doubt about either the setting or the material you wish to clean or repair, eliminate the risk of damage and devaluation by consulting a jewellery expert before proceeding.

Agate

Remove dirt and grease by dabbing with cotton wool dampened with warm, soapy water. If the dirt proves stubborn, gently rub in the soapy water with a toothbrush. Then dab off with clean cold water before drying with a soft towel. Clean agate has a slightly waxy lustre, so don't try to achieve a shine by vigorous buffing with a soft cloth.

Amber

Remove accumulated dirt by gently rubbing with a cotton bud dipped in warm, soapy water. Dry at once with a soft cloth. To revive the sheen, apply almond or olive oil with a cotton bud, wipe off the excess and buff with a chamois leather.
Note: Never allow amber to come into contact with

methylated spirits, white spirit, toilet water, hair spray or perfume, as these will permanently dull it. Never soak amber in water, because this gives it a cloudy look that is almost impossible to remove. You should entrust repair of valuable pieces to an expert restorer. However, you can mend pieces that are less important using a cyanoacrylate adhesive.

Aquamarine

Clean with lukewarm, soapy water and a piece of clean cotton rag. Rinse with clean water. Dry and buff with a soft cloth. Never use hot water, which may crack the stone.

Brass

See 'General care and cleaning', p.210.

Bronze

See 'General care and cleaning', p.210.

Cameos

Clean dirty cameos and intaglios with warm, soapy water and cotton buds and a make-up brush. Rinse with a cotton bud dipped in clean water, and dab dry with terry towelling. To remove heavier dirt, use a small artist's brush moistened with white spirit. Next, add a couple of drops of ammonia to warm, soapy water, and brush this onto the piece. Rinse with the same brush dipped in clean warm water, then dry with a small piece of chamois leather.

Copper

See 'General care and cleaning', p.211.

Coral

Remove dirt with cotton buds or a small artist's brush dipped in warm, soapy water. Rinse with the cotton buds or brush and clean water. Dry with a cotton rag. Remove stubborn marks by making a thin, cream-like paste of crocus powder and water and applying it with a cotton bud. Rinse and dry as before. Never soak coral in water.

To repair clean breaks, use cyanoacrylate adhesive. Repair rough breaks and chips with epoxy-resin adhesive tinted with enamel paints.

Carnelian

Use the method for cleaning agate.

Diamond and artificial diamond

To remove light accretions of dirt from diamond, wash in warm, soapy water, rinse with clean cold water and dry thoroughly. Remove grease and heavier deposits of dirt by brushing with a small artist's brush dipped alternately into methylated spirits and ammonia. Dab dry with a soft cloth or towel. Clean an artificial diamond with a small artist's brush dipped in methylated spirits. Blow on the piece to evaporate the excess alcohol as quickly as possible. Never wash an artificial diamond as these are usually glued in their setting and easily dislodged when wet.

Emerald

Remove grease and dirt by brushing on with a small artist's brush a solution of warm, soapy water and two drops of ammonia. Remove stubborn dirt with the same brush dipped in methylated spirits. Gently buff with a piece of chamois.

Enamel

Always have enamel cleaned by a professional as it is easily damaged.

Gold

Unlike many metals, gold does not tarnish. However, dirt accumulates in flat, curved or raised areas and should be removed by buffing with a dry chamois leather. Clean recessed areas and chain links with a stiff-bristled artist's brush.

Wash gold that is very dirty or greasy with warm, soapy water and then rub it with a cloth or brush. Rinse with clean, cold water and dry immediately with a piece of terry towelling.

Horn and ivory

To clean both horn and ivory, wipe with cotton wool dipped in warm, soapy water. Then rinse with cotton wool and clean water and dry with a soft towel. Revive and polish by gently rubbing almond oil into the surface with a soft cloth.
Note: Both horn and ivory tend to become brittle with age, and exposure to excessive temperatures and immersion in water can split or warp them. After cleaning and drying them, rub a little almond oil over the surface with a cotton bud, leave for two minutes, then wipe off.

Jade

Wipe with cotton wool dipped in warm, soapy water containing two drops of ammonia. Rinse with a cloth moistened with clean water, dry with a soft cloth and buff with a chamois. Use a stiff-bristled artist's brush to remove dirt from crevices. For stubborn dirt, put methylated spirits or white spirit on the brush.

Repair small chips in lightweight, translucent jade with anaerobic adhesive, and repair fine breaks with cyanoacrylate adhesive. Repair heavier, more opaque jade with epoxy-resin adhesive.

Jet

To clean, gently rub with soft fresh bread. Repair fine breaks with cyanoacrylate adhesive. Repair large chips and breaks with epoxy-resin adhesive tinted with black artist's powder pigment.

Mother-of-pearl

Wipe with a soft cloth moistened with milk. Dry and buff with a clean soft cloth.

Onyx

Use the method for cleaning agate.

Opal

Use the method for cleaning pearl.

Pearl

Clean real pearls in a glass jar with a handful of powdered magnesia or potato flour. Shake the jar for three minutes, then leave for 24 hours. Repeat this. Shake again, remove the pearls, and dust off excess powder with a dusting brush. Clean artificial pearls by wiping with a chamois leather moistened with water.

Platinum

To remove discoloration, first add a little olive oil or methylated spirits to jeweller's rouge to make a paste with the consistency of double cream. Rub it on with a clean soft rag, wipe off and buff with a second rag.

Ruby

Wipe with cotton buds dipped in warm, soapy water, rinse with clean water and dry with a soft cloth. Rub with a chamois leather moistened with alcohol.

Sapphire

Use the method for cleaning rubies.

Silver

See 'Washing and cleaning silver', pp.212–13.

Tortoiseshell

Wash with a soft cloth and warm, soapy water. Rinse with clean water and dry with a soft cloth. Moisten a soft cloth with almond oil, add a little microcrystalline wax, and rub in. Buff with another cloth. To remove scratches mix methylated spirits and crocus powder to form a creamy paste. Rub on with a chamois. Wipe with a cloth and buff with a dry chamois. Mend breaks with cyanoacrylate adhesive. Mend cracks and fill in missing inlay by mixing melted wax crayons to match the tones. Press wax into the holes with a spatula.

Turquoise

Use the method for cleaning agate.

Netsuke

Items described as netsuke are made of wood, ivory, horn or stone. You should restrict their cleaning to dusting with a soft brush and buffing with a chamois leather.

If the sheen has dulled, wipe on a little microcrystalline wax and buff with a soft cloth or chamois leather.

Repairing clasps

Antique chains, necklaces and bracelets are all held closed by means of a clasp. There are three basic patterns of clasp: barrel, bolt ring and V-spring. They are all subject to various kinds of wear and tear and need to be maintained in good condition if they are to keep the jewellery secure while it is being worn. Although each pattern of clasp has minor differences of appearance and construction that distinguish it from the others, the principle of operation is basically the same throughout the range of patterns. As a result of this similarity, the basic repair technique that is described below can be used for almost any clasp that you might wish to mend.

YOU WILL NEED:
Flat-nose pliers (two pairs)
Taper-nose pliers (two pairs)
Small pocket knife With a thin, narrow blade.
Cotton rag
Cotton buds
Methylated spirits
White spirit

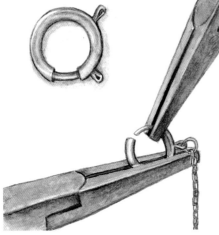

Repairing bolt rings

Metal bolt rings, as seen in the piece shown above left, are a common alternative to barrel clasps, as shown below right. They provide a slightly less secure means of attachment, but when in good working order they are perfectly adequate for holding lighter chains and necklaces closed. They work by means of a sprung metal bolt which is set within a hollow ring that has a small gap in its circumference. The bolt is forced shut by an internal spring, thus closing the gap. To release the clasp, you pull back on a small lever that is attached to the top of the bolt. The lever temporarily compresses the spring and reopens the gap.

● If sustained use has weakened the internal spring, you should have it replaced by a professional restorer. However, if the bolt itself is bent or distorted and will not locate fully into the ring, you can remedy the problem yourself, as described below.
● Gently grip the bottom half of the ring with a pair of taper-nosed pliers and grip the bolt itself with another pair of taper-nose pliers. Gently bend the bolt back into alignment with its housing on the other side of the ring. It is important not to apply excessive pressure with either pair of pliers; otherwise, you risk snapping the bolt out of the ring.

Repairing barrel clasps

A barrel clasp (shown below) is a two-part metal cylinder. Each part is attached to an end of a chain or necklace and the parts screw together to form a secure joint. If the fitting is to work properly, its threads must be clean. Remove dirt and grease with cotton buds dipped in methylated spirits.

● If the screw threads have become burred, you may be able to file them smooth with a needle file. If not, or if the threads have worn away, replace the clasp. Barrel clasps are available from jewellery suppliers. To fit the new clasp, see p.231.

Repairing a V-spring

A V-spring clasp consists of two parts: the spring, which is a piece of thin metal bent into a V or wedge shape, and a small housing. On rigid bracelets, the V-spring is usually welded to one end of the piece and the housing is an integral part of the other end (inset and bottom left). On flexible chains and bracelets (main photo, right), the V-spring and the housing are separate components, each attached to an end of the piece by a metal link.

The clasp works on the principle of friction. The V-spring is compressed as it slides into the housing and the tension in the metal holds it in place. The clasp is released by recompressing the V-spring and pulling it out of the housing. Because V-springs depend on friction, they are the least reliable type of clasp. Repeated compression of the V causes it to lose its springiness. As a result, it does not grip tightly in the housing and can easily pull loose, causing the piece to fall off the wearer. Remedy this problem as described below.

● If a V-spring snaps or fractures along its fold line, replace it. If it is attached by links, you can fit a new one yourself (see 'Replacing links', p.230). If it is welded in place, have it replaced by a professional restorer. In both cases, if the piece of jewellery is valuable, it may be preferable to have the two parts of the original V professionally soldered back together.
● Grip the rear of the bottom of the spring and gently work the thin blade of a pocket knife into the spring, prying the V more open. Do not exert excessive pressure, or open it up too much; otherwise, you may snap the metal at the apex of the V. Also, you should seriously consider having a safety chain fitted; if the V does pull out it will stop the piece from falling off. (For advice on fitting a safety chain, see p.230.)

Repairing brooch pins

The majority of brooches are secured in position by a metal pin. The pin, which is hinged on one side of the brooch, is anchored on the other side either under a metal hook or within a small metal cylinder. If the pin is hooked, the hinge is often sprung, and the resulting tension keeps the pin in place. All the components – pin, hinge, hook or cylinder – are subject to various kinds of wear and tear, which can result in the brooch falling off.

Fortunately, many repairs can be made without recourse to a professional restorer. The exception to this rule is if a piece is rare or very valuable. It is worth noting that many types of costume jewellery that were once relatively inexpensive have, in recent times, become quite valuable. At one time the presence of precious metals and stones was the main determinant of value, but now the designer's status and the quality of the design also confer worth on a piece made of lesser materials.

YOU WILL NEED:
Flat-nose pliers (two pairs)
Taper-nose pliers (two pairs)
Needle-nose pliers

Brooch pins
Below left *A 1930s star-shaped steel brooch decorated with paste diamonds.*
Right *A steel Georgian brooch with garnets and off-cut diamonds.*
Far right *A late-Victorian copper brooch embellished with three large garnets.*

Adjusting hinges

The brooch on the right has a sprung hinge, which was formed by twisting one end of the pin into a small coil. The coil is secured by two metal flanges welded to the back of the piece, one on each side. Each flange has a small dimple that holds the coil in place. A short length of metal, a 'stop', extends from the coil's base. When the pin is in the hook, the stop presses on the back of the brooch and transmits tension from the spring to the pin, holding it in place.

1 Repairing a flattened hinge

• If the hinge has become slightly flattened, so that the stop and the pin are too close together, you must pull them apart slightly to restore tension to the fastening mechanism. Grip the base of the pin firmly with taper-nose pliers, and the stop with needle-nose pliers, and exert gentle outward pressure on both pin and stop.

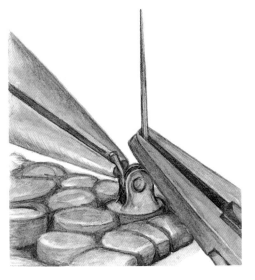

1 Repairing flanges

• If the metal flanges that lie on either side of the coiled spring have become flattened or distorted and the small dimples have disengaged from the spring, straighten the flanges with taper-nose pliers and re-engage the dimples.

Adjusting the pin

In the brooch shown above, the pin seats in an opening in the side of a small metal cylinder. Once the pin is in place, a hollow metal sleeve is pushed down inside the cylinder and over the end of the pin to secure it. As with the hook fastening shown on the opposite page, if the pin becomes bent or distorted, it won't align correctly with its housing. However, it is possible to adjust it.

1 Repairing a flattened pin

● If the pin has been flattened and bends down in the middle and up at the end, grip it just in front of the hinge with needle-nose pliers (this will isolate the hinge from undue pressure). Gently bend it upwards with flat-nose pliers.

1 Repairing a bent pin

● If the pin has become bent to one side, grip it with flat-nose pliers just beyond the hinge. Gently bend it back into shape by applying pressure with your thumb and forefinger. You may need to do this in stages, moving the pliers along the pin as you push out the bend.

Note: Never try to bend back the pin without supporting it with the pliers, as the pressure imposed on the hinge may break it. If it does break, have a professional restorer resolder or replace it.

Adjusting the hook

In the brooch shown in the picture above, the pin seats under an open-sided hook. If the hook is missing or snaps off, have it resoldered by a professional repairer.

1 Straightening a damaged hook

● If the hook becomes crushed or distorted (as in the drawing below), so that the pin won't seat in the opening, hold the hook with needle-nose pliers and bend the metal back into shape. Use only moderate pressure, otherwise you may snap the metal.

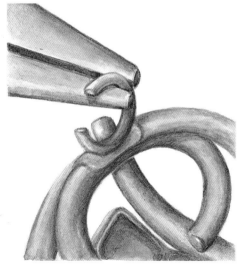

Repairing necklaces, chains and bracelets

The decorative components of most necklaces and many bracelets are either held together by metal links or are strung on a thread. Damaged or worn links and threads must be replaced as soon as possible, because, as with defective clasps or pins (see pp.226–9), it is easy for a piece of jewellery to slip off unnoticed if the means of securing it suddenly fails.

Replacing links

Gold and silver links can be bought from jeweller's suppliers. However, when you are looking for a replacement, it may not be possible to buy one of exactly the right size. If so, you can make links from metal wire – which is available from jeweller's suppliers in various widths and finishes – and fit them as described below.

YOU WILL NEED:

Metal wire Gold or silver, of a diameter to match existing links.

One carpenter's nail A round nail for round-shaped links; an oval-shaped nail for oval links. The nail's circumference should match the internal circumference of the link to be replaced.

Nippers or a jeweller's saw

Taper-nose pliers (two pairs)

1 Making the link

- Wrap the wire once round the nail.
- If you are using nippers, carefully slide the wire off the nail before clipping it. If you are using a jeweller's saw, cut the wire while it is on the nail, then remove the link.

2 Fitting the link

- With two pairs of taper-nose pliers, grip each side of the new link and gently pull apart the opening so that it just fits over the sides of the link in the chain to which it is to be attached.
- Having hooked the new link in place, close up the opening by gently pressing in the sides with the taper-nose pliers.

3 Adjusting the link

- Manipulating the link to attach it to the chain may have distorted its shape. If so, restore by applying gentle pressure around its sides with the taper-nose pliers.

Fitting a safety chain

In addition to carrying out regular inspections for wear and tear which might lead to the loss of a piece, you should consider fitting a safety chain.

Produced in various styles and metals, safety chains are available from most jewellers. Those for a bracelet or watch strap have a link at each end. These can be opened up and fitted to links in the jewellery, then closed again, using the method described in steps 2 and 3 of 'Replacing links' (see left). Some pieces don't allow this method of fitting. In such cases, have the safety chain fitted by a jeweller.

A variant on the safety chain mentioned above is the type for securing brooches in the event of part of the pin mechanism breaking. This has a link at one end for attaching to the brooch, and a safety pin at the other for attaching to clothing. In most cases, because of the lack of an attachment point on the brooch, a jeweller should fit this type of chain.

Safety chain
An early 20th-century brass link bracelet with enamel decoration, a box clasp fitting and a safety chain.

Restringing a necklace

Even if the stringing on an antique necklace hasn't broken, it may be worn and close to giving way. Therefore it is a good idea to inspect periodically the thread where it is visible between the beads (or pearls or stones) to see if there is any rotting or fraying. If there is evidence of either, you should restring the beads to avoid a break.

If the necklace is intact, lay it on a cloth in a tray with raised sides before you dismantle it. Use small scissors or a utility knife to cut one end of the thread where it joins the clasp. If the beads are not individually knotted, carefully slide them off one by one. If they are, you must cut them off one by one. In both cases, note the order in which they are removed and store them so that you will be able to replace them in the proper sequence.

If the necklace has broken and the beads are loose, you have little alternative but to work out the order of stringing for yourself. Generally, beads and graduated pearls get progressively larger towards the middle of the necklace. However, if the piece contains different-coloured beads of similar size, you must make a guess at their sequence and try a trial restringing (without knotting off). If you do not feel competent to undertake this task, seek advice from a professional jeweller or restorer.

YOU WILL NEED:
Small scissors, or utility or craft knife
Silk thread Twice as long as the necklace and no less than half the diameter of the bead holes.
Long needle With a diameter smaller than the holes in the beads.
Needle or hat pin To manipulate knots.
Small tube of PVA adhesive
Small, fine-tipped artist's brush

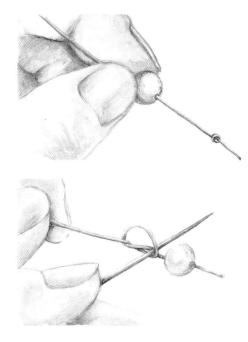

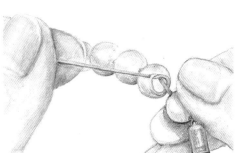

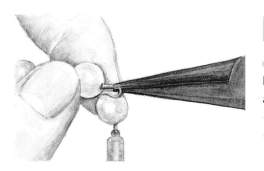

1 Knotting the thread end
● Tie a simple knot approximately 7.5cm in from one end of the thread. The knot should be slightly larger than the holes in the beads.
● Thread the first bead and slide it along to rest against the knot.

2 Knotting the beads
● Tie a loose knot on the other side of the bead. Don't pull it tight.
● Slip the needle or hat pin into the loose knot. Hold the unknotted end of the thread and use the needle to drag the knot close to the bead.
● Remove the needle. Hold the knot against the bead with your thumbnail. Tug on the thread to tighten it.

3 Attaching one half of the clasp
● After attaching the rest of the beads using the above method, thread the silk through the small loop on the end of one half of the clasp.
● Thread the end of the silk through the eye of the needle and pass the needle back through the hole in the final bead.

4 Knotting off
● Pull the spare thread through the last bead and remove the needle.
● Tightly knot the spare thread around the stringing thread, as close as possible to the last bead.

5 Hiding the thread
● Cut the excess thread, leaving a tail half as long as the next-to-last bead. Apply a little PVA adhesive to the tail with a small, fine-tipped artist's brush.
● Push the thread into the second bead from the end.
● Repeat steps 3–5 to secure the clasp's other half.

Repairing earrings

Earrings are designed for either pierced or non-pierced ears. The simplest fittings are for pierced ears and there are two basic types: posts and loops. A post fitting is a short, stiff metal bar that is welded to the back of the earring, passes through the hole in the earlobe, and is secured with a small metal stud that slides onto the end of the post. A loop fitting, commonly used for dangling earrings, is a metal wire formed into a hook or loop. One end of the wire is linked to the top of the earring, the other passes through the earlobe. This style may be open, as in the photograph below, or close in a simple clasp.

The mechanisms that secure earrings for non-pierced ears also come in two types. One is a screw clip, in which a stirrup-shaped bar sits below the earlobe. A small cup at one end of the stirrup sits behind the earlobe. A threaded pin with a small, circular pad on one end is attached to the other end of the stirrup. To secure the earring, the pin is screwed reasonably tightly against the front of the earlobe, in line with the cup behind. Pressure and friction keep the earring in place.

The other type of clip consists of a thin, hinged metal bar. Internal tension in the bar produces a spring-like effect which forces the bar against the back of the earring. When the bar and the back of the earring are placed on opposite sides of the earlobe, the pressure or tension between them secures the earring in place. The tension in the bar can be increased or decreased by adjusting the angle of a small metal prong located either inside or outside the bar.

Adjusting posts

1 **Straightening the post**
● You can usually straighten a bent post by applying gentle pressure with flat-nose pliers.

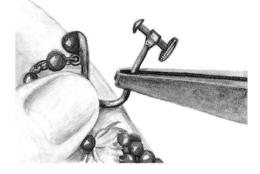

Reshaping ear wires

1 **Bending the wire**
● If an ear wire is crushed or distorted, you can, in most cases, bend it back into shape with gentle pressure from your thumbs and fingers. If the metal is fairly rigid, a finger together with a pair of round-nosed pliers should provide adequate force.

Adjusting screw clips

1 **Straightening the screw**
● If the screw is bent, you may be able to straighten it by applying light pressure with a pair of flat-nose pliers. If this doesn't work, you should have it repaired professionally.
● If accumulated dirt stops the screw in a screw-clip earring from turning freely in the stirrup, clean it with either a cotton bud or a piece of rag moistened with methylated spirits. Apply a drop of lubricating oil and remove any excess with a clean cotton bud or rag.
● If the stirrup has become bent or distorted, and the pad on the end of the screw doesn't align with the cup, grip each side of the stirrup with a pair of taper-nose pliers and apply gentle pressure to ease the metal back into shape.

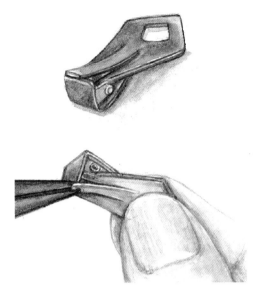

Adjusting spring clips

Sometimes the metal tab of a spring clip earring, as shown above, will not provide sufficient pressure on the ear lobe to hold the earring in place. This is usually a result of the metal prong on the back of the tab becoming crushed or distorted.

1 Bending the clip

● Grip the tab between your thumb and finger. Hold the end of the prong with a pair of needle-nose pliers, as in the drawing above, then gently pull the prong slightly up and away from the tab. Adjustment is a matter of trial and error, so several attempts may be necessary to get it right.

Storing jewellery

You should always store pieces of jewellery separately, either in the small, padded compartments of a jewellery box or in separate boxes lined with acid-free cotton. In both cases each piece should also be individually wrapped in acid-free tissue paper (for method of storing chains and necklaces in this manner, see below). The box or boxes should be kept out of direct sunlight, away from other powerful sources of heat, such as radiators, and in a well-ventilated, low-humidity atmosphere. If the pieces are stored in a humid climate, an electric dehumidifier will prove a good investment.

The most important reasons for taking such precautions are as follows:
● Many gemstones, notably diamonds, are very hard. If they are stored loose with softer stones and metal items, they can easily scratch them, especially when you are rummaging with your fingers to find a particular piece. They can also chip or break brittle stones, and be chipped or broken themselves.
● Some semi-precious materials, such as ivory, bone and horn, react adversely to excessive heat and moisture and extreme changes in temperature. For example, they can swell, shrink, split and crack, and, in damp and poorly ventilated surroundings, may attract mould.
● Regular exposure to strong sunlight bleaches some materials, notably ivory. Restoring the colour may be possible, but must be done by a professional.

Storing a chain

Chains and necklaces often tangle in storage and can break when tugged out. The answer is to wrap them individually.

● Lay a square or rectangular sheet of acid-free tissue paper flat on a tabletop.
● Lay the piece out flat, diagonally across one corner of the tissue paper.
● Wrap the corner of the paper over the middle of the piece, to form a triangle pointing towards the centre of the paper.
● Using the flats of your fingertips, roll both the piece and the paper towards the middle of the tissue paper, and across to the other side. The piece will now be completely covered, and should be laid flat and gently curved within a box or compartment of suitable size.

Preventing damage
Wrap a chain or, as here, a pearl necklace, in acid-free tissue paper to protect it during storage.

Stoneware

Introduction

The earliest examples of figurative art are in the form of stone carvings and date to 27,000 B.C. Ever since, numerous types of rock and stone have been cut, carved or sculpted, and in many cases polished, to produce a wide range of decorative and functional artifacts. The rocks and stones fall into three major categories: igneous, sedimentary and metamorphic. Each category has its own structural characteristics that result in variations in colour, patterning and susceptibility to wear and tear.

Igneous rocks

Formed as molten magma cools and solidifies, igneous rocks are usually uniformly patterned, extremely hard, non-porous and show few structural imperfections. Among this category of rocks are basalt and various kinds of granite and porphyry. Basalt is usually black and, on close inspection, displays tiny, glittering mineral deposits. It has often been used for sculpture. The majority of granites are grey, red or off-white, and can be highly polished. Typically, they have been used to make tabletops, fireplaces and garden ornaments. Porphyries are hard, variegated rocks favoured for sculpture, panelling and artifacts such as vases. Mostly purple and whitish, they contain crystal deposits in a fine-grained ground and respond well to intensive polishing.

Sedimentary rocks

Formed from a sediment consisting of old, weathered rocks and skeletal remains (fossils), sedimentary rocks cover two-thirds of the earth's surface. The minerals within them, such as quartz, turquoise, opal and malachite, produce enormous variations in colour, texture and pattern. Breccias, fossiliferous and variegated limestones, sandstone, gypsums, alabasters and soapstone are typical examples.

Breccias consist of distinctive angular fragments embedded in a finely grained matrix. They can be polished to a high sheen, and are often used for commodes and tabletops. Fossiliferous and variegated limestones are commonly selected for architectural carvings (being relatively soft, they are easy to carve but prone to erosion). They range from greyish-white to light brown, and have a rough, pitted surface. Sandstone is usually honey-coloured and consists of fine grains of quartz and other minerals set in a solid mass. Also presenting a pitted surface, it is even more susceptible to erosion and flaking than limestone.

Gypsums are soft mineral rocks (hydrated calcium sulphate) that provide the basic material for plaster of Paris and other plasters employed in decorative casts and mouldings. Alabasters are either lime carbonates or softer lime sulphates. Smooth, semitranslucent and ranging in colour from white, yellow, light brown

Sandstone vase

A large, Etruscan sandstone vase with classical figures and motifs carved in relief. The rough, pitted surface of this kind of stone makes it particularly vulnerable to weathering and erosion. However, this example has survived in excellent condition.

and pink, alabasters can be highly polished. They resemble some types of marble, but are less durable and more easily scratched. Traditionally chosen for carvings in churches and tombs, over the past three centuries they have also been used in the making of artifacts such as vases, clock cases, fireplaces and ashtrays. Soapstone is a magnesium silicate, similar to alabaster but much softer. Primarily used for small carvings, it appears in a variety of colours, including white, yellow, green, brown, blue-grey and red.

Metamorphic rocks

When heat and pressure combine to recrystallize existing rocks, metamorphic rocks are formed. These make up the classification known as marble. The purest types of marble are composed almost entirely of recrystallized limestone. White Carrara statuary marble is probably the best known and is prized for its smoothness, even colour and almost translucent appearance. However, there are hundreds of other types of marble, each containing highly decorative mineral deposits and displaying enormous variations in colour and pattern. Much of the pattern is produced by mineral deposits that appear as a series of veins lying on or near the surface of the cut and polished stone.

There is not nearly enough space here to list all the varieties of marble. However, among the most popular are white-vein, black-and-gold, Sienna, Red Levanto, Bois Jourdan, Brèche Violet, Serpentine and green onyx. One of the principal characteristics of these and other marbles is porosity. As a result of this quality, they can quickly become discoloured or stained, so general maintenance and cleaning of objects made from them is particularly important.

A 19th-century fireplace
A substantial black marble and granite fireplace, installed in a living room in a New York mansion. It was made c.1842.

Tools and materials

No great expenditure on either tools or materials is required to clean and carry out minor repairs to stoneware. The most expensive item is an electric drill, which you can hire if you don't have one already. Note that a few of the chemicals are caustic, so when working with them, you must wear good-quality rubber gloves, plastic goggles and a face mask to protect your hands, lungs and eyes.

Tools

1 Standard paint brushes Brushes in 2.5cm, 5cm and 7.5cm sizes, for applying various cleaning agents and water.

2 Scrub brush Employ a standard, stiff-bristled type for cleaning certain types of stone. You may need more than one size.

3 Toothbrush A stiff-bristled toothbrush to clean out crevices and mouldings.

4 Dusting brush A fine-bristled dusting brush to remove surface dust from pieces. A large make-up brush is an alternative.

5 Wire brush A medium-size, brass-wire brush for large areas and a toothbrush-sized one (not shown) for small, recessed areas.

6 Rubber gloves Wear chemical-resistant rubber gloves when working with caustic cleaning agents. These are available from specialist suppliers (see Directory of Suppliers, pp.250–1). Household rubber gloves are adequate for soap and water cleaning.

7 Plastic goggles To protect your eyes.

8 Face mask To protect your face and lungs from dust, chemicals and vapours.

9 Electric drill A variable-speed, hand-held type (with a selection of masonry bits) to drill holes for masonry pins, and to power a buffing mop attachment.

10 Buffing mop A lambswool buffing mop can be attached to an electric hand drill to speed the polishing of various types of stoneware.

YOU WILL ALSO NEED:

Plastic buckets and containers To mix cleaning fluids. A choice of sizes from 1 to 4 litres will be useful, depending on the size of the object to be cleaned.

Brass or stainless-steel pins To reinforce repaired breaks in larger or heavier pieces. Available from craft suppliers and many hardware stores.

Cotton buds To clean stoneware. You may also need cotton wool.

Chamois leather To clean stoneware. Can be used whole or cut into pieces according to the size of the area to be treated. Real chamois leather is best, but less expensive, synthetic versions available from car-accessory suppliers are an acceptable substitute.

Garden hose To wash large items of stoneware, particularly limestone and sandstone, outdoors.

Hacksaw With blade suitable for cutting notches in brass or stainless-steel reinforcing pins.

Radiator For warming marble, where specified, before consolidating it.

Hair-drier

Small, flat wooden stick

Small artist's brush To apply paint and acrylic matt.

Materials

11 Adhesive tape To hold repairs together while the adhesive dries. Available in various widths.

12 Blotting paper When mashed to a pulp with distilled water, white blotting paper makes a poultice that will remove various types of stain.

13 Soft lint-free rag To clean and polish stone.

14 Stone sealer A commercial fluid used to protect porous stones from staining.

15 Fillers Two-part epoxy-resin fillers specifically for repairing chips, cracks and holes in stoneware. For pieces displayed indoors, use cellulose fillers. However, these are not weatherproof, nor hard-wearing. Note that neither filler is suitable for repairing alabaster or soapstone.

16 Adhesives Tough epoxy-resin adhesive of a type specified by the manufacturer for mending breaks in stoneware, particularly in larger or heavier pieces. For smaller repairs on lighter pieces, a cyanoacrylate adhesive ('superglue') is an alternative.

17 Wax polish Good-quality white beeswax polish (microcrystalline wax) to consolidate friable surfaces and to buff surfaces to a subtle shine.

18 White candle wax An alternative to wax polish.

THE FOLLOWING ARE USED FOR CLEANING OR REMOVING CERTAIN TYPES OF STAIN:

19 Ammonia Dilute with water.

20 White spirit

21 Bleach

22 Paint stripper

23 Powdered alabaster To mix with adhesives to make your own fillers. Substitute gypsum, kaolin or whiting if alabaster is unavailable. All are available from artist's suppliers and some craft shops.

YOU WILL ALSO NEED:

Distilled water To make poultices for cleaning and rinsing stoneware. If you need to buy distilled water in large quantities, the least expensive sources are generally pharmacists and car-accessory suppliers.

Chloramine T A 2 per cent solution (available from some pharmacists) is a mild bleaching agent.

Sandpaper Coarse, medium and fine grade.

Crocus powder To dry-clean plasters. Available from artist's suppliers and some hardware stores.

Acrylic matte medium To consolidate friable stoneware surfaces. Available from artist's suppliers.

Methylated spirits For mixing with crocus powder to make a cleaning paste.

Liquid soap or detergent For general cleaning, where specified in the text.

Commercial marble polish Available from outlets specializing in garden statuary and architectural fixtures and fittings.

String

Old towels

Plastic sheets

Acrylic paint or oil paint

General care and cleaning

Because most stoneware is porous, it is important to dust it regularly with a soft brush to prevent dirt from penetrating the surface. In addition to this, you should, from time to time, give stone items a general cleaning; the method you use will depend on the type of stone. Always wear rubber gloves, plastic goggles and a face mask when cleaning stoneware.

Basalt and granite

These stones are nonporous, so dirt rarely penetrates them. However, to remove superficial dirt and grime, scrub with a stiff-bristled brush (or wire brush if necessary) and soapy water containing two drops of ammonia. Rinse with clean water and dry thoroughly by dabbing with a towel.

Limestone and sandstone

Position the piece outdoors near a drain or gutter, and set up a hose to spray water over it gently for four or five hours to loosen the dirt. Scrub it with a stiff-bristled brush and a weak solution of warm water and ammonia (one cupful of ammonia to every 4.5 litres of water that is required to remove all the dirt). Rinse the piece with clean water, and towel dry. If the surface is friable, consolidate it as described on the opposite page under 'Friable, flaking and powdery surfaces'.

Gypsum

Before cleaning a gypsum plaster casting, dust it with a soft-bristled brush. Don't use a cloth, because this will rub in the dirt. You can wash the piece with cold water. However, it is much safer to brush a small amount of dry crocus powder over the surface of the casting and into the crevices, then brush it off. If further cleaning is required, use the poultice method (see pp.242–3).

Alabaster and soapstone

Never immerse alabaster or soapstone in soapy water, or you might soften and weaken it. First dust with a dusting brush, then, if necessary, wipe lightly with a cotton bud dipped in warm, soapy, distilled water and then wrung out. Repeat with distilled water to rinse, and dab dry with a towel. Remove dirt in crevices with a small brush or cotton bud moistened with white spirit.

Marble

Dust marble with a soft-bristled brush, then wash with warm, soapy water and a cloth. If this doesn't work, add up to half a cupful of ammonia to every 4.5 litres of water needed to remove all the dirt. Rinse afterwards with clean water, and towel dry. If neither method works, try the poultice method (see pp.242–3).
Note: Before applying any of the above cleaning techniques, you should make sure the surface isn't a painted simulation – faux marble. If it is faux marble, you can safely dust it, as above. In some cases you can also safely clean it by wiping with a mild solution of soapy, lukewarm water and a soft lint-free rag. Afterwards, rinse and dry it as for real marble. However, you must test the soapy solution on an inconspicuous area first. Stop immediately if the paint begins to smear or lift, and seek the advice of a professional cleaner-restorer.

Scagliola

This material is an imitation marble made of gypsum, glue and splinters of real marble or granite. Clean it with the method recommended for marble.

Porphyry and slate

Use the method recommended for marble.

Removing specific stains

Many of the specific stains that stoneware tends to attract will be removed by general cleaning. Some stains will resist basic cleaning methods and require special treatment. To remove them, first try the simple methods listed below. If these don't work, use the poultice method (see pp.242–3).

Oil, wax and grease

Lightly rub with a soft cloth moistened with white spirit or methylated spirits. To remove grease from white marble, use paint stripper.

Nicotine

Make a paste of a little crocus powder and a few drops of methylated spirits. Gently apply with a cotton bud, working in a circular motion. Wipe clean with a rag moistened with white spirit.

Soot

Most soot and smoke stains will be removed from fireplaces by cleaning with soapy water, rinsing with clean water and drying with a towel. However, deeply ingrained stains will require a poultice based on white spirit (see pp.242–3).

Algae and mildew

If the brown-green staining is not too bad, remove it with a cloth dipped in warm, soapy water plus one drop of ammonia. Rinse and towel dry. If this doesn't work, use a cloth to wipe on a mild bleach or a 2 per cent solution of Chloramine T, then rinse. If this fails, try the poultice method (see pp.242–3).

Fly marks

Flies leave small black marks on most types of stone. Never remove them with a scalpel or knife, as this will scratch the surface. Alabaster, soapstone and marble are vulnerable to such damage. Moisten the rounded end of a small, flat wooden stick with white spirit and pry them off. Then rub with a chamois leather.

Protecting and polishing surfaces

Marbles and other hard stones, such as basalt and granite, can be polished after cleaning. Apply a white beeswax polish or a commercial marble polish with a soft cloth. Buff with another cloth or a buffing mop on an electric drill. Both types of polish will help to seal the surface and produce a pleasing soft sheen.

Friable, flaking and powdery surfaces

If they are friable, limestone and sandstone must be consolidated after cleaning. Brush on a solution of one part clear acrylic matt medium to ten parts distilled water, or apply a stone sealer. To consolidate stones such as basalt and marble, warm them slightly in front of a radiator. Use a hair-drier to heat gently a solution of one part melted white beeswax or candle wax to one part white spirit. Brush this over the stone and leave it for an hour. As the piece cools, the spirit evaporates, leaving a wax film. Buff with a soft cloth. **Note:** The wax and spirit solution is flammable, so keep it away from a naked flame or intense heat. The solution slightly darkens stoneware, so never use it on white marble or alabaster, or pale soapstone.

Repairing breaks, chips and cracks

After cleaning, mend any breaks in stoneware with an epoxy-resin adhesive. Follow the maker's instructions on application and drying times. Support the repair during drying with adhesive tape or string. Excess glue on the surface should be wiped off immediately, before it dries. For large breaks you may need to insert brass or stainless-steel reinforcing pins. To add pins, drill aligned holes for them on each side of the break. Cut small notches in the pins with a hacksaw to help the adhesive adhere, set them into one side, then align and glue the other side.

Fill small chips and cracks in marble using a purpose-made epoxy-resin filler. To fill alabaster, use a mix of epoxy-resin adhesive and powdered alabaster. In each case, make the filler higher than the area around it, to allow for shrinkage. Once the filler is dry, cut and sand it. Paint it to match the rest of the piece with acrylic or oil paint, using a small artist's brush.

Painted marble

Since the civilizations of Ancient Greece and Rome, marble has been simulated with paints and glazes. This is usually done to save money or because real marble's density makes it fracture under tension and renders it unsuitable for use in ceilings, overhangs and beams.

Faux marble is sometimes produced so expertly that it is almost impossible to tell it from the real stone. Proceed with caution when you are planning to clean marble: close inspection might reveal a painted finish that would be ruined by the cleaning fluids specified on p.240.

Faux-marble panelling
A fine example of yellow sienna faux-marble wall panelling, and contrasting black and gold faux-marble baseboard, on the hallway staircase at the Sir John Soane Museum in London.

The poultice method

This technique is one of the safest and most effective ways to clean and remove stains from pieces of stoneware. It is widely used by professional restorers to clean valuable statuary and other works of art made of stone. The poultice method is easy to apply, although the preparation stage is somewhat time-consuming, and it is also suitable for use by amateur restorers.

The poultice is made from pulped paper and a cleaning fluid (distilled water, white spirit, or methylated spirits, depending on the type of stone or stain to be treated). It is applied to the surface of the stone, and works as follows. The stone absorbs the cleaning fluid present in the poultice. As the poultice dries, it slowly draws out and absorbs the cleaning fluid along with the stain. The whole process takes about 24 hours, and can be repeated as many times as necessary (with a new poultice), depending on the severity of the ingrained dirt or stain.

1 Dusting

● Remove surface dust from the piece with a fine-bristled dusting brush. Make sure that you don't leave any accumulations of dust lying in crevices and mouldings.

YOU WILL NEED:
Dusting brush
Sheets of white blotting paper
Plastic bucket
Distilled water, or white spirit or methylated spirits
Ammonia
Wooden stake
White terry towelling

YOU MAY ALSO NEED:
Scrubbing brush
Plastic sheets

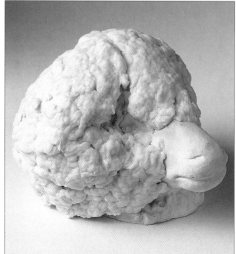

2 Using the poultice

● Shred some large sheets of white blotting paper into a bucket. If you are treating a stone or stain for which water has been specified as a cleaning agent, add warm distilled water to the paper. If water hasn't been specified, add white spirit or, if drastic treatment is required, white spirit plus a little methylated spirits. For mildew and algae stains, use water plus a few drops of ammonia.

● Using a clean wooden stake, mash the paper and fluid to a pulp, adding more fluid if necessary.

● Apply the pulp as a poultice over the stone. Build up a layer about 1–2cm deep, pressing the pulp into the surface. Let it dry, then remove and repeat.

Professional cleaning

The simple poultice method of cleaning has been used successfully many times by professional restorers facing difficult tasks. For example, when the River Arno, in Italy, burst its banks in 1966 and caused flooding in Florence, many Renaissance marble statues were badly discoloured by the large amounts of gasoline and engine oil that escaped into the floodwaters. With poultices containing everyday fluids such as methylated spirits, white spirit and washing soda, the restorers drew out the oil and restored the fine statues to their former glory.

Marble bust

A bust of Ajax, in black-veined, grey, cream, green and white-veined marble. It dates from c.230 B.C. and stands in the Pitti Palace, in Florence, Italy.

3 Rinsing and drying

● Once the second application has dried, remove it and inspect the surface of the stone. If the dirt or stain was deeply ingrained, it may not have been completely absorbed. If this seems to be the case, make and apply a third poultice. However, with the vast majority of stones a third application will not be necessary.

● When you are satisfied with its appearance, rinse the stone with water or wipe it with white spirit on a piece of clean terry towelling. In either case, you must dry it afterwards with clean terry towelling.

Note: You will find that the poultice method is also very effective for drawing out and removing the white crystals (salt deposits) that are frequently found on limestone and sandstone. With a scrubbing brush used with a brisk action, remove as much of these deposits as you can. Then apply a poultice made with distilled water and wrap the entire piece in plastic sheets. Leave the poultice in position for a minimum of two to three weeks. At the end of this period, remove the poultice and, if necessary, make and apply another poultice. Leave this in place for at least two weeks.

Techniques

The techniques described here supplement the instructions given in the earlier chapters, and have been cross-referenced from specific tasks and projects.

However, some of the techniques in this section do not specifically relate to tasks and projects in the earlier chapters. For example, the instructions on how to make a bridle joint, on pp.245–6, are included here because they will prove useful when your carpentry skills develop to a point where you feel confident enough to make structural repairs to not only chairs (see pp.40–51) but also settees. Information is included on soldering, on p.247, as it can be useful to the amateur restorer of metalware.

The following three pages cover a variety of remedial techniques useful for the care and repair of furniture. You will find the main furniture projects on pp.20–65.

Woodworm

Almost all types of wood used in the manufacture of furniture are vulnerable to infestation by various types of beetle. Chief among these are the death-watch, the longhorn, the powder-post and the furniture beetle (the last better known as woodworm). All these beetles can cause major structural and aesthetic damage to wood. However, woodworm is the most prevalent, and it causes damage as follows.

The female woodworm lays its eggs in the cracks and crevices of unfinished wood, especially if these contain dust or dirt. The eggs hatch into larvae, which then gnaw through the wood at a rate of approximately 5cm per year, making a network of interconnecting tunnels and chambers.

Eventually the woodworm larvae change into pupae, which hibernate in the wood for two to three years before attaining adulthood. The adult beetles then tunnel their way back to the surface of the wood, and the process begins again.

You will be able to recognize the presence of woodworm by the exit (or 'flight') holes left by the adults when they emerge from the wood. These holes are about 1mm in diameter. On older pieces of furniture, the presence of flight holes doesn't necessarily indicate that the woodworm is still active – it may have been successfully treated in the past. The signs of active woodworm are flight holes that are lighter in colour than the surrounding wood – older flight holes have invariably darkened to the same colour as the surrounding wood – and the presence of fine sawdust in and around the holes. Pressing the blunt edge of a table knife against the suspect area will also help you to determine the extent of any underlying damage. If the wood feels soft, or if it crumbles under the pressure of the blade, the infestation is serious enough to require treatment. If the woodworm is active, or the damage is extensive, treat it as soon as possible, using the following method.

- If the piece is structurally weakened, seek professional advice. Depending on the rarity and value of the piece, the affected area should either be cut out and replaced, or injected with acrylic resin to strengthen it. The latter should be applied by a company specializing in this work.
- If the damage is superficial, purchase a commercial woodworm-killing fluid (the type contained in an injector can or bottle). Insert the nozzle into a flight hole and squirt the liquid into the tunnels and chambers. Repeat in other holes, spaced roughly 5cm apart, until you have treated the entire affected area.
- Immediately after injecting the fluid, brush a liberal quantity of it over all the unfinished surfaces of the piece, and leave it to dry for 48 hours. Any excess fluid that is not absorbed by the wood will evaporate within this period.
- To further reduce the risk of future infestation, treat all the finished surfaces of the piece with a wax furniture polish which contains an insecticide.

Mortise-and-tenon joints

The joint most often used in furniture construction is the mortise-and-tenon. It is made by shaping the end of a rail (A) into a tongue – the tenon (B) – which starts at the shoulder (C). The tenon fits into a slot – the mortise (D) – cut in a leg (E). There are two basic types of this joint: the 'through' tenon and the 'blind' tenon. A through tenon passes through the leg and is visible on the far side, while a 'blind' (or 'stopped') tenon falls short of the other side of the leg and its end cannot be seen. The size of a tenon can vary, but normally it is one-third the thickness of the rail and the same height. Where the rail lies flush with the top of a leg, the tenon may be cut to slightly less than the height of the rail.

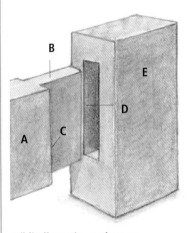

A 'blind' mortise-and-tenon
In this example of the joint, the tenon is the full height of the rail.

A blind mortise-and-tenon

If a rail is beyond repair, cut a new one with tenons at each end. If a leg is beyond repair, cut a mortise in a new one for the tenoned rail. Proceed as follows.

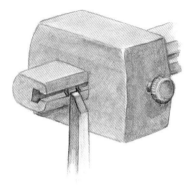

1 Marking the tenon

● Cut, plane and sand the new rail to the dimensions of the original. Then use the original tenon as a guide to the size of the new tenon, and mark its dimensions on the end of the rail. Use a T-square and a penknife to scribe a line around the rail to establish the position of the shoulder or base of the tenon.

Note: Usually, the length of the tenon is two-thirds the width of the leg.

● Set a mortise gauge to the width of the mortise. Then adjust the mortise gauge so that the two pins are centred on the rail. Use the gauge to scribe the outline of the tenon, starting from the shoulder, passing over the end of the rail, and continuing down to the other shoulder.

2 Cutting the tenon

● Secure the rail in a bench vice at an angle of 45 degrees.

● Stand so that the tenon is angled away from you. Hold a tenon saw with its teeth parallel to the work surface and cut down to the shoulder line (A) on the waste side of the gauged lines. Don't cut below the shoulder line.

● Undo the vice, and turn the rail to sit at an angle of 45 degrees in the opposite direction. Repeat the sawing action of the previous stage on this side of the rail.

● Undo the vice, and reset the rail in a vertical position. Make two parallel cuts through the scribed lines down to the shoulder line.

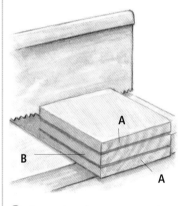

3 Removing the waste wood

● With the rail clamped on its side on a work table, cut along the shoulder line with a tenon saw to remove the waste wood (A). Turn the rail over and repeat the shoulder line cut to make the tenon (B).

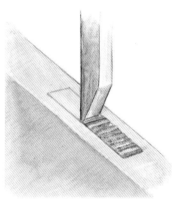

4 Cutting the mortise

● Use a pencil and the newly cut tenon to mark the mortise's length on the leg.

● Scribe the width of the tenon with the mortise gauge.

● Clamp the leg in a vice. Wrap masking tape around the chisel to mark the mortise's depth. Set the chisel in the outline; hold it vertically with the bevel facing the mortise's centre. Working from the centre to the ends, make shallow, closely spaced cuts. Stop about 3mm from each end. Repeat, chipping out waste wood, until you have the proper depth. (If you have a router, a drill press, or a jig that ensures a true vertical, use a bit to bore out the waste wood. Work from the ends to the centre.)

● When you have the correct depth, remove the final 3mm. True the ends and edges with a chisel.

A through mortise-and-tenon

The method you employ to cut a through mortise-and-tenon is different than that used for a blind mortise-and-tenon.

● Mark and cut the tenon overlength (to protrude from the other side of the leg).

● Mark and scribe the outline of the mortise on both sides of the leg.

● With a chisel, cut out half the waste from one side of the leg, and half the waste from the other side of the leg.

● After you have glued the tenon into the mortise, plane the protruding end of the tenon flush with the leg.

A through mortise-and-tenon

Here the end grain of the tenon is visible in the through mortise.

Bridle joints

Intermediate legs on settees are secured to the front and back rails with a bridle joint. To cut a new one, proceed as below.

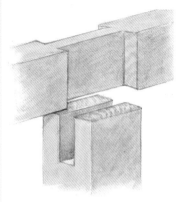

A typical bridle joint

Cutting a bridle joint is easier than cutting a mortise-and-tenon. The housing part of the joint is open on two sides, which makes it easier to cut and pare out the waste wood.

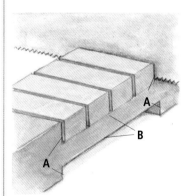

1 Cutting the rail

● With a pencil, mark the width of the leg on the rail.

● Using a T-square and a knife, scribe the shoulder lines (A) all round the rail.

● Set a marking gauge to just less than a quarter of the rail's width. Mark parallel depth lines (B) on each edge of the rail, between the shoulder lines. Make a series of cuts in the waste wood with a tenon saw. Pare out the waste with a chisel or router.

2 Cutting the leg

- Set a mortise gauge to the rail's cut width.
- Mark the shoulder line (A) of the leg to correspond to the depth of the rail.
- Run the gauge line from the shoulder lines across the end of the leg and down the other side.
- Drill from both sides through the bottom of the waste wood. Use a tenon saw to cut down the gauge lines. Chisel waste wood (B) from the housings' corners. Cut across the grain first.

Animal glue

To make animal (or 'rabbit skin') glue when repairing joints, proceed as follows.

- For an average-size chair, place 120g of glue granules in a heatproof container. Barely cover them with cold water, and leave to stand overnight.
- Place the container in a saucepan half-filled with water. Gently heat the pan on a stove until the water is hand-hot. Maintain the temperature and don't let the water boil over or enter the glue mix.
- When the glue has liquified to a creamy consistency and has turned a uniform pale brown colour, it is ready for use. You can apply it with a brush.

Housing joints

The grooves cut into a solid wooden panel to support the ends of shelves are known as 'housings'. The two types of housing commonly cut into the end-panels of case furniture are the 'through' housing and the 'stopped' housing. If you replace an end-panel, you must cut new housings. Proceed as follows.

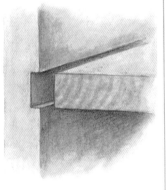

A through housing

In this type of housing joint, the groove that accommodates the end of a shelf runs uninterrupted from the back to the front of the panel. Therefore it is slightly easier to cut than a stopped housing.

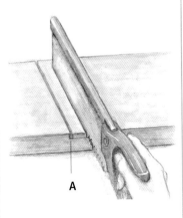

A

Making a through housing

1 Use the original shelf as a template to mark the new housing's width. Measure the original housing's depth and mark this as a depth line (A) on the new panel.

2 Use a T-square and a penknife to scribe cutting lines on the pencil marks.

3 Set a marking gauge to 3mm and scribe depth lines on the back and front edges of the panel.

4 With a tenon saw, cut along the waste side of the cutting lines, down to the depth lines.

5 Remove the waste wood with a chisel or router. Work from the edges to the centre of the panel.

A stopped housing

In this style of joint, the housing is stopped approximately 12mm from the front edge. The corner of the shelf is notched so that its front edge can lie flush with the front of the panel.

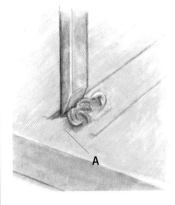

A

Making a stopped housing

1 Mark cutting lines as when making a through housing (see left), but make the lines end at a stop line (A) about 12mm from the front edge of the panel.

2 Mark the depth of the housing, using a marking gauge, on the rear edge of the panel (as in stage 3 of 'Making a through housing'). Set the depth of the gauge to the depth of the original housing. If this measurement is not available because the panel is damaged or missing, set the gauge to about 3mm.

3 Use a sharp chisel to pare out about 5cm of waste wood from the stopped end of the housing. Keep checking the depth with a steel ruler to make sure that you don't cut deeper than 3mm or the depth of the original housing. Make sure that the chisel's bevel always faces the waste wood, to stop the cutting edge from straying.

4 Saw along the waste side of the cutting lines with a tenon saw down to the gauge lines on the rear edge of the panel.

5 Pare out the waste with either a chisel or a router. If you prefer to use a chisel, work from the housing's edges to the centre.

Wooden plugs

Many of the screws used to join components are countersunk and their heads covered with small wooden plugs (see p.42). To gain access to the screw, you must cut out the plug with a chisel. Invariably, the plug is destroyed, with the result that you must make a replacement that matches the wood and, as closely as possible, colour and grain of the original. Cutting new plugs by hand is a laborious task – but it can be done in a matter of seconds if you purchase a plug-cutting bit for your electric drill.

Metalware

Some adhesives specified for repairing metalware (see p.217) are not strong enough for the purpose. If the weight of the object or the load placed upon the bond is too great, or if the surface area of the two parts is too small for the adhesive to grip properly, you must apply solder.

There are two basic types of soldering: soft and hard. Soft soldering, such as is used for repairing lead in a stained-glass panel, is within the ability of an amateur. However, you must observe certain safety measures (see right). Hard soldering, which requires special tools and very high heat, should be left to professional metalware restorers.

Soft soldering involves joining two metals with an alloy – the solder – which melts when it is heated to between 180° and 250°C, and rehardens when cool. The tool used to melt the solder depends on the type of repair. For thick, heavy pieces, use a butane gas blowtorch; for lighter, thinner pieces, use a soldering iron.

Before soldering you must clean the sections to be joined, or they will oxidize when heated, the solder won't flow properly over the surfaces, and the bond will fail. You can clean them with an 'active' or a 'passive' flux. Active flux is a liquid acid that removes all dirt, tarnishing and corrosion. You rinse the surface after soldering to remove traces of acid that would corrode the area surrounding the repair. Passive flux is a non-corrosive paste that will stop the surfaces from oxidizing, but won't completely clean them. It calls for preparatory cleaning work, but it doesn't need to be rinsed afterwards. Use it for repairs where rinsing would be difficult or impossible.

Using an 'active' flux

1 Brush an 'active' flux directly onto the surfaces before soldering.
2 After soldering, rinse the surfaces with clean water and dab dry with towelling.

Using a 'passive' flux

1 Rub the surfaces vigorously with grade-00 wire wool to remove dirt, tarnishing, and corrosion. Wipe off any debris with a clean, lint-free rag. From now on, avoid touching the surfaces with your hands.
2 Brush a 'passive' flux onto the parts to be soldered.

Soldering

Read the safety instructions on soldering (see right), then make the repair with either a soldering iron or a blowtorch, as follows.

Using a soldering iron

1 Clean the copper head, or 'bit', of the soldering iron by rubbing it vigorously with wire wool until it is shiny. Plug the iron into an electrical socket and allow the head to heat to the melting point of the solder. Dip the head into the active or passive flux, then onto the stick of solder. This process, 'tinning', leaves a film of solder over the face of the head. Always tin the iron before soldering.

Note: When soldering an extensive repair, dip the head of the iron in flux from time to time to keep it clean.
2 Clean and apply flux to the two edges to be soldered. Align and secure them in position, using G-clamps or weights. Press the head of the iron against the joint and hold it there to allow the metal to heat to a temperature slightly higher than the melting point of the solder.
3 With your free hand, hold the solder against the tip of the iron and the joint. Almost immediately, the solder will melt and flow into the joint. Withdraw the iron and let the solder cool and harden.
Note: If you are soldering a long joint, simply draw the head of the iron slowly along the joint and push the stick of solder along just behind it.
4 If you used an 'active' rather than a 'passive' flux, thoroughly rinse the joint and the surrounding area with clean water to remove any traces of flux. Pat dry with towelling.

Using a blowtorch

1 Clean the edges to be soldered and brush on the flux, keeping the two halves of the joint separate.
2 Heat one half with a blowtorch. Quickly withdraw the torch and press enough solder along the surface of the edge to create a thin film of solder. Usually the solder will flow freely over the surface. However, occasionally you may have to spread it out by using a short length of wire. Repeat on the other half of the joint. Let the solder cool and harden.
3 Align and secure the two halves of the joint with G-clamps or weights. Apply a fresh coat of flux over the joint. Play the heat of the blowtorch along the joint to melt the two strips of solder and fuse them together. Let the solder cool and harden as before.
4 If you used an 'active' flux, thoroughly rinse the joint and surrounding area with clean water, then pat dry with towelling.

Textiles, Upholstery and Rugs & Carpets

The various stitches and knots called for in the sections on Textiles (see pp.136–51) and on Upholstery (see pp.82–119) are illustrated and described here. Also included are some basic sewing techniques, which will help you to achieve a professional-looking finish.

Sewing techniques

You should bear in mind the following points when repairing antique textiles, upholstery and rugs and carpets.

● On the principle that practice makes perfect, you will find it worthwhile to experiment with specified stitches and knots on fabric scraps before using them on a real piece of work. In order to get a proper feel for what you are doing, always practise on pieces of fabric that are made from the same fibre(s), have the same weave, and are of the same weight, as the antique textile or upholstery that you wish to repair.

● Once you have practised a technique on a scrap and feel confident enough to start work on the actual piece, don't rush the repair. Instead, examine the damage closely – using a magnifying glass if necessary. Antique textiles are very often fragile. Therefore, if you can use existing seam holes with a matching size of needle when restitching, rather than making new holes, do so. In this way you will avoid placing additional stress on the material.

● Take into account the nature of the thread or yarn that you are using to make the repair. For example, woollen yarn has characteristics similar to those of the pile of a rug or carpet: it feels smooth if you pull it through your fingers in one direction, but quite rough if you run it in the opposite direction. As a consequence of this, you will find that your repair will

be smoother, tighter and more compact if you always thread woollen yarn through the needle so that when you pull it between your fingers away from the eye of the needle, it feels smooth. The same is true of cotton thread, which, if it is not run in the right direction, will produce snags and knots.

● It is important to keep the tension of your stitches even when you are carrying out a repair. They should be neither too tight nor too loose. Stitches that are too tight almost always damage the fabric; stitches that are too loose can also cause damage, because once the repair starts to ravel or fall apart, the fabric is more likely to snag on something and tear the stitch holes.

Stitches

When you have practised them a few times, you will find that the following stitches are very easy to execute.

1 Tack stitching

● To tack stitch, insert the needle in and out of both sides of the fabric, as shown in the illustration.

Note: A tacking stitch and a running or basting stitch are similar. The difference is that a running stitch consists of stitches of equal length on each side of the fabric, whereas a tacking stitch is made up of slightly longer stitches on the right side of the fabric and slightly shorter ones on the back.

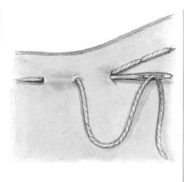

1 Back stitching

Note: A very sturdy line of stitching is formed by moving the needle two steps forward, one step back.

● Insert the needle from the back of the fabric. Reinsert the point about 3mm to the right of the exit point. Slide the needle along the back for 6mm, then push it through to the right side, as shown.

● Continue, inserting the needle at the end of each previous stitch and moving it along by 6mm, until you complete the row.

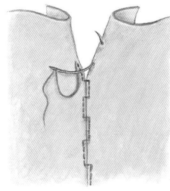

1 Slip-stitching

Note: Although worked on the right side of the fabric, slip-stitching is hidden beneath folded edges and forms an invisible seam. It is helpful to have a steam iron ready to remove puckers and keep a smooth edge.

● Fold and gently press each edge under. Align the two edges.

● Slip the needle inside the fold on one of the edges and secure the thread with a couple of back stitches on top of each other.

● Slide the needle inside the fold for

about 6mm. Push it through the fold into the other piece of fabric exactly opposite where the needle has just emerged.

● Slide the needle under this fold for about ¼ inch. Push it through the fold, across the seam and into the opposing fabric.

● Alternate stitches on each side of the seam until you reach the end of the row. Fasten off. If puckers appear, you may be pulling too tight. Adjust tension; smooth out puckers with finger pressure or light ironing.

Joining threads

When repairing side cords on rugs and carpets (see p.164), you may need to attach a new length of yarn or thread if the original length proves insufficient to complete the repair. To do this, proceed as follows.

● When 7.5–10cm of the original thread or yarn is left, push the needle through the core of the side cord in the direction in which you are overcasting.

● Push and then pull the needle and thread or yarn out of the cord as close as possible to where it joins the main body of the rug.

● Re-thread the needle with a new length of thread or yarn. This time push the needle into the cord 5cm along from the end of the first section of overcasting.

● Push back towards the earlier section of overcasting. When you reach the end of this section, pull the needle up through the inside edge of the side cord.

● Continue to overcast. As you do so, the new thread or yarn will compress the cord, securing the end of the original length and the beginning of the new one.

Knots

These five knots are used to repair upholstery, textiles and rugs and carpets. They are cross-referenced from 'Upholstering a drop-in seat pad', and 'Reupholstering a button-back chair', on pp.94–8 and 99–119, from textile projects on pp.146–50, and from rugs and carpets projects on pp.160–71.

Half-hitch

This very simple knot is made by passing the end of a piece of cord, yarn or thread around itself, and through the loop thus made. It is used to make basic anchors in the repair of both textiles and upholstery.

Double-hitch

This knot provides a means of securing a half hitch (see above) by making another hitch on top of it. It is primarily used to finish off a row of stitches.

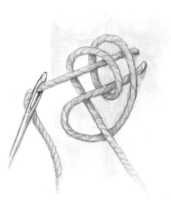

Slip-knot

This versatile knot is particularly useful for starting a row of ties or stitches. Once you have made the loops, pull tight the end of the thread that passes through the eye of the needle.

Clove-hitch (above)

This knot is used specifically to secure laid cord to upholstery springs.

Locked loop (below)

This loop is used to secure springs, but must be knotted off at both ends.

Storing antique clothing

Over the past two decades there has been an upsurge of interest in collecting antique clothing and period costume dating from the second half of the 19th century to the early 1970s.

Unfortunately, of all the categories of antiques and collectables that are covered in this book, costume is probably the most vulnerable to rapid deterioration if it is not handled and stored appropriately. The main reason for this problem is the fact that most costume is hygroscopic: it readily absorbs moisture, and just as quickly loses it, during fluctuations in humidity. An atmosphere that is too humid or too dry will cause damage – the former encourages bacterial growth, the latter shrinkage and loss of natural oils from the fibres. To minimize the risks of damage and decay to antique costume, you should follow the instructions and advice on storage given in the chapter on Textiles (see p.150), but also note the specific requirements for the following items.

A stable humidity level of 55 per cent is suitable for storing most costume, but textiles that are decorated with beads made of soda or potash glass can suffer from a phenomenon known as 'glass disease'. If the clothing is exposed to humidity levels at or above 42 per cent, alkaline mineral salts will leach from the glass. The beads will crack or crumble and the salts will bleach the underlying fabric. If you live in a humid climate, you can prevent this reaction by installing a dehumidifier in the storage area and maintaining the humidity at 40 per cent.

A significant number of 20th-century costumes are made from man-made fibres and fabrics. Dresses made from synthetic polymerics (or 'plastics') such as nylon and other vinyls pose particular problems because of the way in which plastics age: some harden, others become granular and sticky, most give off low levels of corrosive fumes. To minimize deterioration, you should store plastic dresses in a well-ventilated space, at 50 per cent humidity and 18.3°C. Pad them out with acid-free tissue paper, so that they don't harden to the wrong shape, and don't store them with any other textiles, as the fumes can damage their threads and fibres.

Directory of suppliers

You should find little difficulty in obtaining nearly all the tools and materials specified for the projects and tasks covered by this book. They can be bought from retail outlets in most cities and towns. Below is a list of the types of outlet most likely to be able to meet your needs for each of the categories of antiques.

This information is followed by a list of some less well known tools and materials, and the types of outlet where these can be purchased. A few of the tools and materials specified in the book may not be available at retail outlets. To help you locate these items, a list of specialist suppliers and professional restorers is included. Also given are the names and addresses of some useful antiques trade associations.

RETAIL OUTLETS

Furniture tools Hardware shops, DIY and department stores, and timber and builder's merchants.
Furniture materials As above, plus artist's suppliers and chemists.

Canework tools Hardware shops, DIY and department stores, and specialist cane suppliers (see opposite page).
Canework materials Craft shops, artist's suppliers and specialist cane suppliers (see opposite page).

Upholstery tools Hardware shops, DIY and department stores, and specialist upholstery suppliers (see opposite page).
Upholstery materials Haberdashery shops and department stores, and specialist upholstery suppliers (see opposite page).

Leather tools Hardware shops, DIY and department stores, and craft shops and artist's suppliers.
Leather materials Some hardware shops, and specialist suppliers of pre-cut and tooled hides and skivers (see opposite page).

Textiles tools Haberdashery and craft shops, and department stores.
Textiles materials As above, plus chemists and specialist suppliers (see opposite page).

Rugs and carpets tools See Textiles.
Rugs and carpets materials See Textiles.

Ceramics tools Hardware and craft shops, and DIY and department stores.
Ceramics materials DIY stores and craft shops, artist's suppliers and specialist suppliers (see opposite page).

Glassware tools DIY stores and craft shops.
Glassware materials As above, plus specialist suppliers (see opposite page).

Metalware tools Hardware shops, and DIY and department stores.
Metalware materials As above, plus specialist suppliers (see opposite page).

Jewellery tools Hardware shops, DIY and department stores, and jeweller's suppliers.
Jewellery materials Artist's and jeweller's suppliers.

Stoneware tools Hardware shops, and DIY and department stores.
Stoneware materials Artist's suppliers, craft shops and specialist suppliers (see opposite page).

SPECIALIST TOOLS AND MATERIALS

Acetone Chemists and hardware stores.
Acid-free tissue paper Artist's suppliers.
Acrylic matte medium Artist's suppliers.
Almond oil Chemists.
Animal (rabbit-skin) glue Artist's suppliers and some hardware shops.

Benzene Chemists.
Borax Chemists and hardware shops.
Boxwood modelling tools Some artist's suppliers (see also opposite page).

Cane levers (shell bodkins) Cane suppliers and some craft shops.
Carpet shampoo DIY and department stores.
Casters Specialist hardware shops (see opposite page).
Chemical-resistant rubber gloves See Specialist Suppliers on opposite page.
Chloramine T Chemists.
Chrome polish Car accessory shops.
Cold-cure lacquer Artist's suppliers.
Crocus powder Artist's suppliers, jewellers and some ironmongers.
Curled hair Upholstery suppliers.

Dichlorobenzene crystals Some chemists and most professional restorers of leather and textiles.

Epoxy putty Artist's suppliers.
Eucalyptus oil Chemists and herbalists.

Fibreglass matting Car accessory shops.
French chalk Chemists and ironmongers.
Fuller's earth Artist's suppliers, chemists and some ironmongers.

Gesso paste Artist's suppliers.

Gimp pins Haberdashery shops and department stores.
Glover's needles As above.
Gold metallic powder Artist's suppliers.

Hydrogen peroxide (20 per cent volume) Chemists.

Jeweller's rouge Jewellers, artist's suppliers and some hardware shops.

Kaolin Chemists and some artist's suppliers.

Laid cord Upholstery suppliers.
Latex Artist's suppliers.
Latex emulsion Artist's suppliers.
Lint-free cotton rag Artist's suppliers.
Liquid gold size Artist's suppliers.
Liquid metal leaf Artist's suppliers.

Marble polish Outlets specializing in garden statuary and architectural fixtures and fittings.
Marine sponge Chemists and artist's suppliers.
Mattress needles Upholstery suppliers and some department stores.
Microcrystalline wax Some artist's suppliers (see also Specialist Suppliers, right.
Modelling clay Artist's suppliers.

Needle files Some hardware shops, and artist's suppliers.
Nylon monofilament screening See Specialist Suppliers, right.

Oil of spike Chemists and herbalists.
Oxalic acid Chemists.

Polyacrylate resin Some artist's suppliers and leather suppliers.
Potato flour Grocers and chemists.
Potato starch Grocers.
Powdered magnesia Chemists.

Regulators Upholstery suppliers and some hardware shops.

Saponaria Herbalists and some chemists.
Scrim Upholstery suppliers.
Skin wadding Upholstery suppliers.
Solder and flux Hardware shops.
Spirit of salts (hydrochloric acid) Chemists.
Spring needles Upholstery suppliers, haberdashery shops and some hardware shops.
Stone sealer Some artist's suppliers (see also Specialist Suppliers, right).

Tailor's chalk Department stores and fabric shops.
Thymol Chemists.
Titanium dioxide Artist's suppliers and some chemists.
Trichloroethane 1.1.1. Chemists.

Wadding Upholstery suppliers and haberdashery shops.
White ring remover Hardware shops, and DIY and department stores.
Whiting Artist's suppliers and some ironmongers.
Wool detergent Department stores.

SPECIALIST SUPPLIERS AND OTHER USEFUL ADDRESSES

Antique Leathers
4 Park End
South Hill Park
London NW3 2SE
Antique hides and skivers.

Association of Master Upholsterers (AMU)
Francis Vaughan House
102 Commercial Street
Newport
Gwent NP9 1LU

British Antique Dealers' Association (BADA)
20 Rutland Gate
London SW7 1BD
Will provide details of antique dealers and restorers in the UK.

The Cane Store
207 Blackstock Road
Highbury Vale
London N5 2LL
Canework restorer and cane supplies.

Richard Chys
12 Trundle Street
London SE1 1QT
French polishing, furniture restoration and upholstery.

J. Crispin & Son Ltd
92 Curtain Road
London EC2A 3AA
Furniture veneers.

Greenham Trading
Telford Place
Crawley
West Sussex RH10 2TP
Chemical-resistant rubber gloves.

Guild of Antique Dealers and Restorers (GADR)
23 Belle Vue Road
Shrewsbury
Shropshire SY3 7LN

Irish Professional Conservators' and Restorers' Association (IPCRA)
c/o Mr Grellan D. Rourke
The Office of Public Works
51 St Stephens Green
Dublin 2
Republic of Ireland
Will provide details of antique restorers in Ireland.

Liberon Waxes Ltd
6 Park Street
Lydd
Kent TN28 8XU
Specialist furniture waxes and polishes.

Locks & Handles and Interiors Architectural Components Ltd
4-8 Exhibition Road
London SW7 2HF
Suppliers of reproduction furniture and architectural hardware.

London and Provincial Antique Dealers' Association (LAPADA)
535 Kings Road
London SW10 0SZ
Will provide details of antique dealers and restorers in the UK.

London Bullion Ltd
73 Farringdon Road
London EC1
Jeweller's materials.

S.R. Luker Upholsterers
Units 4 and 5
18a Malling Street
Lewes
East Sussex BN7 2EG
Master upholsterer and supplier of upholstery materials (including loose covers).

John Myland Ltd
80 Norwood High Street
London SE27 9NW
Specialist furniture waxes and polishes.

Parry Tyzack
329 Old Street
London EC1V 9LQ
Specialist tools.

Picreator Enterprises Ltd
44 Park View Gardens
Hendon
London NW4 2PN
Nylon monofilament screening and other conservation and restoration materials.

I. & P. Pritchard
17 Heathcote Grove
North Chingford
London E4 6RZ
Chair caning and rush seating.

Rug Restorers' Association
c/o Orientis
Digby Road
Sherborne
Dorset DT9 3NR

Scottish Society for Conservation and Restoration (SSCR)
Sue Wilthew
The Glasite Meeting House
33 Barony Street
Edinburgh EH3 6NX
Will provide details of antique restorers in Scotland.

Alec Tiranti Ltd
21 Goodge Place
London W1P 2AJ
also at:
70 High Street
Theale
Reading
Berkshire RG7 5AR
Craft and artist's tools and materials.

Woolnough (AC) Limited
Units W107-W110
First Floor
Holywell Centre
1 Phipp Street
London EC2A 4PS
Leather restorer and supplier of pre-cut and tooled antique and modern hides and skivers.

Index

Italic page numbers refer to picture captions.

A

acetone damage, on wooden furniture 19
acid-etching 197
acid stains, on furniture 18
acrylic paints 192–3
adhesive stains, on textiles 144
agates 221, 224
air pollution 88, 150, 210
alabaster 236–7, 240
    powdered 239
alcohol stains
    on glassware 201
    on textiles 88, 89
algae, on stoneware 240
alligator skin 122
aluminium 210
amber 221, 224
anaerobic adhesive 199, 203
animal glue 182
    making 246
    softening 42
appliqué *139*
aquamarines 221, 224
armoires 58
arms and armour 210
Art Deco *175, 220*
Ashbury metal 207
assay marks 206
Aubusson 154
Axminster 154

B

back splats 40, *40*
back stitch 248
back-tacking 115
Bakelite *221*
ball-and-claw feet *40*
balloon-back chairs 40, 41, 43
bamboo chinoiserie 68, 69
barrel clasps 226
basalt 236, 240, 241
beads, restringing 231
beadwork 138
bed covers *139*, 146
beds 10
beech, staining 30
beer stains, on textiles 88
beeswax polish 17, 32–3
beet stains, on textiles 144
bentwood chairs 40, 41, *68*
    caned *see* canework
    dismantling 41–2
    reassembling 43
    bergères 68–9
Berlin woolwork 138

biscuit porcelain 175
bleaching, on wooden furniture 18
blind-stitching 104
blood stains, on textiles 144
bloom, on wooden furniture 18, 34, 36
bocage 190
bolt ring clasps 226
bone 233
bone china 175, *175*
bookbindings, leather 122, *123*, 129
bottoming (upholstery) 93
bracelets
    repairing 230
    safety chains 230, *230*
bracket feet *58*
braid, cleaning 89
brass 207
    cleaning 210, 213
    dents 214
    furniture fittings 16–17
    jewellery 220, 224
    scratches 215
breccia 236
bridle joints 245–6, *245*
bridle ties 96, 106, 107
bronze 207, *207*
    cleaning 210
    jewellery 220, *220*, 224
    verdigris 207
brooches *220, 221*, 228–9
    safety chains 230
brown polish 34
bureaux 11, 58
burn or scorch marks
    on furniture 18
    on textiles 145
button-back chairs, reupholstering 99–119
buttoning thread 87
button polish 34
buttons (upholstery) 84–5

C

cabriole legs 40, *40, 52*
calcium carbonate deposits, on glassware 201
calfskin 122, *123, 127*
cameos 224
candle wax
    on leatherwork 126
    on stoneware 240
    on textiles 88
    on wooden furniture 18
canework 66–81, *68*
    antiquing 81
    beading edges 79, 80–1
    bentwood *68*, 69

cane grades 71
cleaning and reviving 72
cushions 68, 69
frame preparation 72
medallion backs *69*
patterns 69, 73
pegging 71, 79
restoring 72–81
six-way standard pattern *68*, 69, 72, 73
canvas work 138
    see also needlepoint
carnelian 224
carpets *see* rugs and carpets
cased glass 197
case furniture 10, 11
    doors 58, 65
    drawers *see* drawers
    frame-and-panel construction 58, 59, 61
    housing joints 246, *246*
    plinths 58
    solid end-panel construction 58–9, 61, 64
    split end-panels 64
    structural repairs 57–65
    tapered laths, fitting 64
    veneered *see* veneers
casters 55, *55*
casting missing components 38, 190
cast iron 207, 211, 217
ceramics 172–93
    care 178
    casting missing components 190
    chipped 178, 186–7
    cleaning 178–9
    crackling 191
    crazing, simulating 191
    decorative techniques 174–5
    dusting 178
    filling joints and holes 186
    glazed 174, 178, 179, 192–3
    grease marks 178
    handles, repairing 183, 188–9
    hand painting 187, 192–3
    lime scale 179
    old repairs, remaking 182–3
    overglaze decoration 174
    regilding 191
    salts 179
    sgraffito 174
    shell chips 186–7
    simple breaks, bonding 180–1
    slip decoration 174
    spouts, remodelling 184–5
    sprigging 174
    stain removal 179

tools and materials 177–8
types 174
underglaze decoration 174
unglazed 178–9
    see also individual wares
chains (jewellery)
    repairing 230
    storing 233
chain stitch 161
chairs 10
    arms 40, 46–7
    back splats 40, *40*
    balloon-back 40, 41, 43
    bentwood 40, 41, 43, *68*, 69
    bergères 68–9
    button-back 99–119
    caned *see* canework
    Chippendale 40, *40*, 88
    cresting rail 40
    dining 48, 88
    dismantling and reassembling 40–3
    dowels, repairing 46–7
    drop-in seats 40, 92, 94–8
    elbows, repairing 46–7
    frame 40, *40, 41*, 43
    hall *29*
    legs, repairing 48–51
    loose joints, repairing 40, 44–5
    mission-style *127*
    Regency style *98*
    Rococo revival *85*
    Sheraton 88
    side *68, 89*
    spindles 41
    sprung seats 40, 92, 100–1, 107–9, 114
    stick 40, 41, 43
    stretcher rails 40, 41, 50–1
    structural repairs 40–51
    tenons, repairing and tightening 44–5
    turned components, repairing 50–1
    upholstered *see* upholstery
    Windsor 40, 43
chaise longue *85*
chamois leather 122
champlevé 210
chandeliers, cleaning 200
chasing 210
chests 10, 11
chests of drawers 32, 58, *58*
chests-on-stands 16–17
chevron caning pattern *73*
chewing gum, removing from textiles 144
chiffoniers 58
chinoiserie 68, 69

Chippendale period *11*, 40, *40*, 88
chocolate stains, on textiles 144
chromium 207, 211
Classical style *206*
clear polish 34
cloisonné 211
clothes presses 58
clothing, antique, storing 150, 249
clove-hitch 249
coffeepots
    ceramic 179, 184–5
    copper *207*
    silver 213
coffee stains
    on ceramics 179
    on silver 213
    on textiles 88
coins 211
copper 207, *207*
    champlevé 210
    cleaning 211, 213
    dents 214
    furniture fittings 16–17
    jewellery 220, 224
    scratches 215
    verdigris 211
copper stains, on ceramics 179
coral 221, 224
cosmetics stains, on textiles 145
cotton 138, 139
couching 138
cow hide 122, 134
crackling 191
crazing, simulating 191
creamware 174
crewel work 138
crochet *139*
cross stitch 149
cross stitch over three holes square 149
crumb cloths 159
cupboards 58
cup casters 55, *55*
cushions 68, 69, 84
cut glass 197
cutlery 217
cutlery boxes 122
cutwork 138

D

damascening 211
damask *98*, 138
Davenports *11*
decanters *201*
    Rodney *196*
delftware
    Bristol 174
    Dutch 174

desks
    Davenports *11*
    ink stains on 19, *19*, 126–7
    leather desktops 122, 130, 134–5
    pedestal 134
diamond-point engraving *196*, 197
diamonds 220, 233
    artificial 224–5
    cleaning 224
dining chairs 48, 88
doors
    hinges and hinge housings 65
    sagging or sticking 58, 65
    sprung 65
double-cone spring 84
double-hitch 249
dowels
    removing 42
    repairing 46–7
drawer guides 59, 61
drawer rails 60
drawer runners 52, 58, 59, 60
    central 61
    double-sided 61
    frame-and-panel construction 61
    replacing 61
    solid end-panel construction 61
drawers
    repairing 60–3
    sticking 63
    in tables 52
    worn 58, 62–3
drawer stops 58, 59, 62
drawn thread work 138
dressers 11, 58
dressing-table sets 206
drop-in seats 40, 92, 94–8
drop-leaf tables 11, 52–3, *52*, 55
dry-cleaning textiles 142
dustboards 58, 59, 62
dust covers (upholstery) 98, 119
dyes
    aniline 131, 138, 155
    leather 123, 131
    textiles 138, 155
    wood stains 30–1

E

earrings *220*, 232–3
earthenware 174, 178, 180–1
    repairing 180–1
egg stains, on textiles 145

electroplating 206
embroidery 138, *139*
emeralds 220, 225
Empire style 68
enamel
    champlevé 210
    cloisonné 211
    enamelled glass 197, 200,
        201
    enamelled jewellery 221,
        221, 225
    enamelled metalware 210,
        211, 213
engraving
    engraved glass *196*, 197
    engraved metalware 211
epoxy-resin
    adhesive 182, 203
    putty 38, 185, 187, 188–90
etching
    etched glassware 197
    etched metalware 211

F
faience 174
fat stains
    on leatherwork 126
    on upholstery 88
feet
    ball-and-claw *40*
    bracket *58*
    pad *52*
fireplaces, stone *237*
flambé glaze *175*
flashed glass 197
flat-woven rugs and carpets
    154–5
    Kelims 154–5, *155*, 171,
        171
    Soumaks 154–5, 171, *171*
    see also rugs and carpets
flux (glassware) 196
flux (soldering) 247
fly marks
    on stoneware 240
    on wooden furniture 18–19
forest glass 196
frame-and-panel construction
    58, 59, 61
frame chairs 40–3, *40, 41*
frames, regilding 38–9
frame tables 10–11, 52–4
French polish 11, 17, 32, 34–7
    applying 36–7
    bloom 34, 36
    deep scratches 21
    disadvantage 34
    filling grain 31
    mouldings and recessed
        areas 37

moss scratches 20
rubbing pad, making and
    using 34–6
satin and high-gloss finishes
    37
staining and colour-matching
    30–1
stripping old finish 29, 36
types 34
waxing 37
fruit juice stains, on textiles
    145
fungus
    on leatherwork 126
    on metalware 211
    mildew and mould on
        ceramics 179
    mildew on stoneware 240
    mildew on textiles 89
furniture 10–65
    acetone damage, treating
        19
    acid stains 18
    beeswax polish 17
    bleaching patchy colour 29
    bleach marks, treating 18
    bloom 18, 34, 36
    bruises 20, 23
    burnt or scorched 18, 24
    candle wax, removing 18
    caned *see* canework
    care 11, 17
    casters 55
    cleaning 16–17
    colour, reviving 17, 28
    colour-matching 30–1
    cracks 20
    dents 20, 22
    figuring and graining,
        enhancing 30, 34
    filling grain and holes 20,
        30, 31
    finishes 11
    fly marks, removing 18–19
    French polishing *see* French
        polish
    gilt frames 38–9
    and humidity 20, 22, 63
    joints 11, 244–6
    maker's stamps *29*
    metal fittings 16–17
    moss scratches 20
    oiled *see* oiled furniture
    painted ormolu *85*
    patina 11, 16, 17, 28, 29,
        29
    reviving 16–17
    scratches, treating 20, 21,
        29
    sealing surface 33
    split panels 64

staining *see* staining wood
stains and marks, removing
    18–19, 126–7
stripping old finishes 28–9,
    36
structural repairs 40–65
tapered laths, fitting 64
upholstery *see* upholstery
veneered *see* veneers
water marks 19
waxed *see* waxed furniture
wooden plugs 246
woodworm *see* woodworm
see also case furniture;
    chairs; tables; upholstery

G
garnet polish 34
gate-leg tables 52–3
gesso 38–9
Ghiordes knot 155, 166–7
gilding
    ceramics 191–2
    frames 38–9
    glassware 197, 200, *201*,
        203, *203*
    gold transfer tape 131
    leatherwork 131
glassware 194–203, *196*
    calcium carbonate deposits
        201
    cased 197
    chandeliers 200
    chipped 202
    cleaning 200–1
    cloudiness 201
    coloured 197, 199, 200,
        203
    core-formed 196
    cut 197
    decorative techniques 197
    drying 200
    enamelled 197, 200, *201*
    engraved *196*, 197
    etched 197
    flashed 197
    flux 196
    forest 196
    free-blown 196
    gilt 197, 200, *201*, 203,
        203
    grinding 202
    holes 202
    iridescence 201
    lattimo 197
    lead-crystal 196
    metal mountings 200
    mirror glass 200
    mould-blown 196
    overlay 197

potash 196
pressed 196–7
    repairing 202–3
    scratches 202
    soda 196
    stained 197, 200
    stain removal 201
    stoppers, freeing 201
    tools and materials 198–9
    trailing decoration 197
glazes (ceramics) 174
    repairing 192–3
    tinting and colouring
        192–3
goatskin 122
gold 206, 214
    assay marks 206
    carat system 206
    chains 230
    cleaning 225
    cloisonné 211
    colour 206
    jewellery 220, 225
    rolled 206, 220
    see also gilding
gold plate 206, 220
granite 236, *237*, 240, 241
grass stains, on textiles 145
grease stains
    on ceramics 178
    on leatherwork 126
    on stoneware 240
    on upholstery 88
    on wooden furniture 19
gypsum 236, 240

H
half cross stitch 149
half-hitch 249
hall chair *29*
hallmarks 206
handles, ceramic
    modelling new 188–9
    repairing 183
harlequin Davenports *11*
harness needles 128
hessian 87, 95
hinges and hinge housings 65
horn 225, 233
horsehair stuffing 84, 93, 95
horse skin 122
hourglass spring 84
housing joints 246, *246*
humidity
    and jewellery 233
    and leatherwork 126
    and textiles 88, 150
    and veneers 22
    and wooden furniture 20,
        22, 63

I
igneous rocks 236
ink stains
    on furniture 19, *19*, 126–7
    on leatherwork 126–7
    on textiles 145
inlaid metalwork 213
inlaid wood
    French polishing 34
    wax polishing 32
insect infestations 126
    mothballs 150
    woodworm *see* woodworm
iron 207, 211
    cast 207, 211, 217
    furniture fittings 16–17
    jewellery *220*
    rust 211
    wrought 207, 211
ironing and pressing textiles 145
iron mould stains, removal 145
ivory 221, 225, 233

J
Jacobean revival 69
jade 221, *221*, 225
jadeite 221
jet 221, 225
jewellery 218–33
    barrel clasps 226
    bolt rings 226
    brooch pins 228–9
    cameos 224
    clasps 226–7
    cleaning 223, 224–5
    dismantling 223
    enamelled 221, *221*
    and humidity 233
    plastic *221*
    precious stones 220–1, 224,
        233
    repairs 226–33
    restringing 231
    safety chains 230, *230*
    semi-precious stones 221,
        224
    storing 233
    tools and materials 222–3
    V-spring clasps 227
jewellery boxes 122
joints (woodworking) 11, 244–6
    loose 40, 44–5
Jufti knot 155, 166

K
Kelim ends 155, 160–2
Kelims 154–5, *155*, 171, *171*
    see also rugs and carpets
knitwear 138

knots 249
knotted pile rugs and carpets
    154, 155
    hand-woven 162, *162*
    knot types 155, 166
    machine-made 162
    repairing pile 166–7
    repiling 170
    reweaving 169–71
    trimming pile 167
    see also rugs and carpets
knuckle joints 53

L
lace 138, *139, 145*
latex emulsion 190
lattimo 197
lead 207, 211
    patina 207, 211
    reshaping 215
lead-crystal glass 196
lead glaze 174, 178, *191*
leatherwork 120–35
    bookbindings 122, *123*
    care 123, 126
    cleaning 126–7, 132–3
    curled edges 134
    desk- and tabletops 122,
        130, 134–5
    dry, consolidating 127, 132
    dyeing 123, 131
    embossed 125
    faded 127
    feeding 133
    fungal growths on 126
    harness needles 128
    insect infestations 126
    lubricating 123
    patching 129–30
    patina *122*, 126, 132
    polishing 132–3, 135
    recolouring 131, 133
    red rot 126
    regilding 131
    repairs 123
    restitching 128, 132
    restoration 123, 126, 132–3
    scratched and scuffed 131
    stain removal 126–7, 132
    suede, cleaning 127
    tanning 122–3
    tooled 125, 131, 134
    tools and materials 124–5
    torn 127, 129
    types 122
    upholstery 122, *122*, 127,
        129
legs
    cabriole 40, *40, 52*
    chair legs, repairing 48–51

pedestal tables, repairing 52, 56–7
sabre *85*
turned, repairing 50–1
Levant 122
lime scale 179
limestone 236, 240
linen 138, 139, *139*
linen presses 11
linseed oil 32, 33
lipstick stains, on textiles 145
lizard skin 122
locked loop 249
looped ties 107
loose covers 88
lowboys 11, 58

M

mahogany *11, 19, 29,* 40, *40,* 46–7, 48, *52, 58,* 68–9, *68,* 72, 134
filling grain 31
French polish 34
staining 30–1, 32
majolica 174
maker's stamps and marks *29,* 206
marble 237, *237,* 241, *243*
cleaning 240
faux 240, 241, *241*
marquetry, French polishing 34
medallion backs *69*
medals 211
Meissen 175
metallic stains, on ceramics 179
metal polish marks, on textiles 145
metalware 206–17
arms and armour 210
assay marks 206
care 210–13
champlevé 210
chasing 210
cleaning 206, 210–13
cloisonné 211
coins and medals 211
cracks and breaks 217
crushed 216
cutlery 217
damascening 211
dents 214, 215
electroplating 206
enamelled 210, 211, 213
engraved 211
etched 211
on furniture 16–17
on glassware 200
hallmarks 206
inlaid 213
jewellery *see* jewellery

mould 211
niello 211
patina 206, 210, 211
repairing and restoring 214–17
reshaping 215
rust 211
scratches 215
soldering 247
storing 210
tarnishing 210, 212–13
tools and materials 208–9
verdigris 207, 211
see also individual metals
metamorphic rocks 237
mildew
on ceramics 179
on stoneware 240
on textiles 89
see also mould
milk stains, on textiles 89, 145
mirror frames, regilding 38–9
mirrors, cleaning 200
mission-style armchairs *127*
Morocco 122, 134
mortise-and-tenon joints 244–5
blind (stopped) 40, 42, 45, 244–5, *244*
dismantling 40–2
hidden wedges 42, 45
open wedges 42, 45
repairing and tightening 44–5
through 40, 42, 45, 244, 245, *245*
moss scratches 20
mothballs 150
mother-of-pearl 221, 225
moth grubs 126
mould
on ceramics 179
on lead 211
musical instruments 122

N

nail polish, removing from textiles 145
Napoleonic motifs *98*
Native American rugs 154
necklaces 230
cleaning 224
restringing 231
storing 233
needlepoint 138, 146
repairing 148–9
stitches 149
nephrite 221
netsuke 225
nickel 207

nickel silver 206
nicotine stains, on stoneware 240
niello 211

O

oak 32, 34
oblique Slav stitch 149
oiled furniture 11, 17, 32, 33
staining and colour-matching 30–1
oil stains
on leatherwork 126
on stoneware 240
on upholstery 88
on wooden furniture 19
onyx 225
opals 221, 225
Oriental rugs 154–5, *155*
ormolu, painted *85*
overcast stitch 161
overglaze decoration 174
overlay glass 197

P

pad feet *52*
paint stains, on furniture 19
panelling, faux marble *241*
Parian ware 175
passementerie 89
patina
on furniture 11, 16, 17, 28, 29, *29*
on lead 207
on leatherwork *122,* 126, 132
on metalware 206, 210, 211
pearls 221, 225
pearlware 174
pedestal desks 134
pedestal tables 11, *11,* 52–3, 56–7
pencil marks, on textiles 145
pendants *221*
Persian rugs 154–5, *155,* 166–7
Persian (Senneh) knot 155, 166–7
perspiration stains, on textiles 145
pewter 207
Ashbury metal 207
cleaning 211
reshaping 214, 215
spotted 211
piano top *11*
pigments, powder 192
pile rugs *see* knotted pile rugs and carpets

pine *11*
oiling 32
staining 30
stripping 28
piping, replacement 91
plank-top tables 52–4
plaster castings 236, 240
plastic *221*
platinum 220, 225
plinths 58
plugs, wooden 246
porcelain 174, 175
hard paste 175
repairing 180–1
soft paste 175
see also ceramics
porphyry 236, 240
pottery 174, 175
repairing 180–1
see also ceramics
poultice method 242–3
precious stones 220–1, 224, 233
purses 122

Q

quilting 138, *138,* 147

R

rabbit-skin glue 182
making 246
rattan 68
ray skin 122
rebates 40, 59, 94
red rot 126
reeding *206*
refectory tables 10–11
Regency stripes *98*
Regency style 68, *85, 98*
regulator (upholstery) 87, 103
ripping off (upholstery) 93, 99
Roan 122
Rococo revival *85*
Rodney decanter *196*
rosewood, faux *85*
rubber-based resin adhesive 182
rubies 220–1, 225
rugs and carpets 152–73
chain stitching fringe 161
cleaning 158–9
colourfastness, testing for 158–9
displaying 159
dusting 158
dyes 155
flat-woven 154–5
fringes and tassels 155, 160–2

hand-woven 162, *163*
Kelim ends 155, 160–2
Kelims 154–5, *155,* 171, *171*
knots 155, 166, 170, 249
knotted pile 154, 155
looms 154
machine-made 162
overcasting fringe 161
Persian 154–5, *155,* 166–7
pile *see* knotted pile *above*
repairing pile 166–7
repiling 170
reweaving 168–71
rewefting 170–1
side cords 155, 164–5, 248
Soumaks 154–5, 171, *171*
split 163
stain removal 158, 159
storing 159
tapestry-type *see* flat-woven *above*
tools and materials 156–7
torn 163
trimming pile 167
Turkish 166–7
washing 158–9
rule joints 53, 55
rummers *203*
rust 211
rust stains
on ceramics 179
on textiles 145

S

sabre legs *85*
salt glaze 174
salts, on ceramics 179
sandstone 236, *236,* 240
sapphires 220, 221, 225
Savonnerie 154
scagliola 240
scraper, cabinetmaker's 28
screw-fitting casters 55, *55*
screws, countersunk 246
seat furniture 10, 84
caned *see* canework
see also chairs; upholstery
secretaires 58
sedimentary rocks 236–7
semi-precious stones 221, 224
Senneh knot 155, 166–7
settees 69
sewing techniques 248
sgraffito 174
shagreen 122
shark skin 122
sheepskin 122, 134
Sheffield plate 206
shellac 15, 17, 34, 47, 182

shell chips, on ceramics 178, 186–7
Sheraton period 88
shield backs *68*
shoe polish stains, on textiles 89
shoes 122
sideboards 11
side chairs *68, 89*
side cords (rugs) 155
repairing 164–5, 248
types 164, *164*
side tables 21, *34*
silicone, wax polish containing 32
silk 138, 139, *139,* 142
silk canvas *98*
silver 206, *206,* 214
assay marks 206
chains 230
cloisonné 211
dents 214
electrochemical dips 212, 213
German (nickel) 206
jewellery 220, 225
polishing 212
Sheffield plate 206
stain removal 213
tarnishing 212–13
washing and cleaning 212–13
silver plate 206, 212–13, 220
skiver 122, 134, 135
slate 240
slip decoration 174
slip-in seats *see* drop-in seats
slip-knot 100, 249
slipping thread 87
slip-stitch 248
smocking 138
snake skin 122
soapstone 236, 237, 240
soda glass 196
soldering 247
solid end-panel construction 58–9, 61, 64
soot stains
on stoneware 240
on textiles 89
Soumaks 154–5, 171, *171*
see also rugs and carpets
spatterware 174
spindles (stick chairs) 41
spongeware 174
spouts, ceramic, remodelling 184–5
sprigging 174
springs (upholstery) 84, 87, 92, 100–1, 107–9
squab cushions 68, 69, 84

stained glass 197
  cleaning 200
staining wood 30, 32, 47
  chemical stains 30
  colour-matching 30–1
  direct dyes 30
  filling grain 31
  oil-based stains 30, 31
  spirit-based stains 30
  water-based stains 30, 31, 32
Star of David caning pattern 73
steam generator 42
steel 207, 211
stick chairs 40–2
stipple engraving 197
stirrup cups 212
stitches
  back stitch 248
  back-tacking 115
  blind-stitching 104
  needlepoint 149
  slip-stitch 248
  tack stitch 248
stoneware 174, 234–43
  breaks 241
  care 240–1
  chips 241
  cleaning 240–3
  cracks 241
  fillers 239, 241
  friable, flaking and powdery 241
  igneous rocks 236
  metamorphic rocks 237
  polishing 241
  poultice method 242–3
  repairing 241
  scagliola 240
  sedimentary rocks 236–7
  stain removal 240, 242–3
stoppers, freeing glass 201
stretcher rails 40, 41, 50–1
stripping old furniture finishes 28–9, 36
suede, cleaning 127
swan-neck handles 58

T

tables 10–11
  casters 55, 55
  dowel joints 52
  drawers 52
  drop-leaf 11, 52–3, 52, 55
  frame 10–11, 52–4
  gate-leg 52–3
  leather tabletops 122, 130, 134–5
  mortise-and-tenon joints 52
  pedestal 11, 11, 52–3, 56–7
  plank-top 52–4

refectory 10–11
  side 21, 34
  structural repairs 52–7
  tilt-top 11, 11, 52–3, 56–7
tacks, upholstery 87
  improved 87
  removing 93
  temporary tacking 101
tack stitch 248
tallboys 11, 58
tankards 214, 215
tanning 122–3
tapered laths, fitting 64
tapestries 138
  cleaning 142
tapestry (upholstery) 84
tapestry-type rugs see flat-woven rugs and carpets
tarnishing 210, 212–13
tar stains, on textiles 145
tea caddies 122
teak, oiling 32
teapots
  ceramic 179, 184–5
  silver 213
tea stains
  on ceramics 179
  on silver 213
  on textiles 89
telescopes 122
tenons see mortise-and-tenon joints
tent stitch 149
terracotta 180–1
textiles 136–51
  cleaning 142–5
  colourfastness, testing for 138, 142
  decorative techniques 138, 139
  displaying 150–1
  dry-cleaning 142
  dyes 138
  embroidery 138, 139
  and humidity 88, 150
  identifying fibres 139
  ironing and pressing 145
  joining threads 248
  knots 155, 166, 170, 249
  linings, attaching 146
  mounting 150–1
  net, supporting with 147
  repairing 146–9
  reproduction fabrics 91, 98
  rugs see rugs and carpets
  sewing techniques 248
  split 146
  stain removal 144–5
  stitches 149, 248
  storing 138, 150–1, 249
  tools and materials 140–1

torn 146
  types 138
  upholstery see upholstery
through ties 108–9
tilt-top tables 11, 11, 52–3, 56–7
tin 207
tin glaze 174, 178
toe casters 55, 55
tools and materials
  canework 70–1
  ceramics 177–8
  furniture 12–15
  glassware 199
  leatherwork 124–5
  metalware 208–9
  rugs and carpets 156–7
  stoneware 238–9
  upholstery 84, 86–7
top-stitching (upholstery) 105
tortoiseshell 221, 225
tourniquets, applying 57
trailing decoration 197
tripods 52, 53, 56–7
tureens 206
turkey work 84
Turkish (Ghiordes) knot 155, 166–7
Turkish rugs 166–7
turned components, repairing 50–1
turquoise 221, 225
twine, upholstery 87

U

underglaze decoration 174
upholstery 10, 46–7, 82–119
  arms 102–6, 114–15, 119
  backs 84, 102, 110–18
  back-tacking 115
  blind-stitching 104
  bottoming 93
  bridle ties 96, 106, 107
  button-back chairs 99–119
  buttons 84–5, 116
  care 88, 119
  cleaning 88–9, 127
  colourfastness, testing for 88
  drop-in seats 40, 92, 94–8
  dust covers 98, 119
  fabric rolls 108
  frame 93, 99
  hard edges 105
  hessian 87, 95
  knots 155, 166, 170, 249
  leather 122, 122, 127, 129
  looped ties 107
  minor repairs 90–1
  piping, replacement 91
  rebates 94

regulator 87, 103
  reproduction fabrics 91, 98
  reupholstering 92–119
  ripping off 93, 99
  sewing techniques 248
  slip-in seats see drop-in seats above
  split 90
  springs 84, 87, 100–1
  sprung seats 40, 92, 100–1, 107–9, 114
  stain guards 119
  stain removal 88–9
  stuffing 84, 87, 95, 96, 103, 106–12
  sunlight, protection from 88
  tapestry 84
  temporary tacking 101
  through ties 108–9
  tools and materials 84, 86–7
  top-covering 114–19
  top fabrics, choosing 98
  top-stitching 105
  torn 90
  trimmings, cleaning 89
  turkey work 84
  twine 87
  wadding 87, 95, 97, 118
  webbing 95, 100, 102

V

veneers 11, 11, 22–7, 58
  blisters 22–3, 24
  burnt or charred 24
  dents and bruises 23
  frame-and-panel construction 58, 59
  French polish 34, 34
  and humidity 22
  patching 24–5, 31
  removing 26
  replacing 26–7
  simulating grain or figuring 31
  splits and cracks 22, 24
  staining 30–1, 32
  wax polish 17, 28, 32
verdigris 207, 211
vetro di cristallo 196
vetro a fili 197
vetro a reticello 197
V-spring clasps 227

W

wadding 87, 95, 97, 118, 146–7
walnut 16–17, 21
  burr 11
  French polish 34, 34
  staining 30–1

wardrobes 11, 58
warp threads 138, 154
  inserting new 162
  mending fringes and Kelim ends 160–2
water marks, on furniture 19
waxed furniture 11, 17, 32–3
  beeswax 17, 32–3
  coloured wax 32
  filling 31, 32
  French polished surfaces 37
  scratches 21, 29, 29
  sealing surface 33
  staining and colour-matching 30–2
  veneers and inlays 32
wax marks see candle wax
weaving
  rugs see rugs and carpets
  textiles 138
webbing (upholstery) 95, 100, 102
weft threads 138, 154
  mending fringes and Kelim ends 160–2
wheel engraving 197
white polish 34
whitework 138
Wilton 154
Windsor chairs 40, 43
wine stains, on textiles 89
woodworm 58
  chair legs 48
  holes, filling 20
  recognizing and treating 244
wool 138, 139
wrought iron 207, 211

Acknowledgements

Author Acknowledgements

For all the skill, effort and dedication that they brought to the production of this book, the author would like to thank: Hugh Johnson (photographer) and assistants Simon Lee and Brett Newnham; Anny Evason (illustrator); Richard Dawes (editor); Simon Bell (designer); Melanie Hulse (US editor); Larissa Lawrynenko (US art director); Stephen Luker (upholstery and furniture repairs); I. & P. Pritchard (canework repairs); Richard Chys (French polishing); Anthony Cullen (leather repairs); Frances Page (textile repairs).

The author would also like to thank the following for supplying the tools and materials used to demonstrate care and repair techniques in this book: Parry Tyzack (specialist and general tools supplier); Alec Tiranti Ltd (craft and artist's suppliers); The Cane Store (canework suppliers); Locks & Handles and Interiors (casters and handles); Woolnough (AC) Limited (antique and modern leathers).

Finally, the author would like to thank the following staff members at Mitchell Beazley for their managerial skills, commitment, and, above all, patience, during the production of this book: Judith More; Janis Utton; Anthea Snow; Nina Sharman; Christina Quigley.

Picture Acknowledgements

p.10 Sotheby's, London; p.11R Reed International Books Ltd./Ian Booth; p.11L Reed International Books Ltd./Ian Booth/Nigel O'Gorman; p.29 Sotheby's, London; p.40 Reed International Books Ltd./Ian Booth; p.52 Reed International Books Ltd./ Ian Booth; p.58 Reed International Books Ltd./Ian Booth; p.84T Reed International Books Ltd./James Merrell; pp.84/5 Reed International Books Ltd./ Ian Booth/Nigel O'Gorman; p.89 Reed International Books Ltd./James Merrell; pp.122/3 Reed International Books Ltd./ James Merrell; p.123 Reed International Books Ltd./Ken Adlard; p.127 Reed International Books Ltd./James Merrell; p.138 Reed International Books Ltd./ James Merrell; p.139 Reed International Books Ltd./James Merrell; p.145 Reed International Books Ltd./James Merrell; pp.154/5 Reed International Books Ltd./ James Merrell; pp.174/5 Sotheby's, London; p.175 Bonhams, London; pp.178/9L Sotheby's, London; pp.178/9R Sotheby's, London; p.196 Reed International Books Ltd./James Merrell; pp.196/7 Reed International Books Ltd./Ian Booth (by permission of Mark West); p.201 Reed International Books Ltd./Ian Booth (by permission of Mark West); pp.200/201 Reed International Books Ltd./James Merrell; p.203R Reed International Books Ltd./Ian Booth (by permission of Mark West); pp.206/7 Reed International Books Ltd./Ian Booth (at Sotheby's London); p.206B Reed International Books Ltd./ James Merrell; p.207B Reed International Books Ltd./ James Merrell; p.220T Reed International Books Ltd./Kevin Summers; p.220B Bonhams, London; p.221T Sotheby's, London; p.221B Reed International Books Ltd./Kevin Summers; p.224 Reed International Books Ltd./Kevin Summers; p.236 Reed International Books Ltd./ James Merrell; p.237 Reed International Books Ltd./Kim Sayer; p.240 Reed International Books Ltd./James Merrell; p.243 Sotheby's, London.

The author and publishers would like to thank the following house-owners, collectors, interior designers, curators and museums: p.84T Melrose Mansion, Mississippi, USA; p.89 Christophe Gollut, London, UK; pp.122/3 Judith and Martin Miller; p.127 Linda and Peter Guber; p.138 Bob Timberlake; p.139 Judith and Martin Miller; p.145 Second House Museum, Gilmartin, Montauk Historical Society, USA; pp.154/5 Judith and Martin Miller; p.196 Judith and Martin Miller; pp.200/1 Judith and Martin Miller; p.206B Mrs Sutherland, Martinsburg, USA; p.207B Lyn von Kirsting; p.220T Steinberg and Tolkein, London, UK; p.221B Linda Bee, Gray's Antique Market, London, UK; p.224 Cobra and Bellamy, London, UK; Steinberg and Tolkein, London, UK; p.236 Guggi and Sarah Sesti; p.237 Bartow-Pell Mansion, New York, USA.